JOURNEY
TO THE 72

(Images from the 72 can be found on my Instagram @theshaunbest)
(Follow me on Twitter @Shaun_Best)

Groundhopping is a hobby that involves attending matches at as many different stadiums or grounds as possible. Participants are known as groundhoppers, hoppers or travellers. Largely a football-related pastime. There is no universal set of rules for counting 'hopped grounds', although a generally accepted one is that a match must have been seen at the ground.

They say that admitting you have a problem is the first step on the road to recovery, so here goes. My name is Shaun Best and I'm a groundhopper. There I said it. I feel better already.

72 games, nine months, thousands of miles to be travelled plus a lot of programmes to sift through. I almost forgot to add an unhealthy number of pies to be digested. Sounds extreme? Just a bit. Nevertheless, challenge accepted!

From the Championship, to Leagues One and Two, the Capital One Cup, FA Cup and last but not least the Johnstone's Paint Trophy on a cold Tuesday evening, all that's left for me to say is go and get your coat and don't forget your hat and gloves (like I did) as it's going to be a long winter.

But first, here's how *Journey to the 72* came to fruition.

Aggborough, August 2013. I'd prized myself away from the sofa and Jeff Stelling on TV for a rare away day with hometown club Chester FC. It wasn't just the taste of the Kidderminster pie that stayed with me that day.

My friends Rich Ward and Danny Broadley were going through a list of grounds they had been to, en route and when it came to my turn, my response was pitiful. In all my 30+ years, I'd probably visited 12 grounds in the whole of England. While I could identify with freezing my balls off on a random Tuesday night stood behind a safety rope at Vauxhall Motors, in truth, I hadn't really been anywhere. Hell, I could count on one finger the number of times I'd even been to London. It was embarrassing. Trips to Old Trafford to see my beloved Manchester United were an extravagance all too rare and far too taxing on the wallet. Thanks to the ever rising cost of the Premier League, I was beginning to feel more like a customer than a fan. This explains the affliction with Chester – the proverbial little brother I started to look out for and occasionally visit.

It hadn't always been like this. As a child I never went without a healthy dose of live footballing activity. In those days, it didn't cost a king's ransom to go and watch a Premier League game. I was bitten by the United bug at an early age, much to the disappointment of my Dad, who tried and failed to convert me into a Liverpool fan. He was the black sheep in an otherwise Everton orientated family. I made several incognito trips to Goodison Park with relatives whenever United came into town. Naturally my team always won, but I wasn't allowed to celebrate for obvious reasons.

I remember my first trip to Old Trafford fondly, as an innocent and inquisitive 12-year-old. It was a memorable match for lots of reasons. Dad couldn't bring himself to drink his pint out of a cup bearing the United logo, so I was given one of my first tastes of the holy water, if only to help him out of his predicament. Sorry Mum. During the game, many of these same cups were used as ammunition to angrily pelt Wimbledon's John Fashanu with after he tried and failed to injure Ryan Giggs. Fash ended up on the wrong side of his own dangerous challenge and was stretchered off, never to play again. On the pitch, Andy Cole scored his first goal for the club following his £7 million move from Newcastle. Back in 1995, that was a lot of money. How times have changed. Come to think of it, how I had changed.

"When was the last time you went to see a Football League game?" My friends had put me on the spot. Fleeting appearances at local sides Crewe, Wigan and Port Vale from years gone by aside, I couldn't give a definitive answer.

"You should look into groundhopping mate. Spend a few seasons going round the grounds," said Rich, a former Everton season ticket holder.

"I'm surprised you came today to be honest," Danny added. He was right. I was making a guest appearance in the blind hope that Chester were going to get off the mark for the season.

Standing behind the goal inside Kidderminster's humble abode, it looked like being a wasted trip when Chester quickly fell behind.

"Sod this, I'm getting a pie," said Danny. "You coming?"
"I don't normally eat at games," I said.
"What? You can't go to a game and not have a pie. Come on!"

It was close to half time and the crowds were queuing to get their hands on Kiddy's famous soup and cottage pies. Naturally, we missed Chester getting a goal back, but the taste of the club's award winning savouries dispelled some of the bitterness – even if it did cost upwards of £4.

Kidderminster ran out comfortable 3-1 winners in the end, yet both the game and experience had been enjoyable. We may have been penned in like sheep, but the fan camaraderie more than negated that. Once again, my friends encouraged me to spread my wings and broaden my footballing horizons. Given my track record, I suspected they were only half serious. They knew that I was the king of starting something and never seeing it through. Several acquaintances who had moved away were always coming to see me, yet I'd never be inclined to return the gesture.

Unsurprisingly, being a lapsadaisical friend and stereotypical lazy football fan went hand in hand. I was a slave to Sky Sports. Picture the scene: It's 4:45pm on a Saturday and the results are almost in. All of a sudden, there's a late development at Watford, a mass brawl at Millwall or even a Mexican wave at Milton Keynes (unlikely, but stranger things have happened) Chris Kamara is like a can of heavily shaken Pepsi and can't contain his excitement. Meanwhile, I'm sat sprawled on the sofa at home checking my accumulator(s) very much feeling like an outsider looking in. On the rare occasion that I'd venture out to Chester, I couldn't help but brace myself for the proverbial late equaliser or winner from the opposition which almost always came. It was a vicious cycle. I needed to break the monotony and have some of what Kamara was drinking. My friends' comments had stuck in my craw. I wanted to tap into my adolescent self, re-discover the buzz and euphoria about going to a match and above all, restore my love of the beautiful game.

Going slightly off-track, I'd been a fan of Italian football ever since the good old days of Gazzetta Football Italia. Many a Saturday morning growing up was spent in the company of James Richardson and his cappuccino in the picturesque setting of an Italian bistro going through the week's goings on around Serie A. Putting my Journalism degree to use, I had started writing weekend match reports in my spare time. The other writers had been trying to arrange a meet-up on the peninsula to take in a game or two. It was approaching Christmas, yet still seemed like the perfect opportunity to put down the pen and add a bit of mileage to the travel clock. You could call it a continental dry run of sorts. Far from a culture shock, being in the front row for Parma's centenary celebrations, plus sitting in the gods of the San Siro to watch the once mighty AC Milan was great. However nice the dream, it probably wasn't realistic to fly over to Italy every other weekend to go and watch football. More importantly, it whetted the appetite and I started thinking about ideas on British shores.

Reading about people spending years visiting all 92 League clubs piqued my interest. However, I wanted to differentiate myself from the pack. 92 games in a season had also already been done. While imitation can sometimes be the sincerest form of flattery, I wanted to put my own spin on things and not cripple myself financially. That's when I had the idea to take my friends' words to heart and visit all 72 Football League clubs over the course of the 2014-15 season. It would still be costly, but very much do-able.

Based in the North West of England meant that I had a cluster of clubs on my doorstep and was just a couple of hours from other hotbeds such as the Midlands and London. Comparitively, if I was doing this from the North East or South West, then the logistics from Geography alone would throw up plenty of problems and add a lot more £ onto the travel costs.

I was in a steady job, albeit one which called for the occasional Saturday to be worked (one in four to be precise) and still held a student card after dabbling in several evening courses. I had a feeling my ID could come in handy during points of the journey. Another factor to take into consideration was the lack of a driving license, meaning I'd be at the mercy of National Rail. These were all minor details when looking at the big picture. Knowing that it would take over my life, I made a pact to still try and make as many social arrangements as possible. I did another trial run and went to see a relegation clash between Crewe Alexandra and Colchester United, which ended in an uninspiring goalless draw. Undeterred, I wasn't put off. Now it was time to let the cat out of the bag to my friends.

Fast forward to the final day of the 2013-14 season. I'd roped in five close friends – Rich, his brother Chris, Danny, Mark Parry and James Sellers to see Chester pull off the great escape and stay up. However, the football gods weren't on our side and Chester were cruelly relegated on goal difference, although thanks to financial irregularities at other clubs, they were given a stay of execution during the close season. As a discarded season ticket book blew past my foot, I decided now was the perfect time to lift the mood and make my announcement.

"Lads, I'm doing a ground tour!"
"We weren't being serious you know," said everyone in unison.
"No, but I am now. I'm going to watch a game at all 72 Football League clubs over the course of next season."
There was stunned silence. Several disillusioned Chester fans could be overheard making plans for visits to Stockport and Chorley. I started thinking further afield. Ipswich, Portsmouth and Cambridge amongst others places flashed through my mind.
"You've probably never been to 72 games in your life," said Mark, ever the comedian and realist. "You'll never do it."

"Maybe I will. I'll never know if I don't try," I said in quick reply. More silence.
"I'll come and join you for a couple of games in the Midlands," said Danny, who lived in the Birmingham area and visits Chester to catch up with family and friends. I sensed he was coming round to the idea. Within minutes, the others also made a pact to come to at least one game with me.

Following several summer pub trips, my friends were fully on board with the idea. Family were receptive too, with Dad showing an interest at coming along to some of the local games. Tentative travel plans were made for the first couple of months when the fixtures came out.

While thrashing out logistics, I set myself a few simple rules to abide by; attend a game at said ground, sample a pie, purchase a programme, and if I'm feeling froggy, have a pint or two along the way. My knowledge of each club ranged from non-existent to average, so attempts to engage with all 72 fanbases would also need to be made.

I was all set. From Brighton Pier all the way to Hartlepool United, it was time to see for myself what Row Z at Yeovil Town and Plymouth Argyle were like. I set off armed with nothing but hope, optimism, excitement and a childlike sense of wonder. Given my inability to read maps, I'd already resigned myself to getting lost a couple of times along the way. Scratch that, make that most of the way. Other than that small detail, what could possibly go wrong?

Getting to know Blackburn Rovers
Anna-Louise Adams (season ticket holder)
www.90minutesmore.co.uk
Twitter: @annalouiseadams
Facebook: www.facebook.com/90minutesmore

Favourite memory as a Blackburn fan?

Although I wasn't at the game, one of my favourite memories was beating Manchester United 3-2 away at Old Trafford. Yakubu scored a penalty and Grant Hanley got the winner after Dimitar Berbatov scored twice in ten minutes.

Best game you've witnessed at Ewood Park?

Whenever Burnley visit - the atmosphere is always unbeatable when your rivals visit. A 1-1 draw with Burnley sticks out, due to a bit of magic from my hero David Dunn in the dying embers of added time.

Best/worst players to pull on a Blackburn shirt?

The worst players I have witnessed in a Rovers shirt are Leon Best and Danny Murphy - two players with absolutely foul attitudes towards Blackburn Rovers, and what I would go as far to say as football as a whole. Both players lacked respect for the fans or the club, especially given the extortionate wage packets they were receiving at the time. Many of the best came before I had time to really appreciate them, however names that stick out to me are obviously Bryan Douglas, Ronnie Clayton, Alan Shearer, Brad Friedal, Matt Jansen, David Bentley (the first time), David Dunn, Tugay and Rudy Gestede.

Best thing about Ewood Park?

I live two hours away from Blackburn so for me the best thing about Ewood Park is feeling like I'm a part of something - I love knowing that everyone else in the ground is a supporter of my club and that we all share a common goal for the club.

Worst grounds you've visited?

I haven't visited a mass of grounds, but I have visited a couple of non league grounds so I would say that Redditch United's ground is fairly poor - the pitch is either waterlogged or dry as a desert! Having said that it's one of my local clubs and I am fond of it.

Enjoyable away days?

The Emirates was a treat to say the least - cushioned seats as opposed to cold, hard plastic! I like Molineux because that was my first proper away day.

Thoughts on ticket prices in general?

This is a subject I can't fully discuss in just a few sentences - it requires pages and pages. Of course, I think ticket prices are extortionate, but the only way I see football clubs reducing ticket prices is for fans to hit them where it hurts - and that's their wallets. Therefore the only way I see a reduction in prices is a nationwide mass boycott of all Football League clubs - which is obviously a huge ask and unlikely to happen.

Famous Blackburn fans?

Matt Smith and Carl Fogarty are fans.

Quirky fact time?

I once wrote an article about how the rivalry between Blackburn and Burnley developed (aside from the geographical location) which explained that there was a big feud regarding cotton mill contracts.

GETTING THE PARTY STARTED

Game #1: The Championship - Friday 8th August 2014
BLACKBURN ROVERS vs Cardiff City - Ewood Park

Here we go. Applying the out of office tag never felt better. No sooner had I exited the workplace, I jumped straight into my Dad's car for the first of 72 journeys. Many people would probably start a two week holiday from work in the pub. Instead, I opted to beat rush hour traffic to get to Lancashire and see the curtain raiser of the 2014-15 season. Convincing my Dad to come was a bonus. In truth, there was no-one else I'd rather begin this adventure with. The first game of the season was moved to the Friday for television purposes and I prayed for the game not to finish 0-0 during the 90 minute drive.

Signing up beforehand to the Blackburn website - no doubt the first of many over the course of the season, I was encouraged by an attractive price for the club's first game of the campaign. Even better was the fact there was no booking fee or distribution charge. Every little helps, especially in my case. I had some money behind me for the project, as well as a portion of my work income, but any saving I could make along the way, no matter how small would be greatly appreciated. Having been put off by the need for loyalty points and fan cards just for a chance to gain entry at Anfield, coming to Blackburn was an easy sell for my Dad, especially when I said I'd cover the cost of a ticket in exchange for petrol.

Ewood Park is well signposted coming off the motorway and parking was pretty easy. We plumped for the 'Fernhurst Pub & Grill' which was literally opposite the ground. Five security guards provided a wall into the car park and deemed us worthy to enter after deciding we weren't hooligans. Decked out in black SWAT gear, I took the Shield at their word when they said they would look after the car and handed over £5 for the privilege. This meant that Dad was definitely buying the pies inside the ground.

The club had unveiled a new 'Parade of Honour' on the link bridges between two of the stands. Images of Alan Shearer and Tim Sherwood holding aloft the Premier League trophy from the title winning season of 1995 and the side's 2002 League Cup triumph are two of its prominent features. Having reaped the rewards of Jack Walker's millions during the 1990s, Blackburn have hit turbulent times. Relegation to the Championship has seen a managerial merry-go-round and fan opinion of current owners Venky's is firmly split.

Despite their fall from grace, there was renewed hope amongst the fans walking in that the club were somewhat of a sleeping giant and this was going to be their season. Even the stewards chimed in, boldly predicting another profitable campaign from top marksman Jordan Rhodes. "Scores when he wants," one stated, as me and Dad were shown to our seats. Dad proudly told the steward about my planned adventures, although I don't blame the staffer for only taking him half seriously. Truth be told, I hadn't completely comprehended the size of the task at hand just yet.

Three sides of Ewood Park have had a facelift and it strikes you as still being a Premier League ground. Dad in particular was impressed by the tidy layout of the ground and the community spirit instilled by everyone working at the club. Nothing was too much trouble – case in point, me being allowed out of the stadium to pick up a programme without any quibble of getting back in. It may have been the buzz of the opening day, but everyone from stewards to catering staff were outgoing, jovial and very helpful.

Seated at the front of the smaller RFS Riverside Stand, we both had a perfect view of the giant TV screen in the corner. Past goals from former alumni were beamed out, before the two teamsheets were displayed, making it easier to get acquainted with everyone on the field. Two piping hot peppered steak pies went down really well and the Cardiff fans adjacent to us were in fine voice, even if there wasn't a single red shirt in sight. "We're Cardiff City, we'll always be blue," they defiantly sung. Owner Vincent Tan clearly hadn't received the memo. His decision at re-branding the club's colours had gone down like a lead balloon.

In a bid to out sing their visitors, the Blackburn fans started singing along to pre-match song 'The Wild Rover.' Ewood Park joined in unison to sing the chorus of 'No Nay Never' with one over zealous fan utilising the gap in between words to kick the hell out of a side panel. While he was in tune with the beat, he was also clearly excited, as was I. We were finally ready to get the new season underway.

Blackburn were denied a penalty in the first minute. Former Cardiff man Rudy Gestede headed against Mark Hudson's hand, but the referee bottled the first big call of the season and awarded a free kick right outside the box.

Despite being privileged to witness the first goal of the campaign going in, the gloss was soon taken off Kenwyne Jones' fine bullet header. An old guy sitting next to Dad decided to witter racist slurs, so Dad quite rightly ripped into him (verbally not literally, unfortunately.) Amazingly, the guy stood by his remarks arguing that as a paying supporter, he could say what he liked. 'Bob' - I didn't catch his actual name went back to munching on his ice cream and talking to himself for several minutes, before getting up and going for a wander. Upon noticing Bob clutching two tickets, and with no friend in sight, I concluded that the guy was crackers. This assumption paid dividends when he wandered past again a few minutes later with his hood up. It wasn't even raining! I know I'm stating the obvious, but there's no place for racism in football.

Blackburn's player of the year Tom Cairney equalised with a peach of a strike before the break, letting rip from 25 yards. Unfortunately, despite the home side's pressing, Cardiff seemed happy to take a draw and frustrated the hosts in a largely forgettable second half. The home fans became more lively as the game went on, but couldn't sing their team to victory. Upon leaving the ground, I passed the same steward who had showed me to my seat and was now taking down his posters to the Jordan Rhodes fan club. I tried a poorly timed joke. "He mustn't have wanted to score tonight mate." I didn't get a reply, just a cursory stare.

The stewards and police operated a first class policy getting into and away from Ewood Park. We were only detained in the car park for five minutes after the game thanks to a well marshalled system. It looked like we would be home in no time. Naturally, I put paid to those plans, giving a wrong direction and a trip through Preston ensured a prolonged return journey. Sorry Dad.

Best chant: "We're sheep shagging bastards, we know what we are." Cardiff City fans beating their Blackburn counterparts to the punch and showing good self-depreciating humour.
Match ticket: £17. Great value!
Match programme: £3. Much like a glossy magazine, packed with plenty of features and a focus on the team.
Cost of food: £12.90 for two pies, two portions of chunky chips and two drinks.
Pie rating: 5/5 - whoa steady on Dad! I clearly made a rookie mistake bringing in a guest judge for the first pie of the season. I think he'd skipped lunch, as I've never seen anybody wolf down a pie quicker than my father. Granted, the pie contained plenty of meat and the gravy was well flavoured with red peppers and peas. However, setting such a benchmark so early in the savoury stakes gave me a nagging feeling that I was making a rod for my own back further down the line.

Final Score:
Blackburn Rovers 1 (Cairney 40)
Cardiff City 1 (Jones 18)
Attendance: 15,625

Getting to know Milton Keynes Dons
Matt W, James D'Arcy and Bingoman
www.concreteroundabout.co.uk - unofficial MK Dons forum

Favourite memory as a Dons fan?

James: Personally, my first game I went to watch against Brighton back in 2009. Ali Gerba nearly scored an audacious overhead kick, we won 2-0 that day and I won't forget the whole amazement of watching the Dons and visiting stadium:mk for the first time.

Do you see the Dons as a continuation of the old Wimbledon or a separate entity altogether?

Matt: Continuation. I sit next to two old Wimbledon season ticket holders and have sat with the Directors of MK Dons and Wimbledon. I have heard everything that happened straight from them directly.

James: Legally at the very least we are the continuation of Wimbledon, but it's something that divides opinion amongst Dons fans. Personally I see Wimbledon as a dead club now and I don't think either us or AFC should try and re-claim the Wimbledon history.

Bingoman: Definitely a continuation. We may have got the league place, but we also got the hard scary debt and the massive wage bill to boot. We were saddled with all the cack that came with Wimbledon as well as the place in the second tier that was lost within months due to the club being in an absolute state.

Are you glad to see AFC Wimbledon back in the Football League?

Matt: Nope, after the years of abuse I have received from their supporters in regards to supporting my local team, been spat at when we first played each other at MK. I look out every week for their results hoping they lose.

James: Only in the sense we are more likely to play each other. Each time we've played them so far the matches have been tight and heated affairs. Other than that I'm not fussed by them, although I admire Neal Ardley for the job he has done there on a tight budget.

Bingoman: They're a club with fans and employees just like any other, including us. I don't begrudge them their success, and they shouldn't begrudge us ours.

Thoughts on ticket prices in general?

Matt: Too high. They should be a maximum of £40 -£20 from Premier League to League Two. Away games cost a fortune. I spend at least £70-120 away from home, it should be affordable and the ticket prices make it unaffordable for some.

Thoughts on owner Pete Winkelman?

Bingoman: Pete Winkelman found a club on its knees and without breaking the bank managed to restore it and create something in the image he always had for our city. There were dark times in Milton Keynes but he stuck at it. Contrary to popular belief, Wimbledon FC was not in full health when he took over; the club had to be effectively rebuilt and he did that, and now we have the rewards. He's also a great guy and a great personality.

Best/worst players to pull on a Dons shirt?

James: Dean Lewington is a club legend and our captain. He is the only player to have been with us from the start in 2004. On the flip side some of the players we had back in 2004 were dross, because we couldn't afford much else and names such as Julien Hornuss and Alex Tapp are best forgotten. James Loveridge was brought in as a striker to score goals, unfortunately he couldn't hit a barn door and didn't score once for us!

Best thing about stadium:mk?

Matt: The family friendly atmosphere. Every time I turn up I still get excited about the stadium and the friends I have made over the years sharing the highs and the lows with them in the stadium.

Enjoyable away days?

James: The Ricoh Arena in Coventry is the only ground I've been to with a casino in it and is well worth a visit.

Bingoman: I quite liked most of the grotty little places we have visited over the years, like Hartlepool United, Exeter City, Dagenham & Redbridge, Yeovil Town.

Worst grounds you've visited?

Matt: Oldham by an absolute mile!

James: Gillingham is the worst ground I've visited in my time watching the Dons. The away end is basically scaffolding with seats and the area around the ground is pretty grim as well.

Bingoman: One place sticks out above all others because I detest the place and that is Swindon Town. It is not a particularly small ground, but it is an absolute hole. You pay £30, get left outside longer before they let you in, get allocated a seat they found at the bottom of a canal, wait for their hostile atmosphere to start, realise they're about as loud as mute mice when you're wearing earmuffs in a soundproof room, and then realise you've got to stay in Swindon for two hours.

Which club serves the nicest pies?

Bingoman: Exeter's pasties were brilliant and became even better when they handed them out for free in the second half. Wigan's offering was very average considering the hype that surrounds it. Hartlepool United, however, found the darkest pits of hell with the food they'd offered. You got it from a bar called the Hungry Monkey, and as far as I could tell it looked like the Hungry Monkey had emptied his bowels on a napkin.

Famous Dons fans?

Matt: Cricketers Darren Gough and James Foster I do believe.

James: Jim Marshall, who developed the Marshall Amp is our most famous fan. He helped us out while we were in a real troubled time by sponsoring us and is fondly remembered by most Dons fans, and since his death the club have held tributes to him.

Bingoman: I think Greg Rutherford (the long jumper) may also be a fan.

Quirky fact time?

Matt: There are police cells under the home end of stadium if required. I believe the stadium has to have them to be able to hold the status the stadium does.

Bingoman: Dons winger Daniel Powell has a brain condition that means he cannot think into the future and therefore he never actually knows what he is going to do next.

Name your MK Dons Dream Team?

David Martin
Dean Lewington
Kyle McFadzean
Antony Kay
Adam Smith
Daniel Powell
Dele Alli
Darren Potter
Stephen Gleeson
Sam Baldock
Aaron Wilbraham

CATCHING A SUN TAN IN MILTON KEYNES

Game #2: League One - Saturday 9th August 2014
MILTON KEYNES DONS vs Gillingham - stadium:mk

Hello train station! It was time to get acquainted with my new best friend for the next nine months. Leaving Chester behind, I was just getting comfortable on board of a Virgin Super Voyager when a text came through. Surely the first of many well-wishers, I thought to myself.

"Coming to the game today?"

My friends had such little faith. In this case, Danny and Rich wanted me to join them for Chester's opening game against Barnet.

"Sorry lads, I'm on the way to Milton Keynes."

"Good! Just checking you haven't backed out."

The sun was shining, the train was moving at a frenetic pace and the mood in the carriage was jovial. Glancing at the seat in front, an equally happy Gillingham fan had his shirt proudly on display, earphones in, with his head swaying from side to side and without a care in the world.

I quickly discovered that Milton Keynes sure loved its roundabouts. Throw in just as many straight roads along with a pretty rough area of sheltered accommodation and that summed up the bus journey to the ground from Milton Keynes Central train station. Based in nearby Bletchley, the stadium is a custom built 30,000 all-seater and located slap bang in the middle of a retail park.

I was due to meet up with Steve Cook from the Full 92 Travel Club, who's doing the complete set of 92 grounds at a much more sensible rate of several years. While I waited for him to arrive, I spied a KFC, McDonald's and Domino's Pizza all within yards of the stadium entrance. With the three main food groups covered, I certainly wasn't going to go hungry.

I got acquainted with Steve, who arrived in a plain blue shirt with the words 'Full 92' on the back. He'd had a few problems parking, due to the attendant assuming by the colour of his shirt that he was a Gillingham fan and giving him directions to the away car park. He's actually a Wolves fan just for the record. As we queued for tickets, we were in earshot of a veteran staffer who was hawking a competition to guess the time of the first goal. His monotonous yelling of "Goal-Don goal" got irritating pretty quickly, so I dove into the club shop to give my ears a rest.

We were unexpectedly stopped from entering the ground by a female steward, who demanded that Steve produce a fire safety certificate in order to allow a simple flag to pass through. He'd unwittingly left the certificate on the kitchen table, so the two of us were escorted through the stadium and told to wait in a corner like naughty school children. After the flag was vetted and we vowed not to pledge our allegiance to fierce rivals AFC Wimbledon, entry was allowed. A quick perusal of the banned objects list also prohibited darts from being allowed into the stadium. If Phil Taylor's reading this, then leave your arrows at home if you ever venture to Milton Keynes.

By the club's own admission, the fanbase is still growing. After all, the team have only been in existence for a little over ten years. Chairman Pete Winkelman's bold and brash decision to move the old Wimbledon to Milton Keynes was a move straight out of the USA's franchise playbook and alienated a lot of fans to say the least. While the club is credited for giving Roberto Di Matteo his start in management, it's also revered and resented by many a football fan upset at seeing a club's identity being changed. When the Dons graduated from a now demolished Hockey ground, they even convinced the Queen to take a break from her royal duties to officially open stadium:mk back in November 2007. However, rumours of Her Majesty being an MK fan are as of yet unfounded.

Shaped like a big black bowl, the stadium is well equipped to host concerts and shows. Spacious leather seats provided extra comfort and ample leg room, while screens in corners of the ground played music videos to keep the crowd entertained. Each Dons player was introduced by a vignette on the screen which was ideal in matching faces to names and numbers. The ground even holds a DoubleTree Hilton hotel on site, so guests can simply open the curtains in their room and get a bird's eye view of the action on the pitch. All for an added charge of course.

The ground was barely a third full, but the sun was out in all its glory. In true northern style, I'd instinctively taken a coat, but that quickly disappeared and I was treated to a pulsating match. Cody McDonald took advantage of a defensive lapse to break clear and fire the Gills in front early on. The forward was then bundled over by Dons goalkeeper David Martin and Danny Kedwell coolly converted the resulting spot kick.

Just as I was commending myself for not placing a home win on my accumulator, the hosts halved the deficit thanks to a comical own goal right on half time. The game then changed completely when Gillingham tormentor McDonald was stretchered off with a knee injury. The visitors lost their collective mojo and conceded three headed goals in a disastrous six minute period. Will Grigg and Kyle McFadzean bagged two of the goals on their full debuts, while the third was credited as another own goal.

It was perhaps a little harsh on the visiting supporters, who had been in great voice throughout the afternoon, but were now well and truly silenced. At least they had some cause to cheer. Back home, it had been slim pickings for both Danny and Rich, as I was to discover upon checking my phone.

"Chester having a shocker, lost 5-0, had a man sent off and missed a penalty. Pathetic!"

I felt bad for them, although I was still buzzing at the game I had been treated to. Six goals in blazing sunshine was a pretty good return for a straightforward two hour train trip down south. Steve saved me a bus ride by kindly dropping me back at the station. We both agreed that a return in the future is very likely. The MK way isn't for everyone, but on days like today, it's hard to argue.

Best chant: "Two nil and you fucked it up." MK Dons fans, who don't beat around the bush or mince their words.
Match ticket: £20 was the flat charge across the board for adults.
Match programme: £3. An informative edition, which gave this reader a crash course in all things MK. Contained a squad picture as its centrefold, although I didn't put it on my wall.
Cost of food: £6.00 for a pie, snack and drink combo.
Pie rating: 3/5. Settled for the chicken balti. The pie was warm and the pastry was a little tough, but the crust was nice and the right blend of spices complemented the generous chunks of meat.

Final Score:
Milton Keynes Dons 4 (Hause 44 og, Grigg 68, McFadzean 70, Legge 73 og)
Gillingham 2 (McDonald 7, Kedwell 29 pen)
Attendance: 7,595

Getting to know Wolverhampton Wanderers
Steve Cook - Chairman of the Full 92 Travel Club
www.full92.wix.com/the-full-92
www.thefull92.blogspot.co.uk

Favourite memory as a Wolves fan?
Probably the play-off final win in 2002/03. First time I'd seen the club in the top division.

Best game you've witnessed at Molineux?
Wolves 4-3 Leicester, October 2003 (we were 3-0 down at half time)

Best/worst players to pull on a Wolves shirt?
Best - Steve Bull and Billy Wright. Worst - Roger Johnson (that I've seen) and probably most of the mid 1980's teams.

Best thing about Molineux?
Location, right next to city centre. And of course the atmosphere (when we're doing well)

Worst grounds you've visited?
Molineux (before redevelopment), Dagenham & Redbridge.

Which club serves the nicest pies?
Wolves, obviously.

Famous Wolves fans?
Robert Plant (Led Zeppelin), Noddy Holder (Slade) Suzi Perry (F1)

Quirky fact time?
Wolves were partly responsible for the creation of the European Cup (Champions League) as the club were one of the first to hold 'floodlit friendlies' at Molineux against European sides in 1950's midweek evening matches. Due to the success of these the competitive European Cup was proposed.

Best/worst Wolves managers?
Stan Cullis, Bill McGarry, John Barnwell, Graham Turner, Dave Jones, Mick McCarthy, Kenny Jackett (good) - Tommy Docherty, Ian Greaves, Graham Hawkins, Graham Taylor, Terry Connor, Dean Saunders, (bad)

Thoughts on ticket prices in general?
All overpriced at every level, especially the top two tiers.

Name your Wolves Dream Team?
Based on what I know from the history books and stats it would have to include Steve Bull and Billy Wright. The rest are all a matter of what era you are. Mine would be:
Matt Murray
Andy Thompson
Denis Irwin
Joleon Lescott
Stan Cullis
Billy Wright
Paul Ince
Robbie Dennison
Matt Jarvis
Steve Bull
Robbie Keane

WANDERING OVER TO WOLVERHAMPTON

Game #3: The Championship - Sunday 10th August 2014
WOLVERHAMPTON WANDERERS vs Norwich City - Molineux

No rest for the wicked. Flying solo for the first time of the tour, I was off to my third game in as many days. After a longer than usual lie-in and miscalculation of train times almost saw me miss the first leg to Crewe, I scrambled on board and was off to the heart of the Black Country for my first visit to Wolverhampton.

There's something strange about Sunday games. Not from a religious point or anything like that. I've just always been one of those traditionalists that looked forward to a full Saturday programme and used a Sunday to catch the foreign leagues on TV. I was sure my tune would change once I was back at work, especially when my Saturday obligation kicked in.

It dawned on me that I had no clue where the ground was, but just like Dorothy followed the yellow brick road in the Wizard of Oz, I simply followed the army of orange shirts. Following a brisk ten minute walk, I found the ground which is located next to the University. I needn't have worried. The sheer size of Molineux, in addition to the roof steelwork makes the ground visible from several miles away.

Former alumni Billy Wright and Stan Cullis both have statues erected outside the stadium and areas of the ground named after them. The Cullis area in particular dominates Molineux in terms of height, with two large tiers towering higher than any other part of the stadium. Former striker Steve Bull is also celebrated with a stand of his own, having scored for fun in a glittering 13 year spell at the club.

The club's two mascots 'Wolfie' and 'Wendy' were out to snap pictures with young fans outside the club shop. I decided against getting a programme for now - a decision which came back to bite me later on and went to collect my ticket. After playing photographer to a couple of selfie-seeking scandinavian fans, security staff were frisking everyone at the entrance.

Having found nothing incriminating, I breathed a sigh of relief at avoiding the rubber glove treatment and took my seat. This was a very different Wolves side from the one I'd witnessed demolish Chester FC 4-1 in a pre-season friendly five days earlier. Kenny Jackett had exiled some of the big earners from his first team squad and put his faith in youth. As a result, Kevin Doyle, Jamie O'Hara and the ever unpopular Roger Johnson were left to train with the reserve team, while the club tried to move them on. In Johnson's case, a Wolves fan told me he'd rather have Roger Rabbit shoring up the defence. He wasn't joking either.

Seated close to the corner flag in the Jack Harris Stand, I was in prime position to see the Wolves players warm up and almost take a few fans out with wayward shots into the crowd. Everyone chose to stand up for the majority of the game. Within seconds of the kick-off, sentiments towards outcast defender Johnson were enforced when he was politely told to go forth and multiply by the vociferous fans within my vicinity. It wasn't sold out, yet Molineux was still a cauldron of noise.

For a team just relegated from the Premier League, Norwich lacked any real bite during a lacklustre first half. The lightning pace of Nouha Dicko - who would give Usain Bolt a run for his money, carried the home side's greatest threat. Although the visitors came out with renewed vigour for the second period, they went down to ten men just as they were in the ascendancy. Defender Martin Olsson was given a second yellow card on the hour, then allegedly placed his hand on the referee. The Swede made it a hat-trick of sins when he kicked out at a water bottle on his way down the tunnel.

Four minutes later, Wolves grabbed the only goal of the game. Debutant Rajiv Van La Parra took full advantage of the space left by Olsson's absence to whip a ball onto the head of an unmarked David Edwards to glance past John Ruddy. Cue the pandemonium around Molineux and the ambitious chants of "we are going up." Steady on lads!

Norwich's fate was inevitably sealed. Their best chance fell to new buy Lewis Grabban, who fluffed a one-on-one after goalkeeper Carl Ikeme kept him out. The forward had been scoring for fun at AFC Bournemouth, but looked out of sorts here. Neil Adams was still waiting for his first win as Canaries boss.

Right on the final whistle, the heavens opened and it took a while to negotiate my way through the crowds and out of the stadium. I cursed myself for not buying a programme when I had the chance. Now it was difficult to see where I could get one from. One final desperate search in the club shop resulted in disappointment when the staff informed me they had sold out and pointed me in the direction of the club website.

Admitting defeat, I made my way back to the station to catch a delayed train home. While the crowds gathered, a couple of drunken fans tried to get a rise out of the Norwich fans standing on the opposite platform by serenading them with songs about former Wolves and current Ipswich Town boss Mick McCarthy. The Norwich fans didn't bite, so the yobs changed tactic. If at first you don't succeed, turn to insults.

"I can't read, I can't write, but I can drive a tractor." Still nothing. Unfortunately, the train was now pulling in so I left the singing group to their own devices and instead ejected a young ginger squire who happened to be sitting in my seat. Rule #1. Always pre-book your seat when making a rail excursion. He was a good sport (although I didn't really give him a choice) and vacated his space next to the female he was probably trying to chat up, although I did feel Ron Weasley's eyes piercing a hole in me from a distance.

Three games in as many days meant I was off to a steady start, although I did decline the offer of a physical game and actual run around when I arrived back home in favour of a roast dinner. It would have been rude to say no to a piping hot meal, plus I needed to get some of my five a day in to balance the pie diet.

Best chant: "He scores with his left, he scores with his right, and when we play the Albion, he scores all fucking night! Stevie Bull." Wolves fans letting their former scoring legend that he's not forgotten.
Match ticket: £23. I expected better quality for the money I paid, especially with Norwich coming down from the Premier League.
Match programme: I finally managed to track down a copy from eBay. The seller even threw in a complimentary match ticket and teamsheet. The magazine's theme for the season was to splash an extreme close-up of one of the squad onto the front cover, whether they were photogenic or not. Contained enough quizzes and reading fodder to make it worth the £3 + postage fee I paid.
Cost of food: £5 pie and drink combo.
Pie rating: 3/5. Steak and ale pie. A tall puff pie, nice and hot with lashings of gravy. Could have done with a bit more meat.

Final Score:
Wolverhampton Wanderers 1 (Edwards 64)
Norwich City 0
Attendance: 22,053

Getting to know Barnsley
Liam Dyson - West Stand Bogs (Barnsley Fanzine)
www.weststandbogs.co.uk
Twitter @ WestStandBogs

Favourite memory as a Barnsley fan?

I've seen my side win promotion to the Premier League, lose at Wembley twice (old and new), win promotion at Cardiff back to the Championship, but the best memory for me was us staying up in the Championship a couple of years ago with a last day draw at Huddersfield Town. The crowd, the atmosphere, the run we'd been on to give us a chance was unbelievable and something I'll never forget. We thought we were on to something - we were obviously wrong.

Best game you've witnessed at Oakwell?

We beat Chelsea 1-0 in the FA Cup Quarter Final in 2008. They had Michael Ballack, John Terry, Florent Malouda, Joe Cole etc and the lad who scored for us we signed from Cheltenham and he only ever got four goals in two years with us. Great night!

Best/worst players to pull on a Barnsley shirt?

There's not enough room to tell you the worst, but the likes of Neil Redfearn, Craig Hignett and Ashley Ward are among the best.

Best thing about Oakwell?

The West Stand. Built in the early 1900s, it's still standing and has character that you don't find anywhere else. It's a little worse for wear, but it's ours and a link to our history that we shouldn't forget.

Worst grounds you've visited?

I like rubbish grounds. They're much better than the new ones. Doncaster's is a soulless DIY flat pack bowl and I never liked Coventry's either.

Enjoyable away days?

Peterborough before they got shut of the standing area was a personal favourite - always a great day out. Other than that, Scunthorpe I enjoy visiting. Not too far away and again a link to a proper football past.

Famous Barnsley fans?

Dicky Bird is the obvious one. John Stones - England international and future captain still comes to games when he's not playing for Everton.

Quirky fact time?

Arsenal got the vote to join the top division instead of us back in the 1920s despite us finishing above them regularly. We could've been watching Mesut Ozil etc now if they hadn't have bought their way in....Rather watch us be rubbish anyway.

TALES FROM SOUTH YORKSHIRE - PART ONE

Game #4: Capital One Cup First Round - Tuesday 12th August 2014
BARNSLEY vs Crewe Alexandra - Oakwell

It was time to get re-acquainted with an old friend. I hadn't set foot in Yorkshire since a relationship went down the tubes three years prior. However, football heals all wounds and today was the day to lay that ghost to rest. Besides, it was the first round of the Capital One Cup, so what better than an overnight stay and taking in two of Yorkshire's finest clubs. First up, a trip to the West Riding of Yorkshire and Barnsley.

I opted to stay in Sheffield due to familiarity of the area. After three relatively short train trips, I checked into my Travelodge. One not so short power nap later and I was dashing back to the station to make my connection to Barnsley. After finding a seat amongst the cluster of work commuters making their journey home, I was hoping for a straightforward half hour journey. Apparently, the toddler running up and down the carriage screaming at the top of her lungs had other ideas. My trusty headphones were back at the hotel, so I smiled through gritted teeth while hoping she would get tired and simply stop. She was like the duracell bunny and kept on going. Thankfully, the obscure town of Chapeltown came to my rescue and she got off the train to continue her screams around the Yorkshire moors.

With my hearing back in tact, I made it to Barnsley and immediately made a beeline for the first fan in a shirt I could find in order to get directions to the ground. I befriended a pleasant chap, (Yorkshire through and through I might add) who was only too happy to guide me to the stadium. My knowledge of the Tykes and their current playing staff was tested as we walked towards the ground, but the conversation flowed nicely. My new friend informed me rather excitedly that Leroy Lita was making his debut tonight. The big striker had just been released by Swansea City and, taking into consideration Crewe's lack of attacking options since the sale of Mathias Pogba, (Paul's lesser talented brother) I boldly predicted a home victory.

Oakwell is situated ten minutes from the train station. Under a bridge, up a slip road, over a hill and there it is smiling at you at the bottom. The surrounding area felt like a throwback to the old Coronation Street set. It's a pretty sweet deal for the locals living in the neighbouring houses to say there's a football ground at the end of their road.

Much of Oakwell has undergone something of a facelift to bring it in line with many other current stadia. However, the West Stand still has one foot in the past, given the sight of a tatty tin roof being propped up by pillars and only partially covering a select few fans from the elements. Luckily for them, it wasn't raining. The players' tunnel was situated in the far corner between the North and West Stands, going against a tradition I was used to seeing of teams emerging from directly by the centre circle.

Admittedly, thoughts of running into famous football folk had popped into my head from time to time. I wasn't expecting Barnsley to be the first place for that to happen. Former Wrexham boss Brian Flynn walked past puffing on a cigar and carrying a leather docket of notes. He was obviously on a scouting mission. I was in a quandary. Given my allegiance to the Chester colours, I couldn't endorse a selfie with a Welsh affiliate, so simply flashed a polite smile as our paths crossed.

The League Cup hasn't been the most glamorous of competitions amongst fans. As an added incentive, sponsors Capital One were running a 'kids for a quid' initiative in order to coax more families to the match. With two of the four stands being open, I took full advantage of the unreserved seating to get a good pitchside seat, opposite the some 200 fans to make the voyage over the Pennines from Crewe.

Upon further inspection of the programme, it transpired that the two teams would meet again in a league fixture at Gresty Road four days later. By Danny Wilson's own admission in his programme notes, the Barnsley boss stated neither side possessed the squad depth to rest all their players, so this game was a dress rehearsal for the weekend. I stuck by my prediction of a home win due to Barnsley's relegation from the Championship and Crewe only securing League One survival late last season.

My Yorkshire friend was right about Lita joining the club. The much travelled forward looked to be carrying some excess timber, but was thrown straight into the team. Lita, along with fellow new signings Keith Treacy and Sam Winnall featured in the thick of the action early on, although it was painfully obvious that the trio had left their scoring boots at home. Crewe soaked up the pressure and hit their hosts with a sucker punch after half an hour. A wayward Liam Nolan shot was turned in by a well-timed Billy Waters slide which further muted an already silent Oakwell.

The Barnsley faithful woke up in the second half, although I suspect it was to mainly dodge the balls that were flying past them. When Winnall did get an effort on target, Ben Garratt got down quickly to smother a powerful header at the near post. Lita lasted an hour, and, after Winnall almost sent another effort into the car park, Barnsley were out of ideas. Crewe made the game safe six minutes from the end with a goal straight from the training ground. This time, Waters turned provider, laying off for captain Matt Tootle to drill a shot past Adam Davies after the right back had sprinted unchallenged down the touchline.

It was time to eat humble pie (which was a lot nicer than the meat and potato offering I sampled before kick-off.) Crewe had played some good stuff and I clearly misjudged them a little bit. They didn't miss Pogba at all. In Barnsley's case, Lita needed to find the gym as much as Winnall needed to locate his scoring boots.

The train journey back to Sheffield was peaceful and a scream free zone. A quick trip to Sainsbury's was necessary to repel the pangs of hunger and replace the disappointing taste left by the half eaten pie I had attempted earlier. Despite a limited schedule on Travelodge TV, I lucked out when the Chase came on, so settled down with my pasta snack and spiked ITV's evening ratings. Party on!

Best chant: "We all hate Leeds scum." A popular chant at grounds not named Elland Road.
Match ticket: £12.
Match programme: £2. Could easily be mistaken for being a Crewe programme, seeing as almost half of the content was dedicated to the visitors. Reduced in price and slimmed down in length due to it being a cup game.
Cost of food: £5.30 for a meat and potato pie and bottle of water. £3 for a grab bag of sweets was too expensive.
Pie rating: 1/5. Very dry and heavy on the stomach. The content was quite bland and it ended up in one of the personalised bins sporting the likeness of club mascot Toby the Tyke. Sorry Toby!

Final score
Barnsley 0
Crewe Alexandra 2 (Waters 32, Tootle 84)
Attendance: 4,391

Favourite memory as a Sheffield United fan?

When I was two years-old and, being the son of a mixed marriage (my Dad supports United, my Mum supports Wednesday) I got the choice of who I wanted to support. At that age, it was more a choice of red or blue and of course, red always wins. Watching United get promoted to the Premiership in 2006 made me really proud to be a Blade. The atmosphere was electric.

Best game you've witnessed at Bramall Lane?

There are far too many to remember, but it was great in the Premiership to face all the big teams like Manchester United and watch Ronaldo miss a pretty much open net.

Best/worst players to pull on a United shirt?

You have to look at the legends such as Tony Currie and Alan Woodward for the best. As for the worst players, I suppose everybody has a few they aren't to keen on, it's personal preference.

Best thing about Bramall Lane?

Not being a pie man, I won't be saying the Pukkas! Just the atmosphere when everybody finds their voice and has something to cheer about. 20,000+ people singing "You fill up my senses" must be terrifying for the opposition.

Worst grounds you've visited?

As a Blade I have to say Hillsborough just for a little dig at Wednesday, but to be completely honest it's not too bad. Barnsley isn't great. I may be biased by the local rivalry though.

Enjoyable away days?

The new Wembley is an amazing stadium, absolutely stunning! Going away from United for a second, Barcelona's Camp Nou is out of this world.

Which club serves the nicest pies?

No idea, I most certainly didn't eat all the pies!

Famous United fans?

Sean Bean (Actor), Kell Brook (Boxer) and Jessica Ennis CBE (track and field athlete)

Quirky fact time?

Brian Deane scored the very first goal in the Premier League (five mins) when Sheffield United beat Manchester United 2-1 on the 15th August 1992.

TALES FROM SOUTH YORKSHIRE - PART TWO

Game #5: Capital One Cup First Round - Wednesday 13th August 2014
SHEFFIELD UNITED vs Mansfield Town - Bramall Lane

A lazy lie-in followed by a chilled out day around town before the match. Well, that was the objective. What is it they say about the best laid plans? Turns out they went right out the Travelodge window. Thanks to the JCB and massive Wilkinsons lorry crashing about outside which woke me up at an early hour. This was going to be a long day. Shooing the cleaner away from my room no fewer than three times, I was determined to utilise the 12pm check-out deadline to the last possible minute in order to kill some time ahead of the evening.

So what did I end up doing to pass the time for the rest of the day I hear you ask? Well, when I wasn't nearly getting run over by trams or buses, I summised that the library was a lot safer than playing in traffic. The pick of the day's reading was Keith Gillespie's autobiography. The Northern Ireland winger graduated from Manchester United's famous 'Class of 92' and also enjoyed a chequered stint at Bramall Lane towards the end of his career. To say the man liked a bet was a bit of an understatement, judging by a reported loss of close to £7million over the years. Digesting that information, I decided to give the accumulator a miss on this occasion and walked past Ladbrokes on the short voyage to the ground.

The sight of Jessica Ennis-Hill's face was one of the better images to greet me as I approached the stadium. The club re-named their Bramall Lane Stand after the gold medal olympian in September 2012. Although the turnstile was a little bit of a squeeze to get through, aesthetically, the ground is beautiful, with all the stands being of the same height. Additional seating, along with a conveniently placed office block has filled in one corner of the ground to give it an enclosed feel. Replacement roofing has also seen some of the view-impeding pillars done away with. Getting to my seat early and taking a gaze around the surroundings, it sunk in that Sheffield United were clearly underachieving. Nigel Clough's minimum objective for the season had to be a play-off place, although I was hoping he had his eyes on the Capital One Cup for my visit.

An electrical fault meant that both video screens were out of order. I took my seat close to the dugouts to watch both sides complete their warm-ups. Thanks to the Pizza Hut buffet I had gorged on earlier in the day, I wasn't too keen on a savoury snack. However, the Pukka pie advertising boards around the pitch did their job and I was sold on the chicken balti option. It was everything that the Barnsley pie wasn't.

Attendance for the game was quite sparse, although the travelling contingent from Mansfield got involved right from the kick-off. The travelling Stags lit up the stadium with their singing and put their Sheffield hosts to shame. Chants of "Sheffield is a shithole, I want to go home," filled the air, while their Yorkshire counterparts sat on their hands for the most part. A half-hearted chant about Sheffield Wednesday was weak in retaliation and never really got going. I sensed that the United fans felt Mansfield were beneath them and were holding back. If the game on show was a League fixture, then I have no doubt that the attendance, atmosphere and volume would all be increased by a few notches.

United dominated the opening period, thanks to wide players Ben Davies and the debuting Jamal Campbell-Ryce bamboozling Mansfield with their pace and trickery on the flanks. Mansfield substitute Sam Clucas almost gave the visitors a shock lead when he headed onto the bar. That was the wake-up call United needed. The Blades sharpened their attack and defender Andy Butler headed home a Davies corner just after half time. Rather than retreat into their shells, Mansfield came back at their hosts and levelled four minutes later. The goal had a hint of good fortune to it. Lee Beevers saw an initial effort deflected into the path of teammate Alex Fisher, whose subsequent rebound took another deflection to wrong foot helpless goalkeeper Mark Howard.

All evening, I had dreaded the game going to extra time. Normally, there wouldn't be a problem, but with a return train to catch, I prayed to the football gods for someone to find a winner. Having waited around all day for the game, I didn't want to be short-changed by having to leave early and missing the climax. Someone must have heard my pleas. Four minutes from the end, Marc McNulty picked the ball up in the area, rode a couple of challenges and nicked the ball past Sascha Studer to net his first goal for his new side and ensure Sheffield United's progression to the next round. Marc, next time I'm in Sheffield, I'll buy you a pint or a whisky. Whatever you prefer. One thing's for sure, I'll definitely return. I'm a big fan of the stadium and the savouries on offer, plus a packed to the rafters Bramall Lane is something I'd like to be amongst.

Best chant: "We're Mansfield Town, we'll sing on our own." A true reflection of the crowd activity.
Match ticket: £10. Very nice gesture by the club. Shame that more fans didn't take advantage of the offer.
Match programme: £2. Another reduced edition, but better than Barnsley's offering the night before. Included a diary of the Blades' pre-season and correctly picked out Mansfield scorer Alex Fisher as one to watch.
Cost of food: £4.80 for a chicken balti pie and bottle of water.
Pie rating: 4/5. Full of flavour and spices, combined nicely with succulent chicken and soft pastry. It loses a mark for the slight blemish in presentation, due to the top of the pie being slightly caved in.

Final Score
Sheffield United 2 (Butler 53, McNulty 86)
Mansfield Town 1 (Fisher 57)
Attendance: 7,929

Getting to know Doncaster Rovers
Glen Wilson - Editor of Doncaster fanzine popularSTAND
www.popularstand.wordpress.com
Twitter @vivarovers

Favourite memory as a Doncaster fan?

I probably give a different answer every time I respond to this question to be honest. For pure drama and joy, the events at Brentford at the end of 2012-13 will take some beating whereby we went from staring a play-off place in the face as Brentford won a penalty deep in injury-time, to winning the title at the other end inside 18 seconds. But my favourite memories are definitely from my formative years on the Pop Side at the old Belle Vue ground - it was a happy escape to be on that terrace and enjoying ourselves and generally larking about as Rovers ploughed up the leagues. For all we've achieved since moving to the new stadium I'd go back there in a heartbeat.

Best game you've witnessed at the Keepmoat Stadium/Belle Vue?

At the Keepmoat probably the 2008 play-off win over Southend; we picked them apart that night, showed everything that was right about the team and style under Sean O'Driscoll, and of course saw the greatest hat-trick I'll ever see live courtesy of Jamie Coppinger. At Belle Vue there's a lot to choose from; the Conference play-off against Chester in 2003 was too important to be enjoyed, despite the incredible late equaliser, so it'd be between the League Cup demolition of Aston Villa in 2005-06, or the 1-0 win over Hull in the league in 2004-05. The latter game didn't mean that much, coming as it did in mid-season, but the atmosphere - whipped up by Rovers' cheerleaders parading the Division Three title trophy we'd pipped Hull to the season before in front of the away end before the game - was incredible, and the roar on Michael McIndoe's winning goal deafening.

Best/worst players to pull on a Doncaster shirt?

It's hard to look beyond Jamie Coppinger in my life-time. Next season, so long as he stays fit, he should beat the club's all-time appearance record. For a creative player to do that is some achievement. His touch, control and vision are still as great as they've ever been. I still get a buzz watching him even now.

Best thing about the Keepmoat Stadium?

Functionality-wise it's great, but it could be so much more with a bit of atmosphere. Hopefully, with the emergence of a new fans' group called Black Bank that might change next season.

Worst grounds you've visited?

The worst experience I've had at a football match is at Reading's Madejski Stadium. Of all the many soulless bowls that have been opened in recent years it ties with Coventry's Ricoh Arena for being the most soulless and most removed from the town it is supposed to serve. The reason Reading's ground wins out though is their stewards and staff gave us the rudest and most unhelpful welcome I've experienced in years. Add in the wall-to-wall Waitrose branding and it is everything that's wrong about modern football.

Enjoyable away days?

I prefer football grounds with a bit of character, so Fulham has long been a favourite.

Famous Doncaster fans?

Apart from the One Direction guy (Louis Tomlinson) none that I'm aware of. At least none who have had any sort of staying power.

Quirky fact time?

Magician Paul Daniels owns the two penalty spots from our old Belle Vue ground. In the mid 90s to help funds, the club sold off pieces of the pitch to fans and supporters. Daniels, whose agent at the time was a Rovers fan, was convinced to buy the two penalty spots. I asked him on Twitter the other year if he'd received them when the club left the ground in 2006, but he said he hadn't.

KEEPMOAT KARAOKE

Game #6: League One - Saturday 16th August 2014
DONCASTER ROVERS vs Port Vale - Keepmoat Stadium

Chester Races always provides a perfect excuse to get out of town for a while. With more drunken idiots in the vicinity than I could shake a stick at, I just needed to plot my destination. Port Vale really caught my eye thanks to their midweek 6-2 thrashing of Hartlepool United in the Capital One Cup. Doncaster enjoyed a resounding 3-0 win at Yeovil Town on the opening day too. With the memories of my midweek Yorkshire jaunt still fresh in the memory, I was sold on a return across the Pennines. Saturdays at Chester train station are always manic. Factor in the Races crowd and it's like a cattle market. Thankfully, I just about managed to beat the queue to pick up my pre-booked tickets and made it to the platform to catch the first of what would be seven trains during the course of the day.

With the Premier League kicking off, there was a mass of various football fans at Crewe station all with their shirts on display ready to travel up and down the country. It was a sight of beauty and reinforced my belief that there's no better thing to do on a Saturday than going to experience the buzz of a live game.

There was a police presence (not for the first time) outside Doncaster train station and the force gave me directions to the ground. Public transport was advised and swiftly ignored. My stubbornness kicked in, as I took off on an unorthodox two mile walk, which isn't recommended. The Keepmoat is situated on the outskirts of an industrial estate and just around the corner from a Tesco factory. It's a relatively new ground, having been in use for seven years. Generous offers of £1 hot dogs (no doubt past their sell by date) were wisely turned down, as I walked past several greasy spoon vendors on the fringes of the stadium. Tickets were easily obtained from a busy window, with queues kept to a minimum. Banners of famous players past and present hung outside various parts of the stadium and there was no bag check upon entering through the turnstile.

I came across Mr T's favourite eaterie, the 'Jibba Jabba' restaurant, which is the stadium's largest events room and located on the second floor of the East Stand. Instead of 'pitying da fool,' I opted for a pauper's snack, then took my seat. The Doncaster fans were pretty quiet, bar three gentlemen sat next to me. Their shouting was directed mainly at the poor linesman all afternoon. Port Vale were rocking their gold and black Barnet tribute kit. When winger Chris Birchall came to take a throw-in, the three man band next to me asked if he had "sprayed his shirt on," before recommending he "lay off the jerk chicken." Birchall got a chuckle out of that and responded with a thumbs up in good jest.

In Tom Pope, Port Vale possessed one of the league's formidable strikers. The 6"3 forward gave Doncaster as many problems on the ground as he did in the air throughout the afternoon. Even 6"7 defender Rob Jones struggled to contain him and extinguish the constant attacks on goal.

The visitors opened the scoring just before the half hour mark. Jed Steer did well to save a Chris Lines header, but Ben Williamson was on hand to nod in the rebound from close range. Pope then got in on the act. The forward's low angled drive squirmed underneath Steer at his left hand post. Two minutes later, the Valiants rubbed salt in the wounds with a third, of which, Lines was involved again. When his corner was only half cleared, skipper Carl Dickinson took advantage by smashing in the rebound. It was very tempting to go and join the travelling support who were bouncing about having a whale of a time, but alas, I stayed in the West Stand where tensions were bubbling.

Doncaster were booed off at the break. A couple of fans missing a few teeth spouted some incomprehensible bile towards the bench. I couldn't make out what they were saying, but it was pretty obvious that the Keepmoat faithful were not happy. Even a half time proposal on the pitch didn't bring much cheer, although a few sarcastic fans did chant "you don't know what you're doing," at the happy couple.

The home side made changes for the second period, but the expected siege on the Port Vale goal didn't really happen. Donny boss Paul Dickov introduced Kyle Bennett as his final substitute, and it was he who pulled back a goal. A speculative 25 yard shot looped over Sam Johnson to give the home side hope. That hope was quickly extinguished when Harry Forrester was given a straight red card for raking his studs across Johnson's face, as the goalkeeper smothered the ball. Donny's hopes of getting something out of the game went down the toilet, prompting the three man band to tune up once again and scream more obscenities at the poor linesman.

The ill feeling seemed to carry over to the streets after the game. A group of travelling youths taunted their South Yorkshire hosts and were escorted to the train station by the Doncaster constabulary. I walked past thinking that would be the last I'd see of them. Wrong! The travelling party just happened to be on the same train back as me and broke into song on the platform. That's when I realised their crime was simply having consumed too much sugar during the game. As the train became more congested and standing room only at Sheffield, the karaoke resumed. Stoke's version of Blazin' Squad treated us all to a rendition of Atomic Kitten's 'Whole Again,' as we made our way over the Yorkshire Moors and back towards Lancashire. Soon enough, the ringleader was trying to get the carriage to do the Okie Kokie and spell out D-I-S-C-O. Following a run through of Steps and 5ive's back catalogue, I decided to take out my earphones, conserve the iPod battery and join in the sing-along through Chinley (and other obscure places.) One grumpy Sheffield Wednesday fan tried to interject, but his claim of the lads "showing everyone up," fell on deaf ears and the "fat bastard" (their words not mine) was put in his place and everyone went back to the hymn sheet.

There was a touch of sadness when the party ended at Stockport and I continued the rest of a low-key journey back to Chester. Despite walking back through a carnage of angry drunken race-goers, I'd had a cracking day out and seen plenty of goals and banter. Bring on the next adventure!

Best chant: "Feed the Pope and he will score." Port Vale fans.
Match ticket: £20. Had a great view of the pitch and the ticket was value for money.
Match programme: £3. Jam packed with player interviews, posters, news from the Junior Rovers and a brief write-up on every other team in the division.
Cost of food: £5.20 for a chicken balti pie and bottle of coke. £2.50 for a sausage roll.
Pie rating: 2.5/5. Pie was a little burnt on top. The chicken didn't have much of a kick to it. More care needed in presentation and less time in the oven. On the other hand, the sausage roll was nice and hot with delicious flaky pastry.

Final Score
Doncaster Rovers 1 (Bennett 74)
Port Vale 3 (Williamson 27, Pope 39, Dickinson 41)
Attendance: 6,437

Getting to know Wycombe Wanderers
Dale Hurman - www.wycombe.vitalfootball.co.uk
Twitter @vitalwycombe

Favourite memory as a Wycombe fan?

The most memorable game probably has to be the F.A. Cup fifth round replay with Wimbledon at Selhurst Park in February 2001, which we won 8-7 in a penalty shoot out having drawn 2-2 after extra time with two players forced off with serious injuries, another sent off and our goalkeeper (Martin Taylor) saving a last minute penalty in front of 4,500 Chairboys.

Best game you've witnessed at Adams Park?

I fell in love with Wycombe Wanderers following a 5-1 thrashing of previous unbeaten leaders Kettering Town in a GM Vauxhall Conference game in front of over 4,000 at Adams Park in November 1990. We played some special football that day. It was certainly matched by the 5-3 win over Brentford in a then third division match in December 2001. We came back from 2-0 and 3-2 down to take the points and it had just about everything.

Best/worst players to pull on a Wycombe shirt?

The best player I have ever seen play for Wycombe Wanderers is Dave Carroll. He might have been nicknamed 'Jesus' because of his hairstyle, but he was a footballing deity. He scored a goal in the aforementioned thumping of Kettering Town which still gives me goosebumps now. He scored exactly 100 goals in 602 appearances. Jason Cousins and Keith Ryan also deserve notable mentions. I am loathe to name a worst player, however Mexican defender Carlos Lopez's solitary appearance in a 2-0 defeat away at Cambridge United in January 2002 has almost transcended into mythology!

Best thing about Adams Park?

I think many visitors to Adams Park would say that the best thing is the picturesque setting within the Chiltern Hills. For me it represents the place where friendships have been made, dreams have become reality and left cherished memories that will live forever.

Worst grounds you've visited?

I struggle to define the word "worst" when used in this context. Colchester United's new community stadium is a hideous anti-septic Orwellian vision which is a total contrast to their vibrant, atmospheric former home at Layer Road. But for the different colour seats it could be Shrewsbury Town's New Meadow. The wind-swept three-sided Kassam Stadium is also a dreadful monstrosity when compared with Oxford United's old Manor Ground, which often felt like an old footballing amphitheatre.

Enjoyable away days?

I loved my one and only visit to Swansea City's former Vetch Field home. It was almost like a museum and I half expected to see the raised hands of John Toshack.

Famous Wycombe fans?

BBC breakfast presenter Bill Turnbull is an avid Chairboy. Whimsical stand-up comedian, actor and presenter Sy Thomas ought to be far more famous than he currently is. He's funnier than you!

Quirky fact time?

We are the only club to have reached the semi-finals of the F.A. Cup, the League Cup, the F.A. Trophy and the F.A. Amateur Cup. We were named Wanderers after the first ever winners of the F.A. Cup in 1872.

Thoughts on ticket prices in general?

Personally I feel ticket prices in England, from the Premier League down into the lower tiers of non-league football, are far too much, represent poor value for money and are generally prohibitive for many working class supporters.

Name your Wycombe Dream Team?

(4-2-3-1 formation)
GK: John Maskell
RB: Jason Cousins
LB: Matt Crossley
CB: Bernard Hooper
CB: Frank Adams
CM: Dave Carroll
CM: Keith Ryan
RW: Len Worley
AM: Noel Ashford
LW: Paul Bates
CF: Tony Horseman

Martin O'Neill - Manager

HITCHING A LIFT TO HIGH WYCOMBE

Game #7: League Two - Tuesday 19th August 2014
WYCOMBE WANDERERS vs Tranmere Rovers - Adams Park

Did I really have to go to Wycombe today? It was a long way to go just for a football game. Those were my thoughts as I pondered my path to Buckinghamshire from the comfort of my bed.

Like a Jose Mourinho press conference, I was giving out mixed messages. Logic and common sense were telling me that perhaps I had bitten off more than I could chew with the ground challenge. Good job, I'd spent most of my life ignoring those two traits. Snapping myself out of a self-doubt mindset, I got my head back in the game so to speak.

Given my lack of a driver's licence, Wycombe wasn't the cheapest or easiest place to get to. This made the decision to swap the train tracks for the luxury of the Tranmere away coach much more feasible and cost effective. I booked a seat for a very reasonable £26, then made a short train commute to Birkenhead in order to link up with the rest of the Rovers contingent for my first taste of travelling on a supporters bus.

The Tranmere faithful were a pleasant bunch and didn't mind a newcomer infiltrating their brigade. As it was still the summer holidays, the attendance was greater than usual. Everyone was happy to mix. The college tearaways blended in with the Dads and lads. Likewise the middle aged couples mingled with the OAPs who had stuck with the club through thick and thin. Reliving Tranmere's famous 3-0 FA Cup victory over Everton from 2001 on the four hour journey down south only served as a reminder to how far the club have fallen. Now back in the fourth tier of football for the first time in 25 years, they were looking for their first win of the season. In contrast, Wycombe barely escaped relegation last season, but had flown out of the gates with two wins from two games.

After a short stopover at Warwick services to stretch our legs, it was back on the coach. With the Tranmere nostalgia finished, someone thought it would be a bright idea to put on last year's Super League Grand Final. It wasn't. My tolerance for eggchasing is quite low - no matter whether it's Rugby Union or League, it doesn't interest me in the slightest, so I decided to take a power nap for the duration of the trip. I awoke as we entered the industrial estate that houses Adams Park and we parked up in a small side street behind one of the units.

Wycombe is famous for its chair factory, hence the club's nickname the Chairboys. They also share their ground with Wasps Rugby club. Whereas home tickets ranged from £17 to £25 for football fans, there was a huge mark-up for the rugby, with the £25 seats costing £45. The club shop is even split into two, but there wasn't much stock on display. That being said, the Wycombe polo shirts did look quite trendy and quite a few fans had them on show as they started to make their way over a wooded hill to the ground. It was a beautiful evening in Buckinghamshire. The sun had its hat on, leaving Adams Park gleaming out against its backdrop of greenfields and meadowland. I summised it was definitely a ground more appreciated in the summer months.

I took my seat in the away end and was probably one of the first people to enter the stadium. A fellow travelling fan was sat a few rows back with his feet up and his head buried in a book. Close to 200 other Tranmere supporters who are based down south came to join us in the Dreams Stand. Thanks to the surrounding greenery, the vociferous chants from my vicinity were echoing back and drowning out any rebuttal from the home fans.

Tranmere were quick to settle and turned the form book upside down by taking the lead. Max Power's low cross was hooked into the top corner by striker Cole Stockton. The strike happened right in front of the Wycombe fans in the Greene King IPA Terrace and doused their enthusiasm.

Naturally, Wycombe mounted a comeback, only to find Owain Fon Williams in fine form. The Tranmere shotstopper looked comfortable saving from long range and collecting crosses - something that the many Tranmere fans stated he wasn't accustomed to. The visitors found a crucial second goal nine minutes after the break. Defender Matt Hill cut in from the left, and he combined with Eliot Richards to find Power. The midfielder drilled a low shot through a sea of players into the bottom corner, then made a beeline for the travelling support.

Operating with a small squad, Wycombe had named the same eleven for the fourth game in a row. Their tiredness had started to show. With games coming thick and fast during the opening weeks of the new season, Tranmere were simply the better team on the night and deserved their victory.

Sadly, there was no time to hang around at the final whistle, as we needed to get back on the road. Traffic was predictably quite congested. I glanced out of the window to see three Wycombe fans making hand signals at me. I think they wanted to know what the score was, so I replied in kind with a lovely v shaped two. That seemed to settle the argument with the little rascals, although I did give them a friendly wave as we pulled away from Adams Park.

As we got back on the coach, I caught wind of a fan conversation talking up a pub called the White Horse, located just over a mile from the ground. I deduced that the establishment was home to 'beautiful' strippers and entry was free, although donations were heartily encouraged for something under the somewhat loose advertisement of 'dances.' Naturally some of the college students piped up wanting to go. Unfortunately, the only itinerary on our coach's return journey was another stop at Warwick services and the only donation I made was towards a packet of Mini Cheddars.

The journey back took another four hours and was relatively low-key. The DVD player remained off and I was thankful at being spared more rugby. The bus dropped the majority of the party back at Prenton Park, but kindly carried on in order to drop a few of us the other side of the Mersey tunnel which was greatly appreciated. A non football fan had kindly agreed to put me up for the night. I repaid that faith by bursting in at 2:30am singing about Max Power. I slept on the floor. Not one of my finer moments.

Best chant: "He's Max Power, he's one of our own." Tranmere fans talking up the promising product of their youth academy.
Match ticket: £20 for an unobstructed view and fantastic atmosphere from the away support. A fair price for travelling supporters.
Match programme: £3. Wycombe's players and staff were bullish in promising there wouldn't be a repeat of last season's relegation struggle. Ironically enough, in the Tranmere portion of the writeup, a fan had picked out both the goalscorers Stockton and Power as two that Wycombe needed to watch out for. They didn't heed the warning.
Cost of food: £6 meal deal for sausage roll, chips and a bottle of coke.
Food rating: 3/5. The pies were given a wide berth in addition to something dubbed 'It's Not Bovril Mate.' To be honest, I didn't want to find out what it was, so played it safe with a sausage roll, which was nice and hot. The chips were crunchy, although there was no vinegar provided. I did conduct some pie research. My guinea pig was Ernie the Tranmere fan. Good old Ernie sampled a meat and potato offering. While it looked a little burnt, he begged to differ and wolfed it down, before declaring he'd get another at half time. He did just that, so I guess it's a thumbs up.

Final Score
Wycombe Wanderers 0
Tranmere Rovers 2 (Stockton 19, Power 54)
Attendance: 3,005

Getting to know Bury
Nick Holt - Manny Road End (Independent Bury supporters website and forum)
www.mannyroadend.co.uk

Favourite memory as a Bury fan?

After our second successive promotion in 1997, we found ourselves in the same league as Manchester City. We'd always been the poor relations and I had loads of friends who were City fans who laughed at me for supporting Bury. We played them at Maine Road on 14th February 1998 and in what has become known as the St Valentine's Day Massacre we won 1-0. It wasn't a massacre in terms of the scoreline, but considering the history, size and status of the two clubs it might as well have been.

Best game you've witnessed at Gigg Lane?

In terms of goals and excitement, we beat Gillingham 5-4 a few years back, but as an occasion it would have to be Manchester City at home in 1998 in a first division match. It was the first and only time I've seen Gigg Lane totally full. The Sky cameras were there and only a late equaliser cost us what would have been a huge win. It finished 1-1 and Georgi Kinkladze missed a penalty for City. Not that I have a hang-up with Manchester City or anything.

Best/worst players to pull on a Bury shirt?

Best - Mark Carter, David Lee, Liam Robinson. Worst - David Healy. Bloody dreadful in a Bury shirt, although my opinion of his awfulness came from the level of expectation we had as a result of his previous exploits.

Best thing about Gigg Lane?

Simply my favourite place on earth. Apart from necessary upgrades, it has hardly changed in years. It's got style and character and thankfully hasn't been transformed into one of those identikit grounds like so many clubs have these days.

Worst grounds you've visited?

Shrewsbury's New Meadow is the very definition of awful modern stadia. It's boring and totally lacking in character and Bolton's Macron Stadium looks like a child's Meccano project gone wrong. I don't like Carlisle's ground because although it's quite unique, it looks unfinished, like it's been poorly planned.

Enjoyable away days?

I like smaller lower league grounds like Cheltenham and Accrington, while Rochdale is always good because it's usually a good occasion and the pubs are dirt cheap.

Famous Bury fans?

Steve Berry (TV presenter) and Mike Read (DJ) claim to be fans but I've never seen either of them at Gigg Lane.

Quirky fact time?

It is alleged that our turf, which was often thought to be the best pitch in the country, originally came from Wembley. Don't know if it's true though.

GIGGING WITH THE SHAKERS

Game #8: League Two - Saturday 23rd August 2014
BURY vs Plymouth Argyle - JD Stadium (Gigg Lane)

East Lancashire is relatively close in geographical terms, yet while I didn't have any Bury fans in my social circle, bizarrely I could count on a Plymouth fan. Dave (everyone's got a friend called Dave) Banks or Banksy as he's more affectionately known hails from the South West and has followed the Green Army for as long as I can remember.

Unfortunately, a prior engagement ruled out Banksy from joining me for the short commute across the North West. Although Bury doesn't have a designated railway station, I didn't anticipate many problems travel wise. I've never wished a train ride to go so quick as the one I faced going to Manchester. Delayed and packed, I somehow scrambled into a vacant seat as part of a bank of four. Pretty soon, it became apparent that the adolescent teen sitting next to me fidgeting with his phone every five seconds, before standing on the furniture to acknowledge his friend several rows back would be the least of my problems.

Barely a third of the way into the journey, I was literally surrounded by a hen party. Normally I wouldn't complain, but these ladies were far from glamorous. The smell of cheap perfume and dirty cigarettes filled my nostrils, while talk of false nails, foot fetishes and vodka hurt my eardrums. I desperately turned up the volume on my iPod to block out my surroundings to no avail. Chantelle asked what I was listening to, so I said with a deadpan expression "music" and hoped that would be the end of our interaction. Enter Lisa, complete with tacky tramp stamps and bolshy manner. She sidled over showing off the wet patch on her pink dress from a toilet break as if it was some sort of badge of honour, before gulping the last of the vodka from her makeshift water bottle. I refused to buckle and hand over my seat out of stubborn male principle. Thoughts of last week's karaoke session with the Port Vale fans came flooding back and I was convinced that this was my karma.

Manchester was packed with all sorts of colourful people. More so than usual. In addition to the usual stereotypical weekend hustle and bustle, the football commuters were also joined by a sea of people flocking towards the annual Pride festival. Fortunately, the trams were still operating frequently and I made the 25 minute journey to Bury's Metrolink without much of a delay. I wasn't exactly sure of where the ground was, so started to follow a group of lads through the city centre. With no football shirts in sight, I asked a passer-by if I was on the correct route and he concurred. We shot the breeze about Bury and his pessimism was disappointing to hear.

"Don't expect much today, they're not very good," he said. I'm more of a glass half full guy, so brushed off negative Nigel, nipped through a side street and came to the ground. All of a sudden, a flurry of white shirts appeared from nowhere. It was like I had gone through the wardrobe and entered Narnia. Now there were football fans everywhere. Relieved that the town of Bury contained a fanbase after all, sounds of the Stone Roses and Happy Mondays blaring out of the stadium speakers brought a smile to my face.

The Shakers were celebrating 130 years with their official history being serialised throughout the season in the matchday programme. Slightly bigger and wider than most, it's produced more like a mini magazine. You really got a feel for the club just by reading it and how much they appreciate their fans. There was still an element of ill feeling towards a debatable decision which cost the club a famous result at Bolton Wanderers in the Capital One Cup. A respectable 2,448 supporters made the trip to the Reebok Stadium which was the largest away following on record during the first round of this year's competition. David Flitcroft's damning verdict of the referee was refreshing to read, as was his revelation of giving fans a lift back on the team coach after.

Staff and stewards were helpful in directing me to a good seat up in the family enclosure, close to the directors area in the Main Stand. I spied a number of executive boxes lying pitchside at the bottom of the stand in a makeshift greenhouse build. I doubt I'd be the first to speculate on how many times the windows have been broken by wayward shots.

Formerly Gigg Lane, the club rechristened their home as the JD Stadium in November 2013 after securing a three year sponsorship deal with JD Sports. If that wasn't chavvy enough, then the sight of JD's slogan 'King of Trainers' splashed across the shirts as the club's main sponsor certainly was. While Gigg is an all-seater stadium, three of the stands still contain a number of supporting pillars. These didn't impede my view, but I can understand them being an issue for some spectators.

Once again, I was blessed by another sunny day. Plymouth had brought a respectable number for the long journey up north which has to be commended and deserves a mention. Sadly, I was situated further away from them than originally planned, so couldn't really make out many chants. Only a small section of Bury fans housed directly opposite in the Les Hart Stand seemed to sing along, although they did beat a drum quite heartily throughout the game.

After falling short of promotion last season, both sides were clearly eyeing a play-off place this time around. For that reason alone, I was expecting an open match. I certainly wasn't disappointed and didn't have to wait long to see a goal. Bury opened the scoring inside five minutes from a set piece, taking full advantage of Plymouth's napping defenders. They may as well have still been on the team bus. Nicky Adams whipped in a teasing cross and an unmarked Tom Soares rose highest to head home. The hosts doubled their advantage ten minutes later. New signing Danny Rose was given the simplest of tap-ins at the far post after Ryan Lowe's low cross zipped past the visiting rearguard.

Plymouth shuffled their pack with a triple substitution early in the second half. The bold move paid off when Pablo Mills was adjudged to have brought down Reuben Reid in the box. It was a soft penalty decision, but Reid picked himself up to rifle in the spot kick and bring the visitors back into the game. Late on, Reid unwittingly blocked a certain equaliser after failing to get out of the way of a goalbound effort. Bury just about hung on to claim a first home victory of the season.

A quick 15 minute walk took me back to the tram station and I travelled into Manchester once more. Thankfully, the horrible hens were nowhere to be seen or heard. I breathed a huge sigh of relief and enjoyed a peaceful train journey back to Chester while reading up some more on the history of Bury.

Best chant: "Lancashire La La La. Lancashire La La La." A simple but effective chant from the young, proud Bury folk.
Match ticket: £15 across the board for all tickets and unreserved seating.
Match programme: £3. The most in-depth programme yet. From community news to fans teams, supporters views, travel tales, player and coach profiles, it really covered all bases.
Cost of food: £5.40 for a steak pie and bottle of coke.
Pie rating: 5/5. A fine offering from the Pukka pie range. Cooked to perfection, the puff pastry was a joy to dig into. Nice soft crust, not soggy at all, nor tough to eat. Bury were quick to re-tweet my appreciation. I was up at half time to indulge in a second offering.

Final Score
Bury 2 (Soares 5, Rose 15)
Plymouth Argyle 1 (Reid pen 66)
Attendance: 3,156

Getting to know Crewe Alexandra
David Law - Crewe Alexandra Mad Facebook Group
www.crewealexandra-mad.co.uk
Twitter@CreweMad

Favourite memory as a Crewe fan?

Beating Brentford 1-0 in the play-off final in 1997 giving us promotion to what is now the Championship. This was run close by winning the Johnstone's Paint Trophy in 2013, because obviously being a Crewe fan doesn't lead to any trophies most of the time.

Thoughts on ticket prices in general?

I think ticket prices are roughly about right in League One - £20-£25 - however my season ticket works out at £12.50 a game which is good. I can't get my head around Premier League prices - £40 + especially when it has been shown that Premier League clubs get so much revenue from TV that they could comfortably afford to only charge £20 and subsidise the fans. Here down in Leagues One and Two, the matchday revenue is probably more important. My own club is slow to reduce ticket prices for unpopular games/mid-week cup replays etc - other clubs in League One do much better.

Best game you've witnessed at Gresty Road?

Difficult to say. There were some crackers while we were in the old Division One playing the likes of Manchester City, Leeds, Stoke etc. I really enjoyed a 2-1 win over Bolton with Dean Ashton scoring the winner, so that is my best home game.

Best/worst players to pull on a Crewe shirt?

Plenty of very good players have been at Crewe including Nick Powell, Danny Murphy, David Platt, Dean Ashton, Rob Hulse, Rob Jones, Neil Lennon, Robbie Savage....... the list goes on and on. Dario Gradi thinks Nick Powell is the most talented and he should know! Richard Walker wins my vote for worst player in a Crewe shirt. A hopeless, gangly centre half with no co-ordination and the first touch of a baby elephant. He was once hauled off by Dario after 30 minutes of the first half after gifting away two goals.

Worst grounds you've visited?

The old Rotherham ground was shocking. Also Macclesfield was an open terrace with no roof.

Enjoyable away days?

Preston is a good away visit.

Best thing about Gresty Road?

The best thing about Gresty Road is that it is a friendly club and most other fans seem to like coming here, so the atmosphere is good. It's also very conveniently located especially by train, being two minutes from the station.

Which club serves the nicest pies?

I'm generally very unlucky when it comes to pies and cannot recommend any. Ours are not too bad, but I've heard Wigan do a mean pie.

EVERYONE NEEDS GOOD NEIGHBOURS

Game #9: Capital One Cup Second Round - Tuesday 26th August 2014
CREWE ALEXANDRA vs Bolton Wanderers - The Alexandra Stadium (Gresty Road)

Passing through Crewe had been second nature so far on the tour. The train station is one of the main travel hubs of the North West, so I thought it was about time I went to check out the football team. The Alexandra Stadium is perfectly situated next door to the train station on Gresty Road, hence the club's nickname the Railwaymen. A short and simple 20 minute train journey was the perfect tonic for taking in a midweek game, especially having started back at work after a lovely two week break.

Coming into the game, Crewe were cemented to the bottom of League One and no doubt welcomed the distraction of a cup tie. Having been in attendance for their first round victory at Barnsley, I had the lovely thought of following the club all the way to the final. Lucky mascot or not, in reality it was still a nigh on impossible dream. Even the most fervent of Crewe fans would agree. However, everyone loves a good underdog story and on this night, I was definitely rooting them on tonight against fallen giants Bolton Wanderers.

A beautiful smell of freshly cooked fish and chips wafted over my nostrils as I passed the 'Gresty Road Chip Stop,' conveniently located directly opposite the ground. Fans were pouring out of the shop and loitering in the street, tucking into their fish, chips and gravy. I spied a few away fans getting involved and mixing with their counterparts.

Given the closeness in proximity, Bolton had brought a healthy following to pack out the aptly named 'Whitby Morrison Ice Cream Van Stand.' I took up my assigned seat opposite in the Main Stand which houses a good 70% of the ground's current capacity and dwarfs the rest of the ground. I was sat just above the team benches. Crewe don't have any dugouts. Instead both sides are given an area of seats right at the front of the stand. I peered over to see Jay Spearing and other Bolton players not involved in the game share out bags of Haribo amongst themselves and appease autograph hunters. Both areas behind the respective goals were empty, although there was still a noisy atmosphere, with the Bolton fans entertaining themselves by passing around a large inflatable white ball.

Crewe showed they weren't overawed and turned the form book upside down with a goal inside two minutes. Bradley Inman sprinted clear and curled a beautiful shot past goalkeeper Andy Lonergan. The away supporters sarcastically clapped when their hapless team managed to string more than two passes together. Crewe were simply playing them off the park. The home side should have gone two up, but struck the crossbar, then inexplicably missed an open goal. Bolton boss Dougie Freedman was far from happy, but got a chance to give his side an early rollicking after the referee pulled a muscle in his leg and had to be replaced. Bolton supporters used the break in play to chant "Freedman, Freedman sort it out." The Scotsman was clearly listening and re-assigned his lacklustre team. The delay disrupted Crewe's rhythm and Bolton equalised before half time, when an unmarked Darren Pratley nodded in at the far post.

Mascot Gresty the Lion entertained fans during the break by taking the ALS ice bucket challenge. Personally, I think it's cruel to tip iced water onto an animal, whether it's of the stuffed variety, real, or in this case a man in a suit. Gresty immediately threw the gauntlet down to Boomer the Dog (mascot to rivals Port Vale) by naming the mutt as one of his nominees. I spent the rest of the interval reading the programme and finding out what happened to former Alex flops Pavol Suhaj and Jamie Moralee. Don't remember them? Neither do I. Inbetween pages, someone with a young child asked to get past. I duly obliged before realising it was ex-Crewe forward Dean Ashton. He made a beeline for director of football and ex-Alex manager Dario Gradi. The two immediately became engrossed in what looked like a father-son style conversation, so I thought better of interrupting their reunion for a gratifying photo.

Crewe looked like they could have done with Ashton's prowess during the second half. An injury to George Ray saw the Crewe defender stretchered off which saw eight minutes stoppage time added on. The person sitting next to me had either seen enough or wanted to beat traffic and duly left. Big mistake! I've never grasped why people pay so much to savour a matchday experience then leave before the end. Boy did he miss out. Jermaine Beckford lashed in a vicious volley in the area to seemingly seal Bolton's path into the next round, but Crewe remarkably pegged them back at the death. Super sub Marcus Haber had caused problems with his large frame since coming on and he nodded in an equaliser to send the game into extra time.

I had never seen a penalty shootout in the flesh before and neither team could be separated during the first 15 minutes. Haber sent an effort onto the crossbar, before Bolton found the killer goal two minutes into the second period. Beckford bagged his second of the night when he reacted quickest to a Lee Chung-Yong pass to deftly touch the ball past goalkeeper Ben Garratt into the empty net. Frustration boiled over on the touchline when the ball went out for a throw and Crewe boss Steve Davis chewed out a hapless young ballboy with a harsh f-bomb tirade. Clearly irritated by the length of time it took for the lad to return the ball, it was still harsh from Davis.

Just like they did in their first round tie with Bury, Bolton needed 120 minutes to get by lower league opposition. Getting out of the ground at close to 10:30pm, I was thankful for the short journey back. Despite being a long day, the match was everything I wanted it to be. Crewe are a footballing side, as opposed to a hit and hope type and that refreshing stance is one of the reasons why I'd certainly come back. Being good value for goals at both ends of the pitch is another.

Best chant: "Tootle, Tootle give us a wave, Tootle what's the score!" The Bolton fans gave Crewe captain Matt Tootle a mountain of stick after not taking too kindly to a spot of simulation right in front of them.
Match ticket: £17.50. A slight reduction from normal matchday prices.
Match programme: £3. Correctly picked out Beckford as the one to watch and contained an entertaining A-Z chat with defender Adam Dugdale, along with some good write-ups on the youth and development squads - two things which are synonymous with the club.
Cost of food: £4.30 for a pie and bottle of coke.
Pie rating: 2/5. The quality between Holland's and Pukka pies is night and day, with the former being the choice of savoury on tonight's menu. Meat and potato pie didn't have much flavour to it. Looked suspiciously like the same snack I'd normally leave on the Tesco shelf. Overdone in the microwave and came apart quite easily.

Final Score
Crewe Alexandra 2 (Inman 2, Haber 90)
Bolton Wanderers 3 (Pratley 40, Beckford 90, 107)
Attendance: 2,642

Getting to know Birmingham City
Oli Osborn - Made in Brum (The Blues Fanzine)
www.madeinbrumfanzine.com

Favourite memory as a Birmingham fan?

It would be difficult for any Bluenose to look past the Carling Cup Final against Arsenal in 2011. The whole cup run was a fantastic experience overall and Obafemi Martins' goal (with a bit of help from Laurent Koscielny and Wojciech Szczesny) in the last few minutes capped off a perfect team performance from the boys. A whole generation of supporters have never seen the club lift a major trophy, so it was a great moment for everyone involved with the club. The resulting European campaign the following season was another highlight, particularly the away victory over Club Brugge, making Birmingham City the first club to win away against the Belgian side.

Best game you've witnessed at St Andrew's?

As mentioned earlier, the Carling Cup run in 2011 was a special period. The two home games against our bitter rivals Aston Villa and the semi-final second leg versus West Ham will be forever engraved in my memory. Plenty of opposition managers down the years have credited the St. Andrew's faithful for their support and those two nights are perfect examples. Both games proved that the "12th man" theory does exist and Birmingham City fans know how to get behind their team during the big occasions.

Best/worst players to pull on a Birmingham shirt?

It will take a lot for a player to take Christophe Dugarry's place as the best Birmingham City player since the turn of the Millennium. The Frenchman was signed on loan in January 2003 and scored five goals in four games to ensure survival during the club's first season back in the Premiership. The World Cup winner's goal against Charlton Athletic epitimises his fantastic footballing ability and the swagger only a Frenchman could pull off! Honourable mentions go to Stephen Carr, Mauro Zarate and Joe Hart. As you will get with most clubs that are not in the Premiership top six, the Blues have had their fair share of awful players. Richard Kingson and Carlos Costly are two players that particularly stand out as both men have played at international level and somehow been involved in three World Cups between them. Other poor players from the club include Darren Ambrose, Matt Derbyshire and Rowan Vine.

Best thing about St Andrew's?

What I enjoy about going to St. Andrew's is the atmosphere on matchday. All of the club staff are friendly and make the ground very welcoming to both sets of supporters. Also, the fans are realistic compared to a lot of other clubs. When we win, few get carried away and after a defeat the majority of supporters will look at the positives. It's something all fans should be like, because the reality is, it's just a game!

Worst grounds you've visited?

It may sound slightly biased given the rivalry between the two clubs, but I've never enjoyed going to Molineux. The orange (closer to yellow now in some areas) seats make the stadium look like a custard bowl and the stands down the sides of the pitch are too far away from the pitch. The away end at Burnley's Turf Moor isn't very inviting either.

Enjoyable away days?

To me, Wigan's DW and Bolton's Macron Stadiums are perfect for any away fan. They are both reasonably new grounds that sell cheap tickets, food and drink and allow clubs to bring big away followings. What more could you want? When it comes to the design then look no further than Arsenal's Emirates and Brighton's AMEX. Brentford's Griffin Park is very much old but gold.

Which club serves the nicest pies?
I not a pie eater myself, but I've heard great things about the food at Brighton's AMEX Stadium.

Famous Birmingham fans?
The only famous fans that come to mind are comedian Jasper Carrott, actor James Phelps (half of the Wesley twins from Harry Potter) and radio presenter Ian Danter. Former Chelsea striker Tore Andre Flo and Watford captain Troy Deeney are also Bluenoses.

Quirky fact time?
In 1906, when Birmingham City moved to St. Andrew's, a gypsy curse was placed on the club after a group of gypsies were removed from the site before it was the club's home. This curse put a 100-year jinx on the side and some managers have blamed it for bad runs of form and poor results. An example of this was in 1996 when Barry Fry attempted to "lift" the curse by urinating in all four corners of the pitch. It didn't work. In the 2006/07 season, when the curse had ended, the Blues were promoted to the Premiership. A coincidence?

Thoughts on ticket prices in general?
Ticket prices are something that a football club and its supporters will never agree on. My own personal opinion is that there is a fine line between a club selling themselves short and the working class fan being priced out of the game. If you look at other forms of entertainment such as the theatre or going to a theme park, then you will see ticket prices very similar to football clubs at the higher end of the market. Some may say that they are "once in a while" trips, but the reality is a football supporter doesn't need to go to every game! The 'Twenty's Plenty' campaign has grown rapidly over recently, but the problem with this could be that lower and non-league clubs who are based close to big clubs could lose a lot of money as a result of higher quality football becoming easily affordable in the Premier League.

SEEING WHAT ST ANDREW'S HAS TO OFFER

Game #10: Capital One Cup Second Round - Wednesday 27th August 2014
BIRMINGHAM CITY vs Sunderland - St Andrew's

The honeymoon period was officially over. Being back at work brought me back down to earth with a massive bump. In addition to re-adjusting to the early wake-up calls, the ridicule coming my way was certainly on par with an under-fire manager.

From the outset, I knew that this adventure would provide a host of challenges along the way and put a strain on many relationships. Now, I don't mind being the butt of some of the jokes in the office, but it was a bit early and certainly harsh to be labelled as being "set up to fail."

My morale was taking a kicking worse than a Sunday League footballer. Birmingham fans could certainly relate. The Blues may have upset Arsenal to win the League Cup back in 2011, but were famously relegated in the same campaign and haven't come close to reclaiming their place in the Premier League since. They only preserved their Championship status on the final day of last season.

Fortunately, the football calendar intervened by providing another game to lift my spirits. What made it even better for me was the fact that I could finally call in some reinforcements. Danny made good on his earlier promise and agreed to come along with his mate Dave Singh. This would be their third game in as many days, having attended the Hawthorns the night before to see West Bromwich Albion edge out Oxford United on penalties and Chester's draw at Kidderminster during Bank Holiday Monday.

Meeting for a swift pint in the city centre, Danny was knocking the drink back just as quick as I was getting around the first ten grounds. Dragging him from the bar, we caught a two minute train from Moor Hill to Bordesley, linking up with Dave, before making the ten minute walk to St Andrew's. Dave informed us that Birmingham had dropped their "extortionate" prices for the game and were expecting a big attendance despite only having three quarters of the ground open. The queues were moving quite quickly, but I declined paying cash on the gate, as I wanted to get my ticket stub. Having to register with the club for the privilege, I decided to kill two birds with one stone and asked the kind ticket clerk for any good food recommendations. He went back to check with the club chef and told me that a chicken balti pie would be my best bet. Armed with that useful information, I high-fived Birmingham's cuddly dog mascot Beau the Brummie en route to entering the stadium.

St Andrew's wouldn't look out of place in the Premier League. At just over 30,000 capacity, all four of the stands are two tiered. Our elevated view in the Tilton Road end provided a nice bird's eye view of the pitch and of the city centre poking out from the opposite corner of the ground. An estimated 2,000 Sunderland fans made the trip from the North East. Certainly good going for a midweek cup game. The over-excited PA announcer rallied the crowd behind the Blues and in a classy moment, former City player Sebastian Larsson was given a warm welcome back to St Andrew's when his name was read out. Sunderland didn't reply in kind to Birmingham boss Lee Clark. Chants of "he's just a fat Geordie Bastard" filled the air, as the gaffer took his place in the dugout. It seems that Clarky's two years spent on Wearside (1997-99) aren't held in high regard by the Sunderland faithful, given his past allegiance to rivals Newcastle United.

Sunderland named a relatively strong side with plenty of top flight experience plus Jozy Altidore. Slow and lethargic, the American looked better suited to playing gridiron based on a woeful shot he sprayed into the heavens. The home side didn't fare much better and rarely tested the debuting Costel Pantilimon in the Sunderland goal, although David Cotterill was unlucky with an effort which hit the post. It soon became painfully clear that Birmingham were bereft of stars or real match winners. They had finally got all the high earners off the wage bill which has turned out to be a necessary evil.

Straight out of the where are they now archives, ex-Manchester United defender Jonathan Spector was brought on earlier than expected to replace the injured Neal Eardley for the home side. Despite the game's dour opening, the Birmingham faithful were quite noisy and that made for a good atmosphere. I'd definitely chosen the right area to be in and shared the optimism that a goal desperately craved by the home faithful would arrive soon.

Danny and Dave needed a pint during the break and braved the crowds to go and queue at one of the heaving concourses. I went along and decided to share a coke with myself. Yes, I finally found a bottle with the correct spelling of Shaun on it. Sometimes it's the small things in life that make you happy. The stroke of good fortune continued when I spotted £10 on the floor. With the rest of the hungry food goers looking at the half time scores, I discreetly placed a foot over the note and swiftly claimed it for myself. Cashback indeed!

Just as the game looked destined for extra time, Sunderland shifted up a gear and netted three late goals, although Birmingham will point to a host of alleged bad refereeing decisions that went against them. The home side stopped as they thought the ball had gone out of play, instantly forgetting the golden rule of playing until hearing the whistle. Jordi Gomez took full advantage with a darting run and precise finish to beat Colin Doyle with a low shot into the bottom right hand corner. Clayton Donaldson almost levelled, but he could only watch his bicycle kick roll agonisingly wide from deep inside the box.

Sunderland sealed the game by hitting their hosts with two cruel sucker punches. Adam Johnson netted a second after Doyle parried from Altidore, before Connor Wickham broke clear to fire an angled shot across the hapless goalkeeper and into the net. The scoreline definitely flattered the visitors and was a bit harsh on Birmingham, whose fans had already started leaving in droves when the second goal went in. Just to rub salt in the wounds, the Sunderland fans graciously asked "Clarky" what the score was.

As we were leaving, plenty of Birmingham fans were still complaining about getting short shrift from the referee, while taking comfort in the fact that they matched their Premier League opponents for most of the game. They quickly turned their attention to the TV when they heard that city rivals Aston Villa had been knocked out by lowly Leyton Orient. As articulate as ever, cries of "shit on the Villa," echoed around the walls of St Andrew's as everyone went their separate ways. There was a small police presence scattered around the city to ensure rival fans didn't clash on the way home. Thankfully, there was no trouble and I caught the red eye train back home. During the trip back, I was comforted by the fact that football and good friends are never far away. Birmingham will need the same unwavering support from their fans if they want to get over their recent struggles and bounce back.

Best chant: "One nil to the referee....Two nil to the referee." Birmingham City fans, who won't be lining up to buy Darren Bond a Christmas card anytime soon.
Match ticket: £12. Around half the price of a usual match ticket.
Match programme: £1.50 for a paper thin edition. Aside from a solitary player interview and short piece on Sunderland there wasn't much readable content, which was disappointing.
Cost of food: £6 meal deal for a pie, drink and mars bar.
Pie rating: 4/5. The pie certainly didn't disappoint and was the best balti I've tasted so far. Firm crust, rich in spices and good quality chicken.

Final Score
Birmingham City 0
Sunderland 3 (Gomez 77, Johnson 87, Wickham 88)
Attendance: 11,245

Getting to know Derby County
David Hinds - DCFC Fans (Derby County Forum)
www.dcfcfans.uk
Twitter@dcfcfans

Favourite memory as a Derby fan?

Has to be that Paulo Wanchope goal v Man Utd at Old Trafford hands down. Robbie Savage leaving comes a close second.

Thoughts on ticket prices in general?

As a Derby fan, I find ours to be quite reasonable and have no complaints. When you look at some of the prices paid at other clubs in the Premier League it's getting silly yet fans are still paying, why? Norwich in the Championship want £40 a ticket! Until fans start voting with their feet we won't see any changes.

Best game you've witnessed at the iPro Stadium?

Does watching on TV count? Derby 5 - 0 Nottingham Forest, 22nd March 2014, won't forget that one for a while, Deforestation!

Best/worst players to pull on a Derby shirt?

Wow, well the best list isn't as big as the worst but I'll try to keep it short! Igor Stimac, Stefano Eranio, Francesco Baiano and Paulo Wanchope are my favourites, no other players have come close, but that doesn't really answer your question. I'm still in love with that Jim Smith team and struggling to move on. It doesn't get much worse than Robbie Savage. I had a few drinks to celebrate the day he left Derby!

Best thing about the iPro Stadium?

Having a Greggs at the stadium. Doesn't get much better than that!

Worst grounds you've visited?

Bolton, purely based on the atmosphere or should I say lack of it. This is maybe slightly harsh as I haven't visited many away grounds. I'm sure there are far worse out there.

Enjoyable away days?

Goodison Park is probably my favourite, even though our bus was pelted with rocks as we left the ground. I'm sure they were lovely lads really. St James' Park was also a decent ground despite being up in the heavens.

Which club serves the nicest pies?

I have no idea. I try to stay off the pies as I've seen what they did to the Mrs's waistline.

Famous Derby fans?

George Clooney is apparently the latest. There's also Jack O'Connell, that one who can't sing in One Direction (Niall Horan), Robert Lindsay and Keiran Lee who's a porn star if that counts?

Quirky fact time?

Derby County have the best online forum for their fans and I'm the man behind it :)

DASHING OFF TO DERBY

Game #11: The Championship - Saturday 30th August 2014
DERBY COUNTY vs Ipswich Town - The iPro Stadium

Scanning an eye across the weekend's fixtures, the Derby-Ipswich pairing was one of the first to catch my eye. Derby had thrashed Fulham 5-1 the week before and also came from 4-1 down to draw 4-4 against Ipswich in this fixture last season. This match had goals written all over it. The iPro was where I needed to be, so I was onto it like a tramp on chips.

I logged on to the Derby website to search for available tickets. The Rams were the first club I came across who were operating a fluctuating ticketing policy. Basically, the price went up and down depending on sales, demand, opponents etc but would never rise/drop below a certain figure. It's hard to understand and even more difficult to explain. I stopped the meter for a seat in the Toyota Stand and set off on my latest journey of self discovery.

Changing trains at my home from home Crewe, I made the simple connection to Derby. Disappointingly, there was only one carriage and it didn't look like it had been cleaned in a week. With rubbish strewn all over seats and crumpled up newspapers lying around, clearly the fine staff over at East Midlands Trains had slacked off. The journey was a slow one, especially with nothing to read. Dropping off a few Port Vale and Stoke City fans en route, gradually more Derby fans got on as we passed Alton Towers and Uttoxeter racecourse.

The iPro became visible as I departed the train station and made my through the swish, impressive Pride Park complex. No-one will ever go without legal advice or hungry for that matter, considering the number of law firms and eateries I passed. I even witnessed first hand a new way to open a bottle of beer, when a lad in front used the sign of Chiquito's to prize open his Carlsberg.

Derby's stadium was recently renamed the iPro as part of a sponsorship agreement (something I'd learn all about throughout the day.) It's very photogenic and, along with a plethora of firms pledging their support on the front of the stadium, the club also pay homage to its history with pictures from former alumni on its outer walls. Ex-club captain and Croatian defender Igor Stimac, (who enjoyed a four year spell at the club in the mid 90s) prominently features and it triggered happy memories of playing as Jim Smith's Derby on Championship Manager back in the day. It's a shame that I never got to see the players of that era - Stefano Eranio, Francesco Baiano and Paulo Wanchope play in the flesh, although in current personnel Will Hughes and Jeff Hendrick, the club do have some exciting prospects at their disposal.

The club boast a Starbucks and a Greggs on site. Sadly, the latter is shut on a matchday so that it naturally doesn't eat into the pie sales from inside the ground. Heading through the turnstiles for my pre-match snack, the eating area and toilet amenities are given ample space. Perfect for someone like myself, who sometimes suffers with mild claustrophobia.

I couldn't have asked for a better seat when I found out I was two rows from the touchline, with a great view and within distance of the fanatical Derby supporters in the adjacent South Stand. In a lovely show of class, the Ipswich players all stopped to pose for a photo with their nervous mascot on their way to change before the game. A motivational team video had the stadium rocking to bring the teams out. Derby's mascot Rammie the Ram looked like he had chugged a couple of cans of Red Bull as he came running onto the pitch and kept the crowd amped up. Having spent much of the pre-match in the stands posing for photos with youngsters, this mascot had been the most passionate I'd witnessed so far.

As for the match, I know it's a cliche, but it really was a game of two halves. Derby's pressure paid off when they went ahead early on. Ipswich failed to clear a cross and goalkeeper Dean Gerken did well to keep out Chris Martin's initial effort. A rebound was foiled on the line, before Martin converted a second attempt. The players made a beeline for Rammie and nearly knocked the poor guy's head off with a team pile-on. Derby lost Hendrick to a serious looking shoulder injury a short time after. The Republic of Ireland international was down in pain for over five minutes before being gingerly escorted from the pitch.

The Derby faithful had sung their hearts out from the first whistle and didn't really give the Ipswich fans a look-in. The away following did have something to cheer about just after the restart when defender Christophe Berra rose highest to head home from a Paul Anderson free kick. Both goalkeepers were called into action more frequently and Derby's fans started to grumble rather loudly about refereeing decisions going against them. "We always get shit refs," could be heard at frequent intervals towards the end. Even the introduction of my namesake - Leon Best couldn't provide a winning goal for the home side and both teams had to be content with a point.

On the whole, the match was quite pleasurable to watch. The only thing that started to grate on me was the constant plugging of this, that and the other all the time. I know a club needs to make revenue, but when substitutions and corners start being sponsored it's a bit too much. Wherever I turned to, it felt like I was watching a run of non-stop commercials. The only pitch I was interested in was right in front of me.

I was informed that some of the roads leading up to the stadium are closed off for 15 minutes after the game to give pedestrians chance to leave without fear of being run over. I was almost caught cold at the station when a platform mix-up led to me just about catching the train back to Crewe. Yet again the East Midlands staff had outdone themselves by only providing one coach, so a group of us were stuck in the lobby and jostling for space. Thank god nobody farted! In that sweatbox, broken wind could have been fatal. With the entrance to the aisle completely blocked off, the banter started flying around which was a good way to pass the time. One bloke enquired when the buffet cart was coming out. Sadly, it didn't make an appearance. Fortunately, the crowd dispensed pretty quickly just two stops in and I made a successful beeline for an empty seat.

There was one final twist in the tales from the train. Pulling away from Stoke-on-Trent, a Potters fan enquired if I had been to the match when he spotted my programme. He seemed friendly enough, so the two of us started talking about various grounds and the cost of games. Being a season ticket holder at the Britannia Stadium, my new friend was bemoaning the cost of a Premier League away day. The conversation was flowing nicely, when he unwittingly missed his stop. It turned out that his girlfriend was waiting to pick him up, as they had reservations booked for a nice meal and now he was going to be late. Unsuccessful attempts were made to contact her until the train pulled up at Kidsgrove a few minutes later. I bid my friend farewell and gave an apologetic look, as he walked along the platform in the midst of an argument with his other half, whom he'd just managed to get hold of. I think it's safe to assume that he picked up the bill for dinner.

Best chant: "Can you hear the Ipswich sing? I can't hear a fucking thing. No noise from the Tractor Boys." Derby County fans
Match ticket: £27. Could have been a bit better, but could have been worse.
Match programme: £3. A handy size, slightly smaller than A5 which fit easily in the pocket. Jam packed with pieces on various players, words from the backroom staff, president, academy update. Contained everything that a programme should.
Cost of food: £6.50 for a peppered steak pie, bottle of coke and mars bar.
Pie rating: 2/5. A bit on the small side, too much gravy and the steak tasted a bit odd. Would have much preferred a Greggs pasty.

Final Score
Derby County 1 (Martin 13)
Ipswich Town 1 (Berra 52)
Attendance: 26,673

Getting to know Oldham Athletic
Ryan Green - OA 95 Athletico Ultras (Oldham Athletic Facebook Community)
Twitter@OA95Athleticos

Favourite memory as an Oldham fan?
Beating Everton away 1-0 in the FA Cup in 2008.

Best game you've witnessed at Boundary Park?
Probably Liverpool in the FA Cup Third Round in January 2013. We won 3-2 against a team with Steven Gerrard and Luis Suarez in it. The atmosphere was electric!

Best/worst players to pull on an Oldham shirt?
Far too many bad players have put a Latics shirt on and then moved clubs and done well such as Adam Rooney and Matt Smith. Best players in my time supporting them has been David Eyres, who was a brilliant winger, and showed great commitment every game. Sean Gregan in defence was a brilliant leader, kept the defence in line all game.

Best thing about Boundary Park?
The history of it. So many clubs have had to upgrade altogether and build a brand new ground. Everything about our ground is historical and unique. The old floodlights, the entrances, even the old wooden seats in the Main Stand upper.

Worst grounds you've visited?
So many awful grounds, mainly due to the lack of atmosphere from some of them. Gillingham was an awful experience, as 300 of us got bunched into a 200 seat section. Most of the newly built grounds I haven't enjoyed due to the lack of atmosphere, although some of them are very impressive to look at.

Enjoyable away days?
Goodison Park is a great stadium with plenty of history. At Loftus Road, you're very close to the pitch, making it a great ground for atmosphere purposes.

Famous Oldham fans?
Paul Scholes is seen on a few occasions thoughout each season. I'd love for him to become our manager one day.

Quirky fact time?
Oldham have been in the same league for 19 years, and I've supported them for 18 of those. As far as I know we hold the record for it. Lucky me!

GOING OLD SCHOOL AT OLDHAM

Game #12: Johnstone's Paint Trophy Northern Section First Round - Tuesday 2nd September 2014
OLDHAM ATHLETIC vs Bradford City - SportsDirect.com Park (Boundary Park)

International breaks are annoying. Everyone tolerates them through gritted teeth. Hanging around for close to two weeks like a bad smell, most of the football calendar goes into shutdown, depriving fans of their weekly fix. God bless the English lower league and thank heavens for the Johnstone's Paint Trophy. You heard that right, I refuse to get on the bandwagon that bashes the competition. Faced with listening to the same monotonous drivel coming out of Roy Hodgson's mouth, I opted for a night out in Greater Manchester to see what the Football League Trophy was all about.

Making my way through the Manchester crowds like a knife through butter, I negotiated the rush hour commuters at a ruthless pace and made my way to the Metrolink in quick time. Surely, there would be lots of other like-minded folk just like myself going to the match tonight. There wasn't, not a soul, nada. Not a single Oldham shirt in sight. I got off the Metrolink at Freehold and it was eerily quiet. I stopped a guy at the bottom of the stairs reading a map in the hope he could point me in the right direction. My prayers were answered when he replied that he was going to the game.

It turned out that Phil (my new acquaintance and travel guide for the evening) was a Bradford fan who lived in the area and was taking advantage of the short commute. The Bantams were in fine form having knocked fierce Yorkshire rivals Leeds United out of the League Cup a week earlier and were eyeing another cup run tonight. Walking along two long straight roads, and ignoring the waft of curry passing over my nostrils from a nearby takeaway we discussed all things Bradford. From Benito Carbone's extortionate wages to bankruptcy, it struck a chord how far they had fallen since hitting the heights of the Premier League at the turn of the Millennium. Like so many others, the club have been to hell and back, so all credit to the supporters for sticking by them. It's a horrible feeling seeing a club fold and a sight no true football fan ever wants to see.

Walking through Chadderton, and past a boarded up mosque, the floodlights to the ground started to peep through as we got closer. However, something was missing and I'm not just talking about the lack of a Main Stand. (a new one was in the process of being built to enhance/modernise the ground after being demolished in 2008.) No other fans were in the vicinity, the floodlights weren't on and I couldn't hear any music in the distance. I started to think that I had the wrong day or maybe the match had been called off. Crossing a muddy field and passing a kids game, it looked as though their attendance would be higher. Alas, I had nothing to worry about as right on the approach to Boundary Park, the fans came swarming out of hidden side streets. It was just like Bury all over again.

The brickwork definitely looked like it had some stories to share. Old summed up the ground perfectly. A short glimpse of the empty away dressing room left ajar brought back memories of the P.E changing rooms at junior school. At the same time, certain parts of the ground seem to be finally getting the TLC it deserves, with only a small part of unused terracing remaining. The slight modernisation continued when sportswear mogul Mike Ashley entered into a corporate sponsorship earlier in the year to have the ground renamed. There was a generous amount of space for people wishing to park at the ground and fans and stewards seemed accommodating. The game was strictly cash on the gate, yet the kind souls at the ticket office still obliged my request for a ticket stub.

At this point, I said bye to Phil, who headed for the away end. I purchased my savoury snack from one of the two food huts in the top corner of the ground, then looked for an unobstructed view, as there were still a couple of pillars in the makeshift Main Stand. The game was unreserved seating, but to be fair, the area around me filled up pretty quickly. The wooden seats were a bit rickety and looked like they could have done with a good dusting down. Right as I took a big bite out of my pie, a mosquito also spied an opportunity to snack under my arm. If that wasn't reason to move, then the Brady Bunch that got a bit too close definitely were. Around five guys and a girl had started at the end of the row, gradually getting closer towards kick-off until the girl was sat right next to me. Unfortunately for her, I came to watch the game and snubbed the chance to play Blind Date. Sorry love, it wasn't you, it's me.

The away fans started in fine voice, out shouting their hosts who were more concerned at swinging their replica tops above their heads and bouncing up and down. It was bloody freezing, so more power to them. Noticeable in the Oldham lineup was ex-Wolves defender George Elokobi and not just for his warrior-esque white headband. The man was quite simply built like a brick wall. He decided that nothing and no-one was getting past him on this night.

I got the feeling early on that there wouldn't be many goals in the game, although Bradford did strike the post early in the second half. Much of the entertainment came from yelling "hoof" whenever the ball was belted into the sky, which was becoming a little bit too frequent. Unlike the Capital One Cup, the Johnstone's Paint Trophy goes straight to penalties if the scores are level after 90 minutes. With a shoot-out looming, Oldham settled a cagey affair thanks to an inspired substitution from young manager Lee Johnson.

Jordan Bove had only been on the pitch for a matter of minutes when he netted his first senior goal. The 18-year-old smashed in a rebound from inside the six yard box after Bantams goalkeeper Jordan Pickford could only parry Carl Winchester's initial cross turned shot. Off came the shirts once more from a small Oldham contingent, seemingly immune to the cold. Bove had pace to burn and almost netted a second almost instantly, nutmegging an unfortunate defender only to be denied by poor finishing.

The streets of Chadderton weren't exactly inviting after dark, so I was thankful for a photographic memory which ensured that I didn't get lost during the brisk walk back to the Metrolink. Sadly, I didn't run into Phil again, but I'm thankful for his help in getting to the ground, plus it's always nice getting to chat to other fans along the way. At the end of the day that's one of the many positives that I'm taking out of this adventure.

Best chant: "Get your spray out for the lads." Bradford fans begging for the use of the invisible spray, which was being trialled during the Johnstone's Paint competition.
Match ticket: £10. A fair price to try and boost attendances for a competition that's looked down on by some managers and supporters.
Match programme: £1 for a hastily put together pull out, perfect fodder for a paper aeroplane. Just joking, I've kept it with all the other programmes.
Cost of food: £4.80 for a pie and soft drink.
Pie rating: 2.5/5. Boldly went for something new, sampling a cheese, potato and onion offering. The onion was overpowering and I contemplated throwing it away to get something else. However, once it cooled down, the other ingredients compensated, so I finished it and slightly changed my stance. Generous half mark added on.

Final Score
Oldham Athletic 1 (Bove 88)
Bradford City 0
Attendance: 2,535

Getting to know Burton Albion
Mark from Burton Albion Fans Forum - Brewers Talk
www.burtonbrewers.proboards.com

Favourite memory as a Burton fan?

The 1986/87 FA Trophy replay at the Hawthorns v Kidderminster was just an incredible game and atmosphere.

Best game you've witnessed at Eton Park/Pirelli Stadium?

Difficult! Eton Park would be a 2-0 FA Cup victory over Staines in the 80's. A complete performance and two top draw goals from Stewart Mell. One of which was a missile of a free kick from inside the centre circle into the top corner. At the Pirelli, it would have to be the FA Cup game against Burscough in the round prior to playing Manchester United. Because our game was postponed on the Saturday, by the time we actually played on the Tuesday we already knew the draw. The sense of anticipation and large crowd, plus a barnstorming performance made it a very special night.

Thoughts on ticket prices in general?

Ticket prices in my opinion are scandalous at all levels of English football. When you think you can watch a game in the Bundesliga for around the same cost as Leagues One, Two and Conference it doesn't make sense. The Premier League and Championship is cloud cuckoo land to me. With all the TV money they don't need to charge those prices, but it shows the greed running through football.

Best/worst players to pull on a Burton shirt?

Worst player was probably poor old Benji Patterson, while the best was undoubtably Ian Storey Moore, a football wizard!

Best thing about the Pirelli Stadium?

The stadium is paid for. It's a nice ground with a good atmosphere and suits what we need with the added bonus that the foundations we built in for future expansion.

Worst grounds you've visited?

Blimey! The worst League grounds are Wimbledon (aka Kingstonian) and Accrington Stanley by some distance.

Enjoyable away days?

The old Wembley, and Plough Lane, where the former Wimbledon used to play.

Famous Burton fans?

The Stig from Top Gear.

Quirky fact time?

The Clough connection. Brian Clough's first game as a manager was an away friendly at Eton Park around 1965/66 as manager of Hartlepool against Burton Albion, who just happened to be managed by his own teammate from Middlesbrough - Peter Taylor. Later that season, Taylor joined Clough at Hartlepool along with some Albion players and a partnership was born and the rest is history. The connection didn't end there though, as when Nigel Clough saw the vacancy for a manager at Albion, he asked his dad for advice. The answer "go on my son, the club has great potential." Brian became a paying season ticket holder who I had the privilege to meet. Nigel went on to realise that potential, but we lost Brian prior to the move to the Pirelli Stadium. Both are held in very high esteem locally and Nigel's ten years in the gaffer's seat have established him as a club legend. We are also the only club who have a drunk as a mascot in Billy Brewer!

HUNGOVER WITH THE BREWERS

Game #13: League Two - Sunday 7th September 2014
BURTON ALBION vs Portsmouth - The Pirelli Stadium

I've already stated that I'm not normally an advocate for Sunday games, purely for the fact that they seem to lack the normal buzz of a Saturday. Although, with it being that time of the month when I needed to show my face in work, I was grateful for the fixture list providing the option of a Sunday game.

I'd never been to Burton before, although I did briefly date a girl from the area back in my late teens. Awwww, the joys and pitfalls of internet dating. To cut a long story short, she came to Chester a few times, but the feelings weren't strong enough to sustain a long distance relationship. Just like the flimsy necklace she once bought me, the bond shattered rather quickly. Needless to say, I wasn't planning on a surprise reunion during my whistlestop stay in Staffordshire. Setting off early in order to make the lunchtime kick-off, I was feeling worse for wear, but that's my own fault for drinking champagne. I'm not normally one to partake in the posh fizz, mainly because the bubbles go straight to my head. That stance went out the pub window when I attended a friend's birthday bash the night before and definitely over indulged. The excited Irish fella decided to mark the occasion in style and very generously splashed out on two bottles of bubbly for the table early doors. That mixed with beer made me feel like I'd done a few rounds with Floyd Mayweather. Irish eyes weren't smiling on my friend, who spent the night in hospital after an untimely faceplant on the dancefloor. Whoops!

A timely McDonald's breakfast at Birmingham New Street started to combat the hangover and allowed the short connection to Burton-upon-Trent to pass smoothly. Ironically, as the train pulled into the station, the first thing I spotted was the Coors factory in the distance. Alcohol was the last thing I wanted to see or taste. Hence Burton's nickname the Brewers. Known as one of the world's 'Brewing Capitals,' I passed numerous pubs on the mile and a half walk to the ground. Plenty of Pompey fans had made the long journey and both sets of fans seemed jovial on the pre-match trek. The Pirelli Stadium has been around for almost ten years now and was built across the road from their old Eton Park home. Three out of the four sides are terraced, so I opted to sit down in the Main Stand, which is all-seated and the largest part of the ground.

Burton just missed out on promotion a few months prior when they were narrowly defeated by Fleetwood Town in the play-off final. Unlike me, the club hadn't suffered from any hangover since May's crushing defeat at Wembley. Having taken 13 points out of a possible 15, Gary Rowett's side had come flying out of the blocks in this campaign. Add two impressive scalps of Wigan Athletic and Queens Park Rangers in the Capital One Cup and the club were definitely primed and ready for all comers.

Portsmouth were being touted as one of the favourites to go up, but aside from veteran defender Nicky Shorey and substitute forward Patrick Agyemang, none of the players really registered with me. Three relegations in four years meant that the club had largely had to start again from scratch in terms of playing personnel.

For perhaps the first time this season, I actually took my coat off at the ground. (Friends know how much I get attached to my jacket.) Bearing in mind that Burton play in yellow, even Stevie Wonder could see that my red shirt stuck out like a sore thumb. The Burton faithful didn't seem to mind that they had a neutral in their ranks and I was allowed to queue for food without any needle from the hometown folk.

I managed to take my seat just before kick-off and quickly realised I was in the naughty corner. I was literally in the very end seat hugging the wall by the exits, no doubt as punishment for leaving my yellow shirt at home. The PA announcer did a great job at getting the fans behind the team by yelling "come on Burton," at the top of his lungs as the teams made their way onto the pitch. Spurred on by the call to arms, the home side went ahead within 90 seconds. Adam McGurk - one of five former Tranmere Rovers players in the starting lineup converted Stuart Beavon's cross turned shot off the underside of the bar.

The goal didn't get the Pompey fans down. In fact, the drummer and bell ringer were non-stop all afternoon. Club mascot Billy the Brewer rallied the home fans when he wasn't trying to get a rise out of the stewards by tapping them on the shoulder and walking the other way. The stewards needed to act when the family next to me complained about an obstructed view due to the substitutes stopping to warm up right in front of us. They were moved higher into the stand at half time and politely told to express any grievances in an email to the club. To be fair, there weren't any raised voices and the situation was handled perfectly.

During the half time break, I saw a fan get lucky on the crossbar challenge with his first attempt. I also learnt that one steward still held Portsmouth - particularly Kanu in contempt for knocking his beloved West Brom out of the FA Cup during Pompey's winning run in 2008. He was convinced that the side from the South Coast were going to nick an equaliser in this game, and they should have. Somehow a goalmouth scramble went begging and Burton punished their visitors with a second goal. Lucas Akins turned on a sixpence to fire a thunderous shot past Paul Jones. To their credit, the visitors kept on pressing, but couldn't find a way past goalkeeper Jon McLaughlin. Burton kept their unbeaten start in tact.

Burton definitely had a team worthy of promotion and a nice little ground to go with it. The capacity, coming in at just under 7,000 is probably right considering the size of the club's current fanbase, although the programme did note that a Canadian family from Calgary, Alberta had recently visited the ground after their young son discovered the club while playing on FIFA.

There was a big queue to get into the club shop after the game, so I didn't get a chance to see inside and instead strolled back to the station. The sun was still out and the hangover was now a thing of the past, yet I still passed on indulging in some famous Burton brew. Much like some of the young England contingent coming back off international duty and joining me on one of the return journey legs, I stuck with the healthy option of water and a mars bar.

Best chant: "One nil down, but it's still early." Portsmouth fans optimistically looking at the glass as being half full.
Match ticket: £18. I was so close to the pitch that I could have blown my nose on the corner flag.
Match programme: £3. 'The Matchday Brew' was presented as a glossy magazine and embraced social media with a "Tweet All About It" feature. The club were very social media friendly, printing one fan's zany tweet that he saw Pele, Luis Figo and Zinedine Zidane doing the conga outside the ground. Now that would be a sight to see.
Cost of food: £4 for a minced beef and onion pie, plus soft drink.
Pie rating: 3.5/5. Pukka kept up their excellent reputation of serving stellar pies. This one gets marked down ever so slightly due to some of the meat being a bit lean.

Final Score
Burton Albion 2 (McGurk 2, Akins 55)
Portsmouth 0
Attendance: 2,980

Getting to know Brentford
Billy Grant aka Billy the Bee
www.beesotted.co.uk
Twitter@billythebee99, @beesotted
www.youtube.com/beesotted1992

Best place to sit/stand at Griffin Park?

Personally, I stand in the Ealing Road. That's where most of the singing takes place. You could also stand in the Braemar Road paddock near the away fans for a bit of atmosphere too.

Best thing about Griffin Park?

It's old school ramshackled-ness. Most away fans love the fact we have a pub on every corner. Personally I love the fact that we're one of the few clubs with terraces still. A massive selling point and it will be a shame when we lose that.

How are plans shaping up for the new ground?

The permission has been granted . Much to the disappointment of the Kew and Chiswick million pound bungalow massive. It's now set to be ready for the start of the 2017/18 season, 20,000 stadium by Kew Bridge , about ten minutes walk from Griffin Park. So it's not going to be one of these out of town soulless numbers, hopefully. There is talk of somehow recreating the drinking den on each corner. That will be interesting.

Best away support at Griffin Park in recent memory?

Hard to say because our away terrace is quite small. It maxes out at 1,600 fans now. Every team that comes down normally sells out. The maddest support we have seen recently was probably Preston on both Gentry days. They came dressed to the nines in bowler hats and suits in honour of recently deceased players or fans. Last year it was dedicated to Sir Tom Finney who died a few months earlier. They were determined to have a good day out.

Worst grounds you've visited?

Been to loads all over the world and non-league too. But the worst ground in the League, there are a few. I don't like going to Oldham at all. Old school, but not a great vibe there. Colchester and Scunthorpe are soulless new(er) stadia. And Franchise AFC aka MK Dons. I've been there quite a few times now including with Charlton and with AFC Wimbledon and it's another smart but soulless stadium no matter who they play and how many people are in the stadium. Quite strangely, it got voted top Division One ground in a football fans survey. Not sure who that was who voted because no-one I know likes going there. Accrington Stanley I've heard is quite bad but the match got called off just as we were leaving the pub across the road so it doesn't count.

Famous Brentford fans?

Natalie Sawyer from Sky Sports is very involved. She goes as much as she can. Dean Gaffney (Robbie from EastEnders), Rhino from Status Quo, Dominic Holland the comedian and Kurupt FM DJs from the cult BBC 3 series 'People Just Do Nothing' is as famous as it gets for us I'm afraid.

Quirky fact time?

Before World War II we were the top team in London - regularly beating the next top team Arsenal. Our pre-war record against them was W5 D2 L1 and in 1935/36 we finished the season above them in 5th position. You never know. If our boys weren't interrupted to go and fight the Germans, we may still have been the number one team in London.

Game #14: The Championship - Saturday 13th September 2014
BRENTFORD vs Brighton & Hove Albion - Griffin Park

It's no secret that I'm as northern as they come. Coat always on, chips and gravy all the way, you get the drift. Aside from a fleeting visit as a youngster, I'd never been to London. My only memories of the country's capital was seeing a couple of waxworks at Madame Tussauds and being afraid of getting crapped on by the pigeons at Nelson's Column. All that was about to change...or was it? The train tickets were booked, but there was a slight hitch with the matchday tickets. No offence to Brentford, but I wouldn't have thought that obtaining a ticket to come and watch the Bees play would be a problem.

Right after signing up on the club's website, I discovered that tickets weren't being released on general sale. In order to buy, I needed to have a purchase history and there lay the problem. I didn't have Tommy the ticket tout's number to hand so resolved to phone the club on my lunch hour the day before the game. With a capacity just over 12,000 and despite not selling out a game this season, the club repeated their stance. Once all of the 1,600 away tickets went, they were under restrictions for health and safety etc. Realising that I was sinking faster than a Big Brother winner's career, I mentioned the ground tour and all of a sudden I was given hope. The sympathetic member of staff took down my details and promised to look into it. True to her word, she called later on and was able to offer me a ticket. To be honest, the club mustn't get many calls from potential fans in Chester, so I appreciated that she made an exception for me. I felt like Cinderella finally being told that she could go to the ball, well if the dance was at Griffin Park and your date was a bunch of rowdy Brentford fans.

I ended up cutting it very fine to make my 7am train to London. Once at Euston, it was bedlam with people coming at me from every direction. No-one batted an eyelid when a woman's suitcase rolled over another poor woman's leg. This was my welcome to the fast paced hustle and bustle of London life. With part of the Northern underground line closed for maintenance, I was like a deer in headlights trying to find the right tube. I was eventually pointed in the right direction and made a quick connection to Vauxhall where Arsenal and Chelsea shirts were out in full force. I could have swore that I saw Danny Welbeck on the platform trying to impress a girl, who couldn't have looked more disinterested. Upon closer inspection, it turned out to be a drunk doppelganger of the Gunners new signing instead. He may have had the swagger, but he certainly didn't have the moves like Jagger.

I finally arrived in Brentford close to four hours after initially setting off, yet the journey didn't feel that long. There was an influx of Polish grocery stores and even a special Polish coupon in the bookies. Coral was full of tattooed loudmouth cockney wideboys speculating on the afternoon's Premier League games. I decided not to take betting advice from someone who had 'Wallop #14' on the back of his shirt and went with my gut instinct instead - I didn't win a bean.

Brentford is quite a small town and I became accustomed to what was where quite quickly. After a pleasant walk around the vicinity, I laughed at the irony of being stopped for directions to the ground. The pair of Brighton fans wore the same innocent yet clueless expression that I had at Euston a few hours earlier. I was glad that I could point them in the right direction and help them on their way. Having corresponded with Vlogger and fan 'Billy the Bee' from the 'Beesotted' fanzine, he had told me about a pub that a lot of the fans go to before the game, so I decided to head over there. Setting foot in the Crown, a bevvy of beauties all dressed in Brentford shirts served thirsty fans. I enquired about Billy who was somewhat of a local celebrity in these parts. The landlord was beaming and working the room like a true salesman and informed me that Billy hadn't come in yet. It turns out that our paths wouldn't cross, although I swear I walked past him on my way back to the ground. Sorry Billy, it was me that flashed a smile as we passed at the traffic lights.

Back at Griffin Park, an announcement came over the PA system just after 1:30pm that the ground was now open. Fans from both sides had gathered outside the Brighton team bus to get pictures with the players and manager Sami Hyypia, who obliged the keen autograph hunters on his way into the ground. My path into the stadium wasn't so simple. I was stopped by foreign security who insisted on doing a bag check. The bottle of water I had been saving for the trip home became a casualty due to the ground staff's insistence of confiscating the cap. I was left with an open bottle full of fluid that would no doubt cause my seal to break at an inopportune time.

Staying on the subject of drink, Griffin Park has a bar situated outside every corner of the ground so no-one will ever go thirsty. Fans from both sides mixed together outside both before and after the game. Taking a perch at the back of the Ealing Road Terrace, I was able to take in the surroundings and have a good read of the programme while the rest of the fans filed in. The away fans were housed in the Brook Road Stand or the 'Wendy House,' as Brentford like to call it, due to the double decker stand having seating on the first tier and a small terrace below.

I was particularly looking forward to watching the battle of the Portuguese loanees, more specifically Brentford's Betinho against Brighton's Joao Teixeira. Disappointingly, only the latter saw action. There was still a host of promising names on show. The visitors had England prospect David Stockdale between the sticks and had recently signed prolific striker Sam Baldock from Bristol City. The sound of 'London Calling,' by The Clash had everyone up on their feet to welcome the two teams onto the pitch.

The away side started the game very brightly. Andrew Crofts smacked a shot against the post and it looked a case of when not if Brighton would find the net. Baldock rounded goalkeeper David Button, but his effort was weak and easily cleared off the line. When the home side finally settled and ventured forward, Brighton got nervous. Lewis Dunk escaped a certain red card when he hauled down Andre Gray and was quite clearly the last man. The referee obviously hadn't gone to Specsavers and only booked the defender. Clearly unnnerved, the away side soon conceded when Moses Odubajo was put through and he found the promised land with an angled drive. Gray doubled the advantage sliding in to score from close range. He clearly knew where the net was after scoring a bucket load for Luton Town last season. However, that was at Conference level and Gray was still finding his feet three divisions higher. After drifting out of the game, he was substituted midway through the second half.

Brighton halved their deficit just before half time. Left back Gordon Greer volleyed in from close range after a corner wasn't cleared. Crofts thought he had equalised moments later from another corner, but the referee ruled it out for an infringement. Undeterred, the Brighton fans chirped "we score when we want." Brentford restored their two goal cushion when Bees midfielder Jonathan Douglas towered above the defence to power a header past Stockdale. Once again, Brighton refused to lie down and ensured a grandstand finish with the goal of the game. Danny Holla sidestepped his marker to curl a beautiful 25 yard effort into the top corner. As soon as it left his boot I knew it was in and applauded the effort. Substitute Kazenga Lualua was inches away from equalising late on when his effort shaved a coat of paint off the post. The final whistle gave everyone chance to catch their breath, myself included. It had been a cracking match for a neutral to watch and the Brentford faithful were a good bunch, constantly singing and gettting behind their team. They'd definitely acquitted themselves well since being promoted in May and they have a very bright future.

There was a police presence at the train station after the game, although the atmosphere was quite upbeat. To be fair, once I got outside mainstream London, I did find the locals a rather pleasant bunch. Me and the local police officer passed the time chatting about lower league football until my train arrived. Once on board, I listened intently to a group of Brighton fans bemoaning how tough the Championship has become and how it's unfair that relegated Premier League sides are still receiving parachute payments. I held my tongue as they unveiled their master plan to copy the Americans and integrate a draft system where the worst teams get the best players. My attention was diverted when the train kept on going past my stop (the announcer didn't mention it was limited stops) and I ended up at Waterloo (sadly without a bucket of vindaloo.) Faced once more with the maze that was the London underground, I regained my bearings and managed to get back to Euston. Once back at the main hub, something didn't feel right. There were a lot of people standing in the waiting area and I mean a LOT! I looked up to see rows of trains delayed or cancelled. Some idiot had decided to throw himself in front of a train around Nuneaton to send National Rail into a frenzy. Getting back home at a reasonable hour was looking very unlikely. Had it not been for a train already on its way into Euston, it looked like it could have been a night on the floor of the station sleeping on top of my bag.

After an anxious wait and listening to a drunken mob show their disdain for Scotland's fight for independence (I think the words went "fuck off Scotland, we hope you vote yes,") the mile long train was ready to board and accommodate almost everyone who had been standing around. A drunken Manchester City fan was being told off by a posh Waitrose shopper - complete with toff voice for his lack of cutlery etiquette. I burst out laughing at the ridiculousness of it all. People passed through my carriage throughout the journey in order to get to their seats. Even Ricky Tomlinson popped by to chants of "my arse," from surrounding passengers. Taking it all in good jest, Ricky quipped back in a sarcastic but witty tone "cheers lads, haven't heard that one today," before shuffling past. Despite the delays, I still made it home in time to catch Match of the Day and the subsequent Football League highlights. Holla's goal was just as good to watch second time around. Hopefully, every future trip to catch a game in London can be just as exciting as this one.

Best chant: "We hate Fulham, we hate Fulham. We are the Fulham haters." Brentford fans showing disdain for their rivals across the River Thames.
Match ticket: £27
Match programme: £3 for a nice glossy programme, which didn't crease upon folding. Provided good photo reviews on the youth, women and development sides.
Cost of food: £5.20 for a chicken balti pie and bottle of pepsi. Steak and kidney was the only other choice of pie. For those looking for an alternative snack, the club offered a £3 deal for a sausage roll and a cup of tea and there was even a pancake stand just inside the turnstiles.
Pie rating: 3/5. The chicken balti option continued to serve me well and satisfy my hunger. The pie came packaged and warm, it was reasonably meaty, not too greasy and had enough spice to satisfy the tastebuds.

Final Score
Brentford 3 (Odubajo 18, Gray 32, Douglas 54)
Brighton & Hove Albion 2 (Greer 40, Holla 60)
Attendance: 10,089

Getting to know Huddersfield Town
Stephen King - Chairman of the Huddersfield Town Supporters Association
www.htsa-online.co.uk

Favourite memory as a Huddersfield fan?

My Dad took me to my first game in the 1979/80 promotion season - a 7-1 win against Port Vale. I cried the next game when we only scored once. I've cried a few more times since! Another fond memory is probably the play-off semi-final second leg away at Brentford in 1995. We won on penalties and went on to win promotion at Wembley!

Best game you've witnessed at the John Smith's Stadium?

There's been a few, but the recent play-off victory against Bournemouth in 2011 would be up there. (Huddersfield won 4-2 on penalties after a 3-3 draw.) Brilliant atmosphere that night.

Best/worst players to pull on a Huddersfield shirt?

My favourite player of all time is probably Steve Kindon. At the moment, another one is Sean Scannell. When Chris Powell came in, the club were on the verge of selling him to Millwall. The worst is Gordon Tucker!

Best thing about the John Smith's Stadium?

The football team that play there ;-)

Worst grounds you've visited?

Our Yorkshire rivals over at Elland Road and Valley Parade, plus Oldham's Boundary Park.

Enjoyable away days?

Molineux, Griffin Park and Bootham Crescent.

Which club serves the nicest pies?

The best food I've had at an away ground was Cambridge United. The worst is definitely Preston. WTF is a butter pie!?

Famous Huddersfield fans?

Sir Patrick Stewart is probably the most well known.

Quirky fact time?

In 1957 we lost 7-6 against Charlton after being 5-1 up with 27 minutes remaining. Charlton had ten men!

Thoughts on ticket prices in general?

Disgustingly expensive.

Name your Huddersfield Dream Team?

Nico Vaesen
Malcolm Brown
Tom Cowan
Dave Sutton
Peter Clarke
Jacob Butterfield
Brian Stanton
Mark Lillis
Anthony Pilkington
Marcus Stewart
Steve Kindon
(sub Andy Booth)

Game #15: The Championship - Tuesday 16th September 2014
HUDDERSFIELD TOWN vs Wigan Athletic - The John Smith's Stadium

The war of the roses! Yorkshire against Lancashire. No, don't worry, I'm not talking about Cricket or Rugby League, although Wigan are more famous for their exploits with the egg rather than the ball. This was a crunch game in the Championship, with both teams looking to kick start their respective seasons. By their own admission, Huddersfield and Wigan had both underperformed thus far. Noting their tendency to leak goals meant that this game was a no-brainer to attend and the pick of the midweek set of fixtures around the Football League.

Anticipating a packed train with rush hour commuters, I did a bit of forward planning and pre-booked a seat for the short commute from Manchester to Huddersfield. However, just like Goldilocks discovered three bears eating her porridge, there was a rather large bear taking up the area in which I had reserved. Flashing an unwelcome stare in my direction, I didn't fancy my chances winning an argument against the rotund lady, so instead plumped myself behind a foreign couple. The train had barely left the station and their spoilt child started complaining about being forced to watch a Spanish version of the Smurfs on her iPad. At that age I would have been happy with a bag of sweets and a comic.

A smattering of the Yorkshire constabulary was present at the station to stamp out any potential trouble, not that there was a hint of any brewing. I had barely begun the walk away from the station when the large steel white tubing on top of the ground came into view. Formerly known as the Alfred McAlpine, and, up until 2012 the Galpharm, the newly christened John Smith's Stadium is one of the more beautiful grounds I've clasped eyes on. It is joined together by four semi-circular shaped stands, while four tall floodlights take up the space occupied by the open corners in between the stands. The green forestry poking out in the background drew comparisons, albeit on a larger scale to that of Wycombe Wanderers' Adams Park ground.

You'd be hard pushed to forget the name of the stadium, given the number of John Smith's banners and slogans in and around the immediate area. The marketing campaign is simple yet very effective. A modest number of Wigan fans clambered out of a lone visiting support bus, which reminded me that the club does have a dedicated fanbase after all. The club shop was divided into two, with equal amount of merchandise on sale for the Huddersfield Giants Rugby League club, who also share the ground.

I walked past the programme sellers and was intrigued to see a bunch of newspapers on the floor. The paper actually turned out to be the programme. The change in format had apparently gone down like a lead balloon, with the Huddersfield faithful flooding the club with complaints. The seller informed me it was cheaper to produce and sell, with the club preparing to ride out the storm. I thought it was unique and definitely a bold move. The size meant it's not practical to put in your pocket, but carrying a rucksack alleviated that problem. Aptly titled 'Give Us An H,' just reading about striker Joe Lolley's addiction to Football Manager alone earned the tabloid a thumbs up from me. I am rather fond of that game.

I needed to walk towards the back of the stadium to gain entry into the lower tier of the Fantastic Media Stand. Once again, the turnstile checkers were quick to inspect the bag, but they didn't find any bottled water this time and I was allowed to pass. I couldn't spy any pies on sale. Instead, I got stung for an overpriced chicken burger from one of the two food vans parked around the side of the entrance. While munching and wondering what might have been from a non-existent savoury selection, the players came out to begin their warm ups. Striker Nahki Wells ballooned a wayward effort over the temporary netting and the ball smacked an unsuspecting female steward on the back of the head. She was able to see the funny side, but did move away for the duration of the shooting session.

Huddersfield were inexplicably already on their third manager of the season. Mark Robins barely lasted the opening weekend, while this was only Chris Powell's second game in charge since taking over the reins from caretaker manager Mark Lillis. The 54-year-old Lillis enjoyed a seven year playing career at Huddersfield in the mid

80s and has had three temporary stints in charge of the Terriers in as many years. Quite simply, the man is seen as a local legend in these parts and was paraded in front of the fans before the game to unveil a new flag in the North Stand. Chants of "there's only one Mark Lillis," rang out around the stadium, before flag wavers and blue and white streamers greeted the teams onto the pitch. From the get go, the Yorkshire faithful were fiercely loyal to their long suffering team, constantly drumming and singing along, while putting a subdued travelling support to shame.

Visiting goalkeeper Scott Carson was almost caught out playing chicken with the ball early on, while Callum McManaman threatened to create something whenever he ventured forward. The Wigan attacker quickly became the pantomime villain when he was booked for simulation in the area. Wigan's German coach Uwe Rosler looked like he was kicking every ball on the sidelines, constantly moving up and down the touchline. His opposite number Powell looked coolness personified, staying perched at the corner of his dugout, mainly keeping to himself.

The home side introduced Sean Scannell for the second half. Straightaway the dreadlocked winger became the go-to guy out wide, beating markers and putting in crosses from all sorts of angles. Sadly, Jonathan Stead couldn't convert the crosses into goals. The gangly forward was in his second stint at his hometown club, but on this performance, Stead didn't look like he could finish his dinner. The wonder that was Scannell managed to squeeze a ball past two markers from the byline, and all it needed was a deft touch from Stead, but a weak effort saw the ball gently roll into Carson's grateful arms. Such was the lack of pace on the final touch that Carson had chance to change direction in mid-flight and smother the ball.

The fans seated directly behind me started to get restless. One fan in particular was cursing his luck, having already purchased away tickets for forthcoming trips to both Fulham and Ipswich Town. Looking for support or some words of encouragement off his friend, the guy simply laughed at him and joked if he'd be setting off two days early in order to get to Ipswich. I laughed, then remembered I hadn't been to Portman Road yet.

I started to get the sinking feeling that there wouldn't be a goal if the two teams played until midnight. The final whistle put everyone out of their misery and ended my hopes of going a whole season without witnessing a stalemate. It truly was a night of firsts. Huddersfield kept their first clean sheet of the season and Wigan picked up their first point on the road. The football gods simply weren't on my side this particular night. Despite the absence of a pie and the lacklustre game, I was far from bitter. The John Smith's Stadium has been one of the better grounds I've visited. Comfy seating, ample cover to shield you from the elements, plus the fans were very passionate and good to be around. At the end of the day, Huddersfield isn't too far away and I wouldn't hesitate to return.

Best chant: "Top tier, top tier, give us a song." The Huddersfield faithful trying to get the upper echelon of fans to join in the singalong.
Match ticket: £22 for unreserved seating and a perfect view of the pitch.
Match programme: £2. Set out like a newspaper, it featured an interview with deadline day signing Mark Hudson and provided a timeline illustration of Huddersfield's loss to Middlesbrough three days earlier. Former Belgian goalkeeper Nico Vaesen featured in the "Where Are They Now" files. He's now a football agent and has fellow countryman and Liverpool goalkeeper Simon Mignolet on his books.
Cost of food: £6 for a chicken burger and bottle of pepsi. What a rip-off!
Food rating: 3/5. Thankfully the chicken was nice and crispy, cooked properly and succulent. The only thing hard to swallow was the price. They could have added an extra piece of chicken or slapped on a bit of cheese at least. I'll bring sandwiches on my next visit here.

Final Score
Huddersfield Town 0
Wigan Athletic 0
Attendance: 11,083

Getting to know Watford
Kieran Callanan - Editor Vital Watford
www.watford.vitalfootball.co.uk.
Twitter @VitalWatford

Best place to sit/stand at Vicarage Road?

Last summer, a group of fans decided to get together and ask the club if there could be a dedicated singing section inside Vicarage Road. They co-ordinated a massive seat movement programme to ensure whoever wanted to join in with the group could sit within a certain block of the ground. This group is called 'The 1881', and it has gone from strength to strength since its inception. It is located on the far right hand side of the Rookery as you look at it from the pitch. It's obvious where they are, as the group has bought a huge amour of flags and there is a banner next to the section that is permanently fixed to the stand.

Best thing about Vicarage Road?

There's history about it, despite the oldest stand (finally) being torn down last year, it's close to the middle of town, and there's character. A lot of modern stadiums these days are almost identikit polished bowls, with little to distinguish one from another but the colour of the seats. At Vicarage Road though, we have a very unique stand in the recently renamed Graham Taylor Stand (it was previously known as the Rous Stand), and it's hard to mistake the ground for anywhere else. We have to deal with the slight embarrassment of having just three sides due to the condemned East Stand remaining untouched for several seasons due to a lack of funds or motivation in previous owners' tenures, but now that this is almost sorted, we should be proud to call Vicarage Road our home. What has been refreshing this season and last as well is the amount of sell-outs and near sell-outs we've had. It's hard to remember a time we've been so regularly close to capacity since the last Premiership season in 2006/07.

Worst grounds you've visited?

I'm sure a lot of Watford fans will want me to say Kenilworth Road, and it isn't a great ground, but at least there's something unique about it. I'm far less impressed with the likes of the Madejski, St Mary's, Ricoh Arena, Keepmoat, King Power, Cardiff City Stadium, and so on. New grounds like these are dull. If I had to pick one ground that's my least favourite to visit it would probably have to be the Ricoh Arena. It might be a different story this season, given the extended period Coventry have had to play away from their home ground, but on the few occasions I've been, it has been a massive disappointment. The ground is huge, and every game at the Ricoh was devoid of any kind of atmosphere. It was hard to get much of an atmosphere going in our end as well, as the size of the place and the amount of empty seats between us and the home fans made it hard for the noise to carry. It's one of the few grounds I've been to where there's a very obvious echo whenever people sing. Hopefully it's different now, I've read about the amount of fans that attended their first game back there and hopefully the next time I go to a match there the momentum from that won't have stopped.

Famous Watford fans?

Of course there's Sir Elton John, who was chairman of the club twice and holds the title of Life President. It's well known he's a big Watford fan and remains so to this day. Without his ownership of the club starting in the 70s, we almost certainly wouldn't be where we are today.

Quirky fact time?

My favourite little story about Watford in recent times is about how Aidy Boothroyd announced his promotion ambitions to the Hornets squad in the summer of 2005. Boothroyd was brought in late on in the 2004/05 season in an attempt to stave off relegation. We were a club with very little money, and in the end we managed to stay in the second tier. Most managers in this position would probably be happy with building on survival the following season, perhaps targeting a top ten finish at best. Not Aidy Boothroyd! He felt he could get promotion the following season, and his way of telling the players this was quite extraordinary. In a room somewhere within one of the training ground buildings, Boothroyd arranged chairs into rows of two, with a single chair at the front in the middle, with all chairs facing the same way. He sat on the single chair at the front, and said to the players, 'This is my promotion bus, who would like to get on board?'In a surreal few moments, the players all sat in bus formation while Boothroyd explained how the club were going to be promoted the following season, and it was not in doubt.

Amazingly, that very next year Watford were promoted to the Premier League following their play-off victory in Cardiff against Leeds United.

Best/worst Watford managers?
I've been lucky in that in my lifetime I don't think I've ever really disliked one of our managers. Gianluca Vialli was around at the time the club took a massive hit on wages and then finished disappointingly in mid table. If you'd ask most fans of my generation who has been our worst manager you'll probably usually be given him as your answer.

Name your Watford Dream Team?
I can only go with who I've seen, so the 80s greats will have to be in someone else's best eleven.
GK: Ben Foster
LB: Peter Kennedy
CB: Steve Palmer
CB: Jay Demerit
RB: Lloyd Doyley
LM: Ashley Young
CM: Richard Johnson
CM: Almen Abdi
RM: Tommy Smith
CF: Troy Deeney
CF: Heidar Helguson

HIGH NOON IN THE HORNETS NEST

Game #16: The Championship - Saturday 20th September 2014
WATFORD vs AFC Bournemouth - Vicarage Road

Today was a day of firsts, like discovering my alarm clock had a 5am wake up time. I was about to take the term 'attack the day' to a whole new level. The powers that be at Sky Sports decided this game warranted a TV slot and a lunchtime kick-off. To be fair, I couldn't fault them. The match had been circled on my calendar for a number of weeks. Two teams who play attractive football and hoped to be in the promotion mix come the end of the season. It was an easy sell for me and the perfect chance to see what Watford was all about.

Lack of sleep and light flu symptoms aside, the commute was fairly swift. Admittedly, the whole carriage was enjoying a brief power snooze during the final leg of the journey until the train conductor gave everyone a rude awakening. Seeing red for a passenger leaving a bike by the door, Mr Angry took the poor lad to Coventry with a cutting lecture then ordered him to chain it up at the said West Midlands station.

Arriving at Watford Junction, a sign pointed out the Warner Bros Studio Tour. Sadly for Bugs Bunny, Daffy Duck and co, time was tight and I had a match to get to. Watford is ideal for pedestrians like myself. The road names all contained directions to various places and a rough number of minutes it takes to get there. Being a power walker meant that I could shave some time off and I was in the city centre in no time. Once again, I subscribed to the Ronald McDonald diet for breakfast, before happily obliging to provide ID for placing a bet on the afternoon's games. The sign in the bookies window predicted a 3-1 Watford victory. Given the Hornets impressive start to the season, it was tempting, but I stuck to a rule of not betting on any games that I was attending.

Supporters from both sides happily mixed and converged towards Vicarage Road. There's no shortage of chip shops or pubs along the way for those who like to indulge. The club shop was in a bit of an odd location. It looks isolated and forgotten about stuck at the side of one of the stands. I got claustrophobic inside and there wasn't really enough room to swing a cat, so I made a hasty exit.

The club DJ served up some classic 80s and 90s pop before the game. Madonna's 'Holiday,' was the pick of the bunch and deserves an honourable mention, although there were many more. Mascot Harry the Hornet was getting quite excited in the build-up to kick-off, hamming it up and dancing in front of the cameras.

Based in the two-tiered Graham Taylor Stand, I was sat directly opposite the players tunnel. Work on a brand new East Stand was well and truly under way and nearing completion. Bournemouth brought a healthy contingent to fill one half of the Family Stand, while the '1881 group' were in fine voice in the dedicated singing section behind the goal. Talking of songs, the familiar sound of Z-Cars (ode to Everton FC) blared out around the stadium to bring the two teams onto the pitch. Harry the Hornet even took part in the pre-game handshakes.

Both sides were sporting new custodians between the sticks. I was dubious of Heurelho Gomes keeping goal for Watford. The Brazilian's reputation preceded him based solely on his calamitous tenure at Spurs. Meanwhile, Bournemouth had loaned Pole Artur Boruc from neighbours Southampton. The away side snuck in a crossbar challenge audition towards the end of their warm-up with impressive results.

The match had barely started when Bournemouth were awarded a penalty. The lightning pace of Callum Wilson took him past Gabriel Tamas, leaving the Romanian with little option but to haul the attacker to the floor. Veteran defender Ian Harte stepped up and inexplicably rolled his spot kick wide of the post. The Irishman was a deft hand from a dead ball situation during his years at Leeds United. If you were going to put your house on anyone to net from the spot, I'd have said Ian, but not now. Okay that was a bit melodramatic of me. Harte could take heart from the fact that he could brush off his disappointment, but the afternoon soon got a lot worse for Tamas, when he was stretchered off with a cruciate ligament injury.

The game was entertaining, but if at any time the atmosphere went a bit quiet, good old Harry the Hornet fetched his drum from the Family Stand and bashed away like there was no tomorrow. In the process, he instantly usurped Rammie the Ram as my favourite mascot.

Gomes was doing his best to get rid of the "calamity" tag I'd given him when he pulled off a top drawer save to keep out a Wilson header. Alas, the shotstopper could do nothing to prevent the Cherries opener, which was something quite special. Midfielder Harry Arter let fly from 30 yards and the ball flew into the top corner to leave an exasperated Gomes clutching at air.

Despite missing top scorer Troy Deeney through injury and more tellingly, new manager Oscar Garcia, who had been taken ill with chest pains after his first game in charge, Watford battled resiliently. The introduction of cult hero Fernando Forestieri had the crowd singing his name to the sound of the White Stripes song 'Seven Nation Army.' With an assortment of nationalities on the pitch (thanks to Watford being owned by the Pozzo family and having used the foreign loan market to their advantage) substitute and Northern Ireland defender Craig Cathcart netted a late equaliser. The ex-Manchester United man beat Boruc with a well executed low volley which went in off the far post and gave the home side a deserved share of the spoils.

Crowd congestion meant there was a delay in getting out of the ground. This gave me a chance to discuss Watford's prospects with a couple of the regulars. Having dropped their first points at home, the general consensus was that Deeney's return would solidify the club's position in the upper echelon of the table. Thankfully, no-one threw themselves in front of a train this week, so there were no delays getting home. A solitary change at Milton Keynes ensured I was back at Chester inside two hours. Although I didn't bump into famous alumni Sir Elton John or Luther Blissett, getting to see Arter's goal up close was wonderful. Vicarage Road gets a solid thumbs up from me. The club also earns extra brownie points for having Football Manager as one of their sponsors. Great taste guys!

Best chant: "We'll sign who we want, we'll sign who we want. From Udinese, we'll sign who we want." Watford fans grateful for Italian feeder club Udinese helping out supplying players.
Match ticket: £26 for a pitchside seat and a great view. I was close enough to tap the cameraman on the shoulder.
Match programme: £3. Quite heavy on nostalgia and flashbacks, I was reminded that Gifton Noel-Williams (a Championship Manager legend) used to ply his trade up front for the club.
Cost of food: £5.30 for a steak and ale pie and soft drink.
Pie rating: 3/5. Meat was quite stewy, the pie had flavour and just enough gravy. The crust was squishy, but in a good way.

Final Score
Watford 1 (Cathcart 83)
AFC Bournemouth 1 (Arter 63)
Attendance: 14,320

Getting to know Shrewsbury Town
Alan from the Blue and Amber Fanzine - www.blueandamber.proboards.com
Twitter @B_and_A_Fanzine

Best game you've witnessed as a Shrewsbury fan?

In all my 50 years as a fan, the memory that is most vivid in my mind is the Second Division play-off second leg against MK Dons at The National Hockey Stadium. Town were the underdogs after drawing the home leg. Francise were managed by Martin Allen (always nice to beat) who was bigging everything up pre match and predicting a convincing home win for his team. Walking into the ground that night there were big posters up imploring MK fans to pre-book their train travel to Wembley for the final because demand was expected to be massive. There were long queues of home fans doing just that, and little old Town went and absolutely spoilt the party in a great way. It had everything that I love about going to the match - gut wrenching emotion, fear, trepidation and a euphoric rush. Suffice to say, all the travel posters had been removed when we finally left the ground.

Best players to pull on a Shrewsbury shirt?

Connor Goldson is a rock at the heart of defence and certain to move onto higher levels of the game. Liam Lawrence is immense, solid, calm and controlled when he's fit. Ryan Woods is our new hero. Youth team product, great range of passing and keeps our midfield ticking over. He's a star of the future for sure. Jermaine Grandison is another. The most entertaining right back we have ever had, and a beast of a player who loves step overs and winning headers. Gets forward all the time and gets the crowd going. Another cult hero.

Best thing about the New Meadow?

It definitely saved the club from following the fate of others that lacked investment and were unable to move with the times and now find themselves wallowing in some obscure semi professional league. Without the ground we would not be here in this form. That said, as match day experience it is pretty dire and the club have to accept their share of the blame for that. Poor facilities given they had a blank page to start from, poor atmosphere simply because of the stupid and always enforced petty regulations that other clubs somehow either ignore or find a way around. Much prefer away games.

Worst grounds you've visited?

Nothing comes close to Edgar Street in Hereford, absolutely shocking and should never have been allowed a safety permit.

Enjoyable away days?

We are lucky in the lower leagues that there are still a lot of good traditional grounds to visit. Always love Spotland, plus Prenton Park is great with a good crowd. Gigg Lane is worth visiting and so is Meadow Lane in Nottingham.

Which club serves the nicest pies?

Don't know about pies, but the best catering you will ever get at football is at Kidderminster Harriers. Fabulous home made soups, big Yorkshire puddings full of meat and gravy, lovely chips (we are not allowed by law to have chips at New Meadow) If you get the chance to visit Aggborough, dont have anything to eat before you get there.

Famous Shrewsbury fans?

We don't do famous fans really. Pete Posthlewaite - the acclaimed actor- was a regular attender at games as he lived local prior to his death.

Quirky fact time?

It was not called Gay Meadow because the inhabitants of the town were predominatley homosexual! In the 1500's a rich Merchant family called Gaye bequeathed the Meadow that they owned alongside the river for the town's poor people to enjoy recreation and fresh air, hence Gaye Meadow. For some reason when the football club moved from their orignal ground on the town's racecourse the 'e' was dropped from the name. And the word 'gay' was hijacked to mean something completely different from its original meaning.

WITNESSING A CUP UPSET IN SHROPSHIRE

Game #17: Capital One Cup Third Round - Tuesday 23rd September 2014
SHREWSBURY TOWN vs Norwich City - Greenhous Meadow

I've really come to grow fond of the domestic cup competitions, especially the League Cup. Although I suffered the indignity of endless TV coverage showing Manchester United get mullered by MK Dons in the previous round, the unpredictability and magic was still clearly evident for all to see. Price reductions also don't harm one bit. With geography being kind to me, I even convinced Dad to come along for his second trip of the season. For this special occasion, he dug out a Shrewsbury Town training jacket that he claims he found at the back of his cupboard.

Funnily enough, the only time I've got lost on my travels this season Dad was with me. No prizes for guessing what happened here. After taking a wrong turn towards Telford, my attempts to cool the tension in the car didn't go down too well. No sooner had the CD player been turned on, 'Eye of the Tiger' was rudely muted mid-song.

Opting for the scenic route through Oswestry, and passing a flurry of mobile cafes, we made it to Shropshire in good time. Despite boasting plenty of spaces, Shrewsbury don't allow parking at the ground, operating a permit only policy. A few neighbouring establishments opted for a similar approach, placing temporary 'no matchday parking' signs up, so the Brooklands pub (a ten minute walk from the ground) became the main beneficiary of the matchday traffic and made a nice chunk of change in the process.

Driving to the game had its benefits. The Greenhous Meadow is situated on the outskirts of the city centre and several miles from the train station. My understanding is that a frequent shuttle bus operates to and from the ground on a Saturday, with a reduced midweek service also in operation. Chairman Roland Wycherley - who has an area of the ground named after him, put the wheels in motion to leave previous home Gay Meadow back in 1999. Opposition from residents meant that the building work didn't commence until 2006, with the club moving to their new home a year later and ending a 97 year association at the Gay Meadow. Unlike their predecessors, the Greenhous Meadow doesn't call on the River Severn as a neighbour, so the worry of flooding and match postponements during the winter months has been somewhat quelled.

We passed a healthy Norwich contingent on the walk to the ground. Clearly, given the long trek up north, the fans were up for the cup and feeling confident. However, thoughts of a cup upset stayed on my mind. Unsurprisingly, Norwich boss Neil Adams rotated most of his squad, whereas opposite number Micky Mellon didn't have that luxury. The omission of Norwich's first choice strike pairing Cameron Jerome and Lewis Grabban was disappointing for me, but this would no doubt galvanise the League Two hosts.

Dad almost choked on his pie and produced a forced smile when 'Eye of the Tiger' came on over the tannoy. The PA announcer even remained quiet throughout so that I could finally enjoy the full version. Dad's attention soon turned to the pre-match warmups. Shrewsbury's #4 Ryan Woods had caught his eye for reasons unknown to me. All I saw was a diminutive red head enjoying the training drills and spraying balls across the pitch. I boldly predicted that Kyle Lafferty would be the one to impress for the visitors. What is it they say about hindsight being 20/20...yeah I thought so.

The Greenhous Meadow is a tidy affair, but it just lacks that certain Je ne sais quoi to differentiate it from some of the other new builds. The four sides are detached from each other for the moment, although it does allow for the corners to be filled in with extra seating at a later date, should the club deem it to be necessary. In keeping with the modern theme, a small electronic scoreboard is present above the away end, while small floodlight pylons sit on top of the side stands.

Norwich treated much of the opening period like a training game, passing the ball around with little substance. Lafferty wasted a golden chance by making a complete hash out of a free header, while Shrewsbury looked reluctant to shoot whenever they ventured forward. The fans were just as adventurous with their chanting. "Salop, Salop," (a slang term for Shropshire) was basically the only home chant I heard all game. Even the old dear sat next to me got involved, screaming down my ear whenever her team got a corner or set piece. The aptly named Jean-Louis Akpa Akpro finally threw caution to the wind and stung Norwich 'keeper Declan Rudd's palms.

Meanwhile, what of Dad's protege Master Woods? The Scholes lookalike was definitely playing like the legendary midfielder. He didn't waste a pass, had an assured touch and was box to box all game. The same couldn't be said for Norwich's Ignasi Miquel. The ex-Arsenal defender looked nervy and out of his depth. Shrewsbury upped the tempo and took a deserved lead. James Collins met a Liam Lawrence free kick to head over Rudd and send the Greenhous Meadow into a mild frenzy.

Norwich's attack looked non-existent. The portly Gary Hooper struggled to make an impression, while Lafferty somehow escaped a red card after two dangerous tackles in the space of a minute. Northern Irish eyes certainly weren't smiling on Lafferty who was quickly substituted for his own good. The occasion clearly got too much for one Norwich fan who had the bright idea to storm the pitch right in front of the police control box. You don't need me to tell you how that one ended. Sadly for the travelling contingent, their side didn't show as much fight and exited the competition with a whimper. Shrewsbury added them to an impressive list of scalps which already included Blackpool and Leicester City.

Leaving the ground, we bumped into the over zealous fan who was now in bracelets and being given a stern talking to by the police. The rest of the Norwich fans were all on the buses ready for the long drive back to Norfolk. Due to a drop in temperature, I didn't hang around to see if the constabulary let the lad off with a warning or insisted he spend a night at Her Majesty's Pleasure.

There was a slight pile-up of traffic which delayed our journey home. We were also distracted by a bright light shining in the sky coming off one of the motorway junctions. On second glance, it turned out to be the illuminated sign of McDonald's lit up like the Bat signal in the sky. We decided to pull over and call in. It would have been rude to just carry on driving. Besides, you can't beat piping hot chicken nuggets at 11pm.

Best chant: "You're not singing anymore." Ironically, the only time Shrewsbury fans deviated from the Salop script was when they scored. Before the goal, it had been the visiting supporters making the most noise.
Match ticket: £12
Match programme: £3. Definitely one of the better programmes I've bought. Contained a great celebrity interview with Norwich fan and BT broadcaster Jake Humphrey, while BBC Radio Shropshire's Mark Elliott summed up beautifully what I'm trying to achieve with a short tale about his journeys to and from various press boxes. Grant Holt got a lot of love and a few pages too, having previously starred for both Shrewsbury and Norwich.
Cost of food: £3.20 for a steak pie.
Pie rating: 2/5. Overcompensated on the pastry, and a lack of advertised peppered steak only gave the pie a slight whiff of flavour.

Final Score
Shrewsbury Town 1 (J.Collins 54)
Norwich City 0
Attendance: 6,187

Getting to know Morecambe
James Main - Morecambe matchday programme columnist
Twitter @Mainylad

Favourite memory as a Morecambe fan?
I have been watching the Shrimps regularly for ten years since the age of five, so I'll go for when we won promotion to the Football League via the play-offs in 2007 at Wembley. I was lucky to be there along with my Dad and my brother. I was only seven at the time but have many memories of that game, and I would go as far to say that it is the best day of my life so far!

Best game you've witnessed at the Globe Arena?
Our 4-3 victory over Chesterfield last season. Chesterfield were cruising in the first half and were comfortably 3-0 up at half time, but the second half was a totally different story and we managed to get a remarkable 4-3 win.

Best/worst players to pull on a Morecambe shirt?
Best players: Kevin Ellison, Stewart Drummond, Danny Carlton and Jim Bentley. Worst: Derek McNiven, Tony Diagne, Zac Aley.

Best thing about the Globe Arena?
Probably the amount of leg room in the Peter McGuigan Stand.

Worst grounds you've visited?
Accrington Stanley and Barnet's old Underhill stadium.

Enjoyable away days?
Stadium of Light, Wembley, Highbury (Fleetwood)

Which club serves the nicest pies?
Morecambe do the nicest pies. They've had many awards for their pies, and had one for their chicken, ham and leek pies not so long ago. They're the best of their kind.

Quirky fact time?
Morecambe have never been relegated in their 95 years as a football club.

MAKING FRIENDS AT MORECAMBE

Game #18: Saturday 27th September 2014 - League Two
MORECAMBE vs Northampton Town - The Globe Arena

So, a Manchester United fan, Ipswich Town follower and two Northampton Town supporters walk into a bar. No this isn't the start of a bad joke. It's actually a true story, yet it wasn't supposed to be like this at all. How on earth did I go from London to Morecambe? Bear with me while I explain. You see, I was all set for a trip to see Leyton Orient take on Rochdale, yet right in the middle of purchasing train tickets, the prices shot up and the folks over at the Trainline wouldn't process my order. After taking a second (and cheaper) look at the fixtures, I packed my bucket and spade and set off for a day at the seaside to see the Shrimps of Morecambe FC.

There was a less significant game going on while I was travelling - the Merseyside Derby at Anfield. Three very vocal Liverpool fans were on the same train bemoaning their team's start to the season. It quickly degenerated into a shouting match, with each voice getting louder and talking over the other. As every opinion became more irrelevant than the last, my ears were finally spared when the future Match of the Day panelists got off at Preston.

Part of the fun of an away day is navigating your way to the ground. A Northampton fan halfway through a six pack of beer looked equally as lost as me and we quickly struck up conversation. A fellow Town fan tried to give us directions which ended up being as easy to comprehend as Chinese arithmetic. After listening politely, me and my new mate Tom decided that he was talking absolute cobblers and sought to find our own way to the Globe Arena. We quickly befriended two more lost souls - Matt and Brad along the way, with me being the odd one out in a group of three fresher students.

Brad - the Ipswich fan had been dragged along by Northampton fan Matt, who in turn swapped war stories with Tom about all things football. I was quickly put on the spot when asked which part of the ground I was going in. Caught cold, I reluctantly agreed to sit in the away end. "You've made a good choice," said Matt confidently, as the stadium came into sight. Little did I know at the time that I had just made a really good choice.

A fairly modern gastro pub - the Flying Hurley lies directly outside the Globe Arena. There wasn't a hint of any hostility between the two sets of fans, with shirts from both sides passing in and out of the doors. Just to be on the safe side though, our pre-match drinks were presented in plastic cups. My new friends bought me a pint, although they had all just scooped student/junior entry to the game while I paid full whack, so I would agree that it was their round. Amazingly, Brad's bushy beard and blatant admittance of craving a pint went unheard by the ticket office, who happily printed him out discounted entry.

A rather intrusive security guard saw fit to open my bag at the turnstile and dip his hand in like he was scooping up pick and mix sweets. All he had to do was ask, and I'd have happily shown him the contents on loan from Chester Library. I'd even have gone the extra mile and recommended a couple of good short stories too. Thankfully, he didn't discover the chocolate stash I was saving for the way home. Given the size of the steward's waistline, he'd probably have pilfered it for a sly half time snack.

The Globe Arena flatters to deceive somewhat appearance wise. Externally, it's quite photogenic, although inside tells a different story. The large all seated Peter McGuigan Stand dominates the ground and houses the majority of the away fans, thus leaving the East Terrace behind the goal empty. I was located in the former, staring directly opposite at an incomplete looking North Terrace. Capacity wise, the uncovered terrace only holds a small handful of fans and has a bricked up building backing directly onto it. On the plus side, the Globe is still relatively new and is free of the view restricting pillars.

The home fans may have bought a drum, but they were drowned out by a small group of hardcore travelling supporters sat directly in front of me. A number of away fans who had simply come to watch the match wanted no part of our singalong and moved away like we all had the plague. Tom ensured I got quickly up to speed. A strange song about a man saying goodbye to a horse became the tune of the afternoon. No-one could explain the reason behind it, they just sung the words over and over again. It wasn't until the second half that a big bald Northampton fan bluntly told us to either shag the horse or shoot it and sing about something else. I did try and get a rise out of my new friends by quietly starting the song up again, but they kept the horse in the stable and moved onto other topics.

The game never threatened to reproduce the nine goals Northampton and Accrington Stanley had shared the previous week in their 5-4 encounter- mainly because Town were a bit light in the forward department due to injuries. The Cobblers had tightened up defensively and did possess homegrown player Ivan Toney in their ranks. The 18-year-old nicked the only goal just past the half hour mark, capitalising on Morecambe goalkeeper Barry Roche's hesitancy to head a loose ball into the net from close range. The 'ultras' singing in front of me fell flat on their backsides after jumping up and down in delight, before shouting their adulation for the youngster who was sporting a Fresh Prince retro style hair-do.

At the other end of the football and hair scale, Morecambe's main threat came from bald, ageing winger Kevin Ellison. The veteran shaved a coat off the woodwork and late on, Alan Goodall saw a looping header tipped over by Town's goalkeeper Jordan Archer. Overall, it had been a disappointing display from the home side who slipped to a third consecutive 1-0 defeat.

During the walk back to the station, I overheard several Morecambe fans discuss their Football Manager-esque plan to blood the entire youth team to teach the senior players a lesson. Talking of seniors, one pensioner decided to answer the call of nature in broad daylight at the end of a bridge. When you've got to go, you simply have to go, especially at that age. He was lucky that the police on patrol were a fair few steps back.

Surprisingly, I didn't indulge in the post game Domino's feast with my new mates. Morecambe's train station is next door to a shopping outlet and the smell of three piping hot pizzas wafted through the two carriages as envious passengers looked on. Tom's pizza was later sabotaged and seized upon by a group of boozers at Lancaster station. A couple of slices had accidentally fallen into a nearby plant pot minutes earlier, but the dirt was wiped off and the slices were put back into the box. The drunks gave their compliments to the chef and proceeded to tell cringeworthy jokes to pass the time to Preston. The joke was on them really. It was at Preston that I bid my new friends a fond farewell. Tom's halls of residence were next door to the station, while Matt and Brad caught a connecting train to Burnley (the lucky buggers had bagged free season tickets to watch the Clarets for doing sports courses.) By my own admission, the match wasn't up to very much, but I discovered that people make the party and thanks to some good fortune, I enjoyed a cracking afternoon's banter.

Best chant: "To his horse, to his horse. He was saying goodbye to his horse. And as he was saying goodbye to his horse, he was saying goodbye to his horse," then repeat. See I told you it doesn't make any sense, yet it was strangely addictive and funny to chant.

Match ticket: £21 (Tom had snared an £8 under 18 ticket, but was quickly forgiven after buying me a pint)

Match programme: £3. Morecambe produced an impressive dossier on Northampton, digging out info on some of their greatest post-war teams and analysing their previous game. AFC Wimbledon were given a scathing review in the 'Traveller's Tales' feature. The wombles hiked up the away support's prices after closing the away terrace, leaving the 40 or so Morecambe fans with a restricted view by the corner flag and a bad taste in their mouths.

Cost of food: £4.70 for a pie and soft drink.

Pie rating: 4/5. Quite small, although the meat and potato offering kept up the North West's tradition of delivering satisfying, piping hot pies. It's no accident that the club were awarded "Best Pie in Football" for their chicken/ham/leek and Bramley apple combinations at the end of last season. Those got snapped up pretty quickly by the hungry fans, although even the leftover meat savouries were just as nice.

Final Score
Morecambe 0
Northampton Town 1 (Toney 33)
Attendance: 1,725

Getting to know Leeds United
Graham Smeaton
www.thescratchingshed.com

Michael Normanton
www.thesquareball.net

Why do people tend to "hate" Leeds so much? Is the reputation unfair or one you thrive off?

Graham: I think it goes back to the basics; successful teams at any time draw hatred. The Leeds "hate" has continued due, in part I guess, to the arrogance of some of the fans who still hark back to the glory years and think that gives us the God-given right to be famous still.

Michael: We've always been an unpopular club, right back to the days when we were known as Leeds City and were caught making illegal payments to players. The bulk of the reputation stems from the Revie era when we were branded as a dirty team, often overlooking the fact that they could also play a bit. Since that point we've also had a high number of what you might describe as "handy lads" following us. As a football fan of the modern era the violence does scare me shitless but it undoubtedly adds to the atmosphere of an away day. People know when Leeds are in town and it's a unique and brilliant part of following the club.

Thoughts on new owner Massimo Cellino?

Graham: You have to respect him. I mean after the recent owners such as Ken 'Capt Birdseye' Bates and GFH - he's at least brutally upfront and honest. What he's said about the team; he's delivered. Oh and he got us £11 million for Ross McCormack.

Michael: He's slowly winning me over. He's undoubtedly a nutter, but he's also clearly a football man. For the first time in years it seems the owner(s) is actually bothered about us having decent players on the pitch.

Best thing about Elland Road?

Graham: The actual banter between genuine fans and not the single braincell morons chanting their outdated drivel.

Michael: Subjectively there's not a lot good about it! I love it because it's full of memories and feels like home.

Worst grounds you've visited?

Graham: Scarborough, the first season they came into the League and a ramshackle third division ground in Spain when I lived there.

Michael: Personally, I hate the new nondescript grounds. I'm thinking the likes of Derby, Middlesbrough, Doncaster etc. that are all built out of town and could literally belong to any club in the country. Give me a bit of character any day, even if it means dreadful facilities.

Best place to sit/stand at Elland Road?

Graham: For Leeds fans - South Stand. Away fans - no idea.

Michael: Traditionally it would be the Don Revie Stand, but there's recently been a movement to get a singing section in the South Stand at the opposite end of the ground. It seems to be working very well so far.

Famous Leeds fans?

Graham: Ricky Wilson (Kaiser Chiefs), Colin Montgomerie, Poppy Morgan - adult star.

Michael: Does Barry George count? The Kaiser Chiefs are probably the most famous, along with an upcoming boxer called Josh Warrington who is possibly about to hit the big time.

Quirky fact time?

Graham: Leeds United failed to win an away game in all the games they played between 18th March 1939 and 30th August 1947.

LIVIN' LA VIDA LEEDS

Game #19: The Championship - Wednesday 1st October 2014
LEEDS UNITED vs Reading - Elland Road

Mention Leeds United to many football fans and it's very likely you'll get a negative response. The 'Dirty Leeds scum' moniker has been around for as long as I can remember. From a personal viewpoint, there was no malice towards the club on my part. However, I do have a chequered past with the actual city. My one and only previous visit was five years prior to catch up with a friend, but it turned out to be a memorable trip for all the wrong reasons. To cut a long story short, I spent a chilly November evening shivering on a friend's doorstep after he got too drunk, went home early and fell asleep. Had it not been for a kind neighbour (high five to Des) offering me some hospitality and a chance to thaw then god knows what would have happened. Had Des discovered the present my less tactful friend left in his bathroom the morning after, I might not be here re-telling the story. Just like Sheffield, it was time to put another Yorkshire ghost to rest.

For some reason, I had a bad vibe as soon as I stepped off the train. I couldn't shake the instinctive feeling that I had picked a bad night to come and watch Leeds United. A pre-booked return ticket meant I needed to be back at the station just after 10pm. Friendly negotiations with the station staff about getting a later train ended up being fruitless. Considering the 7:45pm kick-off, time was definitely going to be tight - much like Dave Hockaday's short-lived reign in charge at the start of the season.

With the ground being a good 40 minute walk and not the easiest to navigate, I heeded the advice provided by the friendly hotel porter (complete with top hat) and opted to go in search of the matchday bus. Luckily for me, I was about to get a helping hand in the form of a tour guide. A lovely woman (of the older generation) called Carmel escorted me to the bus stop. I handed over my £2.50 for a return ticket and within ten minutes we were at Elland Road. Her generosity didn't end there. She showed me where to pick up tickets before advising me on which exit to take after the game, so that I wouldn't get detained with the Reading fans and could catch one of the first buses back into the city centre. Before departing to her seat in the East Stand, I was taken to the statues of former players Billy Bremner and Don Revie, which remain popular hotspots amongst the fans outside the ground. A large number of fans had chosen to wear the club's away shirt over the traditional all white number. The navy blue shirt with white trim resembled something more like a polo shirt and did look quite smart.

Taking a walk past the Peacock pub (where new owner Massimo Cellino often pops in for a pre-match pint) I grabbed some food and headed for my seat in the West Stand. Unfortunately, being pitchside and watching the warm-ups couldn't divert my attention from the disgusting pie I ingested. This was by far the worst pie I've ever tasted. Rock hard from the first bite, it's a miracle my teeth stayed intact. Inside was as black as the ace of spades and looked like a grenade had gone off. Just as I was about to snap a picture of the monstrosity, a lad and his gran took up the seats next to me. Realising that I didn't want to be labelled as weird pie photography guy, I threw it down in disgust. Surprisingly, it didn't cause a crack in the floor. I should've thrown my bottle cap (not confiscated for once) onto the pitch in protest.

Leeds had gone through as many managers as Lady Gaga had outfits. It came as no surprise that the team were still finding their feet under Darko Milanic. The Slovenian coach was taking charge of his first home game, although you wouldn't have guessed it, given the lack of fanfare the poor man was given on his way to the dugout.

With a heavy foreign influence, the team looked steady at the back thanks in part to an assured display from Italian Giuseppe Bellusci, but were ultimately left wanting up front. Souleymane Doukara and Mirco Antenucci were certainly not in the mould of a Jimmy Floyd Hasselbaink or Ross McCormack (more on him in a bit.) Meanwhile, Reading came in off the back of an entertaining 3-3 draw at home to Wolves. Sadly, there was to be no repeat of that performance here. Nigel Adkins set his side up to play for a draw and it made for a disappointing spectacle. The late introduction of Billy Sharp briefly raised Leeds' fans hopes. The substitute went close almost immediately, clearly highlighting the sense of urgency which had been lacking all game. I had no choice but to do what I said I was never going to do (gulp) I left early. While making the bus played a big part, the simple fact was that these two could have played until the weekend and it would have remained goalless. My gut instinct had been right and a poor game was par for the course. Home fans inside the ground were starting to become volatile too when neighbouring spectators wouldn't oblige firm requests for a song to try and spur the players on.

Following Carmel's advice to a tee, I took the right exit out of the ground and made it onto the first bus back. Naturally it was standing room only and I was privy to a whole host of frustrated Leeds supporters unloading their woes. From the lack of a midfield, to Cellino's policy on firing managers, one fed-up fan told the others to "think with your heart, not the head and love the club." When asked why they put themselves through it, one fan revealed he had a season ticket "because he has nothing better to do." That was particularly sad to hear. Surprisingly, given the team's lack of goals, McCormack doesn't seem to be missed too much. The Scottish striker found the net 28 times last season before completing an £11 million move to Fulham. A large section of fans weren't too fond of the high ball philosophy that he fed off. Carmel shared the same sentiment when we reconvened on the platform at Leeds. We agreed to disagree on the philosophy of sacrificing goals for a more attractive style of play. Simply put, the club need to find a happy medium to avoid being stuck in mid table purgatory. Possession doesn't necessarily win you games, goals do. Saying that, attendances have gone up under Cellino's reign, so for the club's sake I hope the fans stick with them. This fan won't be going back for a while. Much like the pie, it will take a while to get the bad taste out of my mouth. As if I hadn't suffered enough, engineering work between Manchester and Chester meant I had to endure the slow scenic train home. Passing through Hale, Mobberley, Northwich and Mouldsworth meant that I didn't put the key in the door until gone 1:30am. Just as well I'd booked the Thursday off work.

Best chant: Typical anti-Manchester United chants aside, the other popular one went something along the lines of "we love you Leeds, Leeds, Leeds." Unfortunately, I didn't share in the sentiment. The fans behind the goal even turned on us in the West Stand when we wouldn't oblige them with a song.
Match ticket: £28. The performance simply didn't justify the price.
Match programme: £3. Leeds love their history and so do the programme writers, reminding readers of a 5-1 victory over rivals Manchester United from 1972. Any excuse to jam a salty thumb into the eye of their Lancashire rivals.
Cost of food: £3.10 for a steak pie. I recommend taking a packed lunch.
Pie rating: 0/5. Even the smart box and napkin wasn't winning this kitchen nightmare a bonus point.

Final Score
Leeds United 0
Reading 0
Attendance: 20,705

Getting to know Nottingham Forest
Jamie Barlow - season ticket holder
*Twitter @JBarlow95_*

Favourite memory as a Forest fan?

The final game of the 2007- 2008 season which saw Forest secure promotion to the Championship by beating Yeovil 3-2. Forest had to rely on results going their way to have any chance of escaping the third tier of English football. Doncaster Rovers accorded to this script by losing away at Cheltenham Town to allow Forest to leapfrog above them into second spot. I strictly recall a roar erupting from A-Block of the Main Stand as fans got wind of Cheltenham taking an early lead, which was made even sweeter after Forest had gone in front. The Reds were majestic that day and threatened to wrap the game up before half time. The scenes after the game were truly unforgettable with fans piling onto the pitch on the cue of referee Fred Graham's final whistle. The buzz from the City Ground was intoxicating.

Best game you've witnessed at the City Ground?

The 5-2 demolition of Derby County in 2010. Any victory against the Rams is sweet, but to hit five against your biggest rivals was unforgettable. The game occurred just days after Christmas on a crisp wintry evening, and the mist literally rolled in from the Trent that night. Steve Bywater in the Derby net was left dumfounded after Forest's ruthlessness in front of goal. Colin Fray's commentary for BBC Radio Nottingham sent shivers down my spine after he exclaimed, 'Forest have hit five against Derby'. What a win!

Best/worst players to pull on a Forest shirt?

I'm unfortunate enough in my era of supporting Forest to have seen some utter dismal players to have pulled on the jersey. The list of players which merit the 'worst player' is endless. Eugene Dadi arrived on a free transfer in 2005 and the so-called Ivorian 'forward' proved that he couldn't hit a barn door in a career which spanned a total of six games. Algerian striker Rafik Djebbour arrived on a reported wage of £30,000 and certainly ruffled a few feathers by being a disruptive influence in the dressing room. Forest did well to get shot of the extortionate flop.

On the other side of the coin, Aaron Ramsey made a huge impression during a brief loan spell in 2010 at a time when he was recovering from a career threatening leg break. The Welshman's first touch was exquisite and it was a joy to watch him instantly stop the ball dead, turn and offload the ball in a majestic like manner. You could tell that he had been schooled by Arsene Wenger as he always appeared to have time on the ball and controlled the tempo of the game.

Best thing about the City Ground?

Forest fans should feel privileged to have arguably the most picturesque stadium in the country as their home ground. My matchday ritual is to park at The Victoria Embankment, situated adjacent to the River Trent, and stroll across Trent Bridge to the City Ground. I always enjoy the unique and refreshing walk along the banks of the River Trent. Unlike modern stadiums which can lack atmosphere and individuality, the beauty of the City Ground is that it is steeped in history and is always well attended.

Worst grounds you've visited?

Luton Town's Kenilworth Road. To get to the Hatters' away stand you have to make your way through an array of terraced houses before eventually reaching the turnstiles. The matchday experience is completely surreal and like no other.

Enjoyable away days?

I always enjoy the trips to Blackpool's Bloomfield Road and Huddersfield Town's John Smith's Stadium. The trip to Bloomfield Road is always thoroughly enjoyable and assembles a party-like atmosphere. The pitch is usually like a beach and incredibly bobbly, but the beauty of an away tie at Blackpool is that you can make a weekend out of it. The John Smith's Stadium is situated on an industrial estate, but in the Terriers' home stadium there is more than meets the eye. Whilst the stadium is arguably moulded to host rugby, the ground is aesthetically pleasing and you are guaranteed a panoramic view of the game.

Which club serves the nicest pies?
If memory serves me correctly then the pies sold at Barnsley and Rotherham United spring to mind as being above average in taste.

Famous Forest fans?
World Champion boxer, Carl Froch often makes guest appearances at the City Ground and used to honour his beloved team by wearing the club's crest on his shorts. England cricketer, Stuart Broad, and golfer, Lee Westwood, are also famous faces who adore the club. The renowned comedian Matt Forde is also a big admirer of the club and has his own column in the club's matchday programme.

Quirky fact time?
Forest signed the first £1 million player in Trevor Francis after Brian Clough paid the seven- figure fee to bring the striker to the club. Francis was signed in 1979 from Birmingham City and the striker shortly repaid Clough's faith by scoring the winner in the 1979 European Cup final against Malmo.

SUNDAY WITH THE SHERIFFS OF NOTTINGHAM

Game #20: The Championship - Sunday 5th October 2014
NOTTINGHAM FOREST vs Ipswich Town - The City Ground

After kicking my heels on the sidelines in work for much of the weekend, a Sunday game was a welcome consolation. Learning from last month's mistake, I steered clear of the Saturday night champagne in order to be bright eyed and bushy tailed for a trip to Robin Hood country. Many a childhood holiday was spent sampling the delights of Sherwood Forest. Nearby Center Parcs always used to be a favourite destination for the family. Oddly enough, I'd never been to a football game in the city, but I was confident that I had picked a great game and top of the table clash to boot.

I'd already witnessed Mick McCarthy's Tractor Boys frustrate Forest's East Midlands rivals Derby County back in August. I desperately needed to see a good game to get the Leeds bore draw out of my system. However, a quick check of the form book created some doubt. Forest had played out three consecutive goalless draws coming into this game. I had every confidence that Stuart Pearce wouldn't allow his side to make it four games without finding the net. The City Ground is only a short ten minute walk from the train station. Once you've passed over Trent Bridge, Forest's home is inbetween the cricket ground and a stone's throw from neighbours Notts County. Hundreds of fans had taken advantage of the fortuitous October sun in order to enjoy their pre-match pints, spilling out into the vicinity around the ground.

After collecting my ticket, a prime location in the Brian Clough Stand was waiting for me. Given my fondness for being close to the action, I was two rows from the front. Sacrificing leg room for a better view was a worthwhile trade. The Ipswich fans were in tickling distance in the lower tier of the Bridgford Stand and looked to have found their voice well in advance of kick-off.

Comedian Matt Forde had a slot in the matchday programme correlating matchday food with overall enjoyment. "Getting a bad burger or pie at a football match ruins the day." Amen to that Matthew! With his chef's hat firmly on, Matt recommended the hot dogs at Millwall, but didn't mince his words when singling out the savouries on offer at Sheffield United. "I had a meat pie there and it still jars with me ten years later. It was the driest pie ever made and I had to pump it full of mustard just to get any purchase on it." Having been to Bramall Lane at the start of the season, I can confirm that the standard has been brought up to scratch. On the subject of food, my review on the Forest pie will come later.

Whoever was in charge of the pre-match music did a good job for the most part. As it got closer to kick-off, the songs were changing at a pace even an ADHD sufferer would frown at, although a brief play of Underworld's 'Born Slippy' did its job of getting the pulses racing. Ipswich wasted no time in getting on Henri Lansbury's back, due to the midfielder's previous playing spell at East Anglian rivals Norwich City. Forest did the same to ex-players Luke Chambers and David McGoldrick, so turnabout was fair play.

The visitors quickly dispelled any fears of a stalemate, going 1-0 up thanks to a fine solo effort from Daryl Murphy. The striker danced past a host of Forest defenders in the box, before curling an effort under Karl Darlow's body into the far corner. Fair play to McCarthy, he played three up front and hadn't come to play for a draw, although Connor Sammon was one of the slowest forwards I'd seen in a while. What he made up for in size and strength, he definitely lacked in pace.

A young couple with their son were sat directly in front of me. The father seemed to be kicking every ball, desperately willing his beloved Forest forward in the search for an equaliser. It finally came when Lansbury shook off the boo-boys to float a corner onto the head of Robert Tesche. Just moments earlier, a premature yell echoed around the City Ground after Forest thought they had scored, only to see the ball desperately cleared off the line. This time, the ball did go in, and the jubilant father hoisted his son in the air in what was a beautiful moment to witness. For me, it was high fives all around with complete strangers as the sounds of the Fratellis 'Chelsea Dagger' rung out around the stadium.

Forest literally set up camp in the Ipswich half. All that was missing was the tent. Everyone could sense another goal was just around the corner. Sure enough, it soon came, but at the other end. Ipswich ripped up the script, breaking clear and punishing their hosts on the counter. Murphy rose highest to meet Tyrone Mings's cross with a fine bullet header, leaving Darlow flapping at air. The Ipswich fans were on cloud nine, while Forest's rotten luck continued. Michail Antonio saw an effort cleared off the line and Dean Gerken pulled off an amazing point blank stop to prevent Britt Assombalonga from knocking in the rebound. The crestfallen lad in front of me was mimicking his father, angrily pounding his fists on his knees in frustration.

Ipswich fans happily waved and chanted "cheerio" to the pessimists who decided to leave early. They were about to be brought back down to earth with a bump, as were the fans walking back along Trent Bridge. Forest found their second equaliser of the day in the 94th minute. Once more, Lansbury was the architect, crossing for Antonio to head in and preserve his side's unbeaten start. The proud father bounced his lad up and down in the air. It was like he himself had just scored the goal. To be fair, a draw was the least that Forest deserved and deep down, I think the Ipswich fans knew that too.

Negotiating my way back through the crowds, the younger fans were buzzing about the late drama, talking to their friends a mile a minute, while no doubt looking forward to replicating the action in the school playground the next day. It was the beautiful game at its finest. I was all smiles on the way back to the station. Even missing my scheduled train didn't put a dampener on the day. I came back through Sheffield, sadly without the karaoke crew. In fact there were no other football fans with me. Everyone was on their Sunday best and the return journey was relatively silent....that is until I got to Stockport. Faced with connecting onto the slow Manchester train or coming back via Crewe, I opted for the latter. The train had barely pulled away when a jovial conductor came to punch my ticket. I wanted to punch him in the face after realising that a free monthly return to Nottingham went out the window right there and then. I mean, who checks tickets at 7:30pm on a Sunday night. That notwithstanding, it was nice to be back amongst the goals. Forest have a top ground and a passionate set of fans. There's a positive vibe around the club and I hope for their sake that the good times aren't too far around the corner.

Best chant: "Stand up if you like this ground." Ipswich fans up on their feet endorsing the City Ground.
Match ticket: £30. The entertainment on display justified the price.
Match programme: £3. A well put together glossy magazine. From the "Face of Forest" feature showcasing a different fan each home game, to the random fact accompanying each visiting player on the teamsheets, it was an enjoyable read.
Cost of food: £6.20 (pie, crisps and drink deal)
Pie rating: 5/5 - Pukka really excelled here, providing a top notch meat and potato offering. Substantially filled, not too dry, soft potato and topped off with a melt in the mouth crust.

Final Score
Nottingham Forest 2 (Tesche 63, Antonio 90)
Ipswich Town 2 (Murphy 19, 71)
Attendance: 24,354

Getting to know Preston North End
Joe - Preston Fans Forum
www.pne-online.net

Favourite memory as a Preston fan?
My Dad's a Chelsea fan, but he always took me to watch Preston as a kid. Having been a Preston fan for 17 years, it brings a lot of disapointment, so most of my memories are of losing play-off semi-finals and finals.

Best game you've witnessed at Deepdale?
My favourite has to be from back in 2001 when we played Birmingham in the second leg of the play-offs. We were 30 seconds from losing when Mark Rankine grabbed a goal to take the game into extra time. We ended up winning the game on penalties. A game I will never forget.

Best/worst players to pull on a Preston shirt?
If you ask any Preston fan who the best player to wear our shirt is, the answer will be Tom Finney, and quite rightly. My favourites would be Sean Gregan, Jon Macken, Graham Alexander, David Nugent and Joe Garner. With regards to the worst, we've had too many, so I will just say Anthony Elding.

Best thing about Deepdale?
When you arrive for a Tuesday night game and see the floodlights. You can't beat Deepdale under the lights!

Worst grounds you've visited?
Carlisle has to be up there with the worst. The stand carries on 50 yards past the byline and makes for an awful view. Another stadium I wasn't fond of was stadium:mk, a lovely stadium, but no character whatsoever, and the atmosphere is non existent.

Enjoyable away days?
Not a fan of soulless bowls so I will go with Valley Parade and Griffin Park. Both grounds have lots of character and always seem to have a good atmosphere.

Which club serves the nicest pies?
Morecambe hands down have the best pies. They've won a few awards.

Thoughts on ticket prices in general?
£20 is plenty!

Famous Preston fans?
Wade Barret (WWE Wrestler) Mark Lawrenson, Kevin Kilbane.

DEEPDALE DELIGHTS

Game #21: Johnstone's Paint Trophy Northern Section Second Round - Tuesday 7th October 2014
PRESTON NORTH END vs Port Vale - Deepdale

Who goes to a game in October without a coat? Oh just me. On the cusp of another tedious international break, I was tempted into a midweek game under the promise of 'Football for a fiver.' Better still, I had company in the form of two mates – James and Mark, making their first appearances on *Journey to the 72*. Both kindly offered to make the hour's drive to Preston and give me a break from National Rail. Never one to look a gift horse in the mouth, I helped hook up the sat-nav. After evading rush hour traffic, the three of us were Lancashire bound.

"Do you know any Preston players?" asked James quizzically (a regular at Anfield with his wife.) I was able to rattle off half a dozen of the current squad, while doing my best to hype up the delights of the Johnstone's Paint Trophy.

"I don't even go and watch Everton in the League Cup," said Mark, a season ticket holder at Goodison Park. Clearly, I had pulled off a massive coup in convincing the two to forego a warm evening indoors for a match with little fanfare between two sides at opposing ends of the League One table.

Deepdale looks fantastic, both up close and from a distance. The crossbow shapes of the steel tubing supporting the pillars in all four corners of the ground appeared in view, just as we came to a stop at a nearby traffic light.

With parking at the ground not an option, we were pointed in the direction of a school at the end of a joining road. Preston are a club that honour their heroes – particularly Sir Tom Finney. The late forward dedicated almost his entire playing career to his boyhood club, and has been rewarded by having the road leading up to the stadium named after him, along with being immortalised with a statue inside a splash water feature outside the ground.

Deepdale differentiates itself from other grounds, going one step further than just incorporating the club initials/name on its seats. While this detail is prevalent on one stand, the other three carry images of celebrated former stalwarts, including Finney, Bill Shankly and goalkeeper Alan Kelly. From our spot in the Alan Kelly Town End, we had a clear view of Shankly's face directly opposite, although this was mainly due to Port Vale not selling out their away allocation. With Deepdale's towering floodlights beaming down and the corners closed off, I felt like I was inside an arena as opposed to a run of the mill ground.

Preston is famous for its butter pie, a real savoury treat amongst Lancashire folk. Consisting of butter (obviously) onions and potatoes, the pie temporarily disappeared from the menu when a new food provider came in. It was reinstated thanks to a successful Facebook campaign by the fans back in 2010 and remains as popular now....well almost among everyone. Sadly, the three of us balked at trying it. I can see you all now shaking your heads in disappointment and I'm sorry for letting the pie team down. The queues were too long to take a punt on something I didn't really fancy, so I stuck with what I knew.

Answering a call of nature before kick-off, I walked past several notices from shirt sponsors Virgin Trains, who were reminding season ticket holders to take advantage of a 25% discount off their travel to and from games. Given the pitfalls of some train companies, it was certainly a commendable offer.

Preston were missing a few players through injury and international call-ups, but took control of the game from the start. Vale came into the game on the back of a barren run and low on confidence, with Rob Page still in a caretaker managerial capacity following the departure of Micky Adams. It came as no surprise when the home side took an early lead. Chris Humphrey received a ball at the far post, quickly cutting inside and firing a low shot past Chris Neal. While there was no music played after the goal, North End fans above me gleefully hummed and banged the tune of Dario G's 'Carnaval De Paris' on the advertising boards. Just like at Oldham, the famous vanishing spray received a rapturous cheer when it made a rare appearance. It was being trialled in the competition ahead of potential use in the league.

Having friends with me certainly took my mind off being cold. Unbeknownst to me, James had taken it upon himself to become my social media representative for the night, spamming Twitter in an attempt to get a retweet from WWE star and famous Preston fan Wade 'Bad News' Barrett. The British grappler was on the shelf with an injury, so James was hopeful of getting a public endorsement of the ground tour from the leader of the 'Barrett Barrage.' Being a true heel, (wrestling talk for bad guy) Barrett ignored the requests. He must have been busy washing his hair or something.

The travelling Vale support were surprisingly quiet, no doubt disillusioned from a fruitless first half. Playing a high ball to target man Tom Pope simply wasn't working, with Preston picking the ball off and treating the game like a training exercise. The hosts should have doubled their lead on several occasions. Chants of "shall we sing a song for you," and "we forgot you were here," were directed towards the away end, when lo and behold, Pope came up trumps. The lanky forward equalised with a well placed header from a Chris Lines free kick. Instead of caving, Preston perked up and put the game to bed with two goals inside six minutes. Joe Garner put the Lilywhites back in front with a sublime lob, before Paul Gallagher tapped in a third after Humphrey ran into the box and cut the ball back into the forward's path.

No longer seeing Port Vale as a viable threat, the home fans turned their attention to hated rivals Blackpool, taking great delight in seeing the Seasiders prop up the Championship table. Gleeful chants of "they're going down" sung to the tune of 'Three Lions,' filled the stadium. A second header by Pope in the final minute proved to be nothing more than a consolation and did nothing to silence Preston's singing parade. Catering staff generously dished out all the unsold burgers for free, with fans doing their best Oliver Twist impressions and greedily asking for more.

I discovered that stewards don't necessarily equal great photographers. The number of blurry shots and pictures covered by the burly man's finger proved my point. Thankfully, a couple of fans helped out with the group photos and made sure we weren't locked in. We even returned the favour, before finally being turfed out. On the walk back to the car, the familiar sound of 'Whole Again,' could be heard and sure enough I was briefly reunited with the Port Vale karaoke crew, who had picked out loanee Stephane Zubar as their latest source of affection. I for one was looking forward to tuning up the band again when it was time to go to Vale Park.

While it was good to get back into the warmth of James's car, I thoroughly enjoyed my first visit to Deepdale. I'd go on record and say it's up there as being the best ground I'd been to so far this season. The closed arena type feel was very appealing, the seats were comfy and the fans made plenty of noise. A return for a Saturday game is a must.

Best chant: "We hate Blackpool. Seaside, seaside shit." The Preston fans weren't too fond of Blackpool, who allegedly flew a plane over Deepdale to "celebrate" the club's relegation to League One. Preston planned on returning the favour at the next opportunity.
Match ticket: £5. Five goals for a fiver and a great night out. Can't argue with that. Cracking value!
Match programme: £1. Another pull-out affair, in what was largely a collage of player pictures.
Cost of food: £4.50 for a pie and a soft drink combo.
Pie rating: Quite a mixed bag and a rare treat having not one, but three "expert" pie tasters on hand.
4/5 (cheese, onion and potato) - not overloaded on cheese, hit the spot and left wanting more (Mark)
2/5 (meat and potato) - quite dry and tasted more like a sausage roll. Maybe I should have opted for the butter pie after all (Me)
3.5/5 (chicken balti) - more meat required, but it provided the heat that was much needed on a cold night (James)

Final Score
Preston North End 3 (Humphrey 13, Garner 63, Gallagher 69)
Port Vale 2 (Pope 51, 89)
Attendance: 3,836

Getting to know Exeter City
Steven Chudley - Some Sunny Day (Exeter fanzine)
www.somesunnyday.org.uk
Twitter @Some_Sunny_Day

Best away support at St James' Park in recent memory?

We don't tend to get massive away followings mainly because of the size of the clubs we're generally playing and our location. However, Portsmouth always bring a good, noisy crowd and during our recent spell in League One clubs such as Leeds and Huddersfield stick in the mind.

Best thing about St James' Park?

It's our home and always has been (as Exeter City anyway). We might not own it, the facilities might not be great and only two sides of it could be considered modern, but it has a charm and character that I'd guess all fans love.

Worst grounds you've visited?

Having read where you're from I apologise now, but I visited the Deva Stadium during our Conference days and hated it. It was a soulless, grey, structure tacked on to the edge of a dull industrial estate with no facilities to speak of despite being quite modern. It didn't help that we lost, the police treated us like international terrorists and that we were spat on from the top window of a double-decker carting home fans back to the city centre as we left, but I don't think I'd have liked it anyway. Home Park, down the road, is also not a favourite. I'm not just saying this because it's Argyle but the away fan experience isn't great to say the least, mainly because of the way that you're forced to leave, channeled up a narrow stretch of land. There is the option to run the gauntlet across the park, but staying where you are is the lesser of two evils.

Is it true that there's a Domino's Pizza chain inside the ground?

There's never been a Domino's outlet as such in the ground, but I think it's still possible to buy from a very limited range of their pizzas from some of the tea huts. I've personally never had one as they're small and expensive.

Famous Exeter fans?

The most famous person that can also be called a proper fan is Adrian Edmonson who lives locally and is a season ticket holder. He even brings his good lady wife along. Other than that, swimmer Liam Tancock seems to take an active interest although I'm not sure he gets to many games. Runner Jo Pavey is too apparently, although I've never knowingly seen her there before showing off her medals. Chris Martin and Joss Stone both grew up locally. The former doesn't seem to have any interest in football and the latter made a brief appearance when we played Liverpool in the League Cup a few years ago but hasn't been seen since. Noel Edmonds used to come sniffing about for any big games but I don't think he lives around here now. Then there was the whole Uri Geller/Michael Jackson/David Blaine/Patti Boulaye circus, but most City fans would rather forget that particular chapter in our history.

Quirky fact time?

The most obvious is that we were the first side to play against a side that was recognised as the Brazilian national team, the centenary of which was marked this last summer. Aside from that, we celebrated ten years of being owned by our Supporters' Trust in 2013, the fact about the largest terrace mentioned earlier, and that nobody really knows where our nickname comes from!

Thoughts on ticket prices in general?

I think most fans have long since come to terms with the fact that football is expensive but, fortunately, in many ways football doesn't operate within "normal" rules of business. That said, it must be a difficult balance to strike with lower league clubs being far more reliant on matchday income than those further up the ladder, as whilst they need to maximise revenue this must be done without alienating fans or making them feel like their loyalty is being taken advantage of.

Keeping attendances up is especially important for our club given the ownership model and that there's no rich chairman putting their hand into their pocket whenever needed. Indeed, lower than hoped season ticket sales in early 2014 (partly thanks to our now former CEO's pricing and marketing "strategy" against a backdrop of pretty terrible home performances) and lower than predicted attendances at just two games during 2013/14 were cited as contributory reasons for us needing to take a loan from the PFA last summer. We also know that it's always likely to be the playing budget that takes the first hit if there's any reduction in income.

The real danger is that people will simply be priced out of going and will either stop entirely or start to pick and choose games and it'll be the clubs and the game as a whole that would suffer. The higher the price the less likely and more difficult it also becomes to attract floating fans or brand new people through the turnstiles.

A very simple solution would be to allow more of the television money allocated to the Premier League to trickle down through the divisions but to get that to happen we would need to convince turkeys to vote for Christmas so I won't be holding my breath.

Name your Exeter Dream Team?
Kevin Miller
Scott Hiley
Shaun Taylor
Rob Edwards
George Friend
Christian Roberts
Matt Grimes
Danny Bailey
Dean Moxey
Tony Kellow
Darran Rowbotham

GOING DOWN TO SEE THE GRECIANS

Game #22: League Two - Saturday 11th October 2014
EXETER CITY vs Hartlepool United - St James' Park

Devon is famous for its clotted cream and Ambrosia rice pudding, perhaps less so for its football. I hadn't set foot in the South West since an ill fated holiday to Newquay in the late 90s where it rained non stop and I cried tears of joy when we came home early. True story. A school friend – John West (not the household name in canned fish) had been living in Exeter for several years, so now was the perfect reason to visit. By sheer coincidence (or not) Exeter City just happened to be playing, so off I went on my longest trip so far to see the Grecians.

The street lights were still on when I left my estate to catch a 7am bus to the train station. I couldn't help but laugh at three pickets holding up signs outside the station. The joke was on me when I linked the protests to the number of trains that flashed on the board as being cancelled. A select number of staff from Arriva Trains Wales had called a 24 hour strike in protest at two workers being sacked whilst off sick. Chester and North Wales were two of the areas affected most and running on a reduced schedule until 12pm. I took one of their leaflets, which was littered with poor grammar and went to investigate. Fortunately, it was still early enough to get to Exeter in time for the game, but I was being diverted via Newport which added an hour onto the outwards journey and scuppered a planned lunch meeting with John.

I slept through most of the grim voyage through South Wales, consisting of rain, hills and some more rain. The on board entertainment got a little better passing through Bristol and Taunton. The train conductor demonstrated some serious anger issues. A group of poor kids got a grilling about how old they were, as the angry man was convinced they were trying to get a cheap fare. To their credit, they didn't flinch and rattled off the convenient dates of birth perfectly.

I was greeted by glorious sunshine upon arriving at Exeter St Davids - just one of Exeter's seven train stations. John assisted in a whistlestop tour of the city, but by his own admission isn't much of a football fan. He opted not to join me for the game, so we made plans to meet up after the match. The ground looked in need of some TLC from the outside and the ticket office resembled something of a tourist information board inside a small hut. The staff were a bit surprised to see me. They obviously don't get many fans travelling down from the North West. I was given a seat close enough to the pitch in the all-seater single tiered WTS Stand. Plenty of home fans had packed out the Thatchers Big Bank Terrace. One of the largest, if not the largest standing terraces in the Football League. Adrian Edmondson (of Bottom and Young Ones fame) was pictured with wife Jennifer Saunders lapping up the chants in the matchday programme. There's a good chance he was here again, although I didn't see him.

Just over 90 fans had made the 700+ mile round trip from Hartlepool, which was impressive given the fact that their side were rooted to the bottom of League Two and managerless after the resignation of Colin Cooper. A few of the travellers were scattered behind the goal at the St James' Road End, which was more of an open terrace than a stand, and drew comparisons with areas of Morecambe's ground. Fans in neighbouring houses get a great bird's eye view of the action.

Exeter operate on a very small budget and a transfer embargo hadn't done the club any favours. Clearly one of the have nots of the footballing world, manager Paul Tisdale had quietly gone about his business, even registering himself as a player during the early part of the season when injuries impacted the small playing squad. Goalkeeper Christy Pym and midfielder Matt Grimes were given special permission to fly back from England Under 20 duty to line up for their club, although according to Exeter fanzine 'Some Sunny Day,' the FA reportedly made the club pay the airfare, due to the players travelling separately from the rest of the squad. If this is true, then that's disgusting behaviour from the men in suits. Main sponsors Flybe (an awesome airline who helped cure my fear of flying last winter) stumped up some of the cash and fans were clearly happy to see the players, enthusiastically chanting "England's number one," at Pym whenever he made a save. Despite being hard up financially, the club did travel to Brazil in the summer to play a Fluminense XI to commemorate the 100th anniversary of the Brazilian national team playing their first ever match against a travelling Exeter City side.

Hartlepool's Michael Woods provided some humour when he couldn't save a ball from going out of play and failed to slow down, resulting in him taking a tumble over the advertising boards. The Big Bank didn't let him off the hook and broke out into a comedic circus chant which quickly caught on. Four-time Olympian and Honiton-born Jo Pavey showed off her gold medal from the recent European Championships during half time, before fans got to show off their vocal chords for charity. The Big Bank took part in the "Make some noise" scheme and officially became the loudest fans in the South West. Rivals Plymouth Argyle had recorded a reading of 100.4 decibels the week before, but Exeter pipped them to the post with 100.5 which really gave them something to sing about.

With his earlier tumble still fresh in the mind, Woods silenced the home fans and ensured he had the last laugh when he gave the visitors the lead. The ginger midfielder netted with a precise volley just four minutes after the restart. In true smash and grab style, Hartlepool effectively sealed the points when they doubled their lead through Charlie Wyke. The forward was given bags of time in the box, and he expertly turned a defender before sending a well placed shot past Pym into the bottom corner. Images of Jeff Stelling doing the Soccer Saturday dance flashed through my mind. His club would no longer be propping up the football pyramid.

Hartlepool's Dan Jones took timewasting to a whole new level, as his side looked to run down the clock. From going down like he had been shot, he even pretended to forget how to tie his shoelaces. The defender really took the cake. Exeter won a free kick when the referee finally wised up to Jones's theatrics. From the resulting set piece, the Grecians halved their deficit thanks to a powerful header from Christian Ribeiro. Exeter should have rescued a point deep into stoppage time, but captain Scot Bennett headed the ball into Row Z, thus ending the club's four game winning streak.

After jumping ahead of various families to get a photo with club mascot Grecian the Lion, who I can concur gives a good hug, I met up with John and we shared a couple of beers in town, for which he picked up the tab. I think he felt a bit bad for bailing on the game. In hindsight, I should have stayed over. There's plenty of vibrant nightlife and good pubs in the city centre to explore.

I had the joy of turfing someone out of my seat for the return train journey. No way was I about to stand up for two and a half hours until changing at Birmingham New Street. A rather well to do woman who was sat opposite couldn't hide her disgust, as I tucked into a savoury treat on the journey back north. Her nose had crinkled so far upwards it was practically touching the ceiling. Rather than offer her a bit of my delicious chicken slice, I ignored her and went back to seeing what the guy in the next seat had on his laptop. Clocking off after an 18 hour day, I now had a better memory of Devon and enjoyed my day out. Despite a tough loss, Exeter seem to be keeping their heads above water. Everyone loves a good underdog story and I'll definitely be rooting for the Grecians from afar.

Best chant: "Have you ever seen a beach?" A postcard of sorts from the 150 Exeter fans who went to Brazil.
Match ticket: £24. Had a cracking view and was shielded enough from the flash downpour of rain.
Match programme: £3. Included an article on beach football stemming from the club's recent trip to Brazil. The published takings from the last four home games detailed both the actual and budgeted figures. Taking Hartlepool's journey into consideration, media manager Richard Dorman wrote a timely piece, putting travel into perspective and reminding fans that most of Exeter's away days are eight hour round trips.
Cost of food: £2.60 for a pie.
Pie rating: 3.5/5 - the chicken balti was encased with chewy pastry and tender chunks of chicken, although it was quite mild in terms of spice.

Final Score
Exeter City 1 (Ribeiro 80)
Hartlepool United 2 (Woods 49, Wyke 66)
Attendance: 3,547

Getting to know Leyton Orient
Jim Nichols - Editor, Leyton Orientear fanzine
www.leytonorientear.com

Best thing about Brisbane Road?
The ground has changed a lot in recent years with all four corners of the ground now occupied by residential flats, some of which are pitch facing and therefore have balconies full of spectators on a matchday.Thankfully, it has retained a certain charm, and much like many other smaller grounds allows fans to feel close to the action.

Feelings on the Olympic Stadium issue?
While there is a feeling of unjustness about the way it was handled in the courts and there is a feeling that West Ham got off lightly, I think most Orient fans are just pleased to draw a line under the issue now. Most seem positive enough that the O's can continue to survive as a football league club in the local area.

Worst grounds you've visited?
One of the main disappointments with missing out on promotion last season was that it left us as the only London side in League One and with a lack of local derbies to look forward to. The three most local grounds remaining are Colchester, Gillingham and Crawley and none of these are enjoyable away experiences.

Best place to sit/stand at Brisbane Road?
The South Stand, being behind the goal, may not have the ideal view of the pitch but is certainly the best place in the ground for atmosphere, not least due to its proximity to the away end. The club's supporters club situated outside the West Stand features in the CAMRA Good Beer Guide and is very popular with both home and away supporters before and after a game. On the subject of refreshments, it takes a brave person to give the club's burgers a try!

Famous Orient fans?
Both of the Lloyd-Webber brothers have been supporters for a long time, with Julian a regular who is often spotted at away games and even named his daughter Jasmine Orienta if only to back up this status! Comedian Bob Mills is another that isn't shy of displaying his affections for the O's publicly.

Quirky fact time?
The O's did spend one season in the top flight in 1962/63, however their stay was brief. One season later they were relegated having finished bottom and have not been back since.

Game #23: League One - Saturday 18th October 2014
LEYTON ORIENT vs Milton Keynes Dons - The Matchroom Stadium (Brisbane Road)

They say in life you only get one chance to make a good first impression. I had barely stepped off the train when my eyes and ears were greeted with the following exchange:

"Fuck off."
"No you fuck off."
"You pushed me."
"No I didn't."
"I'm going to get you arrested."

Oh London, how I'd missed you so. Just to recap, in two visits to Euston, someone's jumped in front of a train and now I was witnessing potential mid-morning violence. The guy at the centre of the controversy threw his hands up like an Italian defender looking to protest his innocence, while two women went on the warpath for an apparent misdemeanour. Their appeals were met with apathy by the public and I certainly wanted no part of their spat. I left them to throw handbags at ten paces as I disappeared into the abyss otherwise known as the London underground.

This was my second attempt at seeing Leyton Orient play, having been priced out of a trip to the capital for the Rochdale game back in late September. I shared the tube with plenty of Arsenal fans (probably paying up to £90 for the privilege) before managing to get lost around Leytonstone. Getting off at Leytonstone High Road and making my way through the place where David Beckham grew up, my senses were heightened. Pairs of unfriendly eyes pierced a hole through me as I made my way past an endless reel of takeaway units and dirty fruit stalls. Everyone I stopped to ask for directions was foreign and I could barely make out what they were saying. I was definitely in the minority in this part of East London. Getting nowhere fast, the staff at William Hill informed me I needed to take a short train from Leytonstone to Leyton, which was where the ground is situated.

Following the directions drawn onto a betting slip to a tee, Orient shirts finally became visible. I was back on the right track. Some fans were lamenting the fact that their team were yet to win at home this season, while kids swung off the train's holding bars under the watchful eye of their approving fathers. A brisk ten minute walk through Leyton and Coronation Gardens reminded me it was somewhere I wouldn't like to be at night, although it did lead me to the ground. Modern apartments piggyback onto Brisbane Road, allowing residents a bird's eye view of the action from their balconies. A series of flags were draped out in support of the struggling O's, who had been in somewhat of a tailspin since suffering the agony of a penalty shootout play-off final defeat to Rotherham United back in May.

Sky Sports cameras were recording vox pops with various fans outside the ticket office, gauging the reaction of now former boss Russell Slade taking over the reins at Championship outfit Cardiff City. For now, Kevin Nugent was the man charged with turning the club's fortunes around on an interim basis. After being snubbed for an on-air role, I took a walk around the ground passing the usual ticket booths, club shop, pharmacy....wait a pharmacy! Yes, the club has a walk-in clinic on hand for anyone needing medical assistance or supplies during the game. I was ready for a pie over a paracetamol at this point, so headed indoors and into a spacious food hall named after ex-player Laurie Cunningham. One of the first black players to represent England at any level, the winger started out at Orient in the early 70's, enjoying a three year stint at the club, before moving to West Brom then Spain and Real Madrid. His life was tragically cut short by a car crash in 1989 at the age of 33. A plaque was unveiled before this exact fixture just over a year ago and various other memorabilia sporting Laurie's face and likeness is visible around the ground.

Taking my seat next to the flat cap brigade and away dugout, MK Dons manager Karl Robinson looked calm and relaxed as he cracked jokes with his coaching staff.

Fans within earshot had pinned their hopes on young winger Shaun Batt. One fan in particular was quite fond of the man, yelling out "go on Batt-Man," whenever he got the ball. Sadly for our Shaun, his first effort was slightly wayward and probably ended up in Gotham City. He did have pace to burn and looked like being Orient's best source of producing a goal. The tough tackling of Dons defender Kyle McFadzean had the Orient supporters up in arms. "Oi ref, have you left your yellow card at home?" screamed an angry cockney a few rows back. Chances were few and far between. Orient's Gary Woods turned a Benik Afobe effort onto the bar, while opposite number David Martin flew to palm over a Shane Lowry screamer from distance. Batt lacked the final touch up top when put clear, stroking a tame effort into Martin's grateful gloves. Holy miss Batt-Man! The fans behind both sets of goals were rather quiet, leaving it up to the travelling MK fans to produce the lion's share of the noise. I didn't think I'd be typing that statement.

Once Batt was withdrawn early in the second half, it was clear that the goals weren't going to come. The cat calls and constant needling of Robinson became the sole source of entertainment for me. While Nugent was quite static on the halfway line, Robinson was up and down like a yo-yo. Cries of "get back in your box," and "your tracksuit is a few sizes too tight," drew a chuckle out of the MK Dons boss who was playing the Orient fans like a fiddle. The exasperated East Londoners turned their attention to poor Mark Randall. As the midfielder was being substituted, one portly fellow decided a backhanded compliment was in order. "Well played Prince Charles, now tuck your ears in. They take up four seats already." Late on, Orient's misery was compounded when defender Mathieu Baudry was dismissed for two needless bookings, proving that the referee did indeed remember to bring his cards.

To their credit, Orient's fans didn't turn on their own players at the final whistle. It was abundantly clear that confidence was down. The same fans screaming abuse all game had suddenly changed their tune. Conversations along the lines of "a clean sheet is massive against this lot," and "at least we didn't get another tonking," could be heard as I was departing. Things would have been a whole lot different had I visited last season. I hadn't exactly got value for money, but looked on the bright side, sharing a tube back with various glum Arsenal fans who had witnessed a disappointing result of their own (2-2 with Hull) at two/three times the price I had paid.

Back at Euston, I forgot about the escalator etiquette, committing the ungodly sin of standing on the left hand side, thus blocking the rushing commuters. By the time the third family chewed me out, I responded with some colourful language of my own. The strange encounters kept on coming. An Essex bachelor was having an engaging chat with himself as he was preening his hair in the bathroom mirror, while a group of Middle Eastern girls decided to sing persian karaoke between Crewe and Chester. I would've joined in, but the chorus didn't fit the rest of the song. The final piece of the jigsaw was the drunken pole sat behind me who kept popping up like a Jack in the box slurring "cheers," with his eyes darting from side to side. As tempting as it was, I didn't poke Lukasz in the eyes. This had definitely been a trip that made me appreciate home a lot more.

Best chant: "We are a franchise, we know who we are." MK Dons fans saying what a lot of people feel about them.
Match ticket: £25. A lack of goals and a low-key performance didn't provide enough bang for my buck.
Match programme: £3. Special mention to super fans Chris Smith and Robert Stone who travelled almost 2,000 miles in less than three weeks to follow the O's in September. They deserved their "League One Fans of the Month" trophy.
Cost of food: £2.50 for a packaged beef and onion pie, £2.20 for a sausage roll.
Pie rating: 3/5 - a touch of blackness on the side, the crust was a little soggy, but contained lovely cuts of mince and wasn't oversaturated with onion. Strong herbs brought out the flavour in the sausage roll.

Final Score
Leyton Orient 0
Milton Keynes Dons 0
Attendance: 5,014

A BLIP ON THE ROAD

Game #24: League One - Tuesday 21st October 2014
PORT VALE vs Scunthorpe United - Vale Park

"So are you going anywhere nice?" asked the taxi driver as we made our way to the train station.
"Stoke-on-Trent for a few drinks and to see Port Vale play," I replied. If only it had been that easy.
I was due to meet up with Port Vale season ticket holder and friend Mike Williams at Vale Park. Everything seemed straighforward, leaving Chester on a busy London bound train and changing at Crewe. It was here where the fun and games started to happen. Hurricane Gonzalo was about to throw a major wrench in my plans.

Heavy winds and vicious downpours had been affecting trains around the country all day and Crewe was no different. My scheduled connection to Longport (closest stop to the ground) via Derby was heavily delayed and then cancelled. A train to Northampton leaving at 7pm looked to be my best bet, as I could get a taxi from Stoke-on-Trent to take me on the four mile journey to the ground. It would be a tight squeeze, but still possible. That train was delayed waiting for a member of staff, so I tried again with the Derby route. The train left Crewe at a snail's pace and it was now gone 7:30pm. After much deliberating, I decided to abort the trip and got off at the first stop - Alsager. I simply wasn't going to make the game and didn't see the point in arriving 30 minutes late.

Stuck in the middle of East Cheshire, my three layers of clothing repelled the biting wind. A train back to Crewe didn't look to be forthcoming any time soon. I checked the latest scores and Scunthorpe had found an early goal. Moments later, Vale swiftly equalised. My decision had been justified. It hurt not being there to see it, but it was simply out of my hands. The Northampton train crept past and the conductor asked if I was going back to Crewe. I nodded and he told me to come aboard, as they were turning around and heading back. The wind on the overhead lines deemed the trip too unsafe, so commuters looking to go as far as Stafford were going to be re-directed in taxis and buses.

I was feeling down at missing out on a game, but my spirits were about to be lifted. Once back at Crewe, I walked past John Hartson who was charging his mobile in the cafe. Big John had also been delayed getting back to Swansea and was more than happy to pass the time and stop for a chat. The man couldn't have been nicer, obliging a photo request, plus he even signed my train ticket. The ex-Wales international has had a rough few years, battling back from the brink of death to beat cancer. Now a beacon of life and enjoying working for the BBC, John even endorsed *Journey to the 72*, in addition to providing a timely lesson in perspective. It had been a minor setback, so I stopped my pity party for one and counted my blessings. What doesn't kill you simply makes you stronger. Thank you John and good health sir!

While it took four times longer than usual to get back to Chester, I kept up to date with the goals flying in all around the country. Vale eventually drew 2-2 and I decided not to let a small gust of wind or a major Hurricane derail my quest to visit the 72.

Favourite memory as a Fulham fan?

Several, thanks to 43 years as a fan, but I can't get past the elation of coming from behind to beat Hamburg 2-1 at Craven Cottage to qualify for the inaugural Europa League final in 2010.

Was Felix Magath as mad as the media suggested?

Definitely, strange tactics, poor handling of players and then there's the cheese incident!

Best game you've witnessed at Craven Cottage?

Hard to assess 'best'. Hamburg, Shakhtar Donetsk, Juventus were all memorable games at the Cottage during our Europa League run, although pretty tense affairs. The same could be said of our match against Lincoln City in the last game of the 1981/1982 season, where the winning side were promoted at the expense of the losing side. In the end, Fulham clung onto a 1-1 draw to edge promotion. Shakhtar were probably the best footballing side we've ever seen at the Cottage. There have been some memorable games over the years. I guess the one that stands out otherwise in recent times, would be the 6-0 demolition of local rivals QPR.

Best/worst players to pull on a Fulham shirt?

Best - Bobby Moore, Gordon Davies, Louis Saha, Dimitar Berbatov, Danny Murphy.
Worst - Steve McAnespie, Mark Cooper, John Watson, Adil Chihi.

Best thing about Craven Cottage?

The uniqueness of the ground and its location by the river with great views across.

Worst grounds you've visited?

QPR is awful for leg room and restricted views. For me, it's usually about the view. I'm happy if I can see the pitch from a good angle/height. Most modern stadium are soulless, but at least provide good views.

Enjoyable away days?

I enjoy all away trips for the varying experiences, seeing different towns, stadia and meeting different fans from around the country.

Famous Fulham fans?

Actors Hugh Grant and Kevork Malikyan, Ray Brookes (aka Mr Benn), MP Steve Pound. I see the latter two quite regularly.

Quirky fact time?

We are the only club to have had terraces (standing) in the Premier League as far as I know.

Thoughts on ticket prices in general?

In general, ticket prices in the UK are too high, especially when you look at other countries such as Germany. With all the money swilling around from TV deals, more should be filtering down to the lower leagues and fans should be getting a better deal? Due to their recent decline, the ticket price reductions at Fulham year on year mean their season tickets are probably excellent value comparatively. Well, they would be if we started playing reasonable football again!

Game #24: The Championship - Friday 24th October 2014
FULHAM vs Charlton Athletic - Craven Cottage

When a Friday night visit to watch Fulham was presented to me, it certainly piqued my interest. Who wouldn't like to spend part of their weekend in a makeshift cottage overlooking the Thames while watching some football? Despite train tickets costing slightly less than a Hammersmith penthouse, I decided to make a weekend of it. Just to make sure I didn't get lost or punched for standing on the wrong side of the escalators, one of my work colleagues Heidi Scammell came along for the adventure. Like me, Heidi's a fellow football enthusiast and Manchester United fan. Plus, she knows about the offside rule. All joking aside, Heidi's one of my best friends and happily arranged the tickets for us, before securing accommodation at her parents' house.

Claustrophobia struck on board the tube which was ridiculously congested and resembled a sweatbox. I could've kissed the sign for Parsons Green (had it not been dirty) such was the relief to get off and breathe a little easier. The Friday tradition for workers in Fulham was seemingly no different to the rest of the UK - to the pub! We settled on the 'White Horse,' a popular choice with many young adults filling the booths and drinking chilled wine. The gastro pub specialised in a wide range of continental ales. Taking a punt on a German ale, I can happily report that the Veltins went down nicely. At £9.95 for two drinks, I should bloody hope so too!

The walk through the leafy suburb to the ground was a pleasant one. With plenty of restaurants to suit every tastebud en route, you won't go hungry. A dimly lit 'Fulham Football Club' gable on the roof soon became visible which meant we had arrived at Craven Cottage. Ground staff outside were helpful regarding access to the right gates. As soon as we were inside, a wall of police complete with sniffer dogs didn't provide as nice a welcome. Stern faces just stared ahead while the mutts did their detective work. Luckily for me, there were no sandwiches in my bag with the rucksack also being 100% slobberproof.

The Craven Cottage pie was Fulham's own stamp on the famous savoury snack. The kiosks did a booming trade and sold out of steak and ale pies before the match even started. Having bottled tasting the butter pie at Preston, I needed to redeem myself. Both of us indulged in the house special and one of us even went up for seconds. Whilst eating in the concourse, rows of Charlton fans went past singing at the top of their lungs to announce their arrival. Current Fulham captain Scott Parker was loudly booed when his name was announced. The midfielder has had his fair share of London clubs and it had skipped my mind that he started out his playing career with the Addicks.

Although the terraces were gone and new floodlights had been installed, Craven Cottage is still unique. The Pavilion building (aka the cottage) above the players entrance may look better suited to Lord's Cricket ground, but adds to the overall character and quirkiness of the stadium. Sandwiched between the Johnny Haynes Stand and Putney End, it immediately stands out. Fulham are also the only club (that I know of) which has a designated 'neutral area.' Located under the cottage, on one side of the Putney End and a safe distance from the away supporters, students, tourists and Joe Publics like myself normally fill the seats. The number of Brits in the immediate vicinity could be counted on one hand, which was a bold statement. How did I know? Simple. As soon as light raindrops began to fall, everyone leapt up and scrambled for a seat higher in the stand. They couldn't move quick enough, acting like the rain would ruin their perfectly coiffed hair or get their designer man bags wet. These foreigners are such divas and clearly not used to the Great British weather.

On paper, this seemed like a lopsided affair. Fulham had been lodged in the bottom three pretty much all season. Suffering from a relegation hangover and a slightly eccentric former manager, the Cottage brass finally pulled the plug on Felix Magath's tenure and handed the reins to the club's Under 21 coach Kit Symons. A former Fulham player, the Welshman had done away with using cheese to heal injuries and running his players into the ground, with the team responding in kind with a run of positive results. It came as no surprise when Fulham opened the scoring just six minutes in. Parker silenced the boo-boys when he met Ross McCormack's cross and fired a half volley in off the underside of the bar. Hugo Rodallega doubled the lead six minutes later, reacting quickest to slot home after McCormack's shot was parried.

By this point, the rain had eased off and fans came out of hibernation. My eardrums started to hurt from the opinionated American sat directly behind me. The bolshy Yank, who I'll call Chad for arguments sake had the worst case of verbal diarrhoea. Amazingly, three fellow female students/acquaintances seemed to hang off this guy's every word. Each statement managed to trump the other in terms of absurdity. Whenever Fulham's Kostas Stafylidis turned his marker, cries of "oh man, your ankles are so gone," polluted the air. Comparing every tackle to a UFC strike, it was clear that the only balls this guy had ever played with were his own. From ideal dates (blonde women with short hair) to ludicrous boasts of, "I'm the most charismatic person at any party," this guy took the proverbial Oreo. Thankfully our American friend wasn't racist. He told us so in no uncertain terms, but categorically "hates the Japanese for killing all the whales and dolphins." Give me strength.

Charlton pressed for a way back into the game, but couldn't turn their corners into goals. They may have looked like Barcelona in their orange/yellow shirts, but the tactic of trying to pass the ball into the net like the Catalans simply wasn't working, although they did hit the post late on. Rodallega put the game to bed in the dying moments. The Colombian netted his second of the game with a wonderful solo finish, dancing past a defender in the box before placing an angled shot past goalkeeper Stephen Henderson into the far bottom corner. By this point, Chad had resorted to doing Forrest Gump impressions. In all fairness, they were spot on. I was tempted to add one of my own in the form of "stupid is as stupid does," but he got up and left early with his entourage. I wasn't sorry to see him go.

Even in defeat, the Charlton fans remained upbeat and were singing for most of the game. In comparison, the Fulham contingent sat on their hands, only taking the Charlton bait on occasions or singing their glee in the direct aftermath of a goal. There was no trouble between the sets of fans after the game, although police on horseback were present. Within half an hour of the match finishing, the club had emailed Heidi asking for our thoughts and if we had enjoyed the experience. We were both impressed with the club's efficiency, as was she with the female restrooms. According to my accomplice, each unit had its own sink, a coat hanger plus ample space. In comparison, the men's facilities were a bit more cramped and had run out of hand towels, but that's just minor nitpicking.

Toffs were forced to mingle with the football folk during part of the Tube ride through Putney. Whereas in the north you get some greasy fast food after a night out, things are a little different in these parts darling. One simply has brioche buns instead. A rather 'fabulous' young couple were fawning over a bag of the savouries, while playfully fighting in their fake accents. Personally, I found the whole 'Made in Chelsea' lah-di-dah crap a bit nauseating, which isn't surprising given that I wasn't born with a silver spoon in my mouth.

Heidi's parents Roger and Angela lived in Oxford and very kindly offered to put us both up for the night. Thankfully, London rarely sleeps and that carries over into the transport links. A quiet train through Reading allowed us both to catch a bit of sleep, before a bus dropped us back at 2:30am. As soon as my head hit the pillow, I was out like a light. It had been a very long day, considering I got up at 6am and did a day's work on top of the travelling. Thankfully, both teams put on a show and I got to see a good game and a few goals too. Heidi proved to be a good omen, she can come again.

Best chant: "Two nil and you're still silent." The Charlton fans trying to wake up their Fulham counterparts.
Match ticket: £30 for a good seat opposite the players entrance.
Match programme: £3.50. Dearest programme yet, but contained several BOGOF and 2-4-1 deals that could be redeemed in the club shop. Historians would appreciate the matchday programme timeline, featuring brief write-ups of six past encounters between the two teams from 1949-2012.
Cost of food: Pies ranged from £3.80 (steak and ale) to £4.20 (cottage)
Pie rating: 5/5. Beautiful whipped potato piping on top with a nice buttery shortcrust pastry on the side. Plenty of gravy kept the pie from being too dry.

Final Score
Fulham 3 (Parker 6, Rodallega 12, 89)
Charlton Athletic 0
Attendance: 17,923

Getting to know Reading
Clyde –Royals Rendezvous (Reading fans forum)
www.royalsrendezvous.co.uk

Best thing about the Madejski Stadium?
The uniform look of the stands and stadium make the stadium look quite pretty when taking photos from the air.

Enjoyable away days?
Millennium Stadium, Nou Camp, Bernabeu, Wembley, Elland Road, Highbury, Upton Park.

Which club serves the nicest pies?
Wigan.

Famous Reading fans?
Bill Oddie ("Rub your beard all over my body")
Irwin Sparkes - lead singer and guitarist for The Hoosiers
Ricky Gervais
Kate Winslet

Quirky fact time?
Reading is the largest town in the UK that hasn't been granted city status. Oscar Wilde spent time in Reading prison.

Thoughts on ticket prices in general?
Far too expensive, especially when compared to other European leagues - where there are cheap matchday and season tickets. Germany has a really good setup where even average teams in the Bundesliga have incredibly large stadiums. This means they can lower ticket prices and still fill the 40,000+ stadiums that they play in.

Name your Reading Dream Team?
Shaka Hislop
Graeme Murty
Adrian Williams
Paul McShane
Nicky Shorey
Jimmy Kebe
Steve Sidwell
Phil Parkinson
Michael Gilkes
Jimmy Quinn
Robin Friday

Game #25: The Championship - Saturday 25th October 2014
READING vs Blackpool - The Madejski Stadium

There are never any certainties in football, yet if ever there was a home banker then this was surely it. Leg two of the weekend down south was about to take me to the Madejski Stadium. Reading had been on the wrong end of a few scorelines in recent weeks, so it must have been a relief for them to be playing the Championship's whipping boys. Blackpool were like a dinghy stranded at the Pleasure Beach, so I was looking forward to seeing them put up a fight and try to prove my theory wrong. After all, it mustn't be much fun for the supporters to travel the country just to see your team get thrashed every week.

Heidi's friend Mark Field was joining us for this game. By his own admission, Mark wasn't the biggest football fan. Scratch that, he wasn't a fan of sports at all, which made it even more surprising that it took little to coax him into tagging along. His only previous game had been Oxford United vs Bury in 199-something, basically a long time ago. This was only his third sporting event in total. I was eager to see what he took out of the day and if modern football could convert him into a fan and get him through the turnstiles a bit more.

Shuttle buses were on hand to transport large numbers to the stadium for a reasonable £4 return ticket. Beefed up security tried to throw their weight around, but in reality no-one was playing up. Everyone just wanted to get to the ground. The jacked up guards just wanted a bit of attention. Having gorged on nothing but fresh fruit for breakfast at Heidi's parents, I felt less guilty indulging in a little pre-match stodge. In addition to pies, Reading sold pizzas. Mama Mia! This was music to my ears and it would have been rude not to indulge. Mark and Heidi had already eaten in town and remarked I'd bought enough to feed a small army. I was happy to share, but neither took me up on my generous offer.

The Madejski is totally enclosed and has that arena feel to it. While it's an all-seater stadium and wouldn't look out of place in the Premier League, there aren't too many bars nearby. There's a Holiday Inn which I suppose would suit some away fans, although I imagine the prices inside there will be pretty steep. Reading share the Madejski with eggchasers London Irish. Sadly, I found the atmosphere lacking somewhat. Sat directly behind the goal in the North Stand, a drummer sat higher up tried his best, but couldn't drum up much support. Fans seemed content to just spectate. The Blackpool fans were so muted, it's as if they had resigned themselves to defeat before they'd even taken their seats. Danny got in touch via text to say he saw Chris Kamara reporting on the game and the stadium looked empty. To be fair to Reading, Soccer Saturday had Kammy positioned at an unflattering camera angle. There were plenty of fans inside the Madejski, they just weren't generating the level of noise you would expect. A wind turbine in the neighbouring business park could be seen poking out from the top of the West Stand, although it wasn't quiet enough for us to hear it spinning.

Reading's Nigel Adkins looked to be a man under pressure, but genuinely seemed to appreciate a chant of "one Nigel Adkins." The former Southampton boss left the dugout and approached the touchline to give the loyal home fans a round of applause. I wondered how much opposite number Jose Riga would appreciate something similar. The Belgian looked stony faced on the Blackpool bench. Given Reading's six game winless run and Blackpool's solitary victory in their first 13 outings, a goalless draw didn't look likely, although painful memories of the Leeds stalemate were in the back of my mind. The home side made hard work of their task, but they allayed my fears by finally breaking the deadlock midway through the first half. Blackpool goalkeeper Joe Lewis could only push Glenn Murray's header into the net after the on loan Crystal Palace man got on the end of Jordan Obita's cross.

While Lewis looked anything but secure, opposite number Adam Federici may as well have been sipping cocktails on the beach and reading the newspaper. He did get out of his deck chair to collect a cross ahead of Ishmael Miller. The tall Blackpool forward went down like he'd been shot, prompting a hoard of young kids in the front row to point their fingers and yell "diver, diver." Moments later, teammate Francois Zoko was in the wars after clattering into his marker at pace. The sickening thud could be heard all the way back in Row Z, but Blackpool weren't even awarded a free kick. The game quickly lost steam, leaving it up to mascots Kingsley and Queensley bear to entertain the restless kids.

Blackpool eventually gifted Reading a second goal. After what looked like head tennis on the training ground, Peter Clarke gave the perfect example of how not to defend in the box when he unwittingly headed past his own despairing keeper. Jamie Mackie took pity on Blackpool when he ballooned over in front of an open goal, but the Seasiders handed Reading another chance to score deep into stoppage time. John Lundstram tripped Nick Blackman in the box and the substitute coolly rolled the resulting spot kick into the net, sending Lewis the wrong way.

We woke Mark up to let him know the game was over and the three of us headed back into town for a much needed drink. The return buses avoided the post match traffic and dropped us back into town pretty quickly. Several Blackpool fans joined us in the 'Three Guineas' pub next door to the train station. One guy's attempt to start a "Sea Sea Seasiders," chant never really caught on, mainly due to some trouble kicking off. We had just sat down and Swansea vs Leicester was in the early stages on TV. One guy demanded El Clasico be shown a bit too forcefully, so the owner had him physically removed. The inebriated one didn't see the two bouncers hook his arms from behind and the three did an all too brief Strictly Come Dancing style Cha-Cha-Cha out of the pub. Ironically, the landlord bowed to peer pressure and promptly switched over so we could see the Spanish senors of Barcelona and Real Madrid strut their stuff.

The beautiful game had failed to capture Mark. He said as much himself. Hopefully he doesn't leave it another 15 years before checking out another match. Six goals from two games was a good return from an expensive weekend down south. It was good to get back on northern soil, even if the half eaten Burger King meal was the first thing I clapped eyes on getting onto the train at Crewe. Before you ask, no I didn't eat it, but give me that over a brioche bun any day. Proper food!

Reading lost any sort of momentum when they slipped back into their old habits and went through a period of poor form. People who pointed their fingers at me cursing the club were only half right. Although it was all sunshine and happiness at this game, the ominous cloud remained over the Madejski. Reading fans didn't need me or the MET office to tell them something that they already knew.

Best chant: "There's only one Nigel Adkins." Not much in the way of chants. They were quite a civilised bunch in Berkshire. Kudos to the Reading fans for getting behind their manager.
Match ticket: £30. I was in the perfect place to assist, should the goalline technology have failed.
Match programme: £3. The recent match reports made for grim reading for home fans, but in happier news, the club sent 23 representatives over to Kenya to help with community projects, which was deemed a success. The well researched Blackpool feature will have cheered up the travelling contingent, reminding them of happier times to temporarily take their minds off the team's dismal plight.
Cost of food: £5 deal on hot food and a drink.
Pie rating: 5/5. Advertised and sold as chicken balti, the pie turned out to be chicken curry inside a pastry shell. The sauce was hot and richly spiced with plenty of succulent chicken. The pizza held up its end of the bargain. Generous sized deep pan pepperoni with creamy tomatoes and melt in the mouth cheese. Delicious!

Final Score
Reading 3 (Murray 23, P.Clarke og 70, Blackman pen 90+4)
Blackpool 0
Attendance: 15,625

Getting to know AFC Bournemouth
Vital Bournemouth - www.bournemouth.vitalfootball.co.uk
Twitter @UTCIAD

What's the secret behind manager Eddie Howe's success?

I'm not entirely sure Eddie himself could put his finger on that one. There's just a very special connection between Eddie Howe and AFC Bournemouth, which inspired fans and players alike. During his first stint as manager he had seen us firstly avoid relegation out of the Football League despite a 17 point deduction. To promotion the following season despite a transfer embargo. Since his return he steered us to promotion to the second tier for only the second time in the club's history and has then secured a club record finish of 10th in the Championship last season. His continued success however is not a secret. It's all down to hard work. Howe is one of the finest young English managers around and Dean Court is his home.

Best away support at Dean Court in recent memory?

I'll plump for Burton Albion in last season's FA Cup. There is a bit of history behind my reason. Burton's Pirelli Stadium had hosted our League Two promotion party in 2010 and despite their season not ending and still having games to play at home, they still welcomed and encouraged a pitch invasion after the game and those scenes will never be forgotten. They certainly weren't last season when our FA Cup tie had been postponed shortly before kick off due to a waterlogged pitch. The Cherries supporters decided to set up a fundraising effort to pay for Burton's supporters coaches for the midweek re-arranged tie. It went viral and instead of part funding one coach, the fund paid for four with extra money donated to charity.

Best thing about Dean Court?

Now that's a difficult one! To anyone else, an away fan or a neutral I'd imagine Dean Court wouldn't really stand out. Perhaps the £1 car parking next to the ground might be a highlight until they realise how long it takes to get out. For home supporters, it's just home, Dean Court and Kings Park has been where we have played for over 100 years, the stadium might have changed and rotated, but it's still home.

Best place to sit/stand at Dean Court?

The majority of the atmosphere is generated in the 'Steve Fletcher' North Stand behind the goal.

Worst grounds you've visited?

Hereford United's toilets have left a lasting memory. Having travelled through the leagues, there are plenty of old grounds in lower league football (some now non league), that could get a mention. Places like Stockport, Macclesfield and Exeter, but they at least all have some character. Instead I'd plump for some of the soulless new grounds with no atmosphere. Places such as Colchester, stadium:mk and the Ricoh are all modern day 'arenas' but all lacking in offering a good footballing experience.

Famous Bournemouth fans?

Harry Redknapp is often considered a fan due to his connections to the club. Otherwise Matt Tong the drummer from Bloc Party is a genuine Cherries supporter.

Quirky fact time?

AFC Bournemouth has gone through many name changes. During the Boscombe era, the players used to use the Portman Hotel pub (mentioned above) as a changing room before walking across Kings Park. The club then evolved from Bournemouth and Boscombe Athletic Football Club to AFC Bournemouth in the early 1970's. The AC Milan red and black stripes were also adopted during this period.

Thoughts on ticket prices in general?

Watching AFC Bournemouth work their way up through the leagues with my rose tinted spectacles on I'm sure I used to be able to get change from a £10 note when walking through the turnstiles and on to a terrace.

Now, I'm not sure how much change I'd get from a £50 note, if I ever had one of those! Add on money for travel and supporting your club home and away in whatever division is no doubt an expensive hobby. Considering the atmosphere of English football is one of its selling points to television broadcasters home and abroad, clearly more could be done with the vast amount of money coming into the sport from TV deals to ensure that grounds are full and supporters are not increasingly over charged.

Name your Bournemouth Dream Team?

Pub debates such as this have been ruined by the sheer success of Eddie Howe's teams. It has to be this season's side, with no exceptions.

Artur Boruc
Simon Francis
Tommy Elphick
Steve Cook
Charlie Daniels
Matt Ritchie
Andrew Surman
Harry Arter
Marc Pugh
Callum Wilson
Brett Pitman

Pitman often shared his role alongside Yann Kermorgant, but as he also played in our two previous promotions and scored the goals to avoid relegation from the Football League following a seventeen point deduction he gets the final nod.

SEEING HOWE THINGS ARE DONE ON THE SOUTH COAST

Game #26: Capital One Cup Fourth Round - Tuesday 28th October 2014
AFC BOURNEMOUTH vs West Bromwich Albion - The Goldsands Stadium (Dean Court)

"So are you doing anything exciting for the rest of the day Shaun?" That was the question several co-workers posed as I hurriedly cleared my desk mid-morning.

"Yeah, I'm going to Bournemouth." Cue the stunned silence and tumbleweeds across the office. I almost had to pick one jaw up off the floor, while I couldn't help but notice several others shaking their heads.

"You're mad," said the majority of my exasperated colleagues, collectively shaking their heads and having a good chuckle. "No, just excited," I replied, picking up my bag before walking out with a jovial "see you all in a few days."

The bond between me and the Capital One Cup was ever growing. Having been to a game in each of the competition's first three rounds, I didn't want to break with the tradition now. Not for the first time, obtaining a ticket proved to be a bit tricky, yet every obstacle can be conquered with a positive mindset. Knowing that I hadn't attended two Bournemouth home games in the last season to qualify, I still tried my luck. An online purchase was subsequently rejected, so I had to fall back on my charming phone manner once again. Because West Brom sold all their allocation, it took a few days for the club to check that I wasn't masquerading as a secret Baggie fan trying to infiltrate the home end. I simply had to respect the club protocol. Persistence finally paid off and I was granted a ticket which was posted out and arrived within a day. I had been looking forward to seeing Bournemouth at home for a few years now. Ever since attending an FA Cup game at Wigan between the two sides close to two years ago, I was taken by the passion of the fans, plus the attractive, positive style of play that had been instilled and became somewhat of a casual fan.

Cherries boss Eddie Howe has worked wonders with the club, taking them from the brink of non league to the upper echelons of the Championship in less than six years. Just days after mauling Birmingham City 8-0 at their own ground, I couldn't have picked a better time to visit the South Coast club. Even the rail staff were getting caught up with the excitement. The conductor stopped to chat for a few minutes, telling me who to watch out for (Matt Ritchie) and giving directions to the ground. The ticket collector had been to watch QPR the night before and explained he couldn't get a pass from his wife on two consecutive nights to watch football. I felt bad for him. The disappointment was evident all over his face. He clearly wanted to tag along. I'm sure he had something to do with the special 'Up the Cherries' message that was displayed on the train.

Given the distance involved, it was natural that an overnight stay would be required. First of all, I needed to drop my bags at the Travelodge before going to the ground. A fishing shop next door to Pokesdown train station guided me to a bus stop across the road. The bus driver informed me he would drop me right outside the door. The man was true to his word and I went to check in. However, there was no reservation. It quickly became apparent that I had arrived at the wrong Travelodge. I needed the one by the seafront, which was precisely what I asked both the bus driver and nautical assistant. The reception staff Declan and Emily both laughed it off, stating this always happened. The hotel showed their class by calling and paying for a taxi to take me to the correct location, passing the pier and illuminations on the way. For a brief moment, it felt like I was passing through the MGM Grand in Las Vegas. A gust of wind which greeted me getting out of the taxi brought me back to reality. An attractive foreign girl on reception was getting chewed out by an angry customer, but she handed me my room key and flashed a continental smile that I'm sure had broken many hearts over the years. Unfortunately for Elena, I didn't have time to flirt. After a quick change I was back downstairs and ready to head to the ground.

No sooner had I got back into a taxi, the driver asked if I minded picking up a few more passengers along the way. The prospect of a cheaper fare sounded attractive and seemed like a no brainer, so we picked up three appreciative West Brom fans. Two middle-aged blokes and a woman crammed into the back (I already called shotgun) and began to speculate on the Baggies lineup in their thick Black Country accents. There was a bit of friendly banter when I told them about the ground tour and my allegiance to the home side, but they didn't hold it against me. In fact, one guy insisted he paid the taxi fare. Never one to look a gift horse in the mouth, I didn't argue.

The ground is located within the concourse of Kings Park in Boscombe (a borough of Bournemouth) with a couple of pubs within walking distance. The floodlights did their job inside the stadium, but that didn't stretch to the outside or the immediate vicinity which looked a little dim. A statue of playing legend Steve Fletcher (there's also a stand named after him) was getting plenty of attention in the club shop, while old team/player pictures were displayed on the walls as you walked around the outside of the stadium. Each corner of the ground has a perspex windshield complete with player photos taken from a prominent match in the club's recent history. I was particularly drawn to the one of Darren Anderton who scored the only goal in his final professional game for the club against none other than Chester City!

Dean Court was packed out for the occasion and there was a great atmosphere as kick-off approached. Both teams practically changed their entire line-ups, such was the squad depth and faith shown by both managers. The train conductor's favourite pacey winger, Ritchie was rested, while West Brom starlet Saido Berahino also started on the bench. His replacement Victor Anichebe threw his weight around literally in the early going without much substance. From TV, Victor never looked very imposing, but in the flesh he was built like a monster truck. The Bournemouth defenders were bouncing off him like rubber pellets.

Bournemouth were happy to mix it up with their Premier League counterparts, opting to play attacking football rather than the hit and hope routine some teams resort to. Both sets of supporters got behind their teams with chants of "you're worse than Birmingham," and "you're only here for the Albion," being two of the more popular taunts. A couple sat next to me got a bit too excited and accidentally kicked a full coke bottle over a poor man's light green jacket and programme. They owned up and he seemed to take it all in his stride, further enforcing the fact that people on the South Coast were a lot more chilled out and easy going.

The home side really gave their fans something to cheer about when they hit the front early in the second half. Junior Stanislas supplied Eunan O'Kane with a perfectly weighted through ball, which the midfielder ran onto and slotted past Boaz Myhill into the far bottom corner. West Brom naturally responded, with boss Alan Irvine throwing on Georgios Samaras, Stephane Sessegnon and Berahino in an attempt to get back into the tie. Cherries defender Tommy Elphick was given a reprieve when the referee played on despite the defender slipping and handling in the box. However, Elphick's luck cruelly turned five minutes from the end when the captain turned a Samaras cross past his own goalkeeper. The Baggies fans were up on their seats chanting "Boing Boing," at the top of their lungs. Straightaway I was taken back to the previous year at Old Trafford when West Brom emerged with a shock victory and I was subjected to the same annoying chant for much of the way home. I couldn't hide my delight when Bournemouth knocked them off their perch just minutes later. Most people had resigned themselves to extra time, but the home side remained confident and knocked the ball forward. Substitute Callum Wilson collected the ball and his shot into the far corner was too powerful for Myhill to keep out. Cue the euphoria in the stands. Jumping up and down, I was the meat in a Bournemouth fan sandwich. This time there was no way back for the beaten Baggies and Bournemouth secured a lucrative quarter final tie with Liverpool. To be fair to West Brom, they took the loss on the chin and their fans kept singing at the final whistle.

It was a nice evening, so I opted to take a leisurely stroll back to the hotel. Having paid attention to the route the taxi driver took to the ground, I followed my instincts back towards the seafront. Walking past rows of West Brom fans either waiting for buses or drowning their sorrows, no comments were made as I wandered past still wearing the Bournemouth shirt I'd purchased before the game. I took a moment to watch and listen to the waves lapping up against the sand. Granted, it wasn't Baywatch and there weren't any red swimsuits running around, but it was nice all the same.

I'd never seen so many hotels as I did on the taxi ride back to the station the next morning. According to the Italian cabbie who dropped me off, lots more were lost during the recession and Bournemouth struggles to accommodate the 1.2million visitors who come to visit each summer. It was a long journey down, and an even longer one back to

Chester, but there are some people and places you would travel to the end of the earth for. Bournemouth was one of those places. I'll remember to bring my bucket and spade next time.

Best chant: "We're AFC Bournemouth, we score when we want." The home fans after Wilson's late winner.
Match ticket: £15. Bargain price and excellent value for money.
Match programme: £2.50. Contained a bonus reprint of the Bournemouth vs West Brom matchday magazine from their FA Cup meeting back in 1999, as part of the club's 'programmes from the past.' A nice walk down memory lane complete with dodgy haircuts. The Bournemouth players proved to be a sophisticated bunch, having formed a Coffee Club to strengthen relations off the pitch. Unlike Fight Club, Coffee Club doesn't have any rules. Everyone is welcome.
Cost of food: £3.50 for a steak pie.
Pie rating: 3/5. Nice taste, albeit a bit on the small side and subsequently not very filling. Had to resort to the cheese sandwiches I pre-prepared as a late night snack back at the hotel.

Final Score
AFC Bournemouth 2 (O'Kane 49, Wilson 86)
West Bromwich Albion 1 (Elphick og 85)
Attendance: 11,296

Getting to know Norwich City
Nathan Tuck - Vital Norwich
www.norwich.vitalfootball.co.uk
Twitter @VitalNorwich

Worst players to pull on a Norwich shirt?

I could give you a list a mile long! Three that stick out are Dean Coney, a striker from QPR who made 17 appearances and scored just one goal between 1989-90. Darren Beckford, another striker bought for £1m from Port Vale (our record signing at the time) in 1991 and sold to Oldham in 1993 for just £300,000. But the worst for me was Raymond de Waard bought by Bryan Hamilton for £225,000 in 2000. He looked like a musketeer but played like Bambi on ice - shocking.

Best away support at Carrow Road in recent memory?

I don't think any of the Premier League fans I've seen recently were great, so I'm going for Luton Town who knocked us out of the FA Cup 1-0 a couple of seasons ago, while they were a non-league side. They thoroughly deserved it on the day and their fans were terrific.

Best thing about Carrow Road?

It's always full! The Championship grounds I've seen on Sky this season are all half empty.

Worst grounds you've visited?

I'm not going to compare clubs from League One with ours, because that's just not fair. So, I'm going to rubbish Selhurst Park - the worst ground in the Premier League by a mile. Awful stadium with poor away fan facilities - looks like it's 1985 in there!

Best place to sit/stand at Carrow Road?

The Barclay stand or, to its right, "The Snake Pit!" How it got that name I have no idea, but that's where the atmosphere is.

Famous Norwich fans?

Delia Smith owns the club and Stephen Fry is a director. Also, Hugh Jackman - seriously.

Quirky fact time?

Norwich City are the only English team to have ever beaten Bayern Munich in the Olympic Stadium and as Bayern have now moved to the Allianz Arena, that record will never be broken!

Best/worst Norwich managers?

Paul Lambert is the best for results that I've known. No other manager has had such an impact in such a short time, despite his acrimonious departure. John Bond was the gaffer when I first started going to Carrow Road and he was a real 1970s character with his sheepskin coat and big cigars. Ken Brown took us to Wembley in 1985 and won the Milk Cup, so he'll always be fondly remembered. When Dave Stringer followed him in the job, he took us to third in the old First Division and an FA Cup semi-final. Mike Walker also did brilliantly to see us finish third in the inaugural Premier League and qualify for the UEFA Cup.

As for the worst, this is an easy one. Glenn Roeder and Bryan Hamilton tie for top spot as the worst City managers I've known. Roeder was an unpleasant man who moaned like hell when he had to face fans at the AGM and answer questions with the Chief Executive and Delia Smith. He was also responsible for failing to give Darren Huckerby a final year contract at Norwich and left it until the close season, thereby denying the fans a chance to say goodbye properly to a hero. He then told Hucks he could train at the club whenever he liked, but changed his mind a few weeks later. Bryan Hamilton came in as Bruce Rioch's assistant and was an ex-Ipswich player and coach. He took the job when Rioch resigned and lasted just eight months, resigning with City in a relegation battle. Luckily, his assistant Nigel Worthington came in and saved the day. Hamilton then went back to coaching at Ipswich and is currently Technical director of the Antigua and Barbuda FA - What a world!

Thoughts on ticket prices in general?

Obviously, away ticket prices are too high. £20 should be set as a maximum at all Premier League away grounds, the clubs could easily afford it. Home tickets aren't cheap either. It certainly isn't affordable for a family to watch Premier League football.

Name your Norwich Dream Team?

GK: Bryan Gunn
LB: Mark Bowen
CB: Craig Fleming
CB: Malky Mackay
RB: Ian Culverhouse
LW: Darren Huckerby
CM: Bradley Johnson
CM: Wes Hoolahan
RW: Neil Adams
CF: Robert Fleck
CF: Grant Holt

HALLOWEEN IN NORFOLK

Game #27: The Championship - Friday 31st October 2014
NORWICH CITY vs Bolton Wanderers - Carrow Road

I've never really been one for Halloween, although passing the poor guards at Chester train station who had been forced to don ghost makeup brought a few chuckles. Trick or treat? You decide. Having witnessed Norwich lose twice on the road this season, I was heading to Norfolk in the hope that my presence would do the trick in reversing the supposed curse. Despite their poor league position, I knew Bolton would provide Norwich with a stern test, more so now they had improved under new boss Neil Lennon.

People tried to explain the unorthodox route in getting to Norwich. My Mum even recalled an old Center Parcs holiday in Elveden Forest that I was too young to really remember. The plan was to go to Norwich for the day, but we gave up halfway through the journey and turned back. Apparently, the road route isn't so clear. Not being a driver myself, I must admit that I didn't pay much attention. Getting the train allows you to lose yourself in a good book, which begs the question, why did I choose Roy Keane's follow-up? In short, he's a miserable bugger and overrated manager, as Ipswich Town fans would agree.

Carrow Road is ideally situated just behind the train station. I was staying a few miles down the road at the 'Oaklands Hotel,' located on a long stretch of road filled with pubs and more carveries than you can shake a stick at. With a bit of time on my side, I ventured into town to have a bit of a look around. I decided to get a taxi to the Oaklands, only to almost jump straight out of the cab when I saw a bald headed driver covered with enough tattoos that would make CM Punk jealous stare back at me. In this case, appearances definitely deceived and he turned out to be quite friendly. Mr Punk was a combination of a Manchester United and Norwich fan. To be fair he'd been watching the Canaries since 1982 and the discussion turned to the club's famous European run from the early 90s, with us both recalling the famous victory against Bayern Munich.

When I told him I was staying at the Oaklands, the driver enthusiastically described the carvery on offer. Had I not been the guy's first job of the night, I have no doubt that he would have parked up, gone inside and grabbed a plate. It was karaoke night at the Oaklands when I rocked up. The girl on reception was doing her best take of Katy Perry's 'Roar.' I tried a bit of X Factor related banter, but was told in no uncertain terms that her singing exploits were strictly reserved for the shower. I enquired about the last carvery sitting, only to be disappointed when I was told that the last orders were 8:30pm. My faith was now solely placed in one of Delia Smith's pies.

Once checked in and refreshed, I followed the crowd of shirts back into town. A well placed Holiday Inn joins the ground and could be seen over my shoulder from my seat in the Jarrold South Stand. Carrow Road is visually impressive, with all sides covered and seated. One of the corner fills has been dubbed the 'Snake Pit' and was quite loud. A small Bolton following were seated not too far from me towards the end of the stand. The club were honouring the Military guard before kick off. Unfortunately, a minute's silence was constantly disrupted by cat calls and mobile phone alerts. Showing respect for a mere 60 seconds was disappointingly too much to ask some folk.

A father sat next to me had brought his two young sons to watch the game. Decked out in Norwich kits, with names and numbers on the back, the youngest didn't really look interested. Constantly fidgeting with his scarf and wriggling on his seat, he looked like he'd rather be anywhere else. All he seemed to want to do was eat sweets. Every time Norwich went on the attack or a decision went their way, the Dad enthusiastically leaned over to explain what was happening. On one side, his excitement was reciprocated, but the other was met with total apathy. Early diagnosis points to young Toby probably being more rugby inclined.

The club were advertising future games on the electronic board. Norwich were one of those who had subscribed to the categorisation of games. Personally, I don't agree with A , B and C type games. Loyal fans are clearly being ripped off. There should just be a flat price for league games and one that's a hell of a lot nicer than the £35 (adult ticket) Norwich were advertising for their upcoming match with Brighton. I looked at the family sat next to me, trying to imagine what the poor guy forked out just to bring himself and his two sons to the game. A full stadium will always quell my argument and I'm not picking on Norwich specifically. I experienced something very similar at Derby County earlier on. Considering the recent BBC study, it's certainly an issue that should be re-addressed across the board.

In Cameron Jerome, Norwich finally looked to have found a prolific striker to fire them back to the Premier League. The much travelled forward bagged a brace and showed the scintillating form which was keeping big buy Lewis Grabban out of the side. Jerome netted his first when he collected a return pass from Jonny Howson and slotted underneath Andy Lonergan. Jerome showed a glimpse of his bad side when he attempted to con the referee with a spot of simulation. The fact that he almost injured himself made me think he'd learnt his lesson.

The crossbar challenge made a welcome return at half time. It's a personal favourite. Showing poise and oozing confidence, the first guy who stepped up impressively struck the woodwork with his first attempt. His friend gave up after a couple of woeful efforts and seemed content to blast a couple of balls into an empty net, which seemed like a smart way to save face.

Norwich resumed their dominance after the break. Nathan Redmond dazzled the Bolton defenders out wide, turning them inside out, collecting a return pass, only to see Lonergan tip his effort onto the post. Not long after, Jerome looked to have made the game safe, meeting Gary O'Neil's corner with a towering header into the net. Lennon was simmering like a steaming kettle on the touchline. It didn't take long for the fiery Northern Irish manager to explode. After taking exception to a throw-in, Lennon refused to give the ball back, eventually throwing it onto the floor before treating everyone to a mini temper tantrum. The Norwich fans ate it up and reminded him "there's only one Neil," referring to their own coach. Mr Adams kept his distance, but seemed amused from his side of the dugout.

Lennon's mood wouldn't have improved when he witnessed Max Clayton run clear, only to fluff his lines and drag a shot wide. Lee Chung-Yong did halve the deficit late on, taking advantage of poor defending to finish from close range. Alas, it was too little too late and Norwich registered a much needed victory. Norwich fans seemed happy to be back on track, as the crowds dispersed into the night. The third time proved to be a charm for me watching Norwich.

Back at the hotel, a sign had been placed on reception to say that the karaoke would be going on until midnight. Accepting that sleep wasn't going to be happening anytime soon, I opened the bathroom door to have a shower, only to discover a trail of blue and green gunk lining across the bath. As Mario Balotelli would say, "why always me?" Needless to say, I didn't take my chances with the slime and grime. Having been treated to an entertaining game of football, the trick was clearly on me for agreeing to a shabby room. Despite the sounds of One Direction coming from under the floorboards, I soon fell asleep. All the lights were on, but hey why not? I wasn't paying the electricity bill.

Best chant: "Who's the pride of Anglia? Norwich, Norwich. Who's the shit of Anglia? Ipswich is their name."
Norwich fans won't be sending their East Anglian neighbours a greeting card this year.
Match ticket: £25 for a Category C game, but it was a Category A performance so I was given value for money.
Match programme: £3. Included a free 2014-15 calendar. I debated sending it to a Norwich fan I know as a Christmas stocking filler. Goalkeeper John Ruddy pulled some strings to get his wife some advertising space for her clothing line.
Cost of food: £3.50 for a pie, £3 for a sausage roll.
Food rating: 2/5. Delia certainly didn't prepare the pies, given the lack of TLC and uneven presentation. The club sold out of the popular three cheese pasty, and the match meat pie was a poor substitute. Too small and the gravy tasted a bit funny. The herbs gave the sausage roll some flavour, but it was still overpriced.

Final Score
Norwich City 2 (Jerome 12, 61)
Bolton Wanderers 1 (Lee Chung-Yong 86)
Attendance: 26,070

Getting to know Colchester United
Thom Denson - Matchday programme contributor
Twitter @thomdenson

How long have you been a Colchester fan?
Actively, since around the turn of the century.

Favourite memory as a Colchester fan?
The seasons between 2005-2007, where we were promoted to, and survived in the Championship.

Thoughts on ticket prices in general?
The guys behind the scenes are very active in terms of gauging opinion and I believe they do a good job at keeping it fair for the punters.

Worst grounds you've visited?
The away stand at Gillingham was half complete when I last went which made for a few frayed nerves. Roots Hall (Southend) for obvious reasons.

Enjoyable away days?
Saw the U's at Charlton for the Capital One Cup last season - wasn't the busiest but one of the bigger stadiums I've seen the U's in!

Which club serves the nicest pies?
Had a cracking Sausage Roll from Brentford's place a year or so back.

Famous Colchester fans?
Legendary Radio DJ Steve Lamacq is a big fan and often attends games - home and away no less.

Name your Colchester Dream Team?
Going to have to keep it to players I've been lucky enough to see play since I've classed myself as a proper supporter:
Dean Gerken
Joe Keith
Joe Dunne
Wayne Brown
Greg Halford
Karl Duguid
David Gregory
Neil Danns
Richard Garcia
Jamie Cureton
Lomana Lua Lua

THE ONLY WAY IS COLCHESTER

Game #28: League One - Saturday 1st November 2014
COLCHESTER UNITED vs Port Vale - The Weston Homes Community Stadium

Coming back from Norwich, my pre-booked route home was through the TOWIE (The Only Way is Essex) district. Fortunately for me, I didn't cross paths with irritating D-List celebrities Amy Childs or Mark Wright. However, it would have been rude not to stop by Colchester and see what was going down. Waking up in my three star hotel room, a full English breakfast did the job of negating the hideous stain left by god knows who in the bathroom. It was a mild morning in Norfolk, perfect for one last stroll into town and onto the train for the short journey into Essex.

I had barely set foot in Colchester when an asian guy rudely barked out "station," and pointed in a forward direction. I was half inclined to send him the wrong way, but fearful of bad karma, explained politely that the station was mere yards away at the top of a short hill. A shuttle bus service (£2.50 return) situated a stone's throw from the station was on hand to take fans to and from the stadium. In stark contrast to Reading two weeks prior, there were barely 20 people on this bus. Claustrophobia didn't come into play and I took advantage of the ample leg room during the ten minute ride to the stadium. A young Port Vale fan innocently asked his Dad if they would get kicked off the bus by the home fans. The locals - a man sporting a grey mullet and a chubby student were hardly menacing. If it came time to throw down fists then my money would be on the lad and Dad tag team.

I could see the reason why the club laid on shuttle buses. Due to a lot of roadworks along the way, the route would have been impossible to walk. After passing through a housing estate, the custom built stadium appears. Sat on a spacious piece of land and seemingly in the middle of nowhere, it draws an instant comparison with Shrewsbury Town's ground. The main difference being that there is a petrol pump sitting outside Colchester's main reception. Well, an electrical re-fuelling station to be exact. In news that will no doubt impress Gary Neville and several other eco-warriors, Colchester are o-zone friendly, although cars weren't exactly queuing to use the service. An enquiry into ticket prices brought mixed results, so I decided to stick with my northern roots and sit with the away fans.

It was a beautiful day in Essex with glorious sunshine beaming down. I remarked to a steward that if this was winter, then long may it continue. Club mascot Eddie the Eagle was walking around greeting fans, but didn't stay in one place long enough to stop for a five second pose. He gave me the slip more than Cristiano Ronaldo does to his marker. I eventually tracked him down hassling the catering staff in the kitchen, so I formed an orderly queue behind a couple of youngsters and their father happily snapped a picture for me.

A-Listers galore were lining up to perform in Colchester. If the advertising boards were to be believed then Robbie Williams, One Direction, and even Elvis himself were due to perform in the coming months. The Weston Homes Community Stadium gets all the headline tribute acts. Entering the ground, my eyes were drawn to a small poster on the wall thanking the away fans for travelling the 426 miles to see the game. I was a long way from home. A healthy following had come to cheer on the Vale, which, given the news that main goalgetter Tom Pope was out injured made me respect their optimism. I'm not sure Colchester's fans knew there was a game on. As 3 o'clock came closer, there weren't that many U's fans in attendance. You could almost hear crickets chirping during the first couple of occasions the poor PA announcer went through the two teams.

Based on their early form, Colchester looked like relegation strugglers. However, the club seem to have benefited (like most do) from a change in management. Tony Humes made the step up from the under 18's to replace the departed Joe Dunne and had subsequently made the club hard to beat.

The home side were awarded a first half penalty when Gavin Massey was sandwiched by two Port Vale defenders. Naturally the Colchester player went down. A lazy spot kick from Freddie Sears was easily saved by a grateful Chris Neal and Vale built in confidence. The away side grabbed the game by the horns and netted a quick fire double in five second half minutes. Colchester goalkeeper Sam Walker somehow allowed Mark Marshall's low shot to creep past him at the near post. Marshall then turned provider for substitute Colin Daniel, who found Walker wanting once again at his near station to give his side a two goal cushion. The word super sub gets banded around all too often, but Daniel could clearly lay claim to the moniker, having been on the pitch barely a minute. The goals gave the Vale fans a brief respite from yelling at the linesman. Given the lack of decisions that went their way, they did have a case for a potential conspiracy theory.

The U's rallied and hit the bar through Sanchez Watt's hopeful effort, before Sears went a little way to appease his earlier penalty miss by tapping in from two yards. It proved to be nothing more than scant consolation. Vale picked up their first away win since the Doncaster game I was in attendance for back in August. It made a refreshing change to bring some good luck to a side. Back on the bus, the Colchester faithful had turned on Sears, lambasting him for his penalty miss. One guy was trying to break the record for the number of time he could get "bollocks" into a sentence. The more the guy talked in his cockney twang, the more convinced I was that Phil Daniels was sitting behind me. Before I could turn around and yell "Parklife," he stood up to reveal a fat, balding man who looked more like Phil Mitchell than anyone else. "You should cut down on your pork pies mate...get some exercise," was what I wanted to say, but common sense prevailed and I kept quiet.

Back at Euston, a couple of Crewe fans helped pass the time on the journey home. Even the 50+ year old woman, whose personal space we all invaded got involved during points of the conversation. From the grim tales of Crawley (where the two had been) to the quirky tale of whether one of the guys ever washed his Crewe mug that he brings to all the games, two hours flew by. Before I knew it, I was back on northern territory. Norfolk and Essex had been very kind to me, but it was nice to get back home to a clean shower.

Best chant: When they weren't chanting "super Vale away," the travelling fans taunted their hosts with calls of "is that all you bring at home?"
Match ticket: £24. Prices ranged between £22-£28, so I found a happy medium.
Match programme: £3.00. Colchester midfielder Alex Gilbey edged out U's fan Stuart Chittock in an egghead related challenge. While both could name where Flamenco music originated (Spain) and that the Queen was the most powerful chess piece, both were stumped when it came to naming the L in URL (Locator.)
Cost of food: £2.80 for a pie, £1.50 for potato wedges.
Food rating: 3/5. A good effort. The wedges were very crispy and tasted even nicer when dipped into the thick sauce provided by the chicken and vegetable pie.

Final Score
Colchester United 1 (Sears 79)
Port Vale 2 (Marshall 56, Daniel 60)
Attendance: 3,571

Getting to know Sheffield Wednesday
Steve Walmsley -"War of the Monster Trucks" fansite
www.warofthemonstertrucks.com
Twitter @SheffWedWOTMT

Who are Wednesday's star players these days?
Tom Lees and Keiren Westwood – defender and keeper which says it all really.

Best/worst players to pull on a Wednesday shirt?
Worst - Archie Irvine (a long time ago), Barrie Watling (another oldie) and Jon Beswetherwick.
Best – Chris Waddle, Roland Nilsson, David Hirst and Des Walker.

Best away support at Hillsborough in recent memory?
In League One a few years ago, Plymouth brought 2000 fans up for a night game which is fantastic and they never stopped singing all night.

Best thing about Hillsborough?
It's a proper old fashioned football ground that can generate a fantastic atmosphere when the Kop is buzzing.

Worst grounds you've visited?
Luton Town, Scunthorpe United and Bristol Rovers.

Best place to sit/stand at Hillsborough?
On the Kop when it's full.

Famous Wednesday fans?
Michael Vaughan, Roy Hattersley, Richard Hawley, Emily Maitlis, Jarvis Cocker.

Quirky fact time?
We hold the record for the fastest recorded shot – David Hirst 114mph on 16/9/96 away at Arsenal.

SHIVERING IN SHEFFIELD

Game #29: The Championship - Tuesday 4th November 2014
SHEFFIELD WEDNESDAY vs AFC Bournemouth - Hillsborough

The Chuckle Brothers, Ant and Dec, Morecambe and Wise are all synonymous double acts. Where one goes, the other predominantly follows. Normally, I would add me and my coat to that list. With the cold snap hitting Yorkshire, I quickly regretted leaving my winter warmer at home. The excuse of it being sunny when I left was a poor one. Worse still, I'd even left my Bournemouth shirt that I'd picked up the week before on the hanger next to my coat.

I couldn't help but eavesdrop on a conversation a group of sixth formers were having during the train journey. It was getting to the time of year where the university applications went in and one lad was talking himself up both academically and romantically. Taking all things into consideration, I concluded that the girls must go crazy for his lazy eye. The young scamp quickly put his UCAS hat on to declare that he had a "couple of unconditional offers," on the female front. I almost choked on my water listening to the youngster's witty boasts.

Unlike their city rivals, Sheffield Wednesday's home is located a couple of miles out of the city centre. This was my first visit to Hillsborough and I was under the impression that there was a shuttle bus service to the ground. On this night, there were no specialist buses transporting fans. Instead, I was pointed in the direction of a tram which takes around 20 minutes to transport fans across town. Getting off at Leppings Lane, my heart sank when I saw that the return tram times weren't correlating with the last train back home. It was too late to book a last minute hotel, so I resigned myself to leaving the game ten minutes before the end to avoid getting stranded. Hillsborough is close to a park and plenty of fans had crammed into a nearby chip shop to get their health fix before the game.

I decided to do a bit of investigating into this mysterious bus service in the hope that it could prolong my stay a little bit. The reception staff couldn't have been nicer and pointed me in the direction of the stewards. Just as I was about to exit, club legend David Hirst was making his way past, no doubt ready to tuck into a plush meal before taking his comfy regular seat in the executive suite. To be fair, Hirst scored a few goals for the club and has achieved legendary status, so the least I could do was hold the door for him. He gave a polite nod, before greeting club officials and walking off into the warm. Around the same time, another familiar looking chap with an army of kids sauntered past. Danny Cadamarteri didn't hold the same status in my eyes, so I decided that he could get the door himself.

Operation bus locator commenced once again, but the stewards gave out conflicting information. Having walked to the other side of the ground, I was told there was a service that operates only a stone's throw across the road from the stadium. The hope I built up was quickly dashed when I was bluntly told that the road in question is closed after a game. It was getting close to kick-off and thoughts of abandoning the game went through my head. It was time to have a discreet chat to myself and make a quick decision. Common sense prevailed and I decided to stay and make the most of the hand I'd been dealt. Besides, I'd already bought a programme, skipped tea and knew deep down I would come to regret my actions by walking away.

Once again, the away end was calling me. With many people already in their seats, there wasn't a queue at the food kiosk. I had barely perused the menu when a small kid asked me what I wanted. At first glance, it looked like he had hopped over the bar, but upon closer inspection it turned out that the laws against child labour had somehow been relaxed and Junior was earning an honest crust. The youngster wasn't fazed, politely recommended one of the freshly cooked pies and even cracked a joke when I almost dropped it. To those that say the kids of today are lazy, I firmly disagree.

Hillsborough is massive and looks out of place in the Championship. Naturally, there were plenty of empty seats, although the ground retains plenty of character – not least for the triangular gable complete with clock placed on the roof. Attempts have been made to fill in the four corners with additional seating, while rooftop lighting makes up for the lack of floodlight pylons.

Within moments of taking my seat, both teams came out to the rocky riffs of 'Waterfront,' by Simple Minds. The 1980s part of my musical education wholeheartedly concurred, as the song blared out over the speakers, doing its job of amping up both sets of supporters. Sat in the upper echelons of the Leppings Lane End, the stand still has a couple of supporting pillars, but these didn't obstruct the view. I appreciated that the roof directly above me stretched out enough to protect me from most of the elements. Unfortunately, falling temperatures wasn't one, with mist and fog soon making an unwelcome appearance.

The match was a meeting between two teams with contrasting fortunes. The Owls were finding goals and points hard to come by, while the high-flying Cherries were enjoying a six game winning streak in league and cup. Wednesday's Keiren Westwood was the busier of the two goalkeepers. The hosts weren't giving their fans much to drum or shout about. Callum Wilson looked like he left his shooting boots back in Bournemouth, with the England Under-21 international showing how not to finish. Ex-Real Madrid midfielder Royston Drenthe was the one asking the questions for the home side - that is until he was sent off. A second booking on the hour forced Royston into taking an early bath and Bournemouth took full advantage. Goalkeeper Artur Boruc threw a long ball out to Wilson, who ran the length of the pitch, before laying off for Andrew Surman to pick his spot and curl an effort into the bottom corner. Moments later, Wilson, having now found his groove turned provider again, this time for substitute Ryan Fraser to prod past Westwood.

It was a double whammy for which Wednesday couldn't recover from. The travelling fans rubbed salt in the wounds with chants of "we can see you sneaking out," to several disillusioned home supporters. I wasn't long behind them, but with ten minutes remaining, I was satisfied that I had got to see the main action. Luckily enough I didn't miss anything else. The amount of Wednesday fans already waiting for the tram at Leppings Lane was surprising. Hoards of fans had left before me and were bemoaning another poor performance. It was around a year ago that then caretaker manager Stuart Gray could do no wrong. However, these particular fans had a short memory. Tram staff were on hand to control the crowds. When I asked if this was the tram back into town, the female staffer remarked "Yes duck." I hadn't been called duck before, but there's a first time for everything I suppose.

No-one should ever go to the match and never come home. #JFT96.

Best chant: "We forgot that you were here." The Bournemouth fans.
Match ticket: £27. Could have saved £3 or £4 by sitting with the home fans in certain sections.
Match programme: £3. Filled with content for new and old fans, you can see why it's won a few awards. From "Best Cover," to "Best Value for Money," the programme has scooped some form of recognition for the past five seasons. Special mention goes out to Wednesdayite (apparently it's a real word) Roger Strain. The 33-year-old had attended 703 and counting consecutive home and away games over a 26 year period, and, excuse the pun, wasn't showing any strain. "Weekends are all about football for me and they always have been," he stated. "Supporting a football team is more than just a hobby to me, it's a way of life and I almost feel like a member of staff the amount of times I've been there!" Amen to that statement Roger. Keep going my friend.
Cost of food: £3 for a pie. Pretty much the standard going rate.
Food rating: 5/5. A piping hot steak pie re-heated the body. Pukka supply both Sheffield clubs and they haven't let this consumer down.

Final Score
Sheffield Wednesday 0
AFC Bournemouth 2 (Surman 65, Fraser 69)
Attendance: 16,881

Getting to know Bolton Wanderers
Chris Mann - Burnden Aces | Administrator & Lead Editor
www.burndenaces.co.uk
Twitter @burndenaces

Best/worst players to pull on a Bolton shirt?
In my lifetime, it's hard to look beyond names such as John McGinlay, Gudni Bergsson, Jay-Jay Okocha, Youri Djorkaeff, Jussi Jaaskelainen, Gary Cahill and Nicolas Anelka as the best players to pull on a Wanderers shirt. But, although he may not be listed as the most technically gifted player, Kevin Davies is perhaps the most fondly remembered of the last decade. Looking back, I think you'd find it very difficult to find a Bolton supporter who wouldn't tell you that Nat Lofthouse was the greatest player ever to represent the club. As for the worst players - we've seen a few. Again, only being able to provide names from the last 15 years, I'm going to stick my neck out and say Gerald Cid, who was one of Sammy Lee's signings during his car crash of a spell in charge.

Best away support at the Macron Stadium in recent memory?
During our Premier League days, I always looked forward to the visits of Newcastle United and Sunderland, both of whom travelled in numbers and contributed to some electric atmospheres. Since our return to the Championship, two clubs that stand out are Leeds United and Sheffield Wednesday.

Best thing about the Macron Stadium?
The road away from it! Just kidding - the traffic after a game is horrendous! 17 years after it was built, the stadium is beginning to lose its tag of being 'new'. Despite that, our fans still think it is one of the best looking stadiums in the country and even though it's a far cry from the days of Burnden Park, we've been here long enough to really call it home.

Worst grounds you've visited?
Without a doubt, the worst ground I have visited is Turf Moor - home of Burnley. Old Trafford is a close second, with the train line behind the away stand meaning United haven't, and maybe can't, complete any sort of extensive development of that part of the ground. As for Turf Moor, it really does feel like you're back in the 70s. The concourse is barely wide enough to contain a queue of five people, the toilets can only hold a queue of three and, as for the seats upstairs, the wood used to make them pre-dates the birth of my grandparents!

Best place to sit/stand at the Macron Stadium?
The atmosphere at Macron Stadium, unfortunately, isn't anything to get too excited about. The obvious decline in attendances since relegation to the Championship hasn't helped, but it's very rare we've experienced an 'electric' atmosphere since moving away from Burnden Park. The best place to sit, or stand, would probably be in the East Stand Lower Tier, underneath the scoreboard - if you can put up with 100 or so illiterate teenagers churning out nonsense for 90 minutes.

Famous Bolton fans?
The famous fans people associate with us seem to be Vernon Kay and Amir Khan - although that boxing friend of ours seems to have taken a like to Manchester United recently. Paddy McGuinness is also a Wanderers fan and perhaps the only one who isn't afraid to admit it on a regular basis.

Quirky fact time?
This is a gutting one - of all the teams to ever play in the top-flight of English football, Bolton hold the record for spending the highest number of years in the division without winning the title.

Thoughts on ticket prices in general?
I think the 'Twenty's Plenty' campaign is a fantastic cause, but, in the modern-day world of profit, we'll struggle to see clubs implement it. After our relegation from the Premier League, in 2012, I was excited at the prospect of visiting some new grounds at a lower price. The reality couldn't be any further from that, though, as most games on the road can cost £30+ before travel expenses are even considered.

Name your Bolton Dream Team?

GK: Jussi Jaaskelainen
RB: Bruno N'Gotty
CB: Gary Cahill
CB: Gudni Bergsson
LB: Ricardo Gardner
RM: Stelios Giannakopoulos
CM: Ivan Campo
CM: Jay-Jay Okocha
LM: El-Hadji Diouf
CF: Youri Djorkaeff
CF: Nicolas Anelka

Other notable mentions must go to the likes of Kevin Davies, Kevin Nolan, Fernando Hierro, Gary Speed, Per Frandsen and probably dozens of others who have been part of the squad since I started watching in 2001.

FRIDAY FIGHT NIGHT (DING DING)

Game #30: The Championship - Friday 7th November 2014
BOLTON WANDERERS vs Wigan Athletic - The Macron Stadium

A Lancashire derby under the lights between two struggling former Premiership middleweights certainly had the potential to be a fiery affair. Throw in a bunch of supercharged Wigan fans on a commuter train to light the powderkeg and I definitely got more than I bargained for.

Workers had downed tools for the weekend and packed the train at Manchester Oxford Road. There were still seats, but given the short journey to Horwich Parkway, I opted to stand by the doors. This turned out to be not such a prudent move. The hoard of singing Wigan cattle bundled on at Bolton, two stops from where the ground was situated. A police presence was futile, with the sheer number of louts easily outnumbering the force.

Dressed as an homage to sporting manufacturers Carbrini and McKenzie, the fans were lagered up - no doubt having started drinking as soon as college finished. These were unlike the happy-go-lucky karaoke singers from Port Vale. These 'fans' were spoiling for a fight. Intimidated commuters were pushed off the train, as the lager flowed, cigarettes were lit and disparaging songs were sung. The train panelling took a pounding and I swear the vehicle was shaking at one point. This journey couldn't go quick enough. One idiot tried to increase the size of his manhood by giving me a death stare. Flanked by a dozen of his flunkies, I could see the stoner was feeling his oats. I took the higher ground and ignored him, keeping all of my body parts in tact.

Police were waiting at Horwich to escort fans to the ground. An illuminated Macron Stadium lit up the sky and was visible from the station. The tubular steel structuring and curvy shape of the stadium makes it one of the more visually impressive grounds both in the distance and up close. A trip to see Bolton is normally perfect to take the Mrs. For interested parties, the club have a hotel based inside the ground. The aptly named 'Bolton Whites' certainly looked plush and was given the seal of approval from my cousin, who has enjoyed a weekend stay with his girlfriend. However, derby days might not be ideal for those with romance on the mind.

In addition to having a retail park and eateries aplenty within the concourse, fans were flocking to the Harvester pub situated between the train station and ground. A wall of security lined up outside to ID fans and keep the peace. From passing by, it seemed to be more of a pub for the home fans. The queues didn't appeal, so I went and got a picture next to the statue of former playing legend Nat Lofthouse outside the stadium.

Without doubt, the Macron is befitting of being in the Premier League, but other matters are currently at the forefront. Growing frustration between the fans and higher-ups over the club's debt and failed takeover bids had been matched by an underwhelming start on the pitch. Things weren't too different down the road at Wigan. Originally touted as promotion contenders, the Latics had slipped into the lower half of the table and were barely keeping their heads above the relegation trap door.

There was plenty of leg room between each row of seats in the stadium and it didn't feel like I was peering over someone's shoulder whenever I leaned forwards. That being said, I felt like throttling the kids between me who couldn't shut up for a minute's silence in honour of the upcoming Remembrance Sunday. Their father didn't rebuke them. In fact, he didn't hold back in yelling obscenities at the Wigan players as the game kicked off. Chants of "break his legs," were aimed at the opposition, specifically Callum McManaman. The Wigan man did everything but score in a first half which saw him rattle both the crossbar and post. Teammate Roger Espinoza looked unrecognisable now he'd shaved off his customary mullet. I was convinced that some of his footballing ability disappeared when his locks fell on the cutting room floor. The Honduran didn't bring much to the party.

Bolton fans weren't impressed with what they were seeing in the first half, judging by the sheer number who got up after half an hour to seek out savoury refreshments. The annoying father decided to change tactics and throw his support behind the home players. Nothing wrong with that, although I don't think Lee Chung-Yong would endorse his new nickname of "noodles." Yes, he's South Korean, but that's a bit of a negative stereotype. Soon enough, the kids were copying their father. Then again that wasn't surprising.

Perhaps he was spurred on by the chants, but nonetheless, Lee proved to be the catalyst for the home side's resurgence after the break. The midfielder played in Max Clayton, who unlike seven days earlier at Norwich, held his nerve to coolly slot the ball under Scott Carson's legs. The goal knocked the stuffing out of Wigan. Soon enough they found themselves two goals down. Liam Feeney's cross was begging to be nodded in and Craig Davies duly obliged with a powerful downwards header at the back post. The Latics proceeded to self destruct. Leon Barnett was off his barnet when he wrestled Matt Mills to the floor in the box in full view of the referee. Lee heaped on the misery by slotting in the resulting penalty.

Substitute James McClean - who opted not to wear a poppy on his shirt for personal reasons which he posted on the Wigan website, came on and made his presence known with a few tough tackles. His doggedness did result in a consolation goal. After holding off his marker and running to the byline, McManaman was able to volley in the resulting cross to finally claim the goal that his performance deserved. Bolton were home and hosed by this point and the goal mattered little. Uwe Rosler looked like a man out of ideas on the Wigan touchline. It came as no real shock when the German was relieved of his duties shortly after the fallout from this game.

Surprisingly, the Wigan fans weren't detained after the final whistle. The result was a hostile stand-off back at the train station. An army of agitated police had been pulled off city centre duty to do a spot of crowd control. Riot vans, dogs and horses were all present to try and keep the peace. One Bolton fan incited the crowd when he straddled the top of a car park entrance to imply that the Wigan fans were incestuous, resulting in glass bottles being thrown. I was in plain colours, but despite my lame attempt to say I hadn't been to the match, I was lumped in with the Bolton fans who were forced to wait for a train back into Manchester. The Wigan contingent were ushered onto the first couple of trains, while the large number of home fans and myself were left to stand in the cold. A lot of miffed Bolton fans rightly asked why they were being punished and forced to wait on their own turf, but the police weren't exactly in the mood to negotiate or provide friendly chit chat. I was just happy to get out of there in one piece and back to Manchester in time to catch a connecting train home.

It may not have been Istanbul or the Old Firm, yet the intensity could be felt both on and off the pitch. Bolton rediscovered their fighting spirit and can boast of having a fantastic ground, while I'll never view Wigan as "just a Rugby town" ever again. Albeit a little too over the top at times, Wigan fans justified that they care just as much about the ball as they do the egg.

Best chant: "Can we play you every week." The Bolton fans.
Match ticket: £26.
Match programme: £3. Some enjoyable nostalgia, reliving players from my earlier years who played for both clubs. Per Frandsen, Scott Green and David Lee brought back memories, although Ryo Miyaichi didn't ring any bells. Club captain Jay Spearing had a feature where he picked his dream team made up of former teammates. Unsurprisingly, 10 of the 11 were Liverpool players, with an honourable mention going to ex-Trotter Marcos Alonso.
Cost of food: £5.10 for a pie/soft drink combo.
Food rating: 3/5. The club have upgraded to Holland's "Big Eat" range of pies, with the steak variation quite meat friendly and more than satisfying the hunger pangs.

Final Score
Bolton Wanderers 3 (Clayton 50, C.Davies 55, Lee pen 61)
Wigan Athletic 1 (McManaman 79)
Attendance: 17,282

Favourite memory as a Coventry fan?
My favourite memory has to be the comeback against Preston in the JPT in 2013. (Coventry netted twice in injury time to win 3-2) The return to the Ricoh Arena was also very special.

Are you glad to be back at the Ricoh Arena?
Yes. It's our home. We shouldn't have to worry if we will be in our city next season.

Did you travel to Sixfields when the club played there?
No. I was a firm believer that CCFC should play home games in Coventry, nowhere else. I attended away games only until our return.

Best game you've witnessed at the Ricoh Arena?
Preston in the JPT, 2013.

Best thing about the Ricoh Arena?
Is there one? We don't own it. There's no atmosphere. Simple design. The best thing about it is the Jimmy Hill Statue outside.

Best/worst players to pull on a Coventry shirt?
Best: Dion Dublin, Steve Ogrizovic, Ernie Machin, Tommy Hutchison, Dennis Wise. Worst, Reece Brown, Kevin Kyle, Roy O'Donovan, Nick Proschwitz.

Famous Coventry fans?
John Stape from Coronation Street, Richard Keys, Eddie Jordan and Christian Horner (F1)

Quirky fact time?
The first ever matchday programme was made for Coventry City. It was produced by a local paper.

Best Coventry managers?
Jimmy Hill is without a doubt the club's greatest manager. He won two promotions with City, bringing us up to the First Division where we would remain for over 30 years. John Sillett is also up there. He won the FA Cup in 1987.

Thoughts on ticket prices in general?
Our ticket prices have actually gone down this season. My season ticket price has dropped by £30. But sadly, this isn't the case everywhere. I'm barely out of my teens. The reason attendances are dropping is the price of tickets. With TV highlights very easy to come by, fans no longer have the incentive to go to the games unless they have a reason to pay the money.

SENT TO COVENTRY

Game #31: Johnstone's Paint Trophy Southern Section Quarter Final - Wednesday 12th November 2014
COVENTRY CITY vs Plymouth Argyle - The Ricoh Arena

You've all heard of the term being sent to Coventry. No doubt everyone has been sent there figuratively by someone else. However, I'd never been to the place literally. Waving the £5 ticket price as the proverbial carrot, I roped in three friends - Banksy, Danny and Rich for the journey. Banksy, as touched upon earlier is a Plymouth fan, so it was an easy sell for him, while Rich loves a good road trip and Danny was keen on adding to his own mini ground hop of the Midlands.

Armed with supplies of chocolate and 90s anthems from Rich's iPhone, we set off through Shrewsbury and stopped off at Birmingham to collect Danny. Early into the trip, Banksy wasn't really feeling the retro tunes, so to appease him, Rich downloaded Plymouth fan chants off iTunes. No doubt, an excited Plymouth received a small royalty cheque as a nice pre-christmas bonus. No fewer than 45 songs, most lasting under a minute were played out in their entirety. From the obvious 'West Country La La La,' to the charming 'You Dirty Northern Bastards,' the melodies were quite hit and miss, although the delightful ditty of fuck off Ian Holloway got the whole car singing. One man absent from the trip was Danny's housemate Richard Doyle. A rabid Coventry fan, Doyle had inexplicably chosen to holiday in Asia and give the excitement of the JPT a wide berth.

Coventry returned to the Ricoh Arena back in September, after settling a dispute with Stadium Operator ACL (Arena Coventry Ltd). A much publicised falling out with the stadium's previous owners - Coventry City Council and the Higgs Charity over rent, saw club owners Sisu move Coventry's home games 35 miles away to Northampton Town. Having spent just over 500 days away and with fans no longer having to make a 70-mile round trip to Sixfields, attendances swelled when the Sky Blues finally returned to their hallowed turf to take on Gillingham. While the novelty quickly wore off and the attendance dropped by more than half for their next game at the Ricoh, most fans were glad to have their home back. Rugby Union club Wasps have since become outright owners of the facility and look set to do a groundshare for the foreseeable future.

Situated around six miles from the city centre and three and a half from Coventry train station, the stadium sits next to a large shopping complex. I understand that a new railway station for the stadium should be functioning soon, if not already. Pubs and relevant eateries are a short walk away, although there is a casino nearby for those partial to a bit of Roulette and Blackjack. Parking the car in a neighbouring facility cost as much as the match ticket. I stuck my neck out and predicted that it wouldn't be a sellout which meant we could sit where we wanted. We made a collective decision to sit in the away end. Banksy pulled out three retro Plymouth shirts from his bag, so me and Danny got involved. Given the number of pies I agreed to eat over the course of the season, it was only appropriate for me to get the Ginsters sponsored shirt.

My friends simply couldn't wait until we got to the stadium for food and stopped by a solitary mobile burger van. I remained sceptical and refused to put my trust in a Turkish food worker wearing a Galatasaray shirt. My instincts were right when Banksy proceeded to order a hot dog and the lazy Turkish chef offered up raw onions. Banksy didn't go for it and even got more change back from his £10. The food gods had obviously analysed his case and decided a swift refund was due.

Walking across a bridge to pass the flyover next to the ground, two Plymouth fans with their girlfriends spotted our jerseys and wandered over for some small talk.

"Alright lads, where have you come up from?"
"Actually, we've come down mate."

The lads looked puzzled, so we connected the rest of the dots for them, before wishing the contingent a pleasant evening. Normally, the club operates a cashless system, but with prices being so cheap and unreserved seating, they were accepting cash on the turnstile.

During the period that football was absent from the Ricoh, singer Bruce Springsteen managed to sell it out. While fans of rival clubs have described the atmosphere inside the stadium as "soulless," I would have to disagree. On this particular night there was a decent sized crowd in making some noise. A lot of teenage Coventry fans had snapped up the £5 offer and were banging on some shutters towards the back of the stadium trying to get behind their team. The West Stand contains a built-in exhibition centre and corporate area which convinces the eye that the stadium is more than a Sky Blue bowl. Granted, the Ricoh branding is very prominent, but that's a minor gripe. Rich was gutted when his phone wouldn't let him place a bet on Plymouth's Reuben Reid to be the first scorer. It turned out to be a blessing in disguise, as Argyle felt the wrath of a team who days earlier had been embarrassed and dumped out of the FA Cup by lowly Worcester City.

Coventry exploited the loan market to their advantage, with a host of unused players from the Championship coming on board to get some much needed playing time. Ryan Allsop (on loan from AFC Bournemouth) almost had egg on his face when he got bored between the Coventry sticks and was almost caught out for being too clever in the penalty area. The Sky Blues got over that scare and made the breakthrough just past the hour. Frontman Gary Madine netted his first for the club since his temporary move from Sheffield Wednesday, heading in a Jim O'Brien corner.

Plymouth tried to come back, but didn't show any threat of adding another League One scalp to their campaign, having put paid to Swindon Town in the previous round. Substitute Marvin Morgan unwittingly contributed to sealing Coventry's win late on when he got in the way of a free kick. The ball bounced kindly for Ipswich Town loanee Frank Nouble to run virtually the length of the pitch, hold off his marker and coolly slot past Luke McCormick. That proved to be the final straw for poor Banksy, whose anger got the better of him and, no pun intended, turned the air sky blue. If he could have pulled his seat out, I'm sure he would have.

Danny took over DJ duties for part of the drive home, opting for Gazza's version of 'Fog on the Tyne,' followed by 'Three Lions.' Nothing like a trip to Coventry to get the patriotic juices flowing. It had been a real team effort from my friends, taking leave from work to help me get my latest football fix. By the time we got back home, poor Rich had been up for almost 24 hours, although you couldn't tell. The guy still had enough energy to put the duracell bunny to shame. At least now he can say he's been to Coventry.

Best chant: "We love City, we hate Sisu." The Coventry fans still have a bone to pick with the club's owners.
Match ticket: £5.
Match programme: £2. A shortened edition, but nothing like the pull-out poster editions I'd received at Oldham and Preston. The programme read like a hopeful hangover cure, with both manager and captain apologising for the Worcester defeat and urging the Sky Blues to bounce back.
Cost of food: £3.50 for a pie or hot dog.
Food rating: Depends on who you ask. There was nothing wrong with my chicken balti pie, although Danny noted that his half time hot dog was crunchy in parts and it gave him a spot of indigestion. On that note, I'll give the food a thumbs in the middle and a generous 3/5.

Final Score
Coventry City 2 (Madine 61, Nouble 85)
Plymouth Argyle 0
Attendance: 7,121

Getting to know Carlisle United
Simon Clarkson - Chairman of the Carlisle Supporters' London Branch
www.carlislelondonbranch.org
Twitter @cusclbontour

How did the London group start and how has it grown over the years?
Established in 1974 during Carlisle's only season in the top flight, the Branch now has over 300 members.

Seeing as you're London based, do you get to Brunton Park much?
Normally we get up only a few times a season, but this season we are going to a lot more games given it's our 40th anniversary. Sponsorship from Virgin trains helps make it affordable.

Best/worst players to pull on a Carlisle shirt?
There's been so many great players. Alan Ross, Stan Bowles, Peter Beardsley, Matt Jansen and Michael Bridges are some of my favourites. We've had far too many sub standard loanees in the past few seasons.

Who's provided the best hospitality for Carlisle supporters in recent memory?
Last time we went to Exeter we got given free pies - that was a nice touch.

Worst grounds you've visited?
Too many to mention, but most recently Boreham Wood.

Famous Carlisle fans?
Helen Skelton, Paul Nixon and Hunter Davies come to mind.

Quirky fact time?
Carlisle has the smallest population of any team to ever play in the top flight of English football.

Thoughts on ticket prices in general?
I'd like to see away fans who are affiliated/members of their club get in for free. They already endure long journeys and significant expense getting to the game. In League Two we are paying up to £25 for some games. This price is widely available in the higher leagues so either they are too cheap or the lower leagues too expensive. My fear is that as the Premier League clubs become less reliant on gate income, they flood the market with cheap tickets and lower league clubs lose income as fans go elsewhere.

Name your Carlisle Dream Team?
Alan Ross
Darren Edmondson
Kevin Gray
Dean Walling
Zigor Aranalde
Chris Balderstone
Stan Bowles
Peter Beardsley
Matt Jansen
Hughie McIlmoyle
David Reeves

FINDING A CHESTER CONNECTION IN CUMBRIA

Game #32: League Two - Saturday 15th November 2014
CARLISLE UNITED vs Accrington Stanley - Brunton Park

You should never leave things until the last minute. Booking games definitely falls into this category. Not for the first time this season, poor planning meant I was scrambling around the night before to find a game to attend. The latest international break threw up a few challenges, but I somehow managed to turn a couple of negatives into a big positive and forge a new relationship which would pay dividends down the road.

The original plan was to go and see Stevenage. With the top two leagues not in action due to international games taking place, the club were offering £10 entry to Premier League and Championship season ticket holders to try and get them off the couch, or out of the pub and through their turnstile for the weekend. My criteria didn't exactly meet the proverbial terms and conditions, but if you don't ask then you don't get, so I tried my luck. A phone call provided no joy, as the operator wasn't sympathetic to my cause and wouldn't grant me the same privilege. I was still mulling over making the journey south, when the fine folk at National Rail intervened yet again to make the decision for me. A late hike on travel costs put the buffers on that trip, so I looked at Plan B.

Unfortunately, there was to be no room at the Swindon Town Inn either. The Robins were hosting West Country rivals Bristol City in a top of the table League One clash, but I had left it far too late to get a ticket. The club shop was closed and online sales weren't available to new members. This left me with Carlisle United - a team I had been saving for a rainy day. Metaphorically speaking, it was now pouring down, so I grabbed my umbrella and set off for Cumbria.

An early morning train provided the best monetary value. Just as I was punching in the code to retrieve my tickets at the station, I heard my name shouted out in vain. I turned to see my friend Tim Sewell almost fall down the stairs and wobble towards me on jelly legs. The dirty stopout had caught the first train back from Liverpool, having pulled an all-nighter after a gig. Still half cut and smelling of booze, he wasn't up for another pint in Carlisle. I told him that sleep was overrated, but he muttered something about looking out for me on Match of the Day (wrong show bless him) before wandering off.

For once, I didn't need to ask for directions to the ground. I had a hunch that a guy sporting a Stobart sports jacket was going to the match, so I followed him down a long stretch of road until he led me to the promised land that was Brunton Park. If there's one thing synonymous with Carlisle, then it's Eddie Stobart's trucks and trailers, who had been long time sponsors and supporters of the club. Virgin Trains had since taken over as the main shirt sponsors.

I didn't fancy drinking on an empty stomach, so opted against a pre-match pint in the 'Beehive' pub directly across the road. You can't help but notice the large skyscrapers between the stands as you come towards the gate. Upon closer inspection, these hold a bank of floodlights mounting up the side. Directly outside the club shop and entrance to the ground, there is a statue of former player Hughie McIlmoyle. The Scottish forward enjoyed three spells with the club over a 20+ year career, with two prolific stints coming during the 1960s.

Not for the first time, I found a club which had some links with Chester. Ex-city boss Keith Curle had taken over the reigns from former player turned manager Graham Kavanagh, who was well on his way to guiding the club to an unwanted second relegation in successive seasons. Upon taking over, Curle didn't mince his words and provided quite the statement in the local press. "I don't mind putting lipstick on and giving people a little bit of loving. Likewise, if someone needs a rocket, I've got a launcher!"

Four wins from his first six games definitely gave Curle a platform to launch the club away from the relegation trapdoor. Meanwhile, opponents Accrington were exceeding expectations and sat comfortably in mid-table, having experienced a similar upturn in fortunes when John Coleman returned to the club to replace James Beattie in mid-September. The two sides met during the early stages of the Johnstone's Paint Trophy at the start of the season. Managerless Carlisle eased to a 3-1 victory in what was one of Beattie's final games in charge of Accrington.

With a ticket easily purchased, a guy in a suit (most likely a sponsor) had gathered a group of kids by the entrance. He asked who'd been to the ground before only to be met by complete silence. "Oh great, this is as real as it gets, proper football," he said. The kids remarkably ate up his words and, before I knew it they were being led on a march around the stadium, cheering their lungs out.

With that ringing endorsement still fresh in my ears, I went through a door, up a flight of stairs and came to a landing. Curious to see what was behind door number one, I was pleasantly surprised when I discovered a bar. A handful of fans had gathered for a pre-match drink and were watching golf on a big screen. There wasn't much of an atmosphere, but my eyes spied that matchday food could be ordered from the bar. Unfortunately, the solitary chicken and leek pie didn't look too appetising. The problem was I'd already ordered it out of haste. Fortunately, the young guy behind the bar wasn't too good at remembering prices and didn't look too enthused to find out. As much as I wanted to run out of the door, I thought of a more subtle escape. When the barman stepped away, I pulled out my phone and pretended to take a call. I motioned to Mr Lazy I would be right back to collect and pay for my pie before ducking out of the door never to return. A helpful steward pointed me in the direction of a food truck outside the ticket office. Fortunately for me it was well stocked and I could put the latest issue of piegate behind me.

I was seated up in the Main Stand just above the players' tunnel. Happily, there was a roof so I was well protected from the elements. The varnished wooden seats had clearly seen better days, but at least there was no chewing gum under my chair. The Warwick Road terrace directly opposite me looked like a garden shed, with its three triangular sections acting as the roof. Directly opposite, the Petterill End drew comparisons with Exeter City for containing only a small area of seating in what was to be a largely unoccupied terrace for this game. Various name plaques were displayed on some of the surrounding seats by me, which meant I was with the hardcore season ticket holders.

While Curle sat below me momentarily to film some pre-match comments for the official website, club mascot Olga the Fox took to the centre circle to perform a Daniel Sturridge inspired dance. As tribute, another fox, this time of the stuffed variety was wheeled out and placed on display during the dance. My inquisitive mind was put to rest when I was informed this was an old tradition as a tribute to John Peel - a 19th century Cumbrian huntsman.

With kick-off fastly approaching, it turned out that I was sat right in the middle of the over 50s club. As Peter greeted Paul and so on, I kept waiting to be rumbled. Surely they wanted to know who this young newcomer was invading their sacred turf. The seat next to me, belonging to Malcolm remained empty - probably a good thing, seeing as I was using it as a table to hold my snacks and drinks. Malcolm certainly wouldn't have approved, but seeing as he was AWOL, I was alright.

Since his arrival, Curle had managed to solve one of the club's main problems - finding a regular goalscorer. He turned to a man who he'd formerly worked with at, you guessed it, good old Chester City. Derek Asamoah had been convinced to give up South Korea for Cumbria (a fair trade) and the diminutive striker had taken to League Two like a duck to water. Signing initially on a short term deal, the frontman had already netted on his debut. Despite his lack of size, the Ghanaian had pace to burn and burst clear early on to slot past goalkeeper Jack Rose for his fourth goal in five games.

It certainly looked like the floodgates were about to open, yet somehow the expected glut of goals didn't happen. Much to their chagrin, Carlisle found Rose in fine form, with the shot stopper making a highlight reel of saves. The visitors sensed their hosts were susceptible on the counter attack, although Stanley's Shay McCartan probably wanted the ground to open up and eat him when he sliced wide from point blank range.

The senior fans seemed to be kicking every ball. One Geordie was spitting venom at poor Matt Robson, who couldn't seem to put a foot right. Carlisle substitute David Amoo looked like a nervous apprentice and didn't seem to have a grasp on basic positioning. However, the light seemed to go on in his head during stoppage time and he came alive. Amoo broke clear and played in Kyle Dempsey, only to see Rose confidently beat the effort away. Amoo went back into his bag of tricks and pulled out three lollipops, before taking aim. This time, a desperate defensive goalline clearance kept Carlisle's lead to a solitary goal. It was pleasing to see that the majority of fans stayed until the end. With fists clenched and heads moving in unison, they were kicking every ball and letting a week of working frustration out while cheering on their team. With a very small away presence, there wasn't much chanting going on and the final whistle brought a wave of relief across Brunton Park.

Checking the results on the way back to the station, Stevenage's 5-1 victory over Cheltenham produced a wry smile. They got all the goals that I should have seen. However, a fire near Wembley station just before England kicked off had thrown most of the train network out of sync. Awaiting my final connection at Warrington Bank Quay, just one train was running on time, which happened to be mine. That was the first spot of good fortune, with the second coming a few days later. Ahead of their 40th anniversary celebration, The London Branch of Carlisle fans replied to an email I had sent and invited me along to watch United's next league match at Dagenham and Redbridge. An afternoon in East London seemed appealing, so never one to turn down a party, I RSVPd and duly bought a train ticket. National Rail weren't going to catch me out again.

Best chant: "Robson, you couldn't catch a cold." A more civilised rant rather than a chant by some of the elder statesmen of Carlisle.
Match ticket: £22. A pre-sale purchase would have saved me £3.
Match programme: £2 and good value. The highlight being a head to head feature, pitting two players against each other answering daft questions. Connor Brown could land a plane in a crisis and missed a family wedding for football, while Tom Anderson would serve up food after it had been dropped on the floor - providing it was within the five second rule!
Cost of food: £3.50 for a pie and soft drink, £1.60 for chunky chips.
Food rating: 3.5/5. A beautiful blend of buttery mash gave the meat and potato some kick.

Final Score
Carlisle United 1 (Asamoah 21)
Accrington Stanley 0
Attendance: 4,069

Getting to know Rochdale
David Chaffey – www.RochdaleAFC.com (Unofficial Rochdale Fan Site)

Favourite memory as a Rochdale fan?
My Dad started taking me as a young boy after my brother stopped taking me to watch Manchester United and I've been going ever since for the best part of 22 years. There are a few memories. The two promotions were obviously well up there, but the best memory I have was that winning penalty at home to Darlington in the play-offs to take us to Wembley. Scenes like we'd never seen before.

Best game you've witnessed at Spotland?
Tough question. In terms of drama, we won a game 5-4 against York at Spotland about 15 years ago in an epic encounter. In terms of most enjoyable, our play-off semi-final second leg against Darlington which we won on penalties gets that award, but I can't fail to mention beating Leeds United last season in the FA Cup. Having a fondness for Manchester United as well, that was particularly pleasing!

Best/worst players to pull on a Rochdale shirt?
There's been a lot of garbage and a lot of top quality. The best players we've seen at Dale include the likes of Rickie Lambert, Craig Dawson, Grant Holt, Adam Le Fondre, Alan Reeves and Will Buckley who have all gone on to play in the Premiership. I'd also include a lad called Paddy McCourt who may be a relative unknown, but he's arguably the best player I've ever seen at Dale. He was a tricky winger who could turn the game on its head with one mazy run. He'd glide past players and went on to play for Celtic. If you type his name into YouTube, it's like a montage of genius wing play. I also have to mention one of the club's most important players, legendary captain Gary Jones, wonderful leader, and midfielder. Reg Jenkins also gets mentioned a lot by the older element, but I'm too young to have ever seen him play. As for the worst, there are several names I could give you. Goalkeeper Matt Dickens, centre back Jon Boardman, striker Paul Tait, defender Simon Coleman. I'll leave it there I think or I could go on forever.

Best thing about Spotland?
It's a very popular away trip for people. We are a friendly bunch, the ground has bags of character and we're not as expensive as most other grounds. Our matchday announcer normally gets loads of praise for the music he plays and lots of fans comment on that. The football on show is also good, as is the groundsman we've had in the past few years. He has produced a magnificent pitch to play good football on.

Worst grounds you've visited?
Anything that's brand new! The likes of Shrewsbury's new ground, or Colchester's are awful. They have zero character and while they might be impressive to look at, they are soulless places and we are worse off for places like this. I used to enjoy going to the old grounds like Gay Meadow which most new or younger fans would class as garbage.

Enjoyable away days?
Old Trafford is brilliant, easily the best ground in the country that I've been to, but as I've mentioned, I used to love going to the old style grounds like Shrewsbury's Gay Meadow, Accrington, Macclesfield or even Barnet's old ground.

Which club serves the nicest pies?
I'll be biased and say our own are the best, but I'll always remember Cambridge United's bacon baguettes which were worth the trip alone. The cottage pies at Kidderminster are also very well thought of.

Famous Rochdale fans?
I hate this question because none of them really have much affiliation to the club. Lisa Stansfield turns up when she has an album to plug, David Bentley turns up to quite a few Dale games and lives in the local area apparently. Apart from that, nobody really!

Quirky fact time?

Tough question, although we once got to the League Cup final! We were beaten by Norwich City in the early 60's. Michael Owen's Dad used to play for us, as did legendary manager Herbert Chapman I think.

Thoughts on ticket prices in general?

I think ticket prices have been on the increase for some time and it's getting to the point where it's pricing fans out of going. Take Hartlepool for example. Two years ago when we went, we were charged £26 to get in. If you've never been to Hartlepool it's a bog standard away end that's really narrow. To charge £26 for that in a League Two game was disgraceful and a lot of us boycotted. For third tier English football, some of the prices are ridiculous.

Name your Rochdale Dream Team?

GK: Neil Edwards
RB: Scott Wiseman
LB: Tom Kennedy
CB: Alan Reeves
CB: Craig Dawson
RW: Paddy McCourt
LW: Ian Henderson
CM: Gary Jones (Captain)
CM: Matty Lund
CF: Grant Holt
CF: Rickie Lambert

That is some team really. I think five of them have played Premiership football, two of which are playing in the Premiership currently in Dawson and Lambert. Some players I didn't want to leave out as well such as Adam Le Fondre, Will Buckley, Jason Kennedy and Paul Simpson for example.

DISCOVERING THE MAGIC OF THE FA CUP

Game #33: FA Cup First Round Replay - Tuesday 18th November 2014
ROCHDALE vs Northampton Town - Spotland

There is no greater cup competition than the FA Cup. A bold statement, but true nonetheless. Even though the importance has dwindled in the eyes of some Premier League clubs in recent years, fans and teams lower down the football pyramid still love the romance of the cup and the possibility of a giant killing. While work commitments prevented me from attending one of the inital first round proper matches, I was all set for a midweek date at Spotland. Northampton and Rochdale had played out a goalless draw at Sixfields ten days earlier to necessitate the replay.

A packed train awaited me at Earlestown en route to Manchester Victoria. Through the corner of my eye, I could see excited youths with tickets clutched in their hands. They must have been as excited as I was to see the clash between Dale's Ian Henderson and Town's Marc Richards. Apparently not. On closer inspection, they were going to see a game featuring Cristiano Ronaldo and Lionel Messi down the road at Old Trafford. It was at this point that I questioned people's loyalty. I mean, who would choose a meaningless friendly over a cup tie which would determine who would face the might of Portsmouth or Aldershot in the second round. Oh right, just me. We'll move swiftly on then.

The final leg of the train journey was full of hassled workers spitting venom at an apparent delay and lack of carriages. The poor train manager dived into the safety of his locked cabinet, as we finally pulled away. I wasn't exactly sure where Spotland was so asked one of the burly police officers on duty outside the station for directions. He advised me to jump in a cab or catch a bus due to the ground being located on the other side of town. Strangely, the Metrolink was right by the train station, but that apparently wasn't an option. To say it was a brisk walk to the bus station would be an understatement. Gangs of youths all with uninviting eyes burnt a hole through me as I passed by a countless number of takeaways and convenience stores. The sanctuary of the bus depot at the bottom of a hill brought a wave of relief.

I spied Rochdale shirts on two other passengers, so simply followed them when alighting. Spotland was situated around the corner from a main road, seemingly in the middle of a terraced housing estate. It was probably for this reason that the club didn't start playing music until half an hour before the game. No doubt the club would want to keep the residents on side whether they were fans of the 'Dale or not. It was pleasing not having to weave in and out of traffic or through a retail park for once to reach the ground. Given the side's recent promotion to League One, the club is in an ideal spot to capitalise on a hike in walk-up business from the locals. However, with the temperatures plummeting, it wasn't too surprising that a lot of people opted to stay indoors. They probably thought that an FA Cup replay against an out of form League Two side would be a given. That being said, a good number of younger fans took up their usual position in the Sandy Lane Terrace behind the goal.

Three modern-ish single tiered sections make up the rest of Spotland, with ample roofing protecting all four sides of the ground. The 'Ratcliffe Bar,' situated just outside was very friendly with a sign saying all fans were welcome. A lot of familiar faces were greeting each other at the bar. True to their word, I sensed a jovial atmosphere inside and nobody batted an eyelid at anyone's shirt colour.

Cold/soft drinks were off the menu, but I was happy as Larry munching on a pre-match pie while listening to a plethora of the finest 90s Indie music. Being close to Manchester, it came as no surprise. They sure know up north what the paying punter likes to listen to before a game. Stewards were very welcoming and happily chatted along to some of the regulars. A young superfan, who seemingly knew what the players had for breakfast was sat directly in front of me. You couldn't help but admire the enthusiasm he showed. A few seats across was someone's gran, again on her own, but wrapped up warm and eyes fully focused on the game. I don't even know if my gran even likes football, let alone what team she follows, plus I doubt she's ever set foot inside a stadium. Rounding out the supporting cast, three chatty guys with thick Lancashire accents (think David Platt out of Coronation Street) occupied the seats directly behind me.

You wouldn't have thought that Rochdale were a division higher than their visitors with the way the first half panned out. It was more like men vs boys, with the League Two outfit using their physicality to bully their hosts. Northampton's Emile Sinclair was built like a tank, yet also had the lightning pace to sprint past his marker. There was an air of inevitability when the visitors went in front early doors. Ivan Toney rose highest to head home from a free-kick, which sent the token Northampton gathering crazy. I couldn't spot any of the fans who I'd befriended at Morecambe. The cold weather must have put them off. Sinclair continued to show off his skills, narrowly missing an ambitious overhead kick. He failed to slow down when approaching the byline and went fully over the advertising boards. I dared not to laugh out of fear he would come over and eat me.

The Rochdale fans weren't impressed and booed their team off at half time. The Lancashire posse behind me summed up proceedings perfectly. "If this were on TV, I'd turn it off," one man said. An older guy sat right at the front was also shaking his head and looking bemused. At least half time brought my ears some respite from his constant chants of "come on Dale," every few minutes.

Rochdale boss Keith Hill must have read the riot act at half time, because his side seemed to come out rejuvenated, while the break in play had the opposite effect on Northampton. All of a sudden, they looked out of ideas and were resorting to time wasting in order to see the game out. Diving and rolling around like they had been shot became the name of the game for the Northampton players. Cries of "he's a flopper," (aka diver) came from the three wise men behind me. Even big Sinclair was no longer the Iron Man. Indeed, with his energy sapped, he was inconspicuous by his absence until manager Chris Wilder decided to replace him.

If they could have got their hands on a residents' kitchen sink, then Rochdale would have thrown that forward. They hit the bar and had an effort cleared off the line. It certainly looked like it wasn't going to be their night. Ten minutes from the end an announcement was made about someone needing to go back to their car. Within seconds, a pensioner was helped from his seat and back into his mobility scooter. I turned to my three Lancashire acquaintances and we all hoped that it wasn't his car and he'd simply left having had enough. Moments later, the breakthrough finally came. Substitute Reuben Noble-Lazarus made it a home debut to remember when he picked his spot and crashed a shot into the top corner to send Spotland into frenzied celebration.

With the momentum fully shifted, talk turned to the possibility of extra time and penalties. However, one look at the Northampton players told me that they were a beaten outfit. The goal had knocked them off their game. Extra time wouldn't be ideal for me, as it would add on more travelling time. I needn't have worried. Rochdale were now riding the crest of a wave and found a deserved winner deep into stoppage time. Defender Olly Lancashire met Michael Rose's cross and the comeback was complete. It was just like the late show at Sheffield United all over again. I shamelessly joined the fans in bouncing around to Madness' 'One Step Beyond,' before high fiving everyone in sight. I could now get home at a reasonable hour.

I made the quick walk back to the bus station, only to discover to my horror that the buses had stopped running. Cursing my luck at failing to check the timetable, I sought out directions back to the city centre and started to make tracks. In unfamiliar surroundings, I decided to chance my luck and ask three fans who had converged on the side of a road. It was at least a long straight mile back into the city centre, but they took pity on this intrepid traveller. Their desire to go for a post match drink in town played into my hands. The kind souls offered me a ride in their taxi to their boozer of choice. Now, to any kids reading this, you shouldn't really accept lifts from strangers, but this was an exception.

The three blokes were season ticket holders and couldn't have been nicer. In addition to picking up the taxi tab and taking an interest in the ground tour, they seemed to know Chester and its racecourse quite well. Had I not had a train to catch, I would have loved nothing more than to stay and chat some more. I asked if I'd seen the real Rochdale and was met by a firm "no" in unison. Injury had kept star man Henderson out, while Blackburn Rovers had refused to allow on-loan defender Jack O'Connell (enjoying a second stint at Spotland) to play in the game.

After expressing my gratitude for the added northern hospitality, we wished each other well and I walked the short distance back to the station. The gang of youths were still out up to no good and waited until I was ten paces past them before shouting a string of obscenities. Their insults fell on deaf ears. The town itself is -let's say a bit rough round the edges, but inside the bubble of Spotland, the fans are a fine and friendly bunch. Walking through the streets of Manchester on my way back to Piccadilly, scores of foreigners went past with their Ronaldo scarves on full display. Without knowing the score, I knew the world's top two players had wowed the crowds with their trickery. I hadn't missed out. Far from it, I was treated to a different kind of magic. The magic of the FA Cup!

Best chant: "If I wanted to see a fairy, then I'd go to a pantomime." A Rochdale fan unhappy at Northampton's second half theatrics. Hopefully his other half didn't get him panto tickets for Christmas.

Match ticket: £12. League prices are quite reasonable, ranging between £15-£20, although the reduction was welcome.

Match programme: £2. Contained a lot of facts and stats about previous meetings with the Cobblers, including a picture of a fresh faced Rickie Lambert lining up for Dale back in 2006. The 'Traveller's Tales' provided an entertaining glimpse of a trip to Leyton Orient, getting used to London prices and the maze that is the London underground. Rochdale's trip to Brisbane Road was a lot more fruitful than mine, producing five goals compared to my stalemate.

Cost of food: £2 for a pie. Cheap as chips, so I got two to celebrate.

Food rating: The steak pie flattered to deceive and offered a paltry amount of meat, so only gets a 3/5. The cheese pie was a marked improvement. Not an onion in sight, just plenty of piping hot melted cheese on a soft crust. 4/5.

Final Score
Rochdale 2 (Noble-Lazarus 85, Lancashire 90)
Northampton Town 1 (Toney 4)
Attendance: 1,717

Getting to know Dagenham & Redbridge
Nick Murphy - Dagenham & Redbridge FC Facebook page

Favourite memory as a Dagenham fan?

In the nine years of being a fan, I've seen us play in the Conference, League One and League Two again now. It has been an absolute rollercoaster, but you wouldn't have it any other way! It's very hard to top that feeling of seeing your team win at Wembley, so our 3-2 play-off final victory over Rotherham United has to be my favourite memory. The 6-0 thrashing of Morecambe in the semi-final is a very close second.

Best game you've witnessed at Victoria Road?

The 6-0 win over Morecambe as mentioned above is the one that stands out for me, although for sheer entertainment value, our 6-6 draw with Brentford in the League Cup was astonishing. Also the 1-1 draw we shared with Huddersfield in League One was pure end-to-end stuff, perhaps my favourite regular league match at Viccy Road.

Best/worst players to pull on a Dagenham shirt?

For best players, there are a number to choose from - Paul Benson, Sam Saunders, Matt Ritchie and Scott Doe all included from my era, but I'd have to go for Tony Roberts who was loved by home and away fans alike. As for worst, how long have you got? Marvin Morgan, Shabazz Baidoo, Chris Dickson and Gavin Tomlin are all serious contenders.

Best thing about Victoria Road?

The feeling that you're a part of the action and that you influence the game. I stand metres from the pitch on matchday. It's an atmosphere and a surrounding that you just can't replicate higher up the league ladder and one you only get at grounds like Victoria Road. It's a dying breed and it's a true shame.

Worst grounds you've visited?

The worst grounds for me aren't your Accrington's or your Dagenham's for that matter, but the new build identi-kit stadiums that have no charm or unique stands to them. For that reason, Oxford, Shrewsbury and Millwall are all awful grounds from my own personal perspective.

Enjoyable away days?

I personally love stadiums that retain an old grandstand, and for that reason Cheltenham's Whaddon Road is always a personal favourite of mine. Aldershot and Southend's away ends also create a fantastic atmosphere, while Chesterfield is by far the best of the new build stadia around. Accrington's also deserves a mention for that uncompromising terrace that I have been soaked and frozen on three times.

Which club serves the nicest pies?

I'm not big on pies I'm afraid, but what I will say is Fleetwood do the nicest pasties and Hartlepool have a good value hotdog! I always hear good things about Morecambe though, so I'll have to go with them.

Famous Dagenham fans?

The best you'll get locally is probably Stacey Solomon unfortunately, although I believe James Buckley of Inbetweeners fame keeps an eye out for our results.

Quirky fact time?

We hold the record for the longest penalty shoot-out with most consecutive kicks scored (27 in a row) 14-13 winners vs Leyton Orient in the 2011 Johnstone's Paint Trophy.

DIGGIN' DAGENHAM

Game #34: League Two - Saturday 22nd November 2014
DAGENHAM & REDBRIDGE vs Carlisle United - The London Borough of Barking & Dagenham Stadium (Victoria Road)

With a stadium name as long as the early morning Virgin Train greeting me, I was off for another foray into the nation's capital for a crunch relegation clash at the foot of League Two. The Daggers had just been dumped out of the FA Cup by Conference outfit Southport (that cup magic again) and manager Wayne Burnett was a man under pressure. He could be forgiven for feeling like a beer or two to steel himself ahead of the game. However, the guys who got on the train at Crewe were on the lager ridiculously early. Knocking back the cans of Carling at 7:30am like there was no tomorrow, it came as no surprise when they were worse for wear by the time we reached Milton Keynes.

Things then went from the drunk to the downright weird. The girl sitting opposite me pulled out a magazine and was soon fully engrossed in its contents. I'd never heard of the Fortean Times, but given that one of its articles led with the line "I used to eat lots of Library books," it's not surprising really. Different strokes for different folks I guess. Rather than go straight through to Dagenham Dock, I stopped off at Barking to meet up with the London Branch of Carlisle supporters who had got in touch after my trip to Brunton Park the previous week. The exiled Cumbrians had just celebrated their 40th anniversary (16th November) and invited me to join them. The pub in question - the 'Barking Dog' was ideally located next to the station. Seeing that the bookmakers across the road had a big crack in the window, I lost all interest in having a bet and dived into the safe haven of the boozer.

The group weren't hard to find. A cluster of Carlisle shirts gave the game away and I quickly became acquainted with members as far from Runcorn all the way to Land's End. I'm probably exaggerating with the latter. However, no matter the distance, the group hold regular meetings and frequently travel up and down the country to see their team home and away. That has to be applauded. I was informed that a team of supporters had beaten their Dagenham counterparts 8-1 earlier that morning, with an 11-year-old getting on the scoresheet and a 64-year-old being given a run out. As the beer continued to flow, the guys were hopeful of this being a good omen for the proper game. Wanting to explore the ground before kick-off, I temporarily excused myself from the group and made the short voyage to Dagenham.

Walking past a vomit laden bus stop and over an array of empty takeaway boxes, a taxi driver proudly wearing his Daggers jersey was bemoaning his club's recent luck to a potential punter. The ground was no more than a five minute walk from the tube station. Being greeted by a funeral director's gazebo at the entrance wasn't exactly the welcome I was expecting, so I cheered myself up with a quick look inside a hut containing a collector's dream of vintage club merchandise. An array of classic matchday programmes, pendants and scarves were all on show, with enthusiastic staff only too happy to chat and accommodate any inquisitive visitors. A new club logo was recently unveiled and would be used on new kit going forward. Ben Cooper's simplified design of two daggers piercing through a blue shield won out from over 100 other entries and he received a £500 cheque for his efforts.

The club were advertising kids for a quid, so I asked for a student price, knowing full well I'd left my pass at home. The cheeky chappy manning the gate (a spit for Jay's Dad off the Inbetweeners) was about to let me through, but then asked to see my ID. Rats! After a brief rummage through my wallet, I informed the staffer of my clumsiness, but he just smirked and said "that's an expensive mistake to make." I flashed a fake smile before being allowed entry into the East London field of dreams. Julie's Fast Food bar was doing a roaring pre-match trade. Hungry diners were stocking up on generous sized bacon baguettes, hot dogs and burgers. Forget the Bridge Street Cafe, or whatever it's now being called in Albert Square. As far as these East End punters were concerned, Ian Beale could stick his sausage butties where the sun doesn't shine.

At first glance, Dagenham seemed to look after the away fans better than some of their own. Travelling supporters are mainly placed behind the goal in the Traditional Builders Stand - an all seated area which replaced a former terrace and can hold just over 1000 supporters. The (main) Carling Stand behind the dugouts only runs three quarters of the pitch, with a smaller family stand bridging the gap between the Builders. Most of the hardcore home fans were squished together in the North Terrace - rechristened by many as 'the Sieve' due to a leaky roof. A small group of Dagenham season ticket holders had found their way into the Builders bit. As part of an initiative and thank you for their support, the full term fans get upgraded for ten games, although that may be due to the fact that the only bar (apart from the social club outside) is housed behind the Builders Stand. One of those said fans - Michael, happened to be sat behind me and was enjoying the upgrade in hospitality, having recently adopted the side. Michael was not long married and, with the growing cost of being a Queens Park Rangers fan, it turned out that he couldn't afford to keep his £600 season ticket. Utilising a cheaper option and embracing a club close to home, his kind wife agreed to invest in a season ticket. Clocking in at £179 it's certainly a bargain buy. However, Michael hadn't reckoned on his generous stag party renewing his QPR season ticket as an early wedding gift. With both sides rarely clashing, he's currently getting the best of both worlds. When I politely enquired as to why he didn't follow West Ham, his reply was short and to the point. "Fuck West Ham, their fans leave a mess outside my house wherever they go. The sooner they fuck off to Stratford the better." That cleared that issue up and I made sure not to bring anything else Hammer related up for the duration of the game.

I was surprised to see 39-year-old Jamie Cureton line up for the Daggers. The nomadic striker has certainly done the rounds in his career and had signed a one year deal back in the summer. The home side made all the early running, but went behind thanks to a quick counter attack. Just like the weekend prior, Derek Asamoah was in the right place at the right time to fire home and give the travelling fans some early cheer. That early optimism didn't last long. The Cumbrians were immediately put onto the backfoot. Just when it looked like goalkeeper Dan Hanford could repel balls all afternoon, he dropped two clangers inside as many minutes. If letting Billy Bingham's grasscutter of a free kick pass him wasn't enough, the shotstopper outdid himself with his next contribution. With a rush of blood to the head, hapless Hanford clumsily bundled over Ade Yusuff in the box after the forward had taken a heavy touch. Had the rebound not fallen kindly for Ashley Chambers to tap in, then Hanford almost certainly would have been sent off. The excitement was too much for a contingent of kids in front of me to take. Decked out in their youth club tracksuits, the happy juniors bounced around merrily doing the Lech Poznan celebration which Manchester City fans famously ripped off. In the meantime, a small boisterous man was walking around the ground yelling "come on you Daggers." Turns out that club Chairman Dave Bennett was just doing his usual rounds. I'd love to see Roman Abramovich take a leaf out of his book.

I could sense a familiar look of "here we go again," appear on the Carlisle fans' faces. Cureton proved that while his legs may have lost a bit of pace, his footballing brain was still razor sharp. The veteran pounced on a timely flick on to send a sweetly struck effort beyond Hanford's reach into the bottom corner. It was one of those efforts that you knew was going in as soon as it left his boot. Having fluffed a couple of earlier efforts, Cureton reminded me that class was indeed permanent.

Keith Curle's half time team talk went right out of the window when Carlisle conceded a fourth barely a minute after the restart. This time, Cureton turned provider, allowing Chambers to net his second of the afternoon from close range. I was on my way back from the concession stand to see the net ripple. Many home fans were still queuing to get their savoury and alcoholic fix and were agitated at missing a goal. Young Carlisle defender Tom Anderson looked to add some more grey to Curle's hair colour when he fouled Cureton in the box. However, the visitors were spared when the striker smashed the resulting spot kick against the crossbar. Carlisle were spurred on by the reprieve and immediately reduced their arrears, when captain and full back Danny Grainger curled a 30 yard free kick into the top corner to stake his claim for goal of the day.

Sadly there were no more goals, but it was a great advert for League Two, a division which I was quickly becoming fond of. Texts came flooding in commending me on choosing the right game. I replied that League Two has a couple of diamonds in the rough for days out. That statement summed up my trip to Dagenham perfectly. The Carlisle fans tried to rationalise their defeat on the way back to Euston by remarking that three of the four relegated sides were now propping up the football pyramid. For Dagenham and their under-fire boss Burnett, they could breathe a sigh of relief....for another week at least.

Catching my usual train home from Euston, I ran towards the front and settled down into a bank of four seats. My personal space was soon invaded by a party of six all carrying bulging M & S bags. The group of chums set their spread across the table and gorged on red wine, Italian meats, olives and calamari amongst other fine delicacies. The obnoxious one got drunk pretty quickly and resorted to belching and swearing until the well spoken one of the group threatened him with blackmail and the revealing an embarrassing secret. I never did find out what it was. They were courteous enough to extend an invite to their tea party, although I politely declined. I did partake in their pop quiz and wiped the floor with them. Shaun 1, Posh folk 0.

Best chant: "Digger Dagger, Digger Dagger, oh oh oh." Dagenham mascot Digger the Dog had the kids in the palm of his paw and they lapped up the chant.
Match ticket: £21, although I'll accept the £6 non student surcharge for the quality of game I was treated to.
Match programme: £3. Defender Billy Bingham was the lucky Dagger to be grilled and ironically played down his goalscoring prowess. In the stats section, Cureton was second in the division for having had a hand in 53% of the club's goals. That stat remained in tact after this game. The Daggers fans proved generous with their cash, with all players, staff and even Digger having their kit and boots sponsored for the season.
Cost of food: £2.50 for a pie, £2 for chunky chips.
Food rating: 4/5. Came in a sealed packet, so brownie points for hygiene. The minced beef and onion offering didn't feel stodgy and warmed the cockles nicely. Kids were fighting over the vinegar and sauces, so I settled for salty chips washed down by a healthy bottle of pop.

Final Score
Dagenham & Redbridge 4 (Bingham 23, Chambers 24, 46, Cureton 39)
Carlisle United 2 (Asamoah 16, Grainger 53)
Attendance: 2,097

Getting to know Southend United
All At Sea Fanzine
www.aas-fanzine.co.uk
Twitter @AllAtSeaFanzine

Favourite memory as a Southend fan?

The 2005 play-off final at the Millennium Stadium. The eight/nine years previous were a real low point in the club's history and I had never dared to dream that Southend could win promotion. To do it after missing out on automatic promotion on the last day was especially sweet.

Best game you've witnessed at Roots Hall?

I remember a 5-2 victory over Bolton back in 1996 when they were top of the league and we were bottom. The 5-3 win over Bournemouth when we scored four in six minutes in 1998 was pretty remarkable too. But for sheer emotion the 2-2 draw which booked us a place in the 2013 JPT final against our rivals Leyton Orient had everything.

Best/worst players to pull on a Southend shirt?

Freddy Eastwood and Adam Barrett were great. Stan Collymore is regarded as our best ever player, but sadly I never saw him play. As for worst, far too many to mention, but certainly none of the current lot are in consideration thankfully. A special mention goes to Alvin Martin for being the worst ever manager in Southend's and possibly football's history.

Best thing about Roots Hall?

Terrific atmosphere for big games, fans close to the pitch and bags of character.

Worst grounds you've visited?

Any of the identikit new ones like Chesterfield/Shrewsbury/Colchester. I still can't tell those three apart.

Enjoyable away days?

Peterborough's away end was the best in the league before they knocked it down. Fratton Park is a great place to watch football too. Carrow Road and Hillsborough stand out from our time in the Championship.

Which club serves the nicest pies?

I don't normally buy football ground food, but I remember Kidderminster Harriers being known for it. Morecambe too apparently.

Famous Southend fans?

Comedian Terry Alderton, singer Alison Moyet.

Quirky fact time?

In 1996, Southend started the second half vs Ipswich with nine men on the pitch. This is because striker Andy Rammell was still in the dressing room trying to find his contact lens, and midfielder Phil Gridelet was superstitious and had to be the last man out onto the pitch. Unsurprisingly, we were relegated that season.

SHRIMPERS, CHIPS & GRAVY

Game #35: League Two - Saturday 29th November 2014
SOUTHEND UNITED vs Northampton Town - Roots Hall

You wait ages for a bus, then two, maybe even three come along at once. Not today. Wandering to the bus stop at the end of my estate, I waited, then waited some more, then started to panic. If I missed the train, the whole day was basically in the Southend Sea. A tad dramatic, but having paid an advance fare, I didn't fancy getting stung by a ridiculously hiked up same day ticket price in its place.

Finally at 6:50am a bus came to save me. There was no traffic and the bus made steady progress into town. There was one other passenger, a rather well to do lady who certainly knew her Ps from her Qs. She alighted two stops before me and wasn't in any rush to get off the bus. What started off as a polite goodbye turned into a full blown conversation with the driver, who thought his luck may be in. I bit my tongue for as long as possible, while she kept talking about things far less important than the League Two game I was hoping to get to. Finally, like a volcano erupting, the words tripped off my tongue. "Excuse me love, but some of us have a train to catch." Just to emphasise my claim, I tapped my watch furiously like Sir Alex Ferguson when he wanted to see his Manchester United side over the line. I was met by an articulate sneer, as Lady Penelope sidled past. I didn't care and shrugged her off. Besides, the bus was moving again and I was able to get to the station on time, print my tickets off and relax in the comfort of my pre-reserved seat.

Once in the capital, I felt like a football hooligan due to all the pushing and shoving going on around a congested Liverpool Street station. Being back on a train felt like a safe haven, as I caught a 45 minute connection to Prittlewell - the closest station to the ground. A sign pointing to Roots Hall is conveniently placed outside Prittlewell. For those that want to check out the city centre, you need to walk through two alleyways which follow the back of the train tracks. If you're lucky, you might even bump into some of the locals. A drunken skinhead approached, swaying from side to side enough to make Cristiano Ronaldo giddy. Suffice to say, it was easy to give him the slip. Another bickering couple then walked past pushing a pram. The guy was looking for a pass to watch the game, but the young mother was having none of it and told him she never promised such a thing. It was anything but love's young dream.

Seagulls and sunshine reminded me I wasn't far from the sea, yet a biting wind was enough of a reminder not to stop for an ice cream. I had heard rave reviews about the 'Fish House,' situated just around the corner from the ground, so decided to stop by. Scores of fans were already outside tucking into fresh fish and chips. The bins were overflowing from happy customers, and I soon joined them, gorging on a proper northern snack of chips and gravy. The request is known to be an alien one in southern parts, but contrary to belief, there was no dramatic pauses or disbelief and I was served up a piping hot treat.

Work commitments had prevented me from visiting Southend for Chester FC's shock FA Cup victory a few weeks prior. Since that defeat, the Shrimpers had put together a run of three straight league victories and held the upper hand coming into this game. However, my allegiances were leaning towards Northampton, so that was where I decided to sit. The North Stand was fenced off, so I had to walk the long way round, going back on myself through the car park and down the surounding roads.

Electronic operated turnstiles and a unique split tier behind the goal provide a nice distraction from a greater problem which faces Roots Hall. The ground is in desperate need of some TLC. Old sheeting, scruffy skirting, dents in the wooden panels were all too clear to see from my spot below pitch level. Another case in point was the Hi-Tec Stand facing opposite. Just by name alone, the brand was outdated even when I was at school. An old P.E teacher was ripped mercilessly for his endorsement of the Hi-Tec label, yet here it was on proud display at a football ground some 15 years later.

Days before the game, Northampton's John-Joe O'Toole had joined Southend on a two month loan deal. According to Phil Brown's programme notes, good old John-Joe was a player he had "been chasing for a couple of years." By his own admission later in the same article, the alice band wearing midfielder said: "It will be a bit of a strange situation to be up against players who I was with until fairly recently. He added: "Things weren't really working out for me at Northampton and sometimes you have to just get out and play football."

In a true baptism of fire, O'Toole lined up against his parent club and almost made it a debut to remember when he fired an early warning sign into the stands. No longer seen as one of their own, cries of "go back to your caravan, you dirty gypsy," could be heard from an exasperated fan sat behind me. The poor guy was acting like his girlfriend had left him. Soon enough, he turned his frustration over to the the fourth official, who just happened to be female. "Get that flag up love, it's not there for decoration." Personally, I think she made the right call. The Southend player in question was definitely onside when the ball was played.

Sadly, the game wasn't showing the same levels of enthusiasm that both sets of fans were. David Worrall had talked up teammate Jack Payne as the "English Xavi Hernandez" in the programme and the midfielder was having a solid, if unspectacular game. Most of the entertainment was going on in the stands. The Northampton contingent – including the familiar faces from Morecambe easily drowned out a small set of ultras who were banging a drum, telling one particular rotund fan exactly where he could stick the instrument. Even the Southend stewards got a chuckle out of that one.

Tottenham Hotspur loanee Jordan Archer was keeping goal for the visitors. His blatant push when defending a corner went unpunished, but a second half blunder proved quite costly for him and his team. Archer spilt a routine cross from Myles Weston, then brought down Barry Corr - the main beneficiary of the rebound in the box. The referee gave the penalty and sent Archer for an early bath. Corr (no relation to the Irish band) stepped up and smashed the spot kick into the top corner.

It was a tough baptism of fire for substitute 'keeper Matt Duke, who was soon picking the ball out of the net for a second time. Southend made the extra man count and Weston laid the ball off for Worrall to sweep in a second. The flat cap wearing Brown punched the air in delight on the sidelines. Sadly, he didn't sing to the fans at the end of the game like he did back in the day at Hull City.

Northampton fans were smarting, but refused to be silenced. Knowing they were beaten didn't stop them looking forward to upcoming away trips and breaking into a chant of "stand up if you're going to Tranmere." On the pitch, Southend were worthy winners. The Fish House was thriving on return business by departing football folk. I didn't indulge for a second time, having had my fill of stodge and soccer for the day.

Best chant: "We're going to score in a minute." Two goals and a man down didn't dampen Northampton spirits. They're clearly glass half full fans.
Match ticket: £14 thanks to my student card. The club offered a £2 saving on most tickets in advance. A walk-up adult ticket would have cost £21.
Match programme: £3. From quizzes, to players taking on fans in Q & A's and picking their favourite five-a-side teams, there was also an entertaining review of Southend's trip to Tranmere. Up there as one of the better programmes picked up so far.
Cost of food: £2.70 for a minced beef and onion pie.
Food rating: 2/5. Substandard meat and nothing to get your teeth into. My recommendation is to stock up at the Fish House instead.

Final Score
Southend United 2 (Corr 69 pen, Worrall 79)
Northampton Town 0
Attendance: 5,500

Getting to know Oxford United
Mark - YellowsForum
www.yellowsforum.co.uk
Twitter @yellowsforum

Best players to pull on an Oxford shirt?
The best players to wear an Oxford shirt to me are Matt Elliott, Dean Windlass, Paul Moody and local lad Joey Beachaump.

Best away support at the Kassam Stadium in recent memory?
This season probably Pompey. They're just down the road, a big club.

Best thing about the Kassam Stadium?
Probably the exit! Only joking, the views of the pitch are great, no restricted viewing, or at least very little.

Worst grounds you've visited?
I've been to some pretty bad grounds in the Conference, the worst being Luton!

Best place to sit/stand at the Kassam Stadium?
Towards the middle/top of the East Stand. It's where most singers are so you get the best atmosphere there.

Best place to get a pre-match drink?
The past two seasons has lost a match day spark. We had a pub called The Priory, just a five minute walk to the stadium. It served home and away fans so you could mingle together. But Mr Kassam's rent forced the landlord out, and it's now sitting empty in a horrible state for a listed building. We have a Bowlplex and Holiday Inn bar, but they are just not the same.

Famous Oxford fans?
Just recently it was confirmed that Tim Henman is a fan. Jim Rosenthal and Timmy Mallett are probably the only other famous fans we have.

Quirky fact time?
Oxford United v Sunderland was the first ever pay-per-view football game in the UK. It ended 0-0!

GOALS, MASCOTS & MALLETS

Game #36: FA Cup Second Round - Saturday 6th December 2014
OXFORD UNITED vs Tranmere Rovers - The Kassam Stadium

FA Cup weekend always throws up some interesting ties. For Oxford and Tranmere, both stuck at the wrong end of League Two, it was a welcome break to engage in a good old fashioned cup tussle. The two teams were no strangers to each other, due to it being just over a month since Oxford strolled to a 2-0 victory in the league, which left Tranmere bottom and handed new boss Micky Adams a real baptism of fire. Credit where it's due, both clubs put together an attractive package for the fans. Tranmere offered a £10 coach and £10 ticket deal, so it came as no surprise to see eight coaches waiting at Prenton Park when I rocked up for the early morning roll call.

Having toured with Tranmere back at the start of the season, I have nothing but good things to say about the volunteers who run the trips. It was a cold morning, but no-one was left outside for long. Envelopes containing coach and ticket stubs were duly handed out and we were soon on our way for the four and a half hour journey south. Based in the middle of the coach, I waited with baited breath to see who would be the first to assume control of the DVD player. That's the only drawback with coach trips - it's one taste for all or tough. Luckily enough, 'John Bishop's 2011 Live Tour' garnered a thumbs up and saw us through to the first service stop. I didn't appreciate the punchline when the comedy was replaced by Ben Affleck and the 'Sum of all Fears.' My opinion was summed up when I reached for the iPod and stole some sleep.

The Kassam Stadium is located inside a mini retail park. Dave Whelan has branched out from Wigan and installed a DW Fitness suite inside the complex. The Oxford fans were also starting to arrive and many headed across to the bowling alley to get a pre-match pint. Sadly, the small bar was struggling to satisfy the large demand of thirsty matchday drinkers, so I turned my attention to the arcades. A decision I would come to regret. Unable to resist the lure of the basketball throwing machine, I stepped up, but ended up being more like Shaquille O'Neal than Kobe Bryant. I threw up so many bricks that two kids passing by shook their heads at the pitiful score I had racked up. Nursing a dead shoulder and wounded pride, I tucked tail and headed towards the ground to seek out a programme seller.

Talking of tails, I bumped into club mascot Olly the Ox. A rather gruff voice from inside the suit obliged my request for a selfie, proving there's absolutely nothing wrong for two grown men to share a five second pose. At that moment, I could hear a voice proclaiming "we're going to win the cup, this is our year." Initially blinded by the guy's bright jacket, it turned out to be none other than Timmy Mallett. To those of you not born in the 80s, Mr Mallett was a staple of any youngster's Saturday morning television, hosting a quick fire gameshow in which the loser would get hit over the head with an inflatable rubber mallet. Good wholesome fun all around. Before I could remark how utterly brilliant (cheap catchphrase alert) it was to see him, Timmy had disappeared through the doors into the VIP section. He had with him a homemade silver replica of the FA Cup which would have made Neil Buchanan and the makers of Art Attack very proud. Sadly, Timmy was without his customary mallet. The original was stolen during a live appearance back in 2002.

The U's share their ground with London Welsh Rugby club and have been at the Kassam since 2001. Ex-owner Firoz Kassam still rents the stadium to the club. The capacity is 12,500 all-seated, although it only has three stands to accommodate a car park and a very low fence behind one of the goals. For the plush cars that had already parked in line with the fence, they were doing so at their own risk. I'd be surprised if a few windscreens hadn't been smashed from stray balls kicked in anger over the years. There were a few grumbles from the away fans about the lack of food available before the game, with supply barely meeting the demand. Premium pies had sold out and fans weren't happy at forking out £4 for a bottle of beer which "tasted like fruit juice."

It's fair to say that Oxford were still finding their feet, following a summer of change in the boardroom and on the bench. Boss Michael Appleton had used the loan system to his advantage by bringing in Peterborough United forward Tyrone Barnett and throwing him straight into the mix.

Surprisingly, it was Tranmere who broke the deadlock. Cole Stockton's opener had a hint of good fortune to it. The forward used gut instinct to flick in a Shamir Fenelon cross. Tranmere fans had suffered more than most thus far, so they took great delight in milking their moment in the sun. Chants of "how shit must you be, we're winning away," rung out around the ground. The sight of male cheerleaders bouncing up and down almost caused me to regurgitate my pre-match cheese and onion slice. Pigtails and skirts didn't mix with beards, tattoos and man boobs.

Oxford's Danny Hylton made a pitch to any Hollywood directors in the crowd when he went down clutching his face from minimal contact. Moments later, Fenelon shook off his marker and ran clear. He had enough time for a shower and a shave, as goalkeeper Ryan Clarke desperately ran out to try and close the angle. With the ball bouncing, Fenelon smashed it over when a simple low shot or lob would have sufficed. It was a pivotal moment and the Tranmere fans knew it. Oxford had been given a get out of jail card and re-emerged from the break a completely different team.

All of a sudden, the same travelling fans who had been singing the Ian Goodison version of the twelve days of Christmas, probably wished that the 42-year-old Jamaican defender was out on the pitch helping them out. The hosts turned the game on its head, with Barnett netting twice inside five minutes. The lanky forward used his trusty barnet to head in from a corner, before showing fancy footwork to pirouette past Marcus Holness and beat Owain Fon Williams with a low finish.

An offside flag came to Tranmere's rescue when Hylton's tap in was disallowed for offside. Just when it looked like the smart money would be on Oxford to win, veteran substitute Jason Koumas rolled back the years with a fine solo run and well placed curling effort to salvage a draw. 'Super Jase' had got his side out of jail and earned a replay at Prenton Park. Oxford's own substitute Alfie Potter almost created a winner when he put the ball on a plate for Barnett, but the striker was denied his hat-trick by a diving Williams save.

A blustery wind had crept into the stadium during the second half. Guess who had forgotten to take a hat and gloves? Fortunately, the coaches were parked just around the back and we made a quick exit to beat some of the traffic. Nobody expressed a desire to stop so an hour or so was shaved off the return journey. Desperate to relieve myself, the unpleasant sight of two drunks urinating in the sink greeted me back at Chester station. I managed to block the image out temporarily, although the toilet humour continued when a glamorous female busker waltzed towards me using a decorated toilet brush as a makeshift microphone. The devil in me was tempted to snatch it away and play an impromptu game of 'Mallett's Mallet,' even though it wasn't befitting of one who'd been to Oxford. The sad fact was that while she may have been dreaming of a White Christmas, I was desperate to find an edible wash basin and some soap. I made a mental note to add hand sanitizer to the festive essentials list alongside the hat and gloves.

Best chant: "Bounce bounce Yellow army." The Oxford fans.
Match ticket: £10. Prices rose by £2 for fans purchasing tickets on the day.
Match programme: £2. The Oxford media team reviewed the facilities of beaten first round opponents Grimsby Town. Friendly staff, a cramped press bench and a pitch described as "Teletubby Hill," summed things up. Oh, the fish is "exceptional" too. Coming from a seaport, that's not surprising.
Cost of food: £3.00 for a cheese and onion slice.
Food rating: 2/5. Although it was something different from the usual pie and contained plenty of cheese, it was a bit too greasy for my liking and not very filling.

Final Score
Oxford United 2 (Barnett 59, 64)
Tranmere Rovers 2 (Stockton 33, Koumas 76)
Attendance: 4,681

Getting to know Bristol City
www.thebountyhunter.bcfcnyc.com
Twitter @BountyhunterBC

Favourite memory as a Bristol City fan?

For such a non-successful club, so many to choose from! Beating Arsenal away, first game in Division One in 1976? Being the width of a goal-post from the League Cup final in 1989? Or winning at Chester in 1984 to secure promotion from Division Four? Let's say all three. Plus many more besides.

Best thing about Ashton Gate?

It still being home to the City. Always has been. Only one home for us. And not moving to Ashton Vale or another identikit bowl.

Best game you've witnessed at Ashton Gate?

Hartlepool United in the play-offs 2004 - 88th minute equaliser and 90th minute winner? Crystal Palace in the play-offs 2008 - 104th minute equaliser, 110th minute winner? Nah! Hereford at home, Freight Rover Trophy semi-final, 1986. Losing 2-0 from the first leg, 0-0 at half time, we won 3-0 by the end of extra time and a Wembley Cup final victory was ours.

Enjoyable away days?

Wembley, Fleetwood, Weymouth (pre-season friendly in 1990.) Any really. We're easy-come-easy-go. If a club owns its own place and has not bought it for £1, we don't mind.

Which club serves the nicest pies?

Blackburn in December 1990 had splendid pies and at ridiculously low prices, 25p or some such. We're not big pie-eaters. If there is good cider, we're happy.

Famous Bristol City fans?

The near 5000 who turned up each week in 1982/83 at our lowest point and prevented us from ever being evicted. Unlike some.

Quirky fact time?

There's only one team in Bristol.

Name your Bristol City Dream Team?

Jan Moller
Gerry Sweeney
Louis Carey
Billy 'Fatty' Wedlock
Geoff Merrick
Micky Bell
Howard Pritchard
Rob Newman
Alan Walsh
Bob Taylor
John Atyeo

Yes 5-3-2: we're playing for a draw!

Game #37: FA Cup Second Round - Sunday 7th December 2014
BRISTOL CITY vs AFC Telford United - Ashton Gate

Re-visiting the past can be a double-edged sword. Sometimes, a trip down memory lane proves to be fruitful, yet at the same time can also leave you with a horrible taste in the mouth after. These statements sum up my feelings on Bristol perfectly. My short affiliation with the Robins began several years ago when I befriended Ben Fotheringham, aka 'the Foth,'- a Bristol City fan who ventured to Chester on a gap year. We kept in touch and I made a first visit to Ashton Gate with him at the beginning of last season.

On that summer's day, Wolves - the eventual champions were in town. While the away side ran out 2-1 winners, the fan experience stayed with me. The Bristolians were in a buoyant and bullish mood having just been drawn against fierce city rivals Bristol Rovers in the Johnstone's Paint Trophy. Chants of "we've got a bye in the JPT," and "stand up if you hate the Gas," dominated the afternoon.

Gashead is the term given to a Bristol Rovers fan. The name stems from the fact that Rovers' old ground, the Eastville Stadium, was next to a gasworks and the deep smell of the gas often wafted across the pitch during matches. In short, this led to the team becoming known as the Gas and the fans as Gasheads.

It was almost as if the Wolves game had been discarded, with fans licking their lips in anticipation of a first meeting in six years against their neighbours. I wasn't in town long enough to witness the frenetic derby experience, but City ended up claiming bragging rights by winning the game 2-1. While post-match celebrations spilt over into a nasty pitch invasion and took some of the gloss off the victory, the earlier West Country experience stayed with me and I was looking forward to re-connecting with some of the non-violent banter on my next visit.

Fast forward a year and everything had changed. The Robins were now sitting pretty perched on top of the League One tree, while bitter rivals Rovers had suffered the indignity of being relegated from League Two on the final day of last season and dropping out of the Football League altogether. Much like Rangers and Celtic, the rivalry had somewhat cooled due to the out of sight out of mind complex. I had enthusiastically booked train and match tickets in advance, only to be informed by Ben that he was unable to meet up due to work commitments. I shook the disappointment off, taking consolation from the fact that it'd just be me having a sing-song with the fans.

City's opponents Telford were sharing residency with Rovers in football's fifth tier, although they were rooted to the bottom and relegation seemed inevitable. Saddled with a stigma of being a "yo-yo club," boss Liam Watson revealed this cup game was a distraction and his real focus was on a subsequent league game with Welling United.

I got the feeling that both clubs saw this game as a bit of a nuisance, yet tried to discard that feeling during a stressful journey into the West Country. It came as no surprise when the Sunday train schedule tried to throw a few spanners in the works. Delays at Stafford and Wolverhampton meant that I'd be cutting it fine to make my connection to Bristol at Birmingham New Street. I politely asked the conductor to check which platform I needed to get to. He flashed a politician's smile and promised to get back to me. He didn't - jerk. To those of you I might have brushed past or caught with my bag straps, I apologise. Blame the idiotic train conductor. A quick scan of the departures board led me to the safe haven of the correct platform with around three minutes to spare.

Ashton Gate is a few miles from the train station. There was less than an hour to kick-off when I alighted at Temple Meads, so walking was out of the question. A bus driver said I'd be best to get a taxi, so I thanked him for his honesty and joined the queue outside the station. Three boozed up Telford fans were getting annoyed at the slow progress of the queue. The negative vibes they were giving off convinced me that it wouldn't be wise to suggest a car share, so I made them wait. I informed the driver of my destination, yet he still asked if there was any football on. Finally, the Indian driver cottoned on to a host of parked cars and suddenly started talking about matchday traffic. I couldn't get out of the cab quick enough and declined the offer of a lift home. Besides, £8 was an extortionate price to pay for a five minute journey. Blue cabs charging black cab prices.

City's home was missing a side to it. The East Stand (which normally houses away fans) had been demolished as the first part of a major redevelopment plan to spruce up all areas of the ground and bring it up to 27,000 capacity. I walked around to hear a loud contingent of Telford fans proudly singing "oh when the whites go marching in." Thankfully, the travelling party got a different memo to their manager and were rightly treating the game as a priority. They had been put up in the Atyeo Stand behind the goal, which was where I had been situated the year before.

Matchday ambassadors were dotted around the car park and proved to be both friendly and helpful. Around these parts the locals sure liked to roll their R's when they spoke. Ben text to say the accent was endearing when you get used to it. I kept on waiting for Worzel Gummidge to come out of the woodwork.

The atmosphere inside was relaxed although far from being a sellout. An elderly couple were sat in my seat having a chat to a group of friends. They appreciated me not kicking up a fuss, plus I didn't want to be rude and interrupt their catch up. There were plenty of seats close by that were going spare and the move didn't affect my viewing pleasure. I'd gone for a normal spec of close to the halfway line. Both dugouts were close and an exit was directly behind me. Food stalls, toilets and a quick getaway were all easily accessible.

Telford got off to an auspicious start when Rod McDonald comically bungled a throw-in by letting the ball slip out of his hands. However, the away side soon settled into a groove and gave as good as they got. Bristol's Jay Emmanuel Thomas seemed content in trying to hit the digger which now occupied the space that was the former East Stand. He failed on more than one occasion. Bristol boss Steve Cotterill named a strong side, yet it took them a long time to move up the gears. 71 league places separated the two teams coming in, although you wouldn't have noticed given the way the game panned out.

There was next to no noise coming from the home fans. A chorus of "shall we sing a song for you," played out from the travelling band. I wished they would. Even a tongue in cheek taunt at endorsing Bristol Rovers failed to wake the City fans from their afternoon nap. Their first bit of activity came just before half time when a large number made a beeline for the concession stand. With pies on their mind, the City faithful were asked if there was a fire drill by the Telford fans. Even the substitutes took a bit of stick. A barbed taunt of "you've only played four times," was aimed at the trio of reserves nonchalantly jogging up and down the touchline.

Jonathan Hedge performed admirably between the sticks for Telford, especially as he was considered the club's stand-in goalkeeper. Equally, Frank Fielding was made to earn his wages in the Bristol goal. Cotterill introduced Luke Freeman onto the field and the pacey winger's darting run into the box almost produced a goal that his side didn't deserve. Fielding kept out an Andy Todd volley late on, as the fourth official indicated six minutes of added on time. City's prolific striker Kieran Agard looked to have left his shooting boots in the changing room when he fluffed a chance on the line. He broke Telford's hearts two minutes into added time, meeting Freeman's corner to knock the ball over the line at the back post. Remarkably, there was still time for one final chance, but Sam Smith headed straight at Fielding to deny Telford the replay they richly deserved.

The Bristol faithful finally found their voice. The words "we only sing when we're winning," were like the salty thumb being jammed into a Telford eye which was all too familiar with the pain of defeat. The City fans demanded a wave from Cotterill. Feeling his oats, he milked the moment for all it was worth, motioning with his hand for the fans to chant louder. He finally gave his supporters what they wanted, even though his team had turned in a far from vintage performance.

A lot of the surrounding roads around the stadium were closed after the game, due to a fireworks display to celebrate 150 years of the Clifton Suspension Bridge being open. Ben's absence and the fact that I was booked on a late train going home meant I had a few hours to spare. The lack of a Bristol City shirt refused me entry into the 'Rising Sun' pub. A sign outside stated "home fans only, proof required." There must have been something in the air that day. When the sun went down it seemed like the oddbods came out to play.

Passing through the city centre, a woman was sat down bawling her eyes out hysterically and cursing life in general with plenty of colourful language. She was scaring passers-by and was oblivious to the fact that impressionable young kids could hear her foul mouth. She seemed a few sandwiches short of a picnic to put it nicely. Good job she hadn't attended the game. That really would have sent her off at the deep end. A few yards away, a fruitcake of the male variety was having a conversation with his imaginary friend. I retreated into the safety of Pizza Hut. Being sat in the middle of a girl's birthday party was definitely the lesser of two evils.

Fireworks from afar illuminated the skyline as I walked off my meal towards the station. The Sunday schedule made another unwelcome visit when I saw that my pre-booked train home was delayed, which would impact a planned connection at Birmingham. Thanks to an understanding train manager, I was permitted entry onto an earlier train which kept me on track.

In a cruel twist of fate, Watson was sacked a week after this game. The Liverpudlian had led his side back into the Conference less than eight months earlier, but in a results orientated atmosphere he fell on his sword. Try and remember the good times Liam. I'll take some of my own advice and do the same with Bristol.

Best chant: "How shit must you be, we're only part time." Telford fans politely reminding Bristol about the gulf in class.
Match ticket: £12. Around half the price of a league fixture.
Match programme: £2. A paltry 16 pages from cover to cover. The bulk of it contained previous match photographs and adverts. There was a small write-up on the away side and a Telford themed wordsearch for fans to do on the journey home. A waste of money and paper.
Cost of food: £3.00 for a pie.
Food rating: 3/5. The catering staff outperformed the playing staff. Perfectly edible steak pie.

Final Score
Bristol City 1 (Agard 90+ 2)
AFC Telford United 0
Attendance: 6,678

Getting to know Tranmere Rovers
Warwick Jarvis - Work colleague and season ticket holder

How long have you been a Tranmere fan?
I've been a Tranmere fan since the age of four, which is the earliest I can remember a game. Dad wouldn't have it any other way.

Best game you've witnessed at Prenton Park?
Got to be the 4-3 win against Southampton in the FA Cup (20th February 2001.) 3-0 down at half time. John Aldridge contemplating suicide live on the pitch, three fans leaving to go for a takeaway 'cause they'd seen enough,' then the comeback of all comebacks. Stuart Barlow scoring the winner, spinning his shirt and Aldo coming over after the game to salute the Borough Road (Johnny King Stand) for their support. It was all the drama of a person's life encapsulated in 90 minutes of football. The hope, bitterness, despair, elation, disgust, pride, and disbelief that any outcome is possible even when there is seemingly no hope of success. I came out of that game thinking I could take on the world. It took me two days to come down off the biggest high I've ever had in football. I take pride that the tattoo on my arm is a Tranmere badge.

Best/worst players to pull on a Tranmere shirt?
Best players: Aldo, Ian Muir (especially Ian Muir), Johnny Morrissey, Clint Hill (because he really did mean it when he kissed the badge), Gareth Roberts. Even at the age of 49, playing in the final of the Mersey Masters against Bolton (and it couldn't get any better than that 'cause we hate Bolton) when that ball came over his shoulder with 30 seconds to go, you knew Ian Muir was going to volley it into the top corner. It was absolutely certain and that's exactly what he did, only Ian Muir was that natural, more so even than Aldo, and I was right behind the goal in the Echo Arena when he did it. Again, I remember hugging complete strangers at James Street train station on the way home, absolutely bladdered!

Worst players: There's been so many. Godwin Antwi - worst player I have ever seen bar none. Also, Kevin Gray (when the manager used him as a water boy after one of his poorer performances even by his low standards, we laughed for a good 20 minutes.)

Best thing about Prenton Park?
The atmosphere when it's full is special. It's a real football atmosphere from the 70's. Then there's the Johnny King statue. When the Borough Road held up his name using cards this year, he saluted us from the Directors Box. It brought a real tear to my eye. And I'm a cold mothertrucker!

Enjoyable away days?
Blackburn is the only ground I've been to with carpeted floor inside the away refreshment area. Everton, just because the only time we've played there we malleted them 3-0 in the FA Cup. Always like to go to Southend. If the weather's nice you can walk to the beach and have proper seaside fish and chips.

Worst grounds you've visited?
Oldham, which is now only half a ground, Rotherham's old ground (Millmoor) was a typical run down northern shithole of the highest proportion. Even a beautiful summer's day would make no difference to it or the town. It made Birkenhead look like Santiago. Doncaster's old ground (Belle Vue) was basically a tip and I mean a tip. Rubble everywhere!

Best place to sit/stand at Prenton Park?
Best place to sit is the Johnny King - the purists stand and my stand!

Which club serves the nicest pies?
Hull City by a mile. Rugby ground you see plus 15 different types of beverage and guest ales. I kid you not.

Famous Tranmere fans?

Elvis Costello and David Dimbleby (so they say)

Quirky fact time?

All Rovers fans who know their history will throw this one out. 1935 Boxing Day, Rovers beat Oldham 13-4 in a league game. The aggregate goal total is still a league record. "Bunny" Bell scored nine in that game, hence why the club bar is called the Bunny Bell.

Name your Tranmere Dream Team?

GK: Steve Simonsen - Before he went to Everton, he was world class. Had everything, England U21, then Everton ruined him.

LB: Gareth Roberts - Tranmere through and through.

CB: Clint Hill - Because he was absolutely nails.

CB: Dave Higgins - Bridged the gap between young and old players.

RB: Steve Yates - Just so honest and a great player.

RW: Johnny Morrissey - There was only one!

LW: Jason Koumas - Super Jase!

CM: Kenny Irons - A midfield god.

CM: James Wallace - Before he got injured, he was the best I've ever seen at Prenton Park, and there have been a few good-uns!

CF: John Aldridge - Legend!

CF: Ian Muir - Every bit as good as Aldridge, trust me.

POPPING MY PENALTY CHERRY

Game #38: Johnstone's Paint Trophy Northern Section Semi Final - Tuesday 9th December 2014
TRANMERE ROVERS vs Walsall - Prenton Park

In all my years as a paying football punter, one thing had eluded me. A penalty shootout. Sure, I'd seen plenty on TV, but never had I bore witness to the test of nerves from the terraces, soaking up the joy, sadness, elation and dejection. A myriad of emotions which makes you want to hug or punch the person you've spent the last 120 minutes sitting next to. There had been a few close encounters so far on this journey, but I was always denied at the death.

Along with Crewe, my trip to Tranmere was as local as I was going to get with the tour. A short half hour train journey to Rock Ferry passed by in no time. A small cluster of Liverpool fans were on the same train, clinging to faint hopes of Champions League progression. However, at the other end of the Mersey Tunnel, fans in Birkenhead were dreaming of something else.....a trip to Wembley! Walsall and a two-legged final against the other northern semi-finalists were all that stood between the Super Whites and a trip to the London Theatre of Dreams to contest the Johnstone's Paint Trophy final. Despite their struggle in League Two, it came as no surprise to see Tranmere thriving in a cup competition. The club were famous for their cup upsets in the late 90s - early 00s. Just ask Southampton (surrendered a 3-0 lead to lose 4-3) or Everton (a famous 3-0 victory at Goodison Park.)

Premier League neighbours Liverpool and Everton unsurprisingly rule the footballing roost in these parts and hold the lion's share of the Merseyside fanbase to boot. Tranmere are very much the little brother on the outside looking in. The club enjoyed higher attendances when they were permitted to play regular Friday night games, welcoming the 'plastic' scouse fans with open arms. These pre-weekend rendezvous still occur, but sadly they're few and far between.

From Rock Ferry, it's a straightforward 20-25 minute walk to Prenton Park. As I walked past the statue of former manager Johnny King at the gates, a small group of youths thought it'd be polite to give the opposition fans a friendly Wirral welcome. Chants of "Super White Army," were meant to be intimidating, but the group of older Walsall fans' nonchalant reaction was almost as cold as the weather. They completely blanked them and carried on with their grown up conversation.

A temporary portakabin was operating ticket sales on the night. If ever I needed an endorsement for matchday food, I was about to find it. I caught the portly concession server red handed with a mouthful of pie. If the pre-game stodge was good enough for him then it was certainly edible enough for me. For those seeking an alternative snack, the 'Villa Venezia' - a fine looking Italian establishment lies across the road, while there is also a Flaming Grill next to the stadium. Both are perfectly viable options and no doubt just as healthy.

Three of the four sides of the ground were operational on the night. I was hoping nobody was watching when I somehow managed to trip over going up the stairs. No such luck. Two elderly people saw the whole thing and were having a good chuckle. A few of the seats higher up in the stands could either do with replacing or being given a lick of paint. Other than that Prenton Park is a perfectly acceptable ground. There was ample space between the seats which also meant plenty of legroom. Still, that didn't deter a steaming drunk from sitting directly next to me. He even joked that I had "the whole stadium," to choose from. The fumes from his breath almost made my eyes water. When he started wittering on about the logistics of the JPT, I gave up and moved to where a group of sane people were.

Despite Walsall being a division higher, Tranmere weren't intimidated and neither were their fans. To stop a ball going out for a throw, a Tranmere fan simply stuck his head out and the ball bounced wickedly off his bald bonce and back into play. The youngster was taken aback - quite literally in his attempt to show off in front of his mates. Walsall certainly didn't know what hit them when Tranmere struck twice before half time. Max Power - Rovers' jewel in the crown underlined his importance to the side when he curled the ball in from the edge of the box.

Power then turned provider for Kayode Odejayi to head in from the midfielder's corner. The gangly forward was getting caught offside more than Filippo Inzaghi used to, but put his size to good use for once.

Chants of "we're going to Wembley," filled the air as Tranmere fans were literally singing in the rain. A vicious downpour showed no sign of letting up as the second half kicked off. Power looked to have sewn the game up when he netted a second. Odejayi had slipped the ball through, but an offside flag was never far away and it came to Walsall's rescue, who then promptly halved their deficit. Substitute Anthony Forde cut inside the penalty box and netted with a low finish. All of a sudden, the Walsall fans cleared the frog from their collective throats and stopped plotting their early trip home.

George Donnelly came on for Tranmere and immediately sent a Walsall player into the dugout with a flying tackle. The bad weather certainly played a part, although that didn't stop a Rovers fan from yelling out "don't get sent off this time dickhead." The youngster was spared, but is no stranger to violent conduct, having been sent off a month prior for kicking out at an opponent during a 1-0 FA Cup victory over Bristol Rovers.

Ten minutes from time, Walsall's momentum brought them level. Michael Cain drilled home an unstoppable effort from 25 yards. Even though I was in the home end, I had to applaud the goal. Credit where it's due, it was a peach of a shot and there was nothing Owain Fon Williams could do in the Tranmere goal to stop it. An all too familiar restlessness started to spread around Prenton Park. While the fans fidgeted and twitched, the goal actually galvanised Tranmere, who finished the game stronger. The hosts saw an effort cleared off the line, before Odejayi actually found the net. Naturally, because it was him, it was disallowed for offside. Substitute Marc Laird was almost the hero, only to get his angles wrong when he rolled an effort the wrong side of the post. The referee blew for time - no not extra time, as the JPT doesn't believe in it. I was finally about to become acquainted with the live lottery from 12 yards.

Walsall fans won the toss and were the main beneficiaries of getting up close with the willing kickers. Tranmere gained an early advantage when Walsall's Ashley Grimes saw his effort saved, only to lose their nerve at the final hurdle. Liam Ridehalgh had the chance to send Rovers through, but went for power instead of precision and gave the crossbar a good smack. It went down to sudden death. Walsall shotstopper Richard O'Donnell saved from Laird and Paul Downing kept his cool to send the Saddlers through.

The Wembley chants started up again, except this time it came from the Walsall fans. Twisting the knife, they serenaded the Tranmere fans out of the ground. Sadly, the closest they would be getting to Wembley now was the aptly named refreshment stall named after England's home. On the walk back to the station, an exasperated kid was remonstrating to his friend about how they had it won. And people still say that the JPT doesn't matter? Young Wayne (I didn't know his actual name) and his friend would certainly disagree. Disheartened Liverpool fans were slumped across the window on the train home. It had been a bad night all round on Merseyside. However, on the flip side, I got to see four goals and a shootout at a knockdown price. I was happy with my lot.

Best chant: "That lad must have been born offside." Me towards the hapless Odejayi.
Match ticket: £12. Dearest price I've paid for a JPT game. The competition still provides some of the best entertainment, so it's always money well spent.
Match programme: £2. "Where there is faith, there is light and strength," is a deep meaning title for a matchday magazine. Contained a flurry of Christmas gift ideas and a much better wordsearch than Bristol City's programme.
Cost of food: £2.50 for a pie or £4 for a whopper burger.
Food rating: 3/5. "Best steak pie this side of the Mersey," according to the seller. He was probably right. A nice little gravy boat with just enough chunky meat thrown in.

Final Score
Tranmere Rovers 2 (Power 37, Odejayi 43)
Walsall 2 (Forde 63, Cain 80)
(Walsall won 5-4 on penalties)
Attendance: 2,355

Getting to know Mansfield Town
Amberheart and Ryan Brooks
www.stagsnet.net

Favourite memory as a Mansfield fan?
Ryan: Hereford away 2012/13 season, 30 seconds away from chucking promotion away before that special goal from Matt Green.
Amberheart: Attaining promotion to Division One (Championship) in 1977/78.

Best thing about Field Mill?
Amberheart: Field Mill is the oldest Football League ground in the world (1861) officially, 1850 unofficially.
Ryan: The location. Near to many pubs. Ideal for when we start losing.

Best game you've witnessed at Field Mill?
Ryan: Mansfield vs Liverpool. To see the team you've seen through all the bad times go up against one of the best teams in the world, and give them a game is such a good feeling.

Worst grounds you've visited?
Ryan: In the conference days, Barrow and Alfreton are up there. Overall, Worksop Town in a pre season friendly. Losing 4-0 didn't help.

Best/worst players to pull on a Mansfield shirt?
Ryan: Best - Liam Lawrence, Lee Williamson and Bobby Hassell. Worst: Fraser McLachlan and Jason White take some beating.

Famous Mansfield fans?
Ryan: Alvin Stardust.
Amberheart: Jason Statham was a Stags fan as a young lad, his family is still local.

Which club serves the nicest pies?
Amberheart: Bury for best pies, while Plymouth do some excellent pasties.

Quirky fact time?
Amberheart: Mansfield were the first club to use floodlights in a competitive match in 1930.

MURRAY MANIA SWEEPS MANSFIELD

Game #39: League Two - Saturday 13th December 2014
MANSFIELD TOWN vs Cheltenham Town - One Call Stadium (Field Mill)

The morning after the work Christmas meal. You know the drill. A feeble excuse of "I'll only stay out for one," rung true. Well, to an extent. It was more like stay out until you're the only one left. Waking up with a sore head, I gingerly set off to Nottinghamshire to see the Stags of Mansfield Town. Contrary to belief, the club's nickname isn't an ode to a group of drunken men about to be wed, rather it's a recognition of the small deer that reside in nearby Sherwood Forest.

Mansfield had shuffled their pack since we last met on the road at Sheffield United back in August. Player turned manager Adam Murray replaced former boss Paul Cox in the dugout. This just so happened to be Murray's first game since being given the job on a permanent basis. To say the new guy got the red carpet treatment would be an understatement. Murray's face was plastered on enough pages of the matchday programme, (including a centrefold) that it would make a Kardashian jealous. Speaking of eye candy, a lovely lass posing in a Mansfield top greeted readers on the first page of the matchday magazine. Taking part in the "Stags' Selfie" will no doubt have warmed the hearts of many a red blooded male on a bitterly cold afternoon. It's not a bad way to start a programme that's for sure.

Ahead of my visit, Mansfield had picked up just one league win in ten games. Murray was forthright in his approach to matters on the pitch. "This will take time," he said. "The main thing now is to pick up points and along the way, we will improve the style." That style in question is "free-flowing, within a disciplined structure."

With Murray's appointment creating a buzz around the club, I'd like to say this played a part in me deciding where to spend my Saturday. Honestly though, my decision was purely financial. With Christmas approaching and presents to buy, I was shopping around for a cut-price ticket. Mansfield were doing a fantastic pre-sale offer for three upcoming games. The club had cut the price of online tickets to £7 and extended the offer to walk-up customers up until 5pm the day before the game. Needless to say, their generous offer trumped everyone else's.

The journey wasn't pleasant. Crewe to Derby ranks as one of the worst train trips that there is. A painstaking 80 minutes on a slow single carriage journey did little to ease a throbbing drink induced headache. Short connections at Derby and Nottingham were more bearable and the One Call Stadium came into view as the train pulled in to Mansfield. Black ice was starting to settle on pavements and surrounding roads, so it was a delicate walk to the stadium. I'd never skated before and didn't particularly want to start here. Fortunately, the ground is just a couple of minutes from the station. Under a bridge, across a road and you're basically there. The neighbouring retail park provides ample space for car parking too.

The One Call may be the name of the stadium, but football isn't the only thing on offer. The club were advertising a Sunday carvery for £5.99 and plugging their own comedy club called 'Hoofers.' They even had a ticket tout. Yes, you read that correctly. A scalper in League Two. Now I'd seen it all. A shifty looking guy leaning against a temporary office booth offered to sort me out with a ticket. I simply pointed to the ticket office and its modest queue of four and politely declined the offer. Besides, I doubt he could have competed with the knock-down prices anyway.

Upon entering through the swish electrical scanners, the catering staff were championing the fact that hot chocolate was reduced to clear at 50p. Was I at a football game or a closing down sale? A concerned mother viably asked whether it was still in date. A jovial reassurance was given, which seemed to satisfy her curiosity enough to make a purchase. Looking beyond the choco milks, I saw that chips had been temporarily scratched off the menu. Pie and mushy peas seemed to be what the cool kids were getting. Several Dads and lads went past with their mountain of green sludge. I didn't bow to peer pressure and stuck with a simple pie.

Since winning promotion back into the Football League from the Conference in summer 2013, Mansfield dutifully revamped parts of the ground. New dressing rooms, fencing and a lick of paint to the floodlights have all been carried out. However, the ground is only accessible to fans on three of its four sides. The Bishop Street Stand - which only runs half the length of the pitch remains out of bounds due to safety concerns. A slew of advertisers are taking advantage of the space, so the club are still making some money.

The players came out to little fanfare. I'd detected the sound of a drum during the warm-ups, but the operator was largely missing in action when the game got underway. I got the feeling that I wasn't the only one who'd been out the night before. The atmosphere was a little bit subdued to say the least and a far cry from the one which the travelling Stags had taken to Sheffield back at the start of the season. Junior Brown was making his home debut after joining on loan from Oxford United. The tiny winger complete with afro perm could have been mistaken for soul singer James Brown, although his poise and ball control suggested Murray had brought the right man to the club. Effortlessly trapping a difficult pass with your first touch is a good way to ingratiate yourself to a new set of fans, as Brown quickly demonstrated. An obnoxious girl sitting a few seats beside me let out an ear screeching roar of "come on you yellows," before standing up and unwittingly exposing her backside. I couldn't believe the bare-faced cheek of it! Clearly, I had seen much more of Mansfield than I had bargained for. Good job my pie had long been digested, otherwise a different shade of yellow would almost certainly have made an appearance.

Cheltenham, like Mansfield had also recently changed their manager. Paul Buckle had been in the job a matter of weeks. Naturally, he was still finding his feet and getting to know his players. Both teams set their stall out not to lose, so in hindsight, it was no surprise that the game finished even. The first half was notable for how many balls had gone into the guttering above the Bishop Stand (two) or stuck in a tree outside the ground (one) Murray kept his substitutes on their toes by making them work out on exercise bikes just by the touchline.

On the pitch, Mansfield's Fergus Bell was mercilessly hacked down by Cheltenham captain Matt Taylor. Considering Bell was clear on goal and Taylor was the last man, a sending off seemed inevitable. However, the referee handed Taylor an early Christmas present in the shape of a reprieve plus a yellow card. Kane Ferdinand had two good chances for the visitors on the stroke of half time. Luke Waterfall's desperate goalline clearance was reminiscent of Kane's cousin Rio in his prime. Kane then channelled the shooting abilities of his elder cousin Les, with a rasping drive which had to be plucked out of the air by Mansfield goalkeeper Dimitar Evtimov.

The game was rescued from the doldrums thanks to two outstanding second half goals. Vadaine Oliver opened the scoring for the hosts with an audacious half volley from 30 yards. The on loan Crewe Alexandra forward was the recipient of a lucky bounce, before turning his marker and looping the ball over Trevor Carson. Just as the fat lady next to me was warming up her voice again, Cheltenham found a late leveller. Substitute Zack Kotwica chested the ball down outside the D and let rip with a rasping effort which flew past Evtimov into the far corner.

Both strikes had brought the entertainment factor up a few notches, which kept me from counting how many more balls flew out of the ground. A biting wind and lacklustre crowd, combined with a frequent lull in action made the game difficult to enjoy. The late equaliser certainly gave Murray plenty to ponder and rocked Mansfield, who thought they had done enough to earn the win. At 1-0, you can never rest on your laurels. Hardly a free-flowing style, but a point was something to build on at least.

My legs felt like clunky boulders thanks to the sub zero conditions. The hot tap in the toilets brought about some much needed feeling in my hands. A combination of black ice and cars leaving the stadium made the walk back to the station an even slower one. With teeth chattering like mad, I blocked out thoughts of the passing cars and the smug looks of the backseat boys keeping warm at my expense.

The journey home was a lot more tolerable thanks to a chance meeting with a work colleague at Nottingham. A couple more carriages had been put on and they even looked like they had been cleaned. The toilet brush busker was back outside Chester station wooing passers by with her feminine charms. I spurned her advances once more in favour of a few pints with friends. The lure of a beer in front of a warm fire was too good to turn down. Sadly, it will probably take a heavily discounted ticket to get me back to Mansfield again.

Best chant: "So come on cheer the boys, Mansfield make some noise. We'll go wild wild wild, we'll go wild wild wild. An ironic boast from the off-key home supporters.

Match ticket: £7. Included a crafty booking fee of £1. Normal adult match prices were £20 in advance, rising to £22 on matchdays.

Match programme: £3. Someone known only as "Stan" sponsored no fewer than eight away and five home kits. What a generous soul. Those players should give him more than a promised autograph at the end of the season.

Defender Liam Marsden took the "Stags Alphabet Challenge." Literature and driving may bore him, but Liam cooks a mean beans on toast and will even come to your party dressed as (Where's) Wally

Cost of food: £2.50 for a variety of pies or £1.50 for a sausage roll.

Food rating: 3/5. Thankfully, there was enough flavour in the beef and gravy to spare me from the splodgy green mushy peas.

Final Score
Mansfield Town 1 (Oliver 55)
Cheltenham 1 (Kotwica 87)
Attendance: 3,324

Getting to know Notts County
Stuart Brothers -Supporters Liaison Officer and Editor of the Black & White Fanzine
www.thenottsblog.co.uk

Best/worst players to pull on a Notts County shirt?

I try not to concentrate too much on the negative side of things – I can mostly find a positive spin on anything. Though if I were to start listing you our worst ever players I dare say I'd be here for quite some time. Each passing season we tend to add another four or five to the ever growing list. Quite where we find them I have no idea, but we've become very good at it! In terms of our best players, the club's all time leading goalscorer is Les Bradd, who now works at the club as an ambassador. Albert Iremonger, a goalkeeper of many years ago has made the record amount of appearances for Notts, whilst we consider Jimmy Sirrel to be our greatest ever manager having led us to the top flight.

Best away support at Meadow Lane in recent memory?

You can't really look beyond the bigger fish in League One really. Away supporters are now housed furthest away from us so it's not as if even the smaller crowds these days can bring much atmosphere our way. A few years back Sheffield Wednesday came in huge numbers, yet spent 90 minutes singing about Leeds and Sheffield United. The best sight in the last few years was Manchester City, who sold out the away seating which made for a great experience in our 1-1 draw with them. We were only ten minutes away from beating them – they went on to win the FA Cup that year and have been mostly unstoppable domestically ever since!

Best thing about Meadow Lane?

Where do I start? Meadow Lane is the great ground in England for me. Aesthetically untouched since it's the birth of the all-seater stadia in the UK. Give me four separate stands over the current trend of new build, identikit dives that plague our game. Which only leads me into your next question....

Worst grounds you've visited?

MK Dons. Even when you can look past their existence, their ground is quite simply soul destroying, everything wrong with modern grounds. It's not even pleasing on the eye such as some, just a dull, lifeless eyesore which just so happens to house a club which embodies such downsides.

Best place to sit at Meadow Lane?

Without doubt, the Kop Stand. Again, as fine an end as you'll find in the Football League and, sadly the only one that will make any noise really. Our Pavis Stand (to the right as you look out from the Kop) is a largely quiet affair housing the older heads, whilst the Family Stand at the far side adds little in terms of atmosphere, numbers or revenue.

Famous Notts County fans?

We do alright musically of late. Stadium filler Jake Bugg counts himself amongst our following, as does fast rising Saint Raymond who always gets to matches whenever he isn't gigging with Ed Sheeran!

Quirky fact time?

Our history is very much an open book sadly so it's doubtful there's anything I could share that isn't already well known. We're the oldest Football League club in the world, we share a proud history with Juventus thanks to us giving them our stripes, and we once got through five managers en route to winning the fourth division!

MAKING UP THE NUMBERS WITH THE MAGPIES

Game #40: Johnstone's Paint Trophy Northern Section Semi Final - Tuesday 16th December 2014
NOTTS COUNTY vs Preston North End - Meadow Lane

National Rail don't really like football fans. Quite a brash statement, albeit a conclusion I had come to on more than one occasion during this adventure. Asking the search engines for a return journey from Nottingham after 9:30pm on a weeknight was akin to asking for a journey to the other side of the country. Friends living in the area were unfortunately away for the night, so I was almost out of options. A fruitless search had me prepared to roll the dice on Late Rooms to try and find a diamond in the rough - or more likely a pokey bedsit, given the tight budget I was still on. However, where there's hope there's most certainly light.

Just like the goalkeeper making one final desperate punt down field, a slight adjustment of the travel requirements brought some optimism. There was a train leaving 15 minutes after the game was scheduled to end, which would get me back into Chester in the early hours. For once, I would be praying that a cup game actually didn't go to penalties. Given the closeness in proximity of Meadow Lane to Nottingham station, if I left straight after the final whistle, then I was confident of getting back all in the same night.

Ignoring the minor details of potential delays, I breathed a sigh of relief at swerving the B & B's and set about booking my journey to visit the Magpies. Travelling via Yorkshire looked a better alternative, but it was double the price of the Derby route, so I settled for my old nemesis instead for the second time in three days.

County are officially the world's oldest Football League club, having been founded way back in 1862. The club are just as famous for their links with Italian giants Juventus. Indeed it was them who supplied the Serie A side with their first set of striped black and white shirts back in 1903, sparing the Turin outfit from a life of playing in pink. County celebrated their 150th anniversary in 2012, prompting Juventus to make the lovely gesture of inviting them to be the first side to play them at their custom built Juventus Stadium. The match finished 1-1.

Having already visited Nottingham to see neighbours Forest play, it was handy to know where I was going. The weather was overcast and there weren't many fans dotted about. The walk to the stadium clocked in at ten minutes, so I put all thoughts of making the return train out of my head to focus on the game. Notts County and Preston were doing battle to earn the right to play Walsall in a two-legged regional final. The JPT had reached the business end and Wembley was in sight. Manager Shaun Derry admitted he was taking the competition seriously in his programme notes. "I'm expecting blood and thunder in a hotly-contested cup tie. I can't wait." After reading those notes, neither could I. Derry sure knew how to sell a game. Now all I needed to do was find some supporters.

Walking around the outside of the stadium, I was just in time to see the Preston fans get off the lone supporters coach. A few stares were exchanged, as they tried to figure out whose side I was on. Hey, I didn't have a beef with either side. The objective for me was simple - to watch a good game with a few goals thrown in for good measure. The ticket officer recommended sitting in the Kop behind the goal. Good choice! Faced with only a couple of supporting pillars, the view was excellent and I was well shielded from the cold. The majority of fans who bothered to turn up had the same idea as me, leaving the rest of the stadium looking quite sparse in comparison. Maybe it was the time of the year, or perhaps fans were still smarting from a 3-0 drubbing by Swindon Town a few days prior. Prices had been reduced for the game, but I suspected that the JPT still has many detractors who see the competition as a Mickey Mouse affair and waste of time.

The 265 Preston fans that made the journey were housed at the far end of the pitch in the Jimmy Sirrel Stand - named appropriately after their late manager who enjoyed three successful stints in charge of the Magpies. Although quite modern, the gable on the roof of the stand gave a tip of the hat to the club's old school roots. It brought back nice memories of Fulham, who also display a similar slogan above Craven Cottage.

Once the game commenced, the lights inside the stand were switched off. At first, I thought Michael Buffer was going to come out and shout "Let's get ready to rumble." That's certainly one way to make an entrance. Like magic, the lights came back on during half time, but promptly went back off when the second half started. It was too much of a coincidence to blame shoddy work from a spark. Perhaps the club had a high electricity bill and were looking to cut back. I don't know. The four floodlights deployed in the corners of the ground provided sufficient light. It wasn't an excuse the players could use to mask poor finishing.

Despite the low attendance, the fans still tried to create a bit of an atmosphere. All two of the Wealdstone Raider's catchphrases were shouted out every couple of minutes. It was kind of ironic boasting that "you've got no fans," given the evening's attendance.

It was nice to be reunited with ex-Manchester United players Roy Carroll and Alan Smith, both now plying their trade with the Magpies. While you can argue that the duo are on their way down the football ladder, Carroll still commands the No 1 spot in goal for Northern Ireland. He even made a mad dash from Romania to Coventry to play two games for club and country in the space of 24 hours. If that isn't dedication to the cause then I don't know what is. Carroll even kept a clean sheet in the 1-0 victory over the Sky Blues to boot.

As for Smith, well I'd always had a bit of a soft spot for ol' Smudger. A no-nonsense player with a take no prisoners attitude, the former Leeds United man leaves it all on the pitch. He deserves great kudos for battling back from a horrific leg break at Anfield and for turning down the MLS when he was between clubs in the summer. "I'd spoken about going further afield to America, but it never really appealed to me because there's no promotion or relegation and I don't like playing for fun." Stick that in your pipe and smoke it LA Galaxy! Now combining his playing duties with a coaching role, Smith was deployed as a defensive midfielder. It came as no surprise when he went straight into the referee's book early on for a typical post-watershed tackle. Some things never change. The electronic scoreboard above the empty Family Stand flashed up Smith's mugshot like he was a naughty pupil, just as it did to other players whenever they were in trouble with the referee or being substituted.

Like a recurring character on a TV show, Jermaine Beckford popped up once again. The forward had joined Preston on loan from Bolton Wanderers to try and rediscover his goalscoring mojo. On tonight's evidence, Beckford's luckless run continued. He was badly off the pace and scuffed more efforts into the ground than towards goal. That being said, Preston did take an early lead, albeit under dubious circumstances. Paul Huntington headed in from close range after a corner caused mayhem in the County box. A group of fans were insisting the ball came off Huntington's arm, but the referee stood firm. It was the right call.

County defender Haydn Hollis headed against the crossbar during a melee in the Preston box. That was as close as the home side came to equalising. Preston seemed happy to sit on their lead and contain their hosts. The dreaded long ball tactic didn't bear any fruit going forward. If anything, it made the ballboys' night busier. A wayward ball found its way into the stand, leaving the befuddled helper looking aimlessly for it. The fans briefly forgot about yelling at the referee to give the lad a helping hand. Clue: It's behind you!

A steady stream of rain was now pelting down. Suffice to say, nobody was singing come the final whistle. The match may have turned out to be a damp squib, but I saw enough of the ground and the few fans to suggest that a league game is worth coming back for. While Preston and their fans were one step closer to Wembley, I resembled a drowned rat back at the station. A quick jaunt through Alfreton and Chesterfield helped me dry out and led me to Sheffield in reasonably quick time. Level one of the journey home was complete.

Going from an East Midlands train to a Northern carriage was like going from a hotel to a tent. Cold, damp, dark and with wetrot settling on the windows, it was all aboard for a slow trek to Manchester through the Hope Valley. A girl sitting in front picked up on my sigh and concurred with a nod of her own. Thankfully, we both had ways of beating the boredom and were on similar wavelengths. Sorry to disappoint, but it's not what you were thinking. She got out her laptop, while I lost myself in a good book. Chris Evans, you loveable ginger rogue. Thank you for keeping me entertained. The fun wasn't over, oh no.

Arriving into Manchester just shy of midnight, the station was deserted and the shutters were down everywhere. Hunger pangs needed to be satisfied. A pilgrimage to an all night Spar allowed me to get something to eat. The inebriated drunk shouting at staff for refusing to serve him ended up providing some bonus entertainment. I asked him if he'd been at Meadow Lane for the game, but he ignored me and carried on ranting at the bespectacled Ron Weasley chap behind the counter.

There must have been two other people plus myself travelling on the 00:30am from Piccadilly to Chester. I was floored when the ticket checker came round. The big red scrawl he left on the ticket ended any hopes of me re-using the ticket. See, I told you National Rail had it in for us football folk. On the plus side, my midweek accumulator came in, recouping some of my travel expenses. Cashback!

Best chant: "I had a wheelbarrow, the wheel fell off, I had a wheelbarrow, the wheel fell off, County, County, County." A simple, clean-cut song which made no sense, yet was equally as endearing and catchy as the Northampton fans singing about their horse. No matter how many times the wheel falls off, the emphatic chant of "County," means the fans will come again for the next game.

Match ticket: £12.00. Adult tickets double in price in certain areas for league games.

Match programme: £2.50. Small in actual size, but contained less adverts and more readable content. Gave the JPT some love with a nice five year history piece for both sides, followed by a through the rounds journey. Stuart Brothers (who kindly helped me with the pre-piece) had a feature, describing his new role as Supporters Liaison Officer.

Cost of food: £2.70 for a chicken balti pie.

Food rating: 2/5. The pie was lukewarm and as soggy as the weather, resulting in the anticipated flavour of the spices falling flat. It ended up caving into a crumbly mess.

Final Score
Notts County 0
Preston North End 1 (Huntington 20)
Attendance: 2,058

Getting to know Crawley Town
Al & Branchy from Redz Bar Chat Podcast
Twitter @redzbarchat

Favourite memory as Crawley fans?

Our FA Cup run during 2011, which included beating Derby and Swindon and playing Manchester United. Also, the back-to-back promotions around the same period.

Thoughts on ticket prices in general?

We have always been within the league average. However they have stated to introduce family tickets which in turn provides better prices for younger fans

Best/worst players to pull on a Crawley shirt?

Matt Tubbs, Sergio Torres, Josh Simpson are among the best. Worst players are Johnny Dixon, Gavin Geddes and Fiston Manuella.

Best thing about the Checkatrade.com Stadium?

Our family friendly atmosphere, great staff, one of the best pitches in the Football League. Oh and the terraces.

Worst grounds you've visited?

Bradford City, Welling and Aldershot Town.

Enjoyable away days?

Old Trafford, Fratton Park.

Which club serves the nicest pies?

Quite simply....us!

Famous Crawley fans?

Dan Walker (BBC)

Quirky fact time?

We've never been to Wembley.

Name your Crawley Dream Team?

GK: Scott Shearer
RWB: Ben Judge
LWB: Ian Payne
CB: John Mackie
CB: Alan Lester
CM: Sergio Torres
CM: Dannie Bulham
CM: Josh Simpson
CF: Matt Tubbs
CF: Ben Abbey
CF: Tony Vessey

Game #41: League One - Saturday 20th December 2014
CRAWLEY TOWN vs Port Vale - Checkatrade.com Stadium (Broadfield Stadium)

"Stop watching the Vale Shaun. You're a curse!"
Those cutting words came courtesy of friend and Port Vale season ticket holder Mike Williams, just moments after I'd posted online the pictures of the Vale JPT defeat at Preston back in October. Did I heed the warning? Of course I didn't. Instead, I subsequently watched Port Vale win at Colchester United at the start of November. Add that to the early season victory at Doncaster Rovers and even Charlie Sheen would admit that I was winning. Wanting to see if I really could be an omen to the Valiants was enough to entice me into making a long journey south to see Crawley Town.

Not many would turn down a three course Christmas meal for £5 in a suave City Centre hotel in favour of a journey to West Sussex. Did I mention there was free booze at this hotel gig? I was placing blind faith in Crawley, while making a loose promise to make it back to Chester in time to cash in some of the drinks vouchers that were very kindly being kept back. On the subject of liquor, familiar faces and usual suspects armed with packs of Foster's joined me at the train station early doors.

London is hectic at the best of times. Add in Christmas shoppers with the usual weekend tourists and regular commuters meant there was barely space to move at Victoria station. From there, the journey to Crawley took an hour, yet felt a lot longer. Stepping outside the station, set taxi fares were fixed to a wall, but I fancied stretching my legs. A brisk walk over the train tracks, through a village and over a hill led me to a special roundabout. I say special, because there was a massive football located squarely in the middle. Behind that lay the mecca that was the home of Crawley Town. Like many, the club had sold the naming rights of their home to sponsors and jazzed it up to the uniquely ridiculous title of the "Checkatrade.com stadium." I wasn't going to forget that name anytime soon, or even the little advertising jingle they used to plug the name on the electronic scoreboard in the lead-up to kick-off.

Before Bruce Winfield became a major shareholder in 2010, Crawley endured a rough and turbulent four year period, where they came perilously close to going out of business. With new investment, the club came to prominence. Just a year later, they reached the fifth round of the FA Cup - going down to a slender 1-0 defeat at Manchester United, before securing the Conference title a few months after. Crawley survived the departure of manager Steve Evans to secure promotion to League One the very next season, which is where the club had remained. While Winfield has unfortunately passed away, the Reds have quite rightly named a stand after the man.

Both sides share a couple of milestones. Port Vale were the first visitors to the Broadfield Stadium when it opened its doors in July 1997. The ground wasn't fully completed and an experimental Crawley lineup were duly hammered 5-0. As fate would have it, Vale wound up being Crawley's first ever League opponents in August 2011. Louis Dodds prevented the Reds from picking up their first victory thanks to a stoppage time equaliser. He would come back to haunt the home side in this game too.

Appearances flattered to deceive when I entered the concourse of the car park. In contrast to the smart looking offices, the match day ticket office and club shop were made up of shipment containers situated towards the back of the car park. I unwittingly entered through the wrong turnstile and came face to face with Vinnie Jones.....or one of his close relatives. Okay, maybe I've exaggerated, but at first glance, it certainly looked like Sir Vincent. Fully expecting to be frogmarched out and told to walk the long way around the stadium, Mr Jones threw me a curveball when he escorted me around the pitch and struck up jovial conversation. A gentlemanly handshake later and he was on his way to confiscate a can of lager from a fan. Tut tut!

Sat in the East Stand was reminiscent of being back at a church fete. Scores of metal poles were barely holding a flimsy plastic cover over the top of everyone. I should have stayed over in the West Stand after all and kept quiet.

Just over half of the ground's capacity is made up of seating. The West Stand is the dominant one which stands out and has windshields on either side. Two small terraces occupy the views from behind the goals. Both of these extend around their respective corners to enclose the stadium to a degree.

Club mascot Reggie the Red came around to hand out sweets. Naturally, the kids all made a beeline for him. Most were polite, but an ungrateful few greedily dipped their own hands into the bucket then pulled at poor Reggie's tail.

Almost on cue, a group of different kids - kitted out in junior strips and high as kites from a mass sugar intake, sat directly behind me. Their poor coach had brought them along for a day out and clearly had his work cut out, trying to calm down and teach his pupils the fundamentals of the beautiful game. For some reason, little Marvin had a fixation with shouting out "epic fail," whenever a chance went begging for either side. The coach was quick to pick up on any showcases of skill, even if the kids couldn't tell a nutmeg from a Cruyff turn.

"Did you see the stepover he did there?" The excitable coach waited with baited breath. Complete silence. I was tempted to interrupt the chirping crickets and tell Marvin that was an epic fail. He wouldn't have listened though. Knowledge is often wasted on the youth.

Crawley were without suspended top scorer Izale McLeod. His absence stood out, as the Reds always looked second best going forward. The Valiants had their fair share of absentees, but the pace of winger Mark Marshall was causing the Sussex club plenty of problems.

Vale's Michael Brown can boast of a storied career. The veteran midfielder has enjoyed the high life of the Premier League and, to say he likes a tackle is a bit of an understatement. Brown is like marmite - you either love him or hate him. There is no middle ground with a man who has collected as many yellow cards as Russell Brand has notches on his bedpost. Brown was enjoying a run of matches at the heart of the midfield and opened the scoring with his second goal in as many games. A first time shot with the outside of his boot was perfectly placed into the top corner. Dodds soon made it two, collecting a return pass and drilling a low shot underneath Lewis Price, after seeing an initial shot saved. Crawley boss John Gregory was flabbergasted on the sidelines. Meanwhile, the junior gaffer sat behind me tried to get his kids to rally behind Crawley.

"Plenty of clapping and banging your feet on the floor," he enthused. That was exactly what my ears didn't need. A high pitched scream of "Crawleeeeeeey" almost drew blood from my hapless eardrums. Fans booed the Reds off the pitch at half time, with some opting to leave as early as ten minutes after the restart. The word fickle certainly came to mind.

Crawley were awarded a generous penalty on the hour when big Marvin Elliott made a meal of Michael O'Connor's high foot. It's a pet hate of mine when players opt for the lazy option and blatantly con the referee. Justice was served when Chris Neal guessed the right way to save Gavin Tomlin's spot kick.

Dany N'Guessan had two bites of the cherry to make it 3-0 and put the game to bed, but Price saved well at the striker's feet in quick succession. Crawley's Sonny Bradley - voted the club's man of the match in the previous game at Bristol City proved that no two games are ever the same. The heavily tattooed defender - who got the feature and poster treatment in the programme, admitted he has hopes of playing in the Championship one day. A terrible showing resulted in Gregory hauling him off towards the end to cap a miserable afternoon for him and the home supporters. Plenty of fans were already in the club's patented 'Redz Bar' drowning their sorrows by this point. They missed the late consolation their side managed to find. Substitute Conor Henderson connected with a fine low volley on the edge of the box to halve Crawley's deficit. The scoreline suggested the game was a close one, although nothing could be further from the truth. Vale picked up their third away victory of the season at a canter, with all three of them coming in front of my very eyes. So much for Mike's alleged curse. Not long after this defeat, Crawley's festive period was disrupted when Gregory stepped down to undergo heart surgery. I hoped for his sake that his former players had the heart for what was shaping up to be a relegation dogfight.

With the game finished, I slipped into Mo Farah mode and jogged back to the station. I'd made the decision to wear shoes and they weren't designed for running. The thought of the free bar countered the winces of pain etched onto my face, as I raced against time to make the first train out of Sussex. Amazingly, everything went to plan and I departed London on the planned 6:40pm express, arriving back into Chester just over two hours later. I discreetly slipped into the hotel just as my colleagues were finishing their main courses. The details after that remain a little hazy, although I can vaguely remember trying to get a "Super Vale away" chant going, while someone else saw fit to start dancing on the table. Honestly, you can't take some people anywhere.

Best chant: "We are going down, I said we are going down." A solitary Crawley fan after the game, who was only half joking.
Match ticket: £20. Adult prices ranged from £18 on the terraces to £24 in the West Stand.
Match programme: £3.00. Visiting supporter David Woakes correctly predicted a 2-1 away win and earns some brownie points. Defender Lanre Oyebanjo took the A to Z Q & A. His footballing idol was Brazilian defender Kafu. Never heard of him. He must have meant Cafu, a damn fine player back in the day.
Cost of food: £3.00 for a chicken balti pie, £2.50 for chips. Crawley were selling a mystery monthly pie, which turned out to be a combination of minced beef, potato and cheese.
Food rating: 4/5. The top part was the only flimsy part of this pie. Underneath lay a proper treat. Packed with large chunks of succulent chicken, combined with tangy Indian spices. Perfect to dip the chips into.

Final Score
Crawley Town 1 (Henderson 88)
Port Vale 2 (Brown 30, Dodds 42
Attendance: 2,320

Getting to know Fleetwood Town
Phil Brown Vice Chairman - Fleetwood Town FC
www.fleetwoodtownfc.com

Favourite memory as a Fleetwood fan?
Winning the League Two play-off final at Wembley Stadium in May 2014.

Best thing about Highbury?
Simply that it's our home and I've had some of my happiest days here.

Best game you've witnessed at Highbury?
Fleetwood Town vs Brigg Town back in April 2006. Fleetwood won 5-1 to win automatic promotion when it looked seemingly impossible to do so.

Enjoyable away days?
Too many to mention, as we've been to some wonderful places on our journey through the leagues.

Which club serves the nicest pies?
Kilmarnock.

Famous Fleetwood fans?
Wes Newton (darts player), Alfie Boe (Fleetwood born and raised), Abbey Clancy (when her brother Sean played for us!)

Quirky fact time?
Fleetwood is the smallest town (population 26,000) currently hosting a Football League club.

Name your Fleetwood Dream Team?
GK: Scott Davies
RB: Phil Robinson
LB: Alan Wright
CB: Phil Clarkson
CB: Steve Macauley
CM: Nathan Pond
RM: Lennie Reid
CM: Jamie Milligan
CF: Magno Vieira
CF: Jamie Vardy
LM: Richie Allen

CHRISTMAS WITH THE COD ARMY

Game #42: League One - Friday 26th December 2014
FLEETWOOD TOWN vs Bradford City - Highbury Stadium

Christmas is a time to eat, drink, be merry and watch football! The UK's festive footy fixture programme is truly like no other. While Europe takes a break, it's all systems go in England. Two games in three days may be a managerial headache and a strain on the players' conditioning, but they're a fans' dream. Despite National Rail's attempts to rain on the parade by not running any Boxing Day trains, help was at hand.

The kind souls at the Football League try to accommodate all 72 clubs by handing out games with minimal mileage involved. A quick perusal of the fixtures led to Dad expressing an interest in visiting Fleetwood. All I had to do was provide pie and petrol money. It seemed like a fair deal, so we set off for the seaside, albeit without the bucket and spade. Far too cold at Christmas time.

Fleetwood are the proverbial new boys on the Football League block, having worked their way up from the North West Counties League (ninth tier) in ten seasons. That's quite a remarkable feat and a classic example of rags to riches. It's even more impressive when you consider that the club went bust for the third time during the latter part of the 90s. Naturally, just like when the new kid in school came in to show off his new trainers, there's a few detractors that point to money being the primary key, but going full time at the start of the 2010-11 season was a key beneficiary compared to other 'bigger name' clubs still stuck in non league purgatory.

I had been checking Fleetwood's progress from afar ever since they poached Chester's midfield lynchpin Antoni Sarcevic. It was he who fired the decisive free-kick in the play-off final back in May to lift the Cod Army into League One.

During the drive, Dad made a passing remark of snow being forecast. I certainly wasn't a weatherman and I brushed off his rather outlandish claim. The skies gave no indication and there were only light drops of rain falling as we passed neighbouring Blackpool and Poulton Le Fylde. There is no train station in Fleetwood, with the closest being Poulton. Just as well Dad had agreed to help me out.

Passing a large Fisherman's Friend warehouse was an appropriate first image of the fishing town. However, to my eyes, there were no signs for the ground. A sat nav would have been handy, alas we didn't have one so had to do without. I spotted some floodlights in the distance, but Dad still decided to ask for directions. Our first impression of Fleetwood folk wasn't good. A rude old woman brushed us off to wait for a bus. Fortunately, a fella on a bike was much more accommodating.

A number of fans were outside the 'Highbury Chippy,' conveniently located outside the ground. The waft of fresh fish and chips was enough to convince me to pay a visit after the game. There were plenty of parking options close by. Given that Highbury is nestled nicely within a housing estate, we managed to find a little hideaway at the end of a quiet road. Even though I'm not a driver, I agreed with Dad when he remarked that free parking and football matches don't exactly go hand in hand.

Highbury is the smallest ground in League One with a capacity of 5,327. "It's all shapes and sizes," said Dad, instantly drawn to a social club tacked on the end of the Highbury Stand, which only runs two thirds of the pitch. He's very much a part of the old school way of thinking that a ground has four sides. Just as well he didn't visit Oxford United. I opted for seats in the spacious Parkside Stand – a curved dome like enclosure. Above me, painted slogans of the club's various league title victories were proudly on display. Club mascot Captain Cod – a walking fish was getting nutmegged by some kids on the pitch. All that was missing was Captain Bird's Eye.

Most of the Bradford fans were squished together like sardines in a tiny terrace behind one of the goals. To be fair, the Bantams had brought a hefty number to the seaside and looked like they could have sold the ground out themselves if given the chance. Fleetwood fans had their own slightly raised terrace behind the other goal, yet every time the ball flew into the stand, I was convinced it was going to put one of the many windows housed above spectators through. Remarkably they managed to stay in tact, so there was no need to get on the phone to Safestyle UK.

Bradford came into the game looking to extend an seven game unbeaten run in League and Cup, while Fleetwood were in the middle of a patchy spell and tucked away in mid-table. I was glad to see Sarcevic line up for the Cod Army, although defender Nathan Pond also deserves a special mention. The man can easily be dubbed as 'Mr Fleetwood' seeing as he'd been with the club every step of the way since the North West Counties days.

Jonathan Stead was the familiar face leading the line for the Bantams, having joined on loan from Huddersfield Town. He was terrible when I went to watch the Terriers earlier in the season and, true to form, fluffed two early chances here. While it looks like I'm singling poor Steady out for stick, his side deserve a fair bit of credit. Having assembled a capable squad on a shoestring budget, the Yorkshire outfit have breathed new life into players cast aside by Premier League outfits. Case in point being full back and captain Stephen Darby. Despite the drop in temperatures, sweat was pouring off the ex-Liverpool defender as he tirelessly ran from box-to-box to try and shut down Fleetwood's forays forward.

Fleetwood midfielder Steven Schumacher was another player re-inventing himself after becoming one of the first casualties under David Moyes at Everton. Speaking in the matchday programme, Schuey admitted there were "eight full internationals," in front of him and he even struggled to get a game in the reserves.

"In the year I got released, the record number of players were released from Everton," he said. "If these lads don't make it at the top level, they can always filter down to the league clubs and have a good career that way," he added. Over 300 league games later (including some for Bradford) the Liverpudlian was looking forward to pitting his wits against his former employers. Unfortunately for him, Fleetwood boss Graham Alexander wasn't into sentiment, and opted to keep Schumacher on the bench as an unused substitute.

Fleetwood dominated the opening stages. To emphasise my point, if this was a Boxing match then the referee would have called for the bell. Full back Danny Andrew shaved the bar with a rasping effort from distance, before succumbing to an injury and departing the field. There was no sympathy reserved for Stead when he went down under an innocuous challenge. Cries of "get up you soft bastard," were aimed at the gangly forward. Fleetwood's Stephen Dobbie had enough chances to fill a highlight reel DVD, yet left his shooting boots at home and the Cod Army were punished for their wastefulness. The Bantams took advantage of a defensive lapse to take the lead against the run of play. James Hanson was left all alone at the back post to nod in a cross to send the travelling away support into a festive frenzy.

Footballs seemed to be in short supply around these parts. Whenever one whistled over the stands, a poor woman was quickly going out to fetch them back in again. Fleetwood's rotten luck continued when a Jamie Proctor screamer ricocheted off the post. Jordan Pickford in the Bradford goal was clasping at air, while the home side were beginning to feel this wasn't to be their day.

Tensions boiled over when a rather tasty tackle by Town's Conor McLaughlin almost sparked a touchline brawl. Bradford boss Phil Parkinson was the first to race over and burst a few blood vessels. The referee must have still been feeling the Christmas spirit, as he let McLaughlin off with a yellow card. This seemed to be the catalyst for all sorts of tackles to go flying in. Bradford soaked up the pressure and wrapped the game up, thanks to a quick counter attack. Stead's ball across the box missed its initial target, but fortunately for him, Filipe Morais was on hand to run in and smash the ball home from close range. It was all too much for the fan sitting in front of me. Dressed as Santa, this old Saint Nick was far from jolly, stopping to call the linesman an "effing banker" (or something along those lines) en route back to the North Pole.

A steady downpour had started for much of the second half. I kept my promise of sampling some of the local fish after the game, although a second miniature pie wasn't such a wise move. It was still half frozen, so I took no chances and tossed it out the window. Scrolling through the scores elsewhere, a quick check on social media confirmed that it was snowing pretty much up and down the country. All I could see was rain. We were making good progress on the drive home....until we hit Wigan! At first it looked like Wigan owner Dave Whelan was just shaking the dandruff from his head, but it quickly became apparent that the arctic white stuff had finally caught up to us. Motorways and traffic ground to a creeping pace. Road signs became completely covered and Dad performed a stellar job in keeping the car from veering off the road. Snow and ice quickly blanketed our view. The radio went off and the car fell silent. I provided an extra pair of eyes and ears to help Dad get us home safely. Although it doubled the length of time to get home, we got back in one piece, which is all that mattered. I'm just glad that Mother Nature was kind enough to delay the big freeze until after the festive games had finished.

Best chant: "*Jingle bells, jingle bells, jingle all the way. Oh what fun it is to sing, when City win away." The Bradford fans.*

Match ticket: £24. The club operated a two-tier pricing structure. Basically, it was cheaper to buy tickets in advance rather than on matchday. An advanced member ticket for where I sat would have been £17.

Match programme: £3.00. The club ran a competition to design the front cover. 11-year-old Bethany Stote's design of club mascot Captain Cod giving a thumbs up in between Christmas candy canes was handpicked by Graham Alexander as the best design from over 160 other entries.Well done Bethany! The League One newboys knock up a decent matchday magazine. Fan profiles, Fleetwood Dream Teams, press anecdotes and plenty of nostalgia pieces all contributed to an interested read.

Cost of food: £5.00 for a meal deal, consisting of a pie, drink, sweets/crisps.

Food rating: 3/5. Slightly bigger than a mince pie. Dad consumed his peppered steak offering in record time although that was down to hunger over the love of the food. He still thinks Blackburn Rovers do the nicest pies.

Final Score
Fleetwood Town 0
Bradford City 2 (Hanson 42, Morais 78)
Attendance: 4,278

Getting to know Wigan Athletic
Peter Walker & Wildheart - This Northern Soul
www.thisnorthernsoul.co.uk
Twitter @TNS_WAFC

Favourite memory as a Wigan fan?

Wildheart: Beating Manchester City with a Ben Watson goal comes as no surprise, but coming back from 3-0 down to beat Port Vale (1979) and Jason Roberts' debut goal after 39 seconds at Preston away are both high on my list.

Thoughts on ticket prices in general?

Wildheart: Too expensive, even ours which are cheap in comparison to other grounds are too high. Chief culprits are Leeds. I'm proud this site was at the forefront of campaign to boycott the game away there on Boxing Day.

Best game you've witnessed at the DW Stadium?

Wildheart: Coming from two nil down to beat Arsenal 3-2 thanks to the mercurial Charles N'Zogbia.

Best/worst players to pull on a Wigan shirt?

Peter: We've had many good ones and even more bad ones. Good ones in recent years are Antonio Valencia and Charles N'Zogbia. From years gone by, Joe Hinnigan and Peter Houghton are my favourites. I won't name the bad ones as they weren't deliberately bad.

Best thing about the DW Stadium?

Peter: It's a concrete monolith, without character. The only special thing is the Wigan public, who are both humorous and sporting. Best place to sit is in E2 and E3 if you can put up with the drum.

Wildheart: Wigan fans are much maligned, but we support our town when it would be easy to follow Liverpool, Manchester United et al.

Worst grounds you've visited?

Wildheart: The old Valley Parade and Old Trafford for its overbearing stewarding and arrogant fans.

Peter: Swindon Town. Their fans and stewards were appalling. Sunderland had very aggressive stewarding.

Enjoyable away days?

Wildheart: Brighton and Middlesbrough. Superb facilities with stewards who treat you like human beings.

Famous Wigan fans?

Peter: Presenter Stuart Maconie and TV newsreader Kay Burley.

Quirky fact time?

Wildheart: Dave Whelan broke his leg in an FA Cup final.

Peter: Our old ground was the widest in the league and used to have trotting races around it.

Name your Wigan Dream Team?

GK: John Filan
RB: John Butler
LB: Joe Hinnegan
CB: Arjan De Zeeuw
CB: Matt Jackson
RW: Antonio Valencia
CM: Jimmy Bullard
LW: Charles N'Zogbia
CF: Jason Roberts
CF: Lee McCulloch
CF: Henri Camara

Game #43: The Championship - Tuesday 30th December 2014
WIGAN ATHLETIC vs Sheffield Wednesday - The DW Stadium

There's a stage in life when everyone comes across that old school friend who seemed to be a good prospect, only for you to discover in later years that said friend has fallen on hard times. This summed up the current state of Wigan Athletic perfectly. Tipped as one of the early season promotion hopefuls, the Latics had lost their way and were knee deep in a relegation fight when I came calling to see in the final game of 2014.

A little over 18 months earlier, Wigan were riding high after upsetting Manchester City in the FA Cup. Okay, they may have been relegated from the Premier League in the same season, but it was unique visiting the DW Stadium on a cold Thursday night for some nicely priced Europa League football. The likes of which probably won't be seen again.

The club made it to the play-offs last season and were one step away from potentially retaining the FA Cup. Add in a gruelling Championship schedule with the demands of the Europa League and it seemed like the hangover had hit a tired squad pretty hard this season. The writing was on the wall for Uwe Rosler after form and results dipped dramatically, and the German was swiftly dismissed following a comprehensive 3-1 derby defeat at Bolton Wanderers - a game you can read all about in the earlier section of *Journey to the 72*. The appointment of Malky Mackay certainly divided opinion amongst the Wigan faithful. The Scot was still the subject of "textgate," following his acrimonious split with former employers Cardiff City.

Earlier in the season, Mark (Parry) had promised to come to see Wigan. All credit to him, he stuck to his end of the bargain, although he was probably regretting it, as we set off on a frosty Tuesday evening.

"No doubt Dave Whelan will be sunning himself at his Barbados retreat right now," I said, as we drove past the DW Stadium. Club owner Whelan might not have been there in person, but he was about to sting us for £5 parking in a big yard overlooking one of his DW Fitness Centres. Mark muttered something derogatory under his breath. I think he wanted to go home. I pretended not to hear. Rows of personalised Sheffield Wednesday number plates had already parked up alongside several coaches. There was a hefty contingent from South Yorkshire in attendance, who clearly smelt blood from a Wigan team low on confidence and seemingly ripe for the picking.

The DW Stadium is located on a retail park with more fast food joints than you can shake a stick at. Previous visits had seen me walk a rather scenic route from the train station, taking in such delights as an industrial estate, scrapping yard and tiny bridge over a filthy river. Maybe the £5 parking charge to be spared that wasn't so bad after all.

Posters advertising 'Festive Footy for £10' were plastered all around the stadium's vicinity. As we approached the ticket office, a steward asked which end we were going in. I thought this was a slightly odd request, so I replied the home end and instantly regretted my decision. The away fans were in good voice and I wanted to be amongst them. Alas, we collected our tickets for just underneath the electronic score board in the Boston Stand. It was only as we tucked into our pies that the plot thickened. The club were charging away fans £25 to get in. Needless to say this went down like a lead balloon with the travelling supporters. A feeble excuse of "they did that to us," from the home fans didn't hold much water with me. Two wrongs don't make a right. Leeds United did this to Reading earlier in the season. Travelling fans should be encouraged and not priced out from supporting their team. The Wednesday fans shook off the disappointment pretty quickly and burst into song. They clearly brought the noise, having taken up almost their entire allocation behind one of the goals.

The game was never going to sell out. Wigan simply don't have the fanbase to sell out the stadium, unless some of the Premier League big boys come to visit. The Latics share the ground with Rugby League's Wigan Warriors, and are undoubtedly one of the better clubs at offering value for money regarding tickets. Having been to the DW on a few occasions in recent years, I'd never paid more than £15 for a ticket.

In an effort to add some character to the four sided single tiered stadium, Whelan has installed a revolving DW slogan which spins around on the roof. Gotham City has the Bat Signal, but in these parts the Wigan head hencho has made sure that he out trumps the Caped Crusader.

Given Wigan's current form and Wednesday being the division's lowest scorers at kick-off, this had the makings of a 0-0 written all over it. Mackay's decision to start Shaun Maloney and Callum McManaman on the bench - the two likeliest source of goals was a definite head scratcher. Roger Espinoza made a second half swansong before packing up and moving stateside to the warmer climate of the MLS. The Honduran was given a polite round of applause, but like I've said before, he's not been the same since chopping off his trademark mullet.

In truth, and I mean this with the greatest of respect, the ability just wasn't there with the current crop of Wigan players. A Fantasy Football feature in the programme hammered this point home. The likes of Leighton Baines, Paul Scharner, Jimmy Bullard and the 'Duke' Nathan Ellington created an enigma around the little club who always seemed to thrive and survive despite punching above their weight. Honourable mentions go out to Antonio Valencia, Roberto Martinez and Jason Roberts who didn't make the fan in question's team. Sheffield Wednesday fans retaliated in kind by naming their all-time five-a-side team on Twitter. Kevin Pressman, Roland Nilsson, Des Walker, Chris Waddle and David Hirst were the famous five to be voted into what would be a formidable lineup.

Quality looked in short supply as the match kicked off. Wigan saw plenty of the ball, yet they seemed hesitant to shoot. Left back Andrew Taylor looked like a deer in headlights, taking two steps forwards, only to panic then pass the ball backwards. Even when he beat his man, the slightest contact saw Taylor go down in a comical heap just a few seconds later. A kid sitting behind me turned to his Dad and asked why their beloved team were playing "like a bunch of boneheads." The Dad just shook his head in disbelief.

Tall Wednesday frontman Atdhe Nuhiu looked clumsy and immobile at first glance. "Even I'm better than him," stated Mark. This was a pretty wild boast from someone who by his own admission has two left feet on the football pitch. Appearances proved to be deceptive, as Nuhiu could certainly move when he wanted to. Ivan Ramis did well to race back and clear an effort off the line from the lanky Austrian.

Bob Marley reassured fans at half time that "everything was going to be alright." For a while it looked like they might be. James McClean had a goal ruled out for offside, then got away with a handling offence, as he darted towards goal and gave Keiren Westwood his first real test.

McManaman was introduced, although he must have grown attached to the bench, because less than ten minutes after coming on he was dismissed for a two-footed lunge on Claude Dielna. McManaman could have no complaints. It was an ugly challenge and worthy of a red all day long. All of a sudden, the Wednesday fans stopped singing for Stevie May to come on and sensed an opportunity to snatch all three points. Nuhiu duly took a chance which was put on a plate, heading in a pinpoint cross from six yards out. The fans went wild and Nuhiu quickly dived in amongst them to soak in the adulation. Maloney was finally introduced for the hosts in the latter stages. Despite being a man down, Maloney's presence shifted the momentum. The substitute created an instant impression when he saw a free kick cleared off the line. Alas, it all came too late. The drummer stopped drumming and Wigan slipped to another defeat - Mackay's fifth out of seven games in charge.

By this point, I was worried for my friend's sanity. Mark hadn't said much during the game, instead opting to retreat further into his scarf and coat as the game wore on and the temperature continued to drop. His car resembled something of an ice block, which is what my two feet felt like on the walk back to the car park. I sensed this was Mark's swansong regarding *Journey to the 72*. Still, I held out hope that I could tempt him back when the Latics contest the Johnstone's Paint Trophy. On this showing, relegation looked a certainty.

Best chant: "You're shit at football, stick to rugby." Sheffield Wednesday fans singing outside the ground both before and after the game.

Match ticket: £10. Prices generally range between £15 and £20 for most games.

Match programme: £3.00. Gary Caldwell didn't half give a menacing stare in the picture for the captain's notes. His presence on the pitch was sorely missed. Wigan's year in pictures was chronicled, as well as various historical "on this day" pieces. The past looked a lot better than the club's current state, so you can't blame Wigan for relying on nostalgia. Chris Kirkland was given a friendly welcome back to the club. Noted as the first Latic to represent England back in 2006, he was also reminded of the 9-1 reverse Wigan suffered at Tottenham Hotspur during the 2009-10 season. "Without a man-of-the-match display from Kirky, it could easily have been 19!" Every cloud and all that!

Cost of food: £2.40 for a pie or £4 for a pie and hot drink.

Food rating: 3/5. I went for the chunky steak option, while Parry opted for cheese. The portion sizes were a little small, but Parry enjoyed the crunchy pastry and gave it the ultimate seal of approval by stating that it lived up to its northern reputation. You couldn't go wrong with the burger van directly outside the ground. Chips and curry sauce was well worth the £3 investment and trumped the pies in my view.

Final Score
Wigan Athletic 0
Sheffield Wednesday 1 (Nuhiu 77)
Attendance: 14,571

Getting to know Rotherham United
Caz Neale - Vital Rotherham
www.rotherham.vitalfootball.co.uk
Twitter @Vitalrotherham

How does the New York Stadium compare with previous homes Millmoor and the Don Valley?
There is no comparison! We all loved Millmoor and were sad to leave but, let's be honest, it had seen better days. Don Valley was the worst place I've ever watched a football match (and I've been to a lot of places.)

Best/worst players to pull on a Rotherham shirt?
I go back a long time! We've had plenty of good players – Bobby Williamson, Alan Lee, Dave Watson to name just three. Alex Revell worked his socks off for the team and is now in the 'Millers legends' after his 'ambitious but brilliant' Wembley goal. If I'm being honest we are really a team of players more than individuals, although I wouldn't ever have encouraged anyone to buy Paolo Vernazza or Brian Wilsterman.

Best away support at the New York Stadium in recent memory?
Middlesbrough brought a very good support to the New York and sang and jumped around all game recently. But Huddersfield Town and Nottingham Forest fans were also very vocal.

Best thing about the New York Stadium?
It's ours! It's iconic (round!) so there are no open corners for the wind to whistle round. It's in the centre of town so easy for everyone to get to. With it being shaped as it is, anywhere is good to sit.

Worst grounds you've visited?
This season it has to be our local neighbours at Hillsborough. I don't think they've given it a clean for years. And have to say I wasn't over impressed with Carrow Road this season either – poor seating. Accrington stands out as a poor ground – we once came home with trench foot from there! Exeter's ground is one to visit if you've never been, they have a tree growing through the ladies toilets while Hereford's is a delight not to go to.

Famous Rotherham fans?
The Chuckle Brothers (Paul and Barry) come, but you won't see them at the moment with it being panto season. Our most famous season ticket holder is England Ref Howard Webb. And Muse bassist Chris Wolstenholme is also a Miller. You might also see The Chaser Mark Labbett, who has been living in Rotherham for a while and is in our local pantomime playing evil Abanazar in Aladdin.

Quirky fact time?
Rotherham United had the first black professional player in Arthur Wharton. There is a project going to have a statue of him at the ground.

Best/worst Rotherham managers?
Best - Ronnie Moore in his first time as manager when he took us up to the Championship in consecutive seasons and, of course, Steve Evans for doing the same thing.
Worst – Danny Bergara who had a poor season with us in the mid-90s and Andy Scott who did little to endear himself to the fans in the eleven months he was with us.

Thoughts on ticket prices in general?
Too expensive. I am a believer that everything in football should be 'capped' meaning that ticket prices should be the same for each league at each ground. I believe £20 is ample for Championship football.

Name your Rotherham Dream Team?
GK: Jim McDonagh
RB: Gerry Forrest
LB: John Breckin
CB: Paul Hurst
CB: Dave Watson
CB: Martin McIntosh
RW: Tony 'Tiger' Towner
CM: Gerry Gow
LW: Alan Crawford
CF: Alan Lee
CF: Shaun Goater

Game #44: FA Cup Third Round - Saturday 3rd January 2015
ROTHERHAM UNITED vs AFC Bournemouth - The AESSEAL New York Stadium

The first FA Cup weekend of 2015 and I was kicking off the New Year in New York. No, not the Big Apple. The New York Stadium, Rotherham to be precise. I traded the transatlantic flight for a transpennine train and was on my way to see the Millers for the first time.

It's a well known fact that the Chuckle Brothers are two of the club's more famous fans. Having been told they were busy doing panto, I shamelessly went fishing for a mention on Twitter. I had heard they were very fan friendly and they didn't disappoint. Well, Barry didn't anyway. Paul must have been busy running an errand for Dan the Van.

Shaun Best @Shaun_Best Jan 3

first time watching the Millers today. I wonder if @BazElliott or @PaulChuckle2 can provide a good luck tweet #tometoyou

Barry Elliott @BazElliott Jan 3

@Shaun_Best @PaulChuckle2 Come on the Millers!!#rufc

Having spent just over 100 years at previous home Millmoor, followed by a temporary stay at stand-in Athletics ground the Don Valley Stadium, the club moved to their custom built new home in July 2012. The catchy, commercial friendly name came about due to the plot of land the stadium was built on being called New York. The AESSEAL branding - from the Rotherham based mechanical company had been recently added for commercial purposes and was the biggest sponsorship deal in the club's history to date.

The River Don runs around the back of the stadium. No doubt, countless flat balls and shopping trolleys are lodged deep in the murky waters. The railway track runs alongside the stadium, so commuters get a great view of the stadium passing through on the way to Rotherham Central. It looks even better when illuminated at night. For a non-driver like myself, it's ideally located and no more than a short 10-15 minute walk away from the station. Just watch out for the odd discarded syringe at the back of one of the neighbouring sidestreets. Luckily for me, I was able to see it in time and step away.

Many will have forgotten the giant strides both sides have made in recent years. It was only 2008 that both clubs were staring at the real possibility of dropping out of the Football League altogether. Saddled with -17 point deductions, both sides survived, kicked on and are now a world away from the same problems.

Two Bournemouth fan coaches had made the trip up to Yorkshire from the South Coast. However, there were still empty spaces galore. Despite a reduction in matchday prices, a slew of supporters were saving themselves for the league meeting between the two teams a fortnight later. Most league games at the New York sell out, which was the case for the club's previous game on Boxing Day. Those who saw this game as a mere dress rehearsal and chose to stay away didn't half miss a corker of a cup tie!

The all red affair that makes up the inside of the New York Stadium is beautiful. The ground is totally enclosed with a transparent see through roof hanging down from the skyline. Two futuristic looking floodlight pylons lie on top of the East Stand, with each one housing a row of lights behind a protective circular disc. A large video screen was over my shoulder in the far corner of the West Stand.

In my haste, I'd put on my Bournemouth shirt before realising that I'd already purchased tickets for the home end. I went incognito and kept my colours hidden. My ticket had been left in a big bowl with the friendly and cooperative stewards outside the ground. Needless to say, I passed a quick security check, followed by a bag inspection. I'd stashed a large bag of Maltesers behind some of my books for the train. Due to the extortionate cost of chocolate (specifically £2.50 grab bags) at grounds, it was more economical and a damn site cheaper to bring my own to games.

Sat two rows from the pitch, I stretched my legs out to watch Rotherham's forwards being put through their paces by first team coach and former player Paul Warne. The Millette cheerleaders nervously practiced their routine just a few yards in front, occasionally turning around and wincing when a wayward ball zipped past them. I can safely say that no cheerleaders were hurt in the buildup to the game - even with Matt Derbyshire taking part in the shooting.

It was fitting that the teams came out to the sound of Frank Sinatra booming out "New York, New York, it's up to you." The rotund Rotherham boss Steve Evans looked like a rabid pitbull, anxiously pacing the touchline from first whistle to last, bellowing out instructions and chewing out players for the smallest of errors. His bark looked every bit as nasty as his bite.

Bournemouth thought they had opened the scoring when Ian Harte crashed a free kick off the underside of the bar. The referee waved play on, which allowed Rotherham to spring a counter attack and go ahead themselves. Full back Richard Brindley collected a pass from Jordan Bowery and saw a deflected effort beat Lee Camp and nestle inside the bottom corner.

Junior Stanislas wasted a golden opportunity to equalise. The frontman was put clear and had enough time to read the paper before applying the finish. Goalkeeper Adam Collin had already committed himself, but Stanislas still lifted his shot wide. The end result was bad enough that even the Bournemouth substitutes stopped their warm-ups to place a hand over their faces and shake their heads. Junior's teammates maintained their composure and kept up with their patient passing football. It finally paid off a minute before half time. Yann Kermorgant played in Shaun MacDonald, who slipped the ball past Collin. The Rotherham fan sitting next to me - most likely a student, threw a minor strop, flailing his arms around and comically shouting "shut up." This would become a recurring theme throughout the game.

The away team dominated after the break. Stanislas made amends for his earlier miss, this time rounding Collin and tapping into an empty net. Minutes later, Rotherham's defence was sliced open again by Kermorgant. The Frenchman's cheeky backheel allowed Ryan Fraser to sprint clear and coolly slot into the bottom corner. Kermorgant himself got in on the scoring party when the Rotherham defence allowed him to blast in umarked on the line. The opportunistic forward nodded in a second after Collin had acrobatically kept out Steve Cook's initial header.

Rotherham really should have reduced their arrears late on. Substitute Derbyshire skied over with an open goal at his mercy. Cue Mr Angry sitting next to me to rant once more: "Get him off, get him sold to Bury." A random statement, but having watched the Shakers I doubt they'd take him to be honest.

To say it had been an enjoyable afternoon is an understatement. Bournemouth had already demonstrated their ability to wipe the floor with teams on numerous occasions. Utilising hungry squad players, Eddie Howe's side played with confidence and re-affirmed their status as English football's top scoring team. I was just happy to be in the vicinity and watch it all unfold. Rotherham were by no means awful. They were simply undone by clinical finishing. The Millers were without star striker Alex Revell for this game, and as it turned out, he was sold to Cardiff City a few days later. His goals were instrumental in getting Rotherham up from League One. I sensed they'd need an adequate replacement to stop them from going back down.

The general consensus in the matchday programme was that a cup run would have been nice, yet the club's main objective was to avoid relegation. Speaking to the BBC after the game, Rotherham assistant manager Paul Raynor stated: "It was a particularly bad day at the office." Fair play, everyone has them, even the Chuckle Brothers. Isn't that right Barry?

Shaun Best @Shaun_Best Jan 3 *Barry Elliott favorited your Tweet*

@BazElliott @PaulChuckle2 oh dear oh dear. Sorry I didn't bring your team much luck today. Cracking stadium though #RUFCvAFCB

Best chant: "6-5, we're going to win 6-5." Rotherham fans giving a tongue in cheek reponse to Bournemouth's boast of "we score when we want."

Match ticket: £15. For league matches, advance adult tickets for the East/West Stands were £25, with concessions £15. Prices increased by £2 for fans who chose to pay on the day.

Match programme: £2.00 for a shortened cup themed edition. Evans looks like he's wearing eyeliner in the close-up picture for the manager's piece, although I'd rather stay on his good side.

Cost of food: £3.00 for a pie or £2.50 for a sausage roll.

Food rating: 2.5/5. The club had named one of their stands after a Pukka Pie, so I was quite hopeful of tucking into a tasty savoury. My chicken balti serving was a tale of two halves. The top half was easy to cut into and produced a strong smell of mint and spices, while the bottom half was quite tough to separate and stuck to the bottom of the foil tray. Very greasy and didn't sit well on the stomach.

Final Score
Rotherham United 1 (Brindley 10)
AFC Bournemouth 5 (MacDonald 44, Stanislas 58, Fraser 63, Kermorgant 67, 71)
Attendance: 5,875

Getting to know Scunthorpe United
Andrew Brown - Scunthorpe United Supporter Liaison Officer
andy.brown@scunthorpe-united.co.uk
Twitter @andyslo58

Favourite memory as a Scunthorpe fan?

As a fan of 53 years, our play-off win vs Crewe in 1992 which gave the Iron the chance to play at Wembley stands out. What a night that was! I never thought that I would see the Iron play at Wembley.

Best game you've witnessed at Glanford Park?

Again, this is a play-off semi-final from 1999 vs Swansea. Losing from the first leg, it was action from the first minute to the last. It had everything - goals, passion sendings off and another trip to Wembley.

Best/worst players to pull on a Scunthorpe shirt?

I have seen many of the best players in my years following the Iron. Some of the modern ones like Billy Sharp, Gary Hooper, Andy Crosby, Cliff Byrne spring to mind. Worst players, there have been too many to remember.

Best thing about Glanford Park?

That we are leaving it soon. There were too many mistakes in the construction of it which has held us back both on and off the pitch. I am greatly in favour in moving to the new ground. You need your ground to be used seven days a week.

Worst grounds you've visited?

Bradford City's toilets and catering facilities are disgusting. At Newcastle United, the view for the away supporters is a joke.

Enjoyable away days?

Fleetwood and Plymouth are both really away supporter friendly.

Famous Scunthorpe fans?

Kevin Keegan, Ian Botham, Tony Jacklin, Ray Clemance, Roy Chubby Brown.

Quirky fact time?

Away supporters think the car park at Scunthorpe is the best they have visited. Easy access and very close to the away end. Home supporters hate it and think it takes too long to get out of.

SEEING WHAT THE IRON ARE MADE OF

Game #45: FA Cup Third Round - Tuesday 6th January 2015
SCUNTHORPE UNITED vs Chesterfield - Glanford Park

The black clouds had been swirling for some time. The day had come and I simply couldn't put the trip off any longer. It was time for a visit to the dentist! Or was it? For various reasons, my routine check-up had been postponed more times than a non league game in the middle of winter. I'd already resigned myself to getting fleeced out of some hard earned £ before football kindly stepped in. Allow me to elaborate.

Back in December, my eyes were glued to the BBC Sport website to watch Scunthorpe edge out non-league Worcester City 14-13 in a back-and-forth penalty shootout after the two teams couldn't be separated over two ties. It was certainly one of the longest, if not the longest shootout in the competition's history, certainly eclipsing Macclesfield's 11-10 victory over Forest Green back in November 2001. Scunthorpe were given a home draw for the third round, but their opponents were yet to be determined. Still, my interest was very much piqued.

The Iron's original opponents were Chesterfield. However, Paul Cook's side were made to replay their second round match at Milton Keynes Dons having fielded an ineligible player. While the rest of the third round games took place and Chesterfield experienced a touch of déjà-vu, Scunthorpe were left kicking their heels. In my mind, I'd been given an extra date to play with, so I was happy. With a legal line-up approved, Chesterfield beat MK Dons for a second time to make a midweek game against Mark Robins' side official. The dentist took news of my umpteenth cancellation well and even asked me to bring him a programme back. I jest.

All joking aside, minutes after moving the date of my check-up, I felt a filling come loose during a break in work. Typical! The receptionist was sick of bringing my file up, as I called in to bring the appointment forward once more. Consoling myself with chocolate probably wasn't the best idea, but it was over three hours to North Lincolnshire, so a little comfort food was more than acceptable.

Thoughts of fillings and flossing disappeared during a short layover at Sheffield. East Midlands Trains had generously installed a piano in the lobby for public use. A pensioner built up an appreciative audience, as he belted out the tune to EastEnders, then pulled out a couple of classics from the Beatles back catalogue. This was a much more enjoyable way to pass the time rather than stare up at a departures board or shiver on a wintry platform.

A floodlit Glanford Park passed by as the train pulled into the station. I had booked into a guest house on the other side of town. A quick search on Google revealed less than favourable reviews from some of the taxi firms. There was no other choice than to choose the best of a supposed bad lot. Ali from AAA Taxis dropped me outside my accommodation, then offered to pick me up to take me back to the ground. Given that there was just over an hour to kick-off, the gesture was much appreciated. A simple task of dropping the bags off and negotiating a quick change took a bit longer than anticipated. I put this down to two factors - one being the massive dog who eyed me up as potential dinner and two being the clumsy identical twins that fumbled their way through my booking. I ended up getting a free upgrade from the owner, so everything turned out well.

I was a little shocked that Ali kept to his word and was waiting to take me to the ground. Apologies for doubting the Scunthorpe hospitality. Unfortunately, the new found friendship quickly fizzled out when it became apparent that Ali wasn't a football fan. The conversation quickly dried up. Fortunately, it didn't take too long to get to the ground. Glanford Park was situated at the back of a busy retail park. With traffic gridlocked and the meter still running, I left Ali to his thoughts and saved the extra cash he was probably counting on. That money was reserved for a programme and pie. Ali once again offered me a lift home after the game and just for a moment, it felt like I had a personal chauffeur. If only I'd done my research and booked the Travelodge that was located only a stone's throw away from the stadium, I could have saved some of the travel hassle.

The placement of the floodlights leaning into the stadium made the exterior of Glanford Park look a little dark. Once through a set of iron gates - complete with club logo, you can't help but take in the array of images capturing some of the club's historic moments which line the outside of the ground. Given that they're only an hour away, it wasn't surprising to hear that Chesterfield had sold out their entire allocation.

Glanford Park is completely enclosed, although the corners don't accommodate any supporters. Still, there were plenty of rabid away fans taking up residence behind the goal, as well as to the side of me, with part of the Clugston Stand fenced off. Planning permission has been sought for a new ground a few miles down the road, despite Glanford Park only being open since 1988. The over-reliance on beams and pillars to support the roof means that there's always going to be a couple of restrictions on matchday viewing. Thankfully, I was close to the touchline and had no such problems.

Scunthorpe punished Chesterfield's defensive lapses and coasted into half time two goals up. When the visitors made a hash out of clearing a goalmouth scramble, on loan Chelsea defender Alex Davey was on hand to lash the ball into the net from the edge of the area. Prolific Chesterfield striker Eoin Doyle was having a good old tussle with Scunthorpe marker Miguel Llera. The frontman went down in the box and shoves were exchanged. The referee calmed proceedings, but didn't award a penalty or present any cards. The Iron doubled their lead with a goal straight out of the route one playbook. Goalkeeper Sam Slocombe booted a goal kick down field, and a poor defensive header from Ritchie Humphreys was seized upon by Lyle Taylor, who ran clear and emphatically smashed the ball home.

The half time entertainment was slightly odd. Willing fans came onto the pitch to spin round a pole ten times, then, if they were still on their feet, got to take a penalty against the 'Scunny Bunny' mascot. I tweeted that the game was all sewn up, which turned out to be a big mistake. I ended up eating those 140 characters with a side order of humble pie.

The phrase 'game of two halves,' summed this game up perfectly. Chesterfield simply camped in the Scunthorpe end for much of the second period. Had it not been for the heroics of Slocombe between the sticks, Chesterfield would not have only come back, but also won the game at a canter. A group of fans tried and failed to get a rise out of Chesterfield winger Sam Clucas. Desperate cries of "ginger" were given the cold shoulder by the red headed wide man, who was delivering quality crosses into the Scunthorpe danger area. It looked like being a question of how long Slocombe could keep the visitors out. The penalty that the visitors had been craving was finally given when Eddie Nolan clumsily pulled Gary Roberts down. The division's leading scorer, Doyle duly sent Slocombe the wrong way, and we now had a cup tie on our hands. Five minutes from the end, Roberts turned provider. His ball across a crowded box was turned in by Jay O'Shea. Manager Paul Cook was on the pitch and punched the air in delight.

Scunny were deflated, but managed to hang on and salvage a replay (Chesterfield would go on to win the replay 2-0 thanks to two extra time goals from Clucas.) Fans openly spoke about "seeing what the January sales bring in," regarding new players. Marquee striker Paddy Madden was unusually quiet, but he still boasted the title of being the most followed person at the club on Twitter.

Yet again, the big freeze had found its way to me, so I ducked for cover inside McDonald's to get a post-match burger. Fans from both sides were already queuing and mixing without throwing food at one another, which I took as being a good sign. A bad sign came when I needed to find a new ride back to the guest house. Ali rudely grunted something about finishing for the night. My new driver looked a spitting image of Andre Royo's character 'Bubbles,' from TV show 'The Wire.' The car stunk of mouldy Indian food and I've never wished for a faster taxi ride in my life.

Back at the guest house, I slept so well that I missed the call for breakfast. It was only when I got into Crewe that the hunger pangs hit and needed addressing. There was one croissant left as I got called to be served. All the girl had to do was drop the pastry into the bag, but she somehow dropped it on the floor. The question was, did I still want it? Ignoring the five second rule, I declined the offer and walked away hungry, yet safe in the knowledge that Sam Slocombe would have shown much better handling.

Best chant: "It's the Spireite boys making all the noise. Everywhere we go." Chesterfield fans sure made themselves heard at the expense of the muted Iron supporters.
Match ticket: £15 special cup price. League games ranged between £20-£23 for adult members and non-members.
Match programme: £3.00. Usurps Bury as the best programme so far. At 76 pages, content was certainly king and I was still reading it on the train home. From catering reports on the road, to international fans, to players putting their least favourite things into Room 101, this had a little bit of everything. Fan Jack Filmer proved he was smarter than Paddy Madden in a quiz, while there were also plenty of player interviews and fan pieces.
Cost of food: £2.80 for a pie or £3.20 including mushy peas.
Food rating: 4/5. After a few dodgy pies, Pukka came to the rescue with their all steak offering. Lovely puff pastry and gorgeous chunks of meat with flowing gravy. I made sure not to drop any of this on the floor. Every last morsel was devoured. There was actual space inside the food corridor to eat without getting stray elbows in the face. An added bonus!

Final Score
Scunthorpe United 2 (Davey 18, Taylor 44)
Chesterfield 2 (Doyle 71 pen, O'Shea 85)
Attendance: 4,307

Getting to know Newport County
Simon Sadler - Newport County AFC Supporters Trust
www.ncafctrust.org

How long have you been a Newport fan?

It's 20 years (1995/96 season) since I began following County religiously. I was 18 and had my first job so I could afford to travel to away games too seeing that I still lived at home. We were climbing up the non-league pyramid at the time and I do miss the non-league scene. So much so that now I have moved to the West Country I'm trying to take in a few Clevedon Town games too.

Favourite memory as a Newport fan?

It would have to be winning the Conference play-off final two years ago at Wembley. Having been a child of the 80's and having Dad taking me to Football League games in Newport, it was amazing to see us get back to the promised land.

Best game you've witnessed at Rodney Parade?

Beating Hereford 2-0 in the league in our first month there. I took the kid for his first game and he fell in love with it. Fantastic game which was a real armwrestle for 75 minutes until Andy Sandell broke the net with the best goal I've seen at the ground.

Best/worst players to pull on a Newport shirt?

My favourite ever County player was Matty Rose. He played for us 10-15 years ago when we were down the pyramid and had a lot of youth products around him. Opposition teams would often try to intimidate the teenagers, but he was on any scene within seconds to tell anyone that they would have to go through him to get to them. Funnily enough no-one took him up on the offer! One of our worst signings was Craig McAllister. He was the top wage earner during his time, but rarely put a shift in and if you didn't play the ball to his feet the others had to win it back again.

Best thing about Rodney Parade?

Its location. It is only a few hundred metres from the city centre, which is great for away fans and the local pub owners (all old school fans so I know them well) get a roaring trade on match day. One of them even has one of my old shirts nailed to the ceiling (I used to be Spytty the Dog, the club mascot).

Worst grounds you've visited?

I didn't particularly enjoy going to St. George's Lane in Worcester over the years. Despite it being one of our shorter trips, it seemed to be the coldest most fragile ground and the facilities for away fans were poor. I believe they don't play there anymore which is a bonus for everyone!

Enjoyable away days?

Before the turn of the Millennium, I used to enjoy going to Moor Green in the Midlands, it had a markedly sloping pitch, but you could get an anorexic cheeseburger for £1 and you were so close to the pitch you could banter with the players and officials (which I did, I was their mascot!). More recently I loved Aggborough at Kidderminster, where the food is top notch and the home team always played attractive football. I still go there every season as my Dad lives near there now and I would love for them to join us in League Two.

Which club serves the nicest pies?

As above, Kidderminster. They are over £4 as I remember, but they are not traditional pastry based pies but more the Cottage Pies in foil. Be careful though as burned tongues are the tattoo of the impatient!

Famous Newport fans?

Newport isn't a city that attracts famous people or the rich. It's a true industrial heartland with salt of the earth working class people. Despite leaving there recently, I still miss how genuine the residents are.

Quirky fact time?

When the original Newport County went out of business in 1989, the Football Association of Wales forced us to play outside of Wales and attempted to force us to play in the League of Wales. We took them to court for restraint of trade and thankfully won to be able to play back in Wales giving rise to our nickname of the 'Exiles' and the English FA welcomed us back into the English pyramid. Despite being passionately Welsh, I will always wish the England national team well for that gesture (that and the fact my better half is English, oh and I now live there!)

GRUDGE MATCH IN SOUTH WALES

Game #46: League Two - Saturday 10th January 2015
NEWPORT COUNTY vs Portsmouth - Rodney Parade

Istanbul, Rome, Belgrade, Milan. Just four of many cities who boast a fierce football rivalry and host hostile derby encounters. You wouldn't think to put Newport and Portsmouth on that list. There may be 136 miles between the two places, yet their League Two encounter was being treated as a bubble match with the heaviest police presence I'd ever seen.

Trouble had blighted this fixture in recent times. August's reverse fixture - a 1-0 Newport victory was marred by violent scenes and flares being set off after the game. One Newport fan was given a three year ban from football for assaulting a teenage Portsmouth fan - leaving the poor guy with a fractured sinus. Sniffing some overtime pay, Gwent police force put in the relevant forms and were subsequently placed on the beat all around the city.

I'd purchased my ticket in advance. Just as well really, as no sales were available on the day. Online sales ceased at 3pm the day before the game, with the ticket office following suit two hours later. Around 1,000 away fans were expected, so nothing was left to chance. Trains carrying the fans were being monitored coming into Newport station, with supporters who were deemed unruly being escorted to the ground.

A long and tedious train journey got me into South Wales by late morning. A short walk led me into the town centre, where the force were out in all their glory. Around every corner, at least three officers with either a rabid dog, horse or riot van were there to greet me. No Pompey fans had arrived yet and a handful of Newport fans were having social drinks in a few of the bars. Their only crime to me was having a good time and sharing banter amongst friends. The constant threat of an afternoon in bracelets and a cell kept many people's emotions in check and I didn't detect any aggravation on the way to the ground.

The Newport city footbridge dominates the surroundings and is the easiest way to reach Rodney Parade. The stadium can be seen slightly from the other side and the steel tubing that supports the bridge reminded me of some of the stadiums I'd already been to. The architecture was a lot better to look at than the floor, which was covered in horse poo. Yet more 'Heddlu,' (Welsh for police) cross examined me as I walked across the bridge and over the River Usk.

Rodney Parade is very much a rugby ground first with football accommodated second. The club began playing there at the beginning of the 2012-13 season, having previously staged games at Somerton Park (now demolished) and athletics stadium Spytty Park. A large playing area is scaled back at Rodney Parade for football matches, making it quite a distance to the pitch for those fans based behind the goal. The club share their current facilities with Newport Gwent Dragons. Outside the stadium, there is a separate fenced off area with a muddy field in the middle and various supporters bars and club shops situated in the far corner. It was from a tiny club shop that I picked up my ticket, which was then scanned through an electronic turnstile inside a small wooden portakabin.

Once inside, a long, dimly lit corridor was reminiscent of being inside a large warehouse. An enlarged picture of the Dragons Rugby squad dominated the area. Up on the wall, a solitary TV was fixed high up so that supporters could crowd around to watch Soccer Saturday. Food stalls were situated right at the back, with a group of kids doing a roaring trade on the side with a busy tuck shop.

Situated in the Bisley Stand, all the seats in my particular area were made up of different colours. A red, yellow and black colour combination was definitely eye catching. The shadow of a towering corporate box loomed over a small uncovered terrace, which accommodates a small number of home supporters. If the action on the pitch gets boring, you can look out over the rest of Newport and see some of the sights from a distance. The teams emerged from what looked like a housing structure, complete with pyramid roof. Its location acts as an ideal divider between the two sets of supporters.

Newport reformed in 1989 after going out of business earlier in the same year. A founder member of the old Third Division, the 'Exiles' won promotion back to the Football League in 2013 for the first time in 25 years. The club were sitting pretty in the play-offs when I came calling, with manager Justin Edinburgh exceeding all expectation on a small budget, having cut his managerial teeth at a number of non league clubs beforehand.

Portsmouth's decline has been well documented. From FA Cup winners in 2008 to three relegations and spells in administration, the club were in the hands of the Pompey Supporters Trust. Despite their plight, the club still flexed their financial muscle to bring in prolific striker Matt Tubbs. Almost the whole of League Two had gone for the player, who had been starring on loan at AFC Wimbledon, before being recalled and released by parent club AFC Bournemouth. Reports had linked Newport with a move for Tubbs, but Edinburgh revealed their offer wasn't lucrative enough.

Speaking to the South Wales Argus, Edinburgh highlighted the gulf in finances between the two sides.

"What Portsmouth are reportedly paying the player is treble what we pay our highest paid player and he's gone there and signed a two-and-a-half year deal. That says it all really."

While Pompey defeated Newport in the financial stakes, given Portsmouth's precarious league position coming into the game, their under-fire manager Andy Awford needed a result to deflect some of the unwanted flak. His players were certainly physical, resorting to WWE tactics which went largely unpunished by the referee. The away side almost gifted their hosts a comical own goal. Paul Jones allowed a Nicky Shorey back pass to run too far and he almost missed out on connecting with a goal kick.

Portsmouth squandered the better chances throughout the game and were unlucky to fall behind thanks to a touch of good fortune. Mark Byrne's hopeful cross evaded everyone in the six yard box and bounced past Jones at the far post. The linesman's flag looked to have come to Pompey's rescue, but the referee overruled him after judging that Aaron O'Connor didn't get a touch on the effort. The Portsmouth protests went on right in front of my eyes, but I was easily distracted by the sight of club mascot Spytty the Dog running around the pitch, wildly waving his arms in the air.

Fans engaged in the usual English/Welsh banter with the sound of each country's national anthem echoing around Rodney Parade. The dreaded chant of "you're getting sacked in the morning," was directed at Awford, alongside a tongue in cheek version of "we're sheep shagging bastards, we know what we are."

Tubbs didn't have much chance to shine on his Pompey debut. At full time, a frustrated Portsmouth coach violently volleyed a wayward ball away in disgust. Newport had recorded a fourth successive victory and completed a league double over their opponents to boot. Media outlets reported that four arrests were made during the game, with two of those being for public order offences.

Standing opposite the Portsmouth fans back at the train station, I could see that they had been given a police escort onto the platform. Still full of energy, they certainly weren't going back home quietly. One final defiant shout of "sheep, sheep, sheep shaggers," was trotted out by the frustrated mob. Ironically enough, it was the travelling pack who were hurried onto the train and sent back to Fratton like a flock of sheep.

All good things must come to an end. Newport's winning streak quickly went south and morphed itself into a four game losing streak. It certainly looked like I had cursed another club. During this barren run, Edinburgh departed to take up the vacant manager's position at Gillingham. It was hard to begrudge the former Tottenham Hotspur defender's decision. Having served his time in the lower leagues, he'd brought Newport back into the Football League and left the Exiles very much in the play-off picture. He'd left them in a good place. Even the most ardent of Newport fans couldn't argue with that.

Best chant: ""Premier League, and you fucked it up." "Championship, and you fucked it up." "League One, and you fucked it up." "League Two, and you fucked it up." Newport fans handing Portsmouth fans a harsh but true history lesson.

Match ticket: £14 for an advance student ticket. Adult tickets ranged from between £18-£22.

Match programme: £3.50. The extra 50p must go towards the printing costs of a 100 page glossy edition. I found myself thumbing through a lot of adverts, although Ismail Yakubu's Q & A was hilarious. His nickname of "King Smug," was quite apt. When asked for three famous people he'd have round for dinner, Yakubu's response was "me, me and me." He listed himself as his all time footballing hero, while boasting of being the snappiest dresser at the club. I'm surprised his head could fit through the dressing room doors.

Cost of food: £2.50 for a pie.

Food rating: 2/5. Minced beef and onion was the only pie option and there weren't many left. Whether the supply couldn't keep up with the demand I didn't know. Unfortunately, the contents were cold, slightly greyish and somewhat forced down due to hunger. The Chicago Town pizza looked like a much nicer alternative.

Final Score
Newport County 1 (Byrne 68)
Portsmouth 0
Attendance: 4,575

Getting to know Cheltenham Town
Leo Hoenig – Longstanding fan, season ticket holder, groundhopper
www.leohoenig.com

Best game you've witnessed at Whaddon Road?

Too many to choose from, but I will give two specific games - a 5-2 win over Plymouth Argyle in September 2000 and a 6-2 defeat by Kidderminster Harriers in March 1986. A special mention though for the 2-1 win at Leeds United in March 2008. Leeds were lucky not to lose by more!

Best/worst players to pull on a Cheltenham shirt?

I do not like to call anyone "worst," although Jason White was clearly a wrong signing. Any of the players in the 1999-2002 window could claim a place in my best list, but Bob Bloomer and Mark (Boka) Freeman were special players in a special group. From earlier eras, I would mention Steve Abbley and Anton Vircavs.

Best thing about Whaddon Road?

The first beer after the game finishes.

Worst grounds you've visited?

I will mention a couple where the away areas are poor, rather than utterly poor grounds - such as Luton Town, AFC Wimbledon and Exeter City. By contrast, Cheltenham is not a very good ground, but has great viewing for away fans.

Best place to sit at Whaddon Road?

The away end. If there are plenty of away fans they will make the best noise.

Which club serves the nicest pies?

Kidderminster - I thought everyone knew that.

Famous Cheltenham fans?

Apart from me, I believe Steve Winwood (Spencer Davies Group, etc) is a fan - he won the 500 club draw once.

Quirky fact time?

A group of Norwegian supporters visit for the last home game of every season, making a presentation for the Norwegian Supporters Player of the Year.

Game #47: League Two - Friday 16th January 2015
CHELTENHAM TOWN vs Morecambe - The Abbey Business Stadium (Whaddon Road)

It's only natural for there to be teething problems when a new manager comes to the helm. From the office to the football pitch, the objectives are the same - forge positive relationships in order to obtain maximum performance from your staff. An early dart from work had been booked in advance, yet it happened to coincide with the arrival of a new boss who let's just say probably won't be ordering a copy of *Journey to the 72*.

Speaking of shaky starts, Robins boss Paul Buckle was still chasing a first home win since being appointed in late November. Meanwhile, opponents Morecambe were yet to find the net in 2015, playing out two goalless draws at home. My gut instinct told me to expect a draw as I settled down to catch up on some sleep during the train journey. It had been a bit of a stressful week due to a spate of unfortunate events which required me to book some last minute accommodation.

Despite having a few friends in the Birmingham and Gloucestershire areas, none of them could put me up for the night. Danny was back in Chester visiting family, while his former housemate Ivor was attending a friend's function. The latter - a very kind soul still offered me a bed for the evening, but I didn't feel comfortable putting a curfew on his night out so politely declined. A trawl around Late Rooms brought up a positive lead which ticked all three boxes - cheap, ideally located in the city centre and plenty of positive reviews. At £29 a night it was a steal, so I promptly booked and thanked my good fortune.

Arriving in Cheltenham mid-afternoon gave me plenty of time to explore. A pleasant walk through the leafy suburbs brought me to the slick district of Montpellier. Fashionable boutiques, distinctive architecture and a chilled out vibe alleviated the stresses of the day. To emphasise how posh the area was, even the Ladbrokes branch that I passed had a canope hanging above the shop. The Cheltenham Festival - held in March is second to only the Grand National in terms of prestige and prize money on the Horse Racing calendar. I've never been one to have a flutter on the gee-gee's. Give me the hallow turf of a football pitch over the pristine grass of Prestbury Park any day of the week!

The Central Hotel lived up to the expectations on Late Rooms and was no more than a 15 minute walk from the ground. Two Morecambe fans had the same idea as me and obviously had great taste in accommodation. We got chatting during the checking-in process. Neither him nor his girlfriend had missed a game so far this season. Given the geography involved in getting around League Two that's impressive. If I'd been wearing my hat, I would have tipped it off to them. Cheltenham and Morecambe had played out a goalless draw at the Globe Arena back in September. However, the Robins had certainly left a lasting impression on my new acquaintance, who made quite a bold statement.

"They played like Brazil, but couldn't put the ball into the net. I'm not worried. We've got Kevin Ellison. Good footballing brain. If he shoots in the area, then it's going in."

With that analogy fresh in the memory bank, I set off to the Maracana of Gloucester to see if Buckle could replicate some of these supposed samba skills. The weather wasn't very Brazilian. Temperatures had unsurprisingly dropped once again and an icy frost had begun to descend. Thank goodness I'd finally remembered to pack a hat and scarf, although a second pair of socks probably would have come in handy too. I was jealous of the locals who could just pop out of their houses and cross the road to get into the ground.

It could well have been the Friday feeling, but the majority of Cheltenham fans I spoke to beforehand were confident that their beloved team wouldn't fall into a relegation scrap. The programme seller had got a bit too excited and unwittingly dropped some of his stock into wet puddles while chatting to anyone within earshot. Parts of the ground had been modernised in the early 2000s, but my seat was very much part of the old school in the Jelf

Stand. The Jelf happened to be the main area and the only two tiered part of the ground. Rusted metal and bits of chewing gum added to the decor of the rickety wooden seats.

Those supporting pillars also made another appearance, but didn't impede my view. Two modern floodlights complimented two older looking telephone pole type lights at either end of the stadium. The lights inside the stand went off when the game was in play.

Some of the steps leading up to the seats were frozen over and became a safety hazard. Despite repeated warnings from the PA announcer, a VIP rushing through the turnstiles tripped coming up the stairs from the entrance and was lucky not to be hurt. Several scouts, sponsors, members of the press and club officials were close by. I was minding my own business tucking into my pre-match pie, when one of the scouts made themselves known.

"Is that the award winning pie you're eating?" A definite icebreaker if ever I heard one, even if I nearly choked on a mouth full of savoury from trying not to laugh. The man in question - Phil Holder was on a scouting mission from Queen's Park Rangers. In addition to being Harry Redknapp's eyes and ears, Holder was also a friend of Buckle's. He was in attendance to run the rule over three Liverpool loanees in the Cheltenham side - defender Lloyd Jones, midfielder Kevin Stewart and striker Jack Dunn. Stewart and Dunn had already hit the ground running, notching debut goals in a 2-1 win at Oxford United two weeks prior to this game. All three lined up to make their home debuts, with Dunn the first to make an impression from the penalty spot. Lee Vaughan outpaced his marker before being felled in the area. Dunn stepped up and coolly sent Andreas Aristidou the wrong way. The diminutive striker was very much in the Michael Owen mould, with pace to burn and unfazed at mixing it up physically with his markers.

Similar in size and stature, Jack Redshaw carried Morecambe's main attacking threat. There was no sign of Ellison. My thoughts went out to the couple from the hotel, no doubt disappointed at not seeing their favourite veteran bald eagle. Dunn continued to star and give the scouts plenty to scribble about. After spinning on a sixpence and firing over from close range, the forward forced Aristidou into an instinctive fingertip save.

Morecambe began to press in the second half. Cheltenham goalkeeper Trevor Carson took flight to flick a Padraig Amond header from out of the top corner. It was definitely a save worthy of being seen on the Sky cameras - just a shame there weren't any there. The visitors earned a penalty of their own when Craig Braham-Barrett clumsily tripped Jamie Devitt in full view of the referee. Devitt dusted himself down to take the spot kick himself, but Carson guessed the right way and saved it. The rebound fell kindly to Devitt, who inexplicably rolled his next effort against the post with the goal at his mercy. Devitt redeemed himself when he won his side a second penalty. His cross was handled by Vaughan - who had gone from hero to villain for his side. This time, Amond took up the responsibility from 12 yards and placed his penalty under Carson's body to earn his side a share of the spoils.

Lack of ice skates meant that the walk back to the hotel took slightly longer than anticipated. In front of me, I noticed a father grip his young son's hand tightly. Just as well, given that the nipper was slipping and sliding about the place like a penguin. The cold facts didn't make good reading for Cheltenham fans, with a small section booing their team off. Buckle was left waiting for his first home win in charge. Sadly for him it didn't come and he departed the club not long after, having spent just 79 days in charge. A record of one win in 13 meant that the writing was on the wall for the much travelled manager. Players had been brought in and shipped out like musical chairs, with those who departed being less than complimentary towards Buckle and his managerial style. Cheltenham's teething problems ended up being more deep rooted and Buckle became a mere temporary filling which unfortunately needed extracting.

Best chant: Nothing, zilch, nada! Nothing really caught on apart from something along the lines of "the referee's a banker," predictably when Morecambe were awarded their spot kicks.

Match ticket: £7 student ticket, also valid for those aged 18 and under. Adult tickets were priced at £20 with a £2 increase for 'Category A' matches.

Match programme: £3. Much was made of a rare Friday night game under the lights, but chairman Paul Baker had swanned off on a skiing holiday. Buckle tried to gloss over a report of the team not applauding travelling fans after a defeat at Hartlepool United. Morecambe were given a generous mention for their delicious pies. On that note.....

Cost of food: £3.20 for a pie.

Food rating: 2/5. Could learn a thing or two from Morecambe's chef Graham Aimson. The beef and onion pie won out over the chicken and mushroom option, but was lukewarm and the meat was cold. I only managed half a bottle of a flat Pepsi to try and wash it down. By full time, the discarded cola resembled black ice.

Final Score
Cheltenham Town 1 (Dunn 18 pen)
Morecambe 1 (Amond 83 pen)
Attendance: 2,122

Getting to know Swindon Town
Gary Stanley - Former Editor of Vital Swindon
www.swindon.vitalfootball.co.uk
Twitter @VitalSwindon

Favourite memory as a Swindon fan?

I started going in 1983 with my Dad. Ironically, I believe I cheered the away team's goal at my first match. Ooops! I was only three years old mind.

Any good Paolo Di Canio stories during his time in charge (2011-13)?

He galvanised the Town when we needed it. We had just come off relegation with Paul Hart, who has the personality of a brick wall. We needed a boost and Paolo was that man. Okay, he spent a stupid amount of money, but his antics of rallying the crowd and signature of raising the Town scarf aloft following matches bring back good memories. The thump when he slammed his fist into the dugout was also a memory fondly looked back upon. Paolo was Paolo and he got us promoted at the first chance of asking by winning League Two. We would have won League One if he stuck around the following season. I'm convinced of it.

Best game you've witnessed at the County Ground?

Our 2-1 FA Cup win over Wigan Athletic, who at the time were in the Premier League during the 2011/12 season. We looked comfortable under the leadership of Di Canio. It was such an enjoyable day and we got some much needed publicity.

Best/worst players to pull on a Swindon shirt?

Charlie Austin. Quite simply he oozed class and you can see it to this day. The boy knows where the goal is and will continue to take the Premier League by storm. Simon Cox was a great goalscorer down here too. For whatever reason he has been played out of position since leaving us so hasn't found that midas touch again. Shaun Taylor and Colin Calderwood were good back in the day. Both rock hard defenders who would get stuck in.

Best thing about the County Ground?

It hasn't lost its identity. It may be dilapidated and in desperate need of repair, while some would say it's a dump, but it's our dump. Plus it still has four awesome floodlights which were a staple of football grounds from an era gone by. Our ground has character unlike many of the modern stadia which are all too similar to each other.

Worst grounds you've visited?

The Withdean Stadium in Brighton was miles from the pitch. The away end was near a long jump pit. You couldn't see the other end of the pitch. Awful place to watch football, but that wasn't the fans' fault. Colchester United's identikit, soulless ground would also make the top two. Awful place! Pitch is awful, the car park was flooded, no pub near the ground.... in fact there was nothing near the ground. The place is out in the middle of nowhere. Histon's ground in the FA Cup would round off the top three. The result (a 1-0 Histon win back in 2008) probably made the ground worse than what it is.

Enjoyable away days?

Accrington Stanley – tiny ground, but the nicest most hospitable fans you will meet in the Football League. The Crown pub was also very welcoming. Wouldn't want to visit on a wet day mind. Millwall – there is always a tense atmosphere there, although it's not as intimidating as it once was. Love a feisty crowd.

Famous Swindon fans?

TV presenter and former glamour model Melinda Messenger, plus singer Jamie Cullum are both known to be Swindon Town fans.

Quirky fact time?

We are the only club in the country to have a Rolex watch keeping time of our games.

Thoughts on ticket prices in general?

The prices in the Premier League and some Championship sides are absolutely disgusting. They are not for the working man and are clearly set up to maximise profit thanks to the stupid money dished out by media outlets. More and more you are seeing opposition fans boycotting games to make a point about ticket prices in the higher divisions. Leagues One and Two for the most part have nice priced tickets to allow families to attend and watch live football.

Name your Swindon Dream Team?

GK: Fraser Digby
LB: Paul Bodin
CB: Shaun Taylor
CB: Colin Calderwood
RB: Nicky Summerbee
LW: Don Rogers
CM: Ross Maclaren
CM: Martin Ling
RW: Mike Summerbee
CF: Alan Mayes
CF: Andy Rowland

WALTZING ALONG IN WILTSHIRE

Game #48: League One - Saturday 17th January 2015
SWINDON TOWN vs Chesterfield - The County Ground

Riding high at the top of League One, things going great guns. That meant Swindon were due a visit from yours truly. A lucky charm to some and a damned curse to others. The statistics didn't lie. While my presence had galvanised certain teams, others saw me as the proverbial screwdriver, loosening the bolts just enough to ensure the wheels came flying off in the wake of playing in my presence. The cold snap had led to a few clubs up and down the country drafting in helpers to remove covers and snow from pitches. Thankfully, the white stuff had given Swindon a wide berth and I was off to see a second set of Robins inside 24 hours.

Thanks to the overnight stay in Cheltenham, the journey to Wiltshire was a short one. Just as well. An obnoxious guy sitting behind couldn't keep still for most of the hour long journey and kept digging his feet into the back of my chair. I don't know what was worse, that or the fact that he didn't think to offer a chocolate digestive out of the packet he was scoffing.

I'm happy to report there were no back spasms during the short walk from the station to the stadium. Following the signposts to the County Ground proved to be both interesting and dangerous. What started as a pleasant walk past swish upmarket office blocks turned into a stroll through foreign territory. Polish delicatessens, an Istanbul market and Masala bazaar all featured, while reckless taxi drivers neglected to indicate as they hurtled around corners. The *Journey to the 72* almost didn't make it to #48, so I breathed a sigh of relief when I finally spotted Swindon's home, situated behind the 'County Ground' hotel.

Collecting tickets from a small grating in a wall felt like visiting time at prison. I gave the relevant information and was handed my visiting card - I mean envelope containing my ticket. Taking a walk around the back of the stadium, a professional graffiti artist had produced a mural with four ex-playing alumni either side of the club's latest badge. Out of the four players, the only one I recognised was Norwegian striker Jan-Aage Fjortoft, complete with outstretched arms doing his customary aeroplane goal celebration. Anyone old enough to remember Swindon's 1993-94 Premier League stint will know who and what I'm referring to.

Queuing for food, I overheard a guy bragging to his mate that he had chips for tea on Tuesday, Thursday and yesterday. I was about to ask what he had on Wednesday, but the server was ready to take my order. With food in hand, a father of three was trying to get his three sons into betting by holding a game of predict the score. A grand total of £1 made up the cashpot, as the three lads - no more than six or seven years old at a guess came up with 3-0, 3-1 and 2-0 in favour of the home side. Before Ray Winstone could reveal the odds, one lad wanted to cash out in favour of a bag of Fruit Pastilles. Smart kid!

Only three sides of the County Ground were in operation. The uncovered Family Stand was mostly covered up, although a small Rolex clock situated next to the electronic scoreboard is apparently the first and only one of its kind you'll find inside a football ground. I was based in the Lower Tier of the Don Rogers Stand which gave me a great view of the pitch, and I was directly opposite the players' tunnel and dugouts. Most of the noise was coming from the Town End - a small old school traditional stand complete with supporting pillars behind the goal. Speaking of noise, the sounds of UB40's 1993 hit 'Can't Help Falling in Love,' greeting the teams onto the pitch was both funny and surreal. I'd literally deleted the track from my iPod a couple of days earlier, but to hear a few thousand fans singing the chorus was enough to get the pre-match adrenaline pumping. And yes, before you ask, the track has now been restored to my music library.

Swindon were without international duo Yaser Kasim and Massimo Luongo, who were busy making headlines over in Australia at the Asian Cup. Luongo in particular ended up playing a key role in leading the Socceroos to the trophy. Back in Wiltshire, midfielder John Swift was making his home debut after joining on loan from Chelsea. There was a real buzz around the ground that Swindon had bagged a real jewel in the crown. A feature in the matchday programme revealed that after being released by the Premier League giants, an impressive performance in a Sunday League game led to a swift (no pun intended) reunion with Chelsea. Having experienced a brief taste of the first team towards the end of last season, the "next Frank Lampard," was ready to impress a new set of fans. Siblings Nathan and Louis Thompson also deserve a mention for being Swindon's version of the Neville brothers. Both came up through the Swindon ranks, with defender Nathan captaining the side and Louis occupying the midfield.

The home fans didn't have long to wait before they were up on their feet. Chesterfield showed how not to defend a set piece, when Harry Toffolo's cross was nodded in by an unmarked Jack Stephens. Swindon had gone close with a similar effort moments earlier and, in truth any one of three or four players could have put away the chance.

Chesterfield manager Paul Cook had made the strange decision to start the division's highest scorer Eoin Doyle out wide to accommodate the larger Armand Gnanduillet up front. While Doyle took time to settle into his new position, fellow winger Sam Clucas had the bit between his teeth. When Cook switched Clucas to the opposite side, the ginger ninja quickly drew the Spireites level. Clucas was given far too much time and space to run at goal and fire a low shot into the bottom corner from the edge of the box. It was another one of those efforts that you knew was destined for the net as soon as it left his foot. I got caught up in the occasion and stood up to applaud the goal. A few disapproving eyes flashed in my direction, before Swift quickly rescued me from the angry mob.

Just three minutes after conceding, Swindon restored their lead. Chesterfield goalkeeper Tommy Lee rushed out to snuff out a chance, only to leave himself exposed, enabling Swift to spin his marker and fire into the net. It was a really open game and great for a neutral like me. Chesterfield almost drew level once again, but Jimmy Ryan's thumping volley riocheted off the underside of the crossbar. Cook was lucky not to be sent to the stands when he blew a gasket in reaction to a rash challenge on the touchline. His opposite number Mark Cooper wisely kept his distance, while the red mist descended. Swift did little to improve Cook's mood when he turned provider to seal the game. A perfectly weighted pass released Andy Williams, and the prolific Swindon frontman skipped past his markers to slot in his 18th of the season. I found myself humming along to the UB40 lyrics once again with the rest of the jubilant crowd. Entertaining, free-flowing football is easy to love.

"We're playing like Barcelona," remarked one fan a few rows back. A slight exaggeration, but the result did keep Town on top of the League One pile, albeit on goal difference. The crazy taxi drivers were caught up with the rest of the post-match traffic, so the route back to the station was relatively safe. I managed to make the first train out of Swindon by the skin of my teeth. With a four and a half hour commute back to Chester, adding another hour's wait wasn't really appealing. "It's getting a bit too easy now," said one Swindon fan to his mate. Uh-oh, I began to fear that the Robins were about to be knocked off their perch. Lo and behold, the unlucky horseshoe struck again. Swindon would go on to lose four of their next five games. Sorry lads!

Best chant: Anything other than UB40 wouldn't be right, so I'll stick with that.
Match ticket: £19 student ticket. Adult tickets ranged from £18-£27 depending on seat location/match category.
Match programme: £3. Swindon superfan Paul Jackson got a small mention. He started following the club in 1969 and had just finished watching Town at all current 92 league grounds. Well done Paul! Chesterfield were given a generous six page spread, while the squad lists were bumped from the traditional back page slot to make way for sponsor adverts. The club were flogging a programme/FourFourTwo magazine combo for £5. I'd have been all over this had I not just received a subscription as a Christmas present.
Cost of food: £3.40 for a steak and ale pie.
Food rating: 5/5. Maybe it was because I was doing dry January, but the ale was prominent in almost every mouthful, adding flavour to an already delicious savoury snack.

Final Score
Swindon Town 3 (Stephens 17, Swift 25, Williams 47)
Chesterfield 1 (Clucas 22)
Attendance: 7,981

Getting to know Gillingham
Daniel Storey - Gills Fansonline Editor
www.fansonline.net/gillingham

Thoughts on Peter Taylor's departure?

It was time for him to go. The football being served up was dreadful to watch and turning fans away from watching the club. Ok, you can argue he was getting results, but most football fans want to be entertained at the same time and his tactics and formations were just setting us up to avoid defeat even at home! Also towards the end of his tenure he started having a go at the fans and once you start doing that you're never going to win people around. They say you should never go back and Peter Taylor should have followed that advice. His second spell as manager from late 2013 to the start of 2015 won't be remembered quite like his first promotion winning spell.

Best game you've witnessed at the Priestfield Stadium?

I've seen plenty of memorable games in my twenty years watching the club. The Championship winning game against AFC Wimbledon at the end of the 2012/13 season immediately springs to mind. There won't have been too many people inside Priestfield that afternoon who would have witnessed our first Football League Championship winning season in 1964, me included, so to see Adam Barrett lift the trophy in front of a packed Priestfield full of smiling happy faces meant so much to so many, including me. Cherish it as it may never happen again in some of our lifetimes.

Then there was the play-off semi final win against Preston in 1999. A night when Priestfield simply shook to the noise and passion of over 9000 Gillingham fans who knew the team were just 90 minutes away from their first ever visit to Wembley. Over 1000 Preston fans struggled to make themselves heard above the din inside Priestfield that night. After just two minutes, Andy Hessenthaler sent us all wild with delight to give us a 1-0 lead on the night and 2-1 on aggregate. For the next 88 minutes plus injury time, the team defended for their collective lives whilst the rest of us nervously chewed every nail off our finger tips. The final whistle reduced some to tears as history was made in front of the old Rainham End which was making its last stand. What a way to see her off.

Finally, a 5-0 massacre of Swindon Town in August 2009. The Wiltshire lot may not be that bothered by us these days, but Gillingham fans of a certain age will forever hate Swindon Town. This victory may have been bitter sweet seeing as we were relegated at Wycombe nine months later, but at the time in the glorious Priestfield sunshine it was like all our Christmases had come at once as Swindon trundled back down the M4 with their tails well and truly between their legs. All together now, "We will fight forever more because of Roy McHale". Sorry I'm getting carried away now.

Best/worst players to pull on a Gillingham shirt?

Cody McDonald is still the main source of goals and has the ability to create goals out of nothing. Stuart Nelson in goal is also a hero for the fans and has been our saviour many times since he signed in the summer of 2012. Worst players, wow where to start. Mark McCammon - a striker on his CV, but we all lie on our CV's don't we? The same applies to Lee Matthews. Neil Masters was a sick note of epic proportions and became a laughing stock in the mid 90s, as he was injured more times that he was fit! Stuart Thorgood was a signing from non-league and that's exactly where he should have stayed.

Best thing about the Priestfield Stadium?

The atmosphere when the place really gets behind the team.

Worst grounds you've visited?

Dagenham and Redbridge is a pretty soul destroying place. The new grounds at Shrewsbury, Colchester and Chesterfield are all identikit, bland, dull and lacking in any kind of atmosphere. Accrington Stanley is another ground I won't be rushing back too neither.

Best place to sit at the Priestfield Stadium?

The Rainham End when it's at full voice.

Best place to get a pre-match drink?

The Cricketers near the ground, but it's for home fans only. However, the beers on tap are not great and it could do with bringing in some more real ales.

Which club serves the nicest pies?

Walsall.

Famous Gillingham fans?

The commentator Brian Moore. We even had a fanzine named after him.

Thoughts on the club winning best programme in League One?

Fair play to all involved in The Gills match day programme for winning the award. I have to say it's a good read with a good mix of club and supporter contributions throughout. I do rather like this year's book style format which is minus the annoying staples.

Quirky fact time?

We once won five trophies in one season back in the 1945/46 season.

Name your Gillingham Dream Team?

GK: Vince Bartram
RB: Mark Patterson
CB: Adrian Pennock
CB: Chris Hope
LB: Dominic Naylor
CM: Paul Smith
LM: Nicky Southall
CM: Andy Hessenthaler
RM: Mark Saunders
CF: Robert Taylor
CF: Carl Asaba

PARTY TIME AT THE PRIESTFIELD

Game #49: League One - Saturday 24th January 2015
GILLINGHAM vs Oldham Athletic - MEMS Priestfield Stadium

"So what are you doing for your birthday this year Shaun?" A question posed by many a friend.

"Well, I've booked a table at my favourite Chinese restaurant on the Friday, or you can join me at the Gillingham game the day after?" Cue the awkward silence on the end of the phone.

With the votes tallied, the result was a full table on the Friday followed by empty seats on the train to Kent the next day. The sweet and sour pork was all well and good, but sometimes my friends don't know what they're missing out on.

Sober as a judge (thanks to dry January) and with a friend's butchering of Oasis hit 'Cigarettes and Alcohol,' still ringing from my ears, I caught the early bird express to London, optimistic of bearing witness to a second birthday weekend treat.

You had to go back to the first day of the season for the last time me and Gillingham were acquainted. Surrendering a 2-0 lead to go down 4-2 at MK Dons, the Gills certainly entertained. While they may have left stadium:mk empty handed, they had left a lasting impression on me. Since that sunny August day, it had been a case of the more things change, the more they stayed the same.

Following a period of conceding as many goals as they scored, Gillingham chairman Paul Scally didn't even wait for Big Ben to bring in the New Year. Instead, he chose to relieve Peter Taylor of his managerial duties mere hours before the phone lines became jammed with several hundred drunken renditions of 'Auld Lang Syne.' The appointment of Justin Edinburgh was still a few weeks off, so in the interim, a party of four - Steve Lovell, Andy Hessenthaler, Darren Hare and Mark Patterson occupied the hotseat. Rumours of the substitutes playing shotgun for a space in an already crowded dugout proved to be unfounded.

Getting on the train at London St Pancras, I was almost blinded by the sight of a flourescent high vis jacket, complete with 'Sports Direct' slogan across the middle. On closer inspection, it was just an Oldham fan decked out in Mike Ashley wear braving his side's away colours.

Priestfield Stadium is well signposted as soon as you come out of the station. The scaffold poles which prop up the uncovered Brian Moore Stand (named after the late commentator and lifelong fan) come into view as you approach the end of a cul-de-sac. From a distance, the area does resemble something of a construction site. I wouldn't like to sit in one of the high seats, especially on a windy day. Passing through a hole in the wall doesn't transport you to Narnia. Instead it brings you around to the other sides of the stadium. Photos of former greats and past achievements (including a shot of jubilant players holding the League Two title aloft in 2013) proudly hang on the walls of the offices and inside the club shop. A conference and banqueting venue is situated towards the back of the stadium and close to where I was located. For those looking for something a bit less upmarket, there is a Rock Cafe too. My bag got caught in the ultra thin turnstile that a size zero model would barely get through. Luckily for me, a local kindly pushed my bag over so that I didn't get further mangled.

Away fans get the rough end of the deal being based in the Brian Moore Stand - the only part of the ground without a roof. The two-tiered Medway Stand is the newest of the three stands, after being opened at the start of the millennium. The Rainham End, situated behind the goal and directly opposite the Brian Moore area has been updated from a terrace and is where you'll find the most noise from home fans.

The Gills bagged a victory before a ball was kicked in anger, when the club were announced as having the best programme in League One by *Football Programme Magazine*. Bound tightly and presented with a laminate finish, the victory was down to the edition's "strong and unified branding." Unfortunately, they won't be winning any prizes for their food anytime soon. I'll dig my chef's hat back out later for the pie report.

Gillingham's PA announcer took a page out of the NBA playbook, making a big deal out of the player introductions while trying to whip the crowd into a wild frenzy. Little anecdotes were thrown in as I was introduced to "the goal machine," Cody McDonald amongst others. In contrast, the announcer couldn't have named the Oldham side any quicker and with any less gusto.

McDonald had been a main source of goals for Gillingham, but here he was very much the assist machine, helping his side race into a two goal lead. McDonald's slide-rule pass enabled loanee John Marquis to run at goal unchallenged and bury a shot into the far corner. Marquis quickly bagged his second of the game when he beat goalkeeper Paul Rachubka at his near post. The ex-Manchester United shotstopper really should have done better.

A sense of déjà vu swept over me when Oldham were awarded a penalty not long after. Bradley Dack was punished for two needless fouls in the box. Although Danny Philliskirk saw his effort saved, Liam Kelly was quickest to react and put the ball under Stuart Nelson's legs. Moments later, the away side had pulled level. Nelson came under the microscope again, mis-controlling a routine backpass with his knee, allowing Dominic Poleon to nip in, pick his pocket and slot the ball into an empty net.

It was shaping up to be just like MK Dons all over again. The Gills surrender a two goal lead before going down to yet another defeat. However, this time it wasn't like that at all. Dack ripped up the script and made up for his earlier mistake by netting the winner. Oldham failed to clear a Gavin Hoyte cross and the bearded wonder volleyed an unstoppable shot into the top corner from the edge of the box.

A five goal thriller was a great birthday present. Some overzealous Oldham fans had been kicked out for removing their shirts and attempting to obstruct the game, but the majority were well behaved. A small group could be heard talking about the lack of curry sauce to go with their chips to several puzzled looking younger Gillingham fans on the train home. It's a northern thing lads.

Best chant: "You dirty northern bastards." Not exactly an original chant, but given my roots and location I had to laugh. Oldham's hard nosed approach and tough tackling didn't exactly go down too well with their southern counterparts.
Match ticket: £21 and worth every penny. Taking advantage of a discounted pre-match purchase, adult tickets went up by £3-£4 if purchased on a matchday.
Match programme: £3. According to the club's website, two full-time members of staff put together each edition. Well presented and strong enough to withstand a few accidental drink spills, a rollercoaster 2014 is reviewed, while some of the smaller Kent based clubs also got a few lines and generous coverage. Last but not least, the Gillingham Ladies team were afforded some column inches and had just as many sponsors as the men. Good to see equality on display.
Cost of food: £3.30 for a pie, £2.00 for chips, £3.80 for a burger, £3 for a sausage roll. Before you go jumping to conclusions, I didn't consume all of that....just half, although in hindsight I now regret that.
Food rating: 2/5. The chips were burnt and tasted like leftovers from the previous home game. The steak and ale pie was only marginally better, although the flavour quickly wore off and you're definitely short changed on the meat content. Go and watch Gillingham play football, but don't forget to take a packed lunch.

Final Score
Gillingham 3 (Marquis 7, 14, Dack 70)
Oldham Athletic 2 (Kelly 20, Poleon 23)
Attendance: 4,959

Getting to know Chesterfield
Stuart Basson - Chesterfield FC honorary historian
www.cfchistory.com
Twitter @StuartBasson

Favourite memory as a Chesterfield fan?

Probably coming back from the Old Trafford FA Cup semi-final, and seeing the homemade banners of congratulations that had been stuck on fences and lamp posts as we came through Stockport.

Thoughts on ticket prices in general?

They're too high. Our £24-ish per game tickets for Division Three (let's call it what it is) is too much, but it pales in comparison to the £50 or so that Sheffielders being asked to pay for one division above. At our prices, I will have to pick and choose. £16 would be fairer for our league, but I doubt the players and agents will ever voluntarily suck less from the game in order to make that possible.

Best game you've witnessed at the Proact Stadium?

There have been quite a few, perhaps surprisingly the 5-5 draw with Crewe in 2010-11 comes readily to mind.

Best/worst players to pull on a Chesterfield shirt?

The best ones are not always the most gifted. I used to like players like Steve Williams, the Mansfield forward that Chesterfield converted into an attacking full-back in the 1990s, because he always played to the absolute top of his game, limited though that was. Of the current lot, Drew Talbot fits the same profile. Conversely, the players I disliked are the ones who seemed to fail to understand the opportunity they had, and looked as though they couldn't be bothered. I once saw Mark Randall nesh a tackle that led directly to an opposition goal, while I recall Jonathan Grounds coming off the field after we had been beaten at home, laughing with an opposition player. You need to know that it hurts them as much as it hurts us.

What was the best thing about old ground Saltergate?

Leaving it behind. The low roofs over the home standing areas helped create an atmosphere, especially at night matches, but that atmosphere was often quite poisonous if the team weren't doing well. It was emotional to leave a place where football had been played since 1871, but the startling rate at which it deteriorated, once left unmaintained, made the point about having to go.

Best thing about the Proact Stadium?

You get a decent view from almost every seat; the place is light and airy, so there is no hiding place for the morons and racists.

Worst grounds you've visited?

I went to a lot in the days of fencing. 'Doncatraz,' on the Belle Vue away end, was dreadful, but Halifax also had a caged area down one side that rather shamed the game. The view from the standing bit of Everton's old away end (opposite the Gladwys Street end) was a strong contender for the worst view in Association Football. The Don Valley Stadium as used by Rotherham United was awful. I once paid to sit in the old main stand at Crewe and found my seat to consist of a plank wide enough only for a one-buttocked man. But I called Saltergate my home, so who am I to have a pop?

Enjoyable away days?

The Victoria Ground, Stoke; Roker Park, Sunderland; Fratton Park; Meadow Lane is always good. Of the newer ones, Huddersfield's is probably the best. In the days of standing, the Holte End at Villa Park and the Kippax at Maine Road were good to experience, when full.

Which club serves the nicest pies?

I'm afraid my pie-munching days are behind me. I'm told ours are quite good, being locally made.

Famous Chesterfield fans?

None that I'm aware of, which is actually quite a good claim to fame, since it implies that we don't stand for any of that poncy, celebrity stuff up here.

Quirky fact time?

January 30th, 1946: In an effort to help European clubs back to their feet after the war, the club agreed to send a set of old shirts to some Dutch outfit called 'Ajax.' What became of them, I wonder?

Name your Chesterfield Dream Team?

Of those I have seen play:
GK: Billy Mercer
CB: Sean Dyche
CB: Steve Blatherwick
RB: Gary Bellamy
LB: John Ryan
CM: Thomas Hitzlsperger
CM: Sam Morsy
RM: Marcus Ebdon
LM: Jamie O'Hara
CF: Kevin Davies
CF: Ernie Moss

SNEAKING OFF TO SEE THE SPIREITES

Game #50: League One - Tuesday 27th January 2015
CHESTERFIELD vs Crawley Town - The Proact Stadium

You wait ages for a bus then two come along at once. Or in my case, you wait until January to see Chesterfield play, then watch them three times in less than a month. You'd think I'd be on first name terms with manager Paul Cook and his playing staff by now. Sadly for me that wasn't the case.

Thanks to Chesterfield's recent FA Cup adventures, this game was moved to a midweek slot. A hastily put together holiday request was met with as much enthusiasm by my employers as a David Moyes greeting card at Old Trafford. Thankfully, a compromise was eventually met. Sacrificing a lunch break and going hungry in the hope of seeing a game full of goals was the hand that I played. Chancing my arm further with the roulette of the bus timetable, a prompt service got me to the station in time and I was off to see the bright lights of Chezvegas baby!

Fleeting visits had been made towards the Proact over the years, but an ex-girlfriend's tolerance for football was non existent. As a result, we always ended up in the neighbouring Tesco instead. Passing through South Yorkshire and the neighbouring villages did bring back some familiar sights. Sadly it didn't jog my memory in terms of directions to the ground. Walking across a busy flyover and past the famous crooked spire on top of the parish church, I looked for signs, but instead got something much better....a superfan!

A girl decked out in a Chesterfield club shirt, jacket, hat, scarf and badge was walking towards me. Working on the safe hunch that she was going to the game, Emma ended up being my tour guide for the evening. Familiarity with the team's recent performances helped me pass the initiation/ light interrogation during a lengthy walk down a long dipping road, passing such delights as the 'Donkey Derby' pub and 'Chester's fish bar' along the way. By the way, these two eateries come highly recommended by Emma for those wanting to break the journey up to the ground.

Having seen the team draw and lose, this was my chance to see Chesterfield complete the set and pick up a win to stay in touch with the play-off chasers. The club famously reached the semi-finals of the FA Cup back in 1997. Unfortunately, there was no chance of a repeat performance this year. Their current run had just been ended at the fourth hurdle by Derby County days earlier.

The Spireites moved to their new £13 million stadium in 2010, with IT company Proact acquiring the naming rights from B2net. Former home Saltergate - the scene for many of those 1997 memories has now been demolished and turned into a housing estate. However, a piece of the club's history still remains, following a successful fan vote to name the street on the new development 'Spire Heights,' as a play on the club's nickname.

Shaped and presented like a mini changing room, the Chesterfield club shop made use of its small space to create a unique surrounding. Temporary access to the posh executive area was also granted for a quick look at the trophy cabinet, with the Johnstone's Paint Trophy and League Two title being recent additions.

It was ironic that Crawley boss Dean Saunders was being advertised for a sporting dinner at the stadium six days after this game. With all due respect, Deano's managerial career hasn't really reached the same levels as his playing days. Given that Crawley were rooted to the bottom coming into this game and the fact that Saunders tasted relegation with his last two club sides - Doncaster Rovers and Wolverhampton Wanderers, he definitely looked like he was hedging his bets with his after dinner speaking commitments.

Once inside, the Proact is a simple but neat four sided affair. The curved roofs of both the Main and East Stands seem to be inspired by Huddersfield Town, albeit on a smaller scale. If you squint then you can just about make out the small electronic scoreboard which sits on the roof of the away end behind the goal. I was sat in and amongst the hub of the noise and 'Yogi' the drummer, directly opposite the handful of optimistic away fans who had made the long journey up from West Sussex. Happily, there wasn't a supporting pillar in sight, although the open corners of the ground meant it was easy for the wind and winter chill to make its presence felt.

Crawley barely threatened and were swept aside by a well-oiled Chesterfield display. The division's top scorer Eoin Doyle had brought his shooting boots and took centre stage, in what proved to be his penultimate appearance for the club before a deadline day move to Cardiff City. A section of fans were already resigned to losing one of their prized assets when they informed me that the club were still paying off the Proact and needed to balance the books.

Doyle netted his first after running onto an Armand Gnanduillet flick-on, turning his marker inside out and burying a low shot past Lewis Price. Crawley's flimsy resistance was then ripped apart by two early second half goals. Jay O'Shea was given full licence to run at goal and it came as no surprise when he buried his effort into the far corner. The Chesterfield fans had barely stopped singing when Doyle netted his second of the night. Pressuring his marker into a weak header, the 'fox in the box' picked up a loose ball and applied the close range finish. Doyle really should've taken home the match ball, but spurned the chance of a hat-trick by rolling his next effort the wrong side of the post. As the Spireites amped up the noise levels, poor old Saunders cut a lonely figure on the touchline, with the magnitude of the task he'd taken on just starting to hit home.

In truth, the referee should have ended this mercy killing long before the 90 minutes were up. I certainly didn't envy the Crawley fans making the long trip home after sitting through a fruitless night. Mind you, I had my own journey back to contend with and was on a tight deadline. Declining an offer of a fish and chip supper at Chester's, I bid Emma farewell and headed back up the dipping road towards the town centre. Taking a wrong turning at the church certainly wasn't in the plans, but that's exactly what happened. I just had to get a couple of pictures of the famous spire. Running in work shoes and a heavy backpack was a necessity to avoid a six hour layover and the possibility of using a station bench as a makeshift bed. Through sheer good fortune, I made it back to the station minutes before the train came into sight. On a positive note, I think I managed to run off the pie.

Best chant: "Eooooo-in Doyle, ooh aah. I want to know how you scored that goal." Sung to the tune of DJ Otzi's 2001 hit "Hey Baby," the Spireite version caught on pretty quickly and was fun to sing along to.
Match ticket: £20 was the cheapest adult ticket for a prime position behind the goal in the South Stand. Tickets went up to £24 for a seat in the West Stand, while there was a £2 increase across the board for Category A games.
Match programme: £3 - American fan Vinny Plateroti discovered the club on FIFA back in 2008, forged a connection through Facebook and watched a couple of JPT games online. Now a fully fledged fan, Vincent sports the shirt when he goes to watch his local side New York Red Bulls. However, he is still to visit the Proact. Get yourself down here lad!
Cost of food: £3.50 for a chicken hot pot pie.
Food rating: 2/5. The glazed pastry looked promising, but it went downhill from there. The crushed vegetables and white chicken sauce was bland and lacking any type of flavour.

Final Score
Chesterfield 3 (Doyle 34, 53, O'Shea 51)
Crawley Town 0
Attendance: 5,329

Getting to know Walsall
Kevin Paddock - Vital Walsall Editor
www.walsall.vitalfootball.co.uk
Twitter @VitalWalsall

Favourite memory as a Walsall fan?

It's quite simple for me. The Ray Graydon years. He took over the club in 1998/99 and, up to that point we had cup runs but not much else. Ray brought professionalism to the club and instantly we had success. In his first season we got promoted over the likes of free spending Stoke, Wigan and Man City - that season we were favourites to go down! The next season we battled against all odds and went down on the very last day - after the game Ray said "we will come again" and we did the following year as Ray took us up via the play-offs beating Reading in extra time. He was sacked into his fourth season, but to this day he is my idol!

Best game you've witnessed at the Bescot Stadium?

There's been a few! When we beat Torquay 8-4, beating Premier sides Sheff Utd and Forest while we were in Division Two, but for me it would have to be Stoke at home which clinched our place in the play offs in 2000-01 when we beat them 4-2. As one of our rivals, it was nice to win, but the atmosphere was incredible.

Best/worst players to pull on a Walsall shirt?

The best would have to be Jimmy Walker and Jorge Leitao. Jimmy was our shot stopper for ten years and went on to make over 500 appearances for the club. If he was slightly taller he would have played at the very top and even for England. Jorge was a surprising £150,000 signing from a lower league Portuguese side. Not only were we surprised at how good Jorge was, it was the fact we paid a transfer fee which was more surprising. He went on to be top scorer for the club in four years and he wore his heart on his sleeve. Recently the fans helped pay for him to come back to England to play for our legends side.

Best thing about the Bescot Stadium?

Its location probably. It's on the border of the M6 and uses that with its constant advertising. The stadium was built ten years too early and is showing her age.

Worst grounds you've visited?

Worst ground I've ever visited is probably Northampton's cricket ground in the 90's. There was literally a speed bump in both goal areas and the pitch sloped towards the canal. Quite surreal.

Enjoyable away days?

For me it would have to be Molineux - Wolves. Given it's only a ten minute bus ride, we always enjoy our local derbies - the wins in 2008 and last season are still some of my fondest memories in football

Which club serves the nicest pies?

I'm biased, I'd say ours. We introduced the first Balti pie into England and they're bostin!

Famous Walsall fans?

Musical moguls Pete Waterman and Nigel Jenkins are Walsall's most famous fans. Jenkins once watched a Walsall game in America with Britney Spears and Justin Timberlake!

Quirky fact time?

Our record transfer fee is still over thirty years old when we paid £185,000 for Alan Buckley.

Game #51: League One - Sunday 1st February 2015
WALSALL vs Gillingham - The Banks's Stadium (Bescot Stadium)

The Premier League cameras were being packed away and Sky were winding down another weekend of football, but all was not settled. Not by a long shot. There was still the matter of a mid-table game in the Midlands to be decided. Having missed out on my usual Saturday football fix due to work commitments, I jumped at the chance to sample some early evening action and prolong the Monday blues for at least a couple of hours. A 6pm kick-off was as random as it was fortuitous, especially on a Sunday. Still, Danny was game to come with me and offered to pick me up from Birmingham.

So why the late Sunday kick-off time I hear you ask? Two reasons. The first being that a lucrative Sunday market takes place in the Bescot area, which is very financially viable for Walsall. The second and main reason for moving the game from a Saturday was due to Gillingham only playing the second leg of their Johnstone's Paint Trophy semi-final at Bristol City on the Thursday evening.

Danny had clearly done his research on the Saddlers. "First club to sell the balti pie," he confidently stated as I got into the car. Cheers mate. That was my meal selection sorted. Danny didn't need much convincing to brave the arctic wintry temperatures. The Bescot was the final stop on his own mini ground tour of the Midlands. The work Christmas party he attended in the function room apparently didn't count.

For those travelling to and through Walsall, it's nigh on impossible to miss the Bescot Stadium. Situated off the M6 motorway, a large digital advertising board will certainly draw your attention to the ground. For me, it's always the smiling amphibian along the top of the Tile Choice Stand which I try and look out for.

Five days on from securing a place in the Johnstone's Paint Tropy final, Wembley fever had gripped Walsall. Fans were queuing around the block, lining up to get tickets for the club's first ever appearance at England's national stadium. A hastily arranged sign pointed out that tickets weren't on sale yet, but most of the pack stayed back to take in the upcoming game. Opportunists were handing out flyers at every corner, offering to put alternative transport on and clearly make a tidy chunk of change in the process. After conveniently parking at the neighbouring Bescot Station (behind the away end) we joined the queue.

Getting tickets wasn't as easy as first thought. Sorry, I should rephrase. Getting tickets for the correct game wasn't easy. A quick scan of the tickets in our possession revealed advanced entry for the Rochdale game in eight days. That's what having four or five different windows open on your computer leads to. Skipping the queue to point out the mistake, the tickets were duly corrected, although there was now an added charge. The guy behind the glass looked a lot like Billy Zabka out of the first Karate Kid movie. Appeals for a price freeze out of goodwill fell on deaf ears, so me and Danny coughed up the extra few pounds each. 1-0 to the Cobra Kai!

Unfortunately, because of the faffing over tickets, there was no time for a pre-match pint. A small number of fans were still looking to carry on the party from midweek. That being said, attendance was way down from the 10,000 who were here five days earlier. Given the magnitude of this game, plus the number of other clubs in close proximity, and not forgetting the odd kick-off time, that wasn't very surprising.

Gillingham had brought a healthy, boisterous following. The rowdy bunch conveniently took up residence in a segregated part of the Community Stand, not too far away from me and Danny. They didn't care that it was a freezing cold Sunday night and their enthusiasm soon spread.

It's hard to ignore the fact that the Tile Choice Stand behind one of the goals dwarfs the rest of the ground and is the only part without supporting pillars. Efforts have been made to fill in the corners with advertising boards to give the stadium that fully enclosed feel. Danny pointed out the hospitality area and recalled a drunken tale of dancing on the tables at Christmas as the two teams came out.

Walsall's James Chambers was given an early headache when Gillingham's Gavin Hoyte literally pushed him into the advertising boards. The ball had long gone, yet Hoyte was lucky to escape with only a caution. Walsall dominated, but found Stuart Nelson in inspired form. The Gills keeper flew to palm an effort out of the top corner, saved an effort with his legs and even channelled his inner Peter Schmeichel by running out to thwart a one-on-one. The travelling support broke into chants of "England's #1." Unfortunately, I don't think Roy Hodgson was there, but I could certainly vouch for Nelson's performance. Walsall's bad luck continued when they lost Tom Bradshaw to injury, after the striker aggravated his hamstring when meeting a shot on the turn.

Naturally, Gillingham soaked up the pressure and took the lead in classic smash and grab fashion. Bradley Dack ran onto a long ball over the top of the defence and coolly slotted the ball underneath Richard O'Donnell. Moments later, the Gills were livid when the referee waved away a penalty attempt. Cody McDonald had gone down a bit too cheaply and was unhappy at being caught. He still gave the referee an earful, who responded in kind with a yellow card. Pipe down son!

Just when I thought I was about to see a rare Gillingham clean sheet, Doug Loft didn't take too kindly to being nutmegged and needlessly raised an elbow. From the resulting free kick into the box, Ashley Grimes bundled in from close range to give Walsall a deserved equaliser. The Saddlers missed a couple more chances late on, with fans and stewards all noticeably aggrieved at the end. Cries of "we should have won that," were heard more than once during the short trip back to the car.

It had been a chilly night and I was only too glad to feel the heating on my legs once back in the car. "I could have used the Bovril for my feet," said Danny as he dropped me back off in Birmingham for a quiet commute back home. The beefy snack isn't really my cup of tea, so I'll just stick to wearing two pairs of socks for the rest of winter.

Best chant: "If you're all going to Wembley clap your hands." Walsall fans. "We've been three times." Gillingham fans in response.
Match ticket: £22.50 for a Category B game. Could have saved £2 by buying in advance, while a Category A game would cost £22 in advance or £24 on the day. Family tickets (one adult, one child) ranged from £22.50-£26.
Match programme: £3. Lots of Wembley related reaction and pieces from everyone connected at the club, which was to be expected. In an interesting tidbit, Walsall first played on a Sunday in January 1974, beating Wrexham 3-0. Admission was free because it was a Sunday, although fans had to buy a teamsheet at the turnstiles to get in. How times have changed!
Cost of food: £3.00 for a balti pie. Steak and kidney was never going to be an option.
Food rating: 3/5. Foil packed for freshness, the exterior was a little tough. Inside was warm enough and the chicken was marinaded with enough spice to give it a bit of a kick. Not a bad effort.

Final Score
Walsall 1 (Grimes 74)
Gillingham 1 (Dack 69)
Attendance: 3,951

Getting to know Northampton Town
Dan Pearce - The Hotel End (Northampton Fans Forum)
www.thehotelend.co.uk

Favourite memory as a Northampton fan?

My first game was Exeter City at home in 1997. The Cobblers won the game 4-1 and I was hooked. I thought that every game would be that easy. 18 years of suffering later, I realise that this wasn't totally correct! Other than that, winning promotion at Torquay in 2000. We won the last six games that season to steal third spot from Darlington, and seeing Cobblers fans invaded the pitch from all three stands that day is something that I'll never forget. The Torquay fans were first class as well, I've had a soft spot for them ever since.

Best game you've witnessed at Sixfields?

There's only one choice for this. Bristol Rovers at home in the play offs. May 1998.

Best/worst players to pull on a Northampton shirt?

The best in my life time is without doubt Martin Smith. The most technically gifted player I've ever seen wear the claret shirt. The worst has too many candidates sadly. But, Gary Johnson considered Bas Savage to be an ideal replacement for Billy McKay. Him or Chris Arthur.

Best thing about Sixfields?

The intimidating atmosphere.

Enjoyable away days?

Hillsborough is my favourite ground. It has a great mix of traditional and modern stands, and had a superb atmosphere. But a favourite for most NTFC fans has to be "The London Borough of Barking and Dagenham Stadium". Cobblers have played there five times, won five times, and not conceded a goal. They're great hosts.

Famous Northampton fans?

Des O'Conner, Jo Whiley, and Dan Roan of the BBC.

Quirky fact time?

Joe Mercer, the Manchester City manager in the 60s said, "The miracle of 1966 was not England winning the World Cup but Northampton reaching Division One".

Thoughts on ticket prices in England?

Ticket prices have been beyond a joke for too many years, and because of people like us who pay the prices regardless, nothing will change. I read that some championship teams are charging £52 a game this season. Championship teams!

Name your Northampton Dream Team?

GK: Keith Welch
RB: Kyle Walker
CB: Ian Sampson
CB: Luke Chambers
LB: John Frain
RW: Michael Jacobs
CM: Ian Taylor
CM: Brent Rahim
LW: Martin Smith
CF: Jamie Forrester
CF: Eric Sabin

TALKING COBBLERS

Game #52: League Two - Saturday 7th February 2015
NORTHAMPTON TOWN vs Morecambe - Sixfields

Meeting fans along the way has not only been rewarding, but it's also made me care about clubs whom I shared no affinity with before starting out on my journey. Northampton Town is probably the best example of this. Long story short, had it not been for the chance meeting with some lost fans in Morecambe back in September, then I wouldn't be the honorary Cobbler that I am now. With that touch of nostalgia fresh in the memory, it was only fitting that I would go and watch the return league meeting between the two teams.

Fan experiences can heighten or dampen the mood anywhere you go. From the liveliest of arenas, to the dampest of squibs, you're all in it together for 90 minutes. The last time I was with the Cobblers, they were screaming abuse at poor John-Joe O'Toole, who had just been loaned out to Southend United. Now back at his parent club, the fans had done a complete 180 and were even planning on honouring the long haired wonder with an official day named after him at the club's next away game.

Registering on fan forum 'The Hotel End,' the night before the game, I was guided in the direction of the North Stand in terms of best matchday atmosphere and was optimistic of tracking down my fellow acquaintances. Changing trains at Rugby was ironic, if only to come into contact with several fans of the eggchasing sport. Northampton Saints were playing at home and scores of replica jerseys were proudly on show, while there wasn't a single claret football shirt in sight.

Alighting at Northampton, I was faced with more rugby fans. The only time I ever choose the egg over the ball is at Easter, and even then it's the chocolate variety. Out of the corner of my eye, I spied a loved-up Morecambe couple studying a map and plotting their route to the stadium. Finally, some kindred spirits. I trailed behind them and popped the earphones in for the two mile walk to Sixfields. As long as it isn't tipping down with rain, I'll always opt for a walk over taking a bus or a taxi. Passing several warehouses, I did a double take when walking past a random Greggs outlet sandwiched inbetween in the middle of nowhere. Certainly not a prime location, unless the canteen food in the warehouses is crap.

Carrying on down a long dipping road took me past Franklin's Gardens (the home of the Saints) and finally onto Sixfields, located at the bottom of a hill with a retail park sitting above it. The ground is currently operational on three sides, while a new East Stand is being built. Reconstruction work had temporarily been halted over a contract dispute, leaving the club in limbo due to the stop/start negotiations. As it currently stands, it's anyone's guess when the new stand will be completed and opened.

The junior team were out in force with their buckets, trying to raise funds in order to play a lucrative game in Spain. Hopefully my donation went towards flights and not sweets. The Cobblers onesie took pride of place front and centre inside the club shop. Throw in some bling and it wouldn't look out of place in an urban music video. As advised, I took my seat behind the goal and dodged many wayward shots from the Northampton players warming up. The rows of seats had been assembled like a table football set, not that I did much sitting down. Right on cue, and true to their word, the merry crew I was familiar with made their arrival, singing along and shaking hands with fellow fans along the way. Anti Peterborough United songs quickly filled the air, before a rendition of Harry J Allstars' 'The Liquidator,' welcomed the two teams onto the pitch, with Northampton singing it with much more gusto than Chelsea currently do.

Morecambe looked like they were still in the changing room when Northampton hit the front after less than 30 seconds. Slack marking allowed Town full back Brendon Moloney licence to run unchallenged into the Morecambe box and goalkeeper Andreas Aristidou could only push the ball into the path of Joel Byrom, who tucked it away from close range. Fans were still filing in, while others rushed from the pie stands to share in the adulation.

To their credit, Morecambe didn't wilt. The Shrimpers had drawn every game they'd played in 2015 before today and got themselves level, although their equaliser had a hint of good fortune to it. Matt Duke used his legs to thwart Jack Redshaw, but the ball looped into the air and Jamie Devitt leapt highest to head the rebound in off the post. Faint noise could be heard from the travelling Shrimpers fans, but this was soon drowned out by the home support. In Marc Richards, Northampton boasted one of League Two's top marksmen. It came as no surprise when the forward bagged his 16th of the season, getting on the end of Evan Horwood's cross-shot to turn the ball into the bottom corner.

The Cobblers had the chance to make the game more comfortable when Ricky Holmes charged into the box and was bundled over. Surprisingly, Richards wasn't as potent from 12 yards and had a sketchy record. I even pointed to where he should place the kick, but he fluffed his lines and struck the post. That gave Morecambe hope and they too hit the woodwork late on. Alan Goodall let rip from outside the box and the ball ricocheted off the base of the post and back off Duke's head, before rolling to safety.

Northampton boss Chris Wilder put a proverbial pin in the fans' balloons when he took off O'Toole towards the end. The midfield mullet had been solid if not spectacular. Besides, he was probably saving himself for his famed day at Mansfield the following week. A fleeting thought passed through my mind where I thought it would be funny if he got sent off during that game. Would you believe me if I said he did? Because that's exactly what happened. The script wrote itself, as O'Toole let the emotion and occasion get to him and fell foul of the referee, bringing a premature end to his big day.

The final whistle handed Northampton their fifth win on the bounce and kept them in touch with the play-offs. Quite a remarkable turnaround considering that the club lost every game in December and were being touted as relegation candidates. Finally, I was bringing some good luck to a team. I was in good spirits as I set off on the journey home. With a delicious Subway sandwich in hand, I was looking forward to losing myself in a good book. Not for the first time this season, a fatality on the line at Leighton Buzzard changed all that. National Rail ground to a halt as services up and down the country were pushed back and cancelled. Accepting that I was stuck at Milton Keynes for a while, I was informed that my train had already left London, so it was just a case of waiting it out. That didn't stop some people from buzzing around like pesky flies every time I tried to get into my book. Particularly annoying was an Energy Consultant who wouldn't shut up about missing a meeting with an important client in Manchester. In his own words, he was supposed to schmooze a German colleague with a meal and some women. Well, I was missing Match of the Day, so we were all going to have to make some sacrifices.

Forensics must have finished their investigations early, as my train turned up only 90 minutes later than scheduled. I was expecting a longer delay, but the kind souls at Virgin Trains still reimbursed half of my train fare under the delay repay scheme. I even made it home for Match of the Day. Back of the net!

Best chant: "You'll always be non-league." Northampton fans taunting all 128 of Morecambe's modest travelling contingent.
Match ticket: £22.00 standard adult ticket.
Match programme: £3. A real community club, everyone from journalists, to students on work placements and even the assistant club chaplain had a voice in the matchday programme. The University (and shirt sponsors) wrote a piece encouraging young people to get out and vote in the upcoming elections. More importantly, big defender Ryan Cresswell put forth his case for the the team to run out to Jeff Beck's "Hi Ho Silver Lining."
Cost of food: £3.10 for a steak and ale pie.
Food rating: 3.5/5. Very crusty and big on pastry. Weak on the ale, although plenty of steak. I didn't appreciate the pie seller wedging a fork deep into the pie before passing it over. That's my job.

Final Score
Northampton Town 2 (Byrom 1, Richards 54)
Morecambe 1 (Devitt 41)
Attendance: 4,307

Getting to know Bradford City
Tom & Don from Bantams Banter (Bradford City podcast)
www.bantamsbanter.co.uk
Twitter @bantamsbanter

Jason McKeown - Width of a Post
www.widthofapost.com
Twitter @TheWidthofaPost

Thoughts on current boss Phil Parkinson?

BB: He is the messiah. We and every other Bradford City fan worship him. He has worked miracles to take over a team that was for all intents and purposes doomed and turn them into a giant killing, promotion winning side. He has a knack for putting together teams that work well and bond with the fans. Seriously, as a club we were at risk of falling out of the Football League and it was all thanks to poor managers, both named Peter.

Best game you've witnessed at Valley Parade?

BB: Beating Liverpool to stay in the Premier League and that game against Aston Villa in the League Cup. We won 3-1, nobody saw it coming and the crowd were sensational, like nothing I've seen before.

Jason: A 2-1 victory over Barnsley in 1998 probably pips it. With three minutes to go, City were trailing 1-0 despite battering the visitors. Then Gordon Watson came off the bench to score twice within the space of 150 seconds. The celebrations were incredible. The last great day before the Kop terrace was demolished to make way for an all-seater stand. What made the story more romantic was Watson being the hero. He had been out of action for 18 months after breaking his leg, and to see him return and score two goals was emotional for everyone. An amazing day.

Best/worst players to pull on a Bradford shirt?

BB: Some big names have worn the famous claret and amber - Beni Carbone, Chris Waddle, and even Stan Collymore played for us for half an hour-ish, but no player has ever come close to Stuart McCall. He could control the game from central midfield, pull a team out of the gutter and the fans LOVED him. As for worst…the list is endless, Stand out disappointments came in our Premier League stint when we signed Bruno Rodriguez, Jorge Cadete and David Hopkin. All coming in with big reputations, all turning out to be utterly crap.

Best thing about Valley Parade?

Jason: The character of the place. Each stand is a testament to different eras. The basic Bradford end behind the goal (known as the TL Dallas Stand) was constructed in 1991, which were modest times financially. It shows! Then the Midland Road Stand was overhauled in 1996, midway through City's rise from the third tier to Premier League – representing progress. The Kop and Main Stand were redeveloped during the Premier League days, and they tower over the rest of the ground. An uncomfortable reminder of past financial recklessness perhaps, but a great legacy nonetheless. All four stands are very close to the pitch and, when there is a big crowd present, it can feel as though they are on top of the players. The result is we can produce brilliant atmospheres and generate a lot of noise.

Worst grounds you've visited?

BB: Brighton's old Withdean Stadium. Not really a football ground so the away fans were sat about 300 meters from the pitch on seating the club had borrowed from Wimbledon tennis court! Also, I really don't like Elland Road, not just because I dislike Leeds United, but because it's just weird. It has a weird 1970s depression feeling about it.

Jason: Morecambe's old Christie Park ground – horrible! Macclesfield's Moss Rose and Accrington's Crown Ground are fairly dismal, although I always enjoyed them. They have more going for them than some of the identikit modern stadiums.

Which club serves the nicest pies?
BB: Well, we were lucky enough to visit the Chelsea press room recently and the food in there would easily win Masterchef, but for pies alone, Morecambe's aint half bad.
Jason: Without doubt Morecambe. They are too good to be served at football matches. Worth the admission fee alone.

Famous Bradford fans?
BB: Dynamo (magician), some woman who was in London's Burning about 20 years ago, George Layton (famous in the 70s) and Ed Sheeran, he's originally from the area and although he's not a football fan there is a picture circulating online of him wearing a Bradford City shirt.

Jason: The most celebrated seems to be a local weatherman called Paul Hudson. Another notable "fan" is the Dalai Lama. He was presented with a personalised Bradford City shirt when visiting Yorkshire in 2012, and many of us joke that the subsequent rise and rise of Bradford City is due to his divine intervention!

Quirky fact time?
BB: The club once had a player called Harry Potter and as you may now realise, the wizard is also a fan of claret and amber...the team colours of Gryffindor! Sadly Bradford City's Harry Potter lost his life during the First World War.
Jason: First winners of the current FA Cup trophy? First fourth tier side to reach a major Wembley final? Nah, the most interesting fact is that the cult football film ID was in part filmed at Valley Parade!

Thoughts on ticket prices in general?
Jason: Bradford City's 2015/16 season tickets are £149. We are so lucky to support a club that is committed to affordable prices. It is staggering how much other clubs charge their fans. For ticket prices themselves, they are too high. Unfortunately for us football fans, clubs take advantage of our loyalty and push up the prices knowing people will pay it. I think they are too expensive even in League One.

Name your Bradford Dream Team?
GK: Gary Walsh
RB: Stephen Darby
CB: David Wetherall
CB: Darren Moore
LB: Wayne Jacobs
RM: Jamie Lawrence
CM: Gary Jones
CM: Stuart McCall
LM: Peter Beagrie
CF: Lee Mills
CF: Robbie Blake

VERTIGO AT VALLEY PARADE

Game #53: League One - Monday 9th February 2015
BRADFORD CITY vs Milton Keynes Dons - The Coral Windows Stadium (Valley Parade)

Falling ill sucks, especially at the start of a week. Having gone to work feeling slightly under the weather, by the time I got to the train station, I felt tempted to turn back and abandon the latest mission. That would have been the sensible option. Knowing what I do now, that would definitely be the only option. Without the benefit of hindsight, plus knowing that the game was being televised, the thought of missing out on a potential five goal classic played on my mind. I decided that I didn't want to watch the game from the couch. Besides, I'd never been to Bradford. What could possibly go wrong? Don't answer that. Read on. Before I knew it, I had a return ticket in hand and was Yorkshire bound to see the Bantams.

The trip to West Yorkshire was far from plain sailing. The first leg to Manchester was fine, but then it all started to unravel. With a chesty cough now accompanying a headache, lethargy began to set in. The fast train which I needed to connect at Piccadilly was about to leave. Heavy legs made it impossible for me to run, so I was just in time to wave off the last carriage. Predictably, the rush hour train which stopped at Huddersfield was delayed and lacking seats. That had a knock-on effect when I finally reached Huddersfield, with a conductor taking great pleasure in saying I had an hour to wait for the next train. A quick scan online exposed the conductor as a liar. I could get a Northern Rail (aka slow) train to regional station Mirfield, then connect to Bradford Interchange. A painstaking dash under a tunnel got me to the required platform at Mirfield just in time to see my fourth train come into view. The final leg of the journey turned out to be my first trip on the Grand Central Network, which had Monopoly and chess boards moulded into some of the seats. I had left my dice at home unfortunately, so couldn't partake.

Three hours after I'd set off, I finally made it to Bradford. As the carriage doors opened, I befriended a Bradford fan on his way to the game. Andrew ended up being good company and had called in a debt from a friend in order to attend the match. The poor lad had recently been given an ultimatum by his girlfriend - football or her. Upon choosing the former, he came home from a game to find his girl cheating on him. He swiftly kicked her into touch and now Andrew's only love was the football club.

There are a couple of hills to negotiate on the way to the ground, which sits behind a petrol station. Reaching my destination, I bid farewell to my latest acquaintance, who went to meet friends opposite to where I would be housed. On first inspection, Valley Parade looks like two stadiums joined together. Half of the ground is fully enclosed and towers over a more traditional stand and another smaller double decker type. Okay, it's a bit rough around the edges, but is a far cry from being soulless and boring.

The club finally seem to be getting onto an even keel. This coming after two spells in administration, numerous relegations and a plethora of financial troubles, mainly stemming from carefree spending during their two year Premier League tenure between 1999-2001. Getting to the final of the League Cup back in 2013, followed by promotion from League Two a season later shows steady progress and is a sign that happier times are on the horizon. Phil Parkinson's ability to assemble a competitive squad on a shoestring budget also deserves plaudits. Fans who were accustomed to the extravagance of Benito Carbone and Stan Collymore have now got used to the more modest pairing of James Hanson and Jonathan Stead. The latter duo's wages may be nowhere near the reported £40,000 a week Carbone was on, but their goal return is a lot higher. See, I can say nice things about Stead. His goal which helped knock Chelsea out of the FA Cup softened my stance towards him.

With pie in hand, I made my way through the spacious lobby and looked to track down my seat. Pointed in the direction of a red door, I climbed some steps, followed by more steps and a few more steps just for good measure. At the end of a corridor, I passed through some double doors and proceeded to go as white as a sheet. Hello vertigo!

I'm not too good with heights at the best of times and could feel my head starting to spin. Wanting to push the steward out of the way to grab the small yellow bars in front, I needed to steady myself. Thankfully, I guided myself away from the edge and once I was able to sit down and get my bearings, the dizziness stopped. The view from the rafters may have afforded me a look out into the bright lights of Bradford city centre, but inside the noise levels were reminiscent of the Nou Camp. The Kop broke into their version of 'Take Me Home,' to welcome the two teams onto the pitch.

Much of the first half was spent negotiating with myself to eat my pie. The queasy feeling in my stomach was getting less about the vertigo, but I still managed to finish it by the time half time rolled around. Up until then, there hadn't been much action to write home about. Danny Green had gone close with a free kick for the Dons, but the majority of the players were struggling to get to grips with a badly cut up pitch. Weak shots meant the ball was getting caught up in the turf and neither goalkeeper was sufficiently tested.

It took a goalkeeping mistake to open the scoring. Bradford's Jordan Pickford sent out a poor pass which was easily intercepted by the opposition. A square ball to an unmarked and Tottenham Hotspur bound Dele Alli was duly tucked away under Pickford's legs. The small MK Dons support, which had been quiet up until now surprisingly weren't as tongue tied. The goal woke Bradford up and finally opened up the game. Two minutes after going behind, the Bantams levelled things up. Billy Clarke timed his run perfectly to latch onto Gary Liddle's cushioned header and fire the ball through David Martin's legs. Bradford then found a winner, although it was slightly tainted. Stead's use of an arm to bring down a high ball went undetected, before a slide-rule pass sent Hanson clear. Martin rushed out to narrow the angle, but the striker guided it past him to net the spoils and City's first home league win of 2015.

With the game heading for an exciting climax, I realised that I'd neglected to get any pictures. The mood changed in an instant. No sooner had I snapped my first shot, the same steward who had assisted me to my seat and even shared a joke over my delayed pie eating, came over looking all serious. The following uncomfortable exchange took place.

"You'll have to stop that. You can't take pictures."
"OK, why not?"
"You can't take pictures."
"Can I ask a reason?"
"You can't take pictures."

I was getting nowhere fast with this guy, who now had a wry smile on his face. No-one at the other 52 grounds had even batted an eyelid when I went to take a picture. I'd even hazard a safe guess that no other club in the Football League will take this stance either. This stupid schmuck was just being an arsehole for no apparent reason. Not wanting any trouble, I put my phone away, yet couldn't help but notice a second steward now standing a few feet away. Moments later, a third guy all mic'd up was a few rows behind me too. This behaviour was disgusting! The fourth official put up his board for stoppage time and I decided that I'd had enough of being made to feel like a criminal. Besides, I didn't have the energy for an argument or a fight. I simply packed up and left, cursing the three stooges under my breath all the way down the blasted stairs and out of the stadium.

Walking back up the hill, my feet were dragging and every step hurt. Freezing cold with a fever was not a good combination. Seeing a taxi parked up by the petrol station, I limped in and could hear the final whistle sound along with one last roar of the crowd as I closed the door. The taxi driver couldn't shed any light on cameragate, so I decided to try and get some answers from the club about their policy on flash photography. Tweets were sent out, but went unanswered, thus doing nothing to eradicate the bitter taste left in this paying fan's mouth.

Shaun Best @Shaun_Best Feb 9

so @officialbantams don't let you take photos inside the ground. Made to feel like a criminal by the stewards and spoilt a good night.

If all that wasn't enough, the four hour commute home was brutal. In between shivering and waiting for delayed connections, the escalators had been shut off at Leeds. Getting up the stairs while coughing my guts up was a bit of a struggle. Forget 32, I looked and moved more like a 62-year-old. Doubled over and clutching my chest didn't endear me to the late night folk, whose demeanour was as cold as the evening temperature. I looked and felt as rough as a badger's you know what, yet people still jumped to the wrong conclusion of assuming I was someone who'd had one drink or pill too many. Resting my feet against the heaters briefly stopped the shivering between Leeds and Manchester. I pre-booked a taxi when I got close to Chester. Walking simply wasn't an option. Crawling through the door at 2am, I gobbled down a couple of painkillers and finally took solace in bed. Home sweet home! It'll be a long time before I go to Bradford again, if ever.

Best chant: "Take me home, Midland Road. To the place that I belong. To the Valley, to see the City. Take me home, Midland Road." The Bradford fans. I simply wanted to go home towards the end.
Match ticket: £20 across the board for adults. Good value.
Match programme: £3. The Parader was one of the few editions to track down an away fan for a detailed interview. There's a touch of sarcasm directed at Sky for ignoring Bradford's FA Cup run and overlooking their ties for TV coverage.
Cost of food: £3.20 for a steak and ale pie.
Food rating: 3.5/5. Plenty of steak to get your teeth into. The ale was non-existent, but the pie stayed warm despite the delay in consumption. Puff pastry predictably led to a bit of spillage. Didn't feel like I could stomach a pie, but a bonus half point gets awarded for the easy digestion.

Final Score
Bradford City 2 (Clarke 56, Hanson 70)
Milton Keynes Dons 1 (Alli 54)
Attendance: 11,948

Getting to know Stevenage FC
Pete - Editor of BoroGuide
www.boroguide.co.uk

Favourite memory as a Stevenage fan?

We've had our moments in the sun over the years, but it'll be difficult to beat clinching the Conference title (again) at Kidderminster in 2010. It was as perfect a day as you'd want.

Best game you've witnessed at the Lamex Stadium?

It's a close call between the demolition of Sheffield Wednesday in League One or brushing past Newcastle United in the FA Cup. Both were games that underlined how good we were at those respective times, considering the relative strength of the opposition.

Best/worst players to pull on a Stevenage shirt?

There have been some wonderful players to pull on a Stevenage shirt: George Boyd is the stand-out name, but Barry Hayles, Efetobore Sodje, Mark Smith, Steve Morison, Mark Roberts and Martin Gittings won't be far off the lists of most supporters. Worst? Plenty of them too – we collected bang average centre midfielders in the late 1990s and early 2000s including Ray Houghton (yep, him), Steve King, Darren Fenton, Ian King... oh, and then there's strikers such as Brian Quailey and Jefferson Louis.

Best thing about the Lamex Stadium?

There are many visitors who'll say the opposite, but the best thing about our ground is how close it is to the pitch. It's smaller than most too, which makes you feel more closed in when you're out there. It does lead to some great atmospheres, especially at night.

Worst grounds you've visited?

I've never been a massive fan of the Crown Ground, Underhill or Kenilworth Road. And the Vetch Field was pretty run down when we went there in the FA Cup a decade ago.

Enjoyable away days?

York is one of the best away days on the circuit, but that might have more to do with the city as a whole rather than the ground. By the same measure, you could also say Southend.

Which club serves the nicest pies?

Kidderminster Harriers, hands down.

Famous Stevenage fans?

Ken and Barbara Follett are about as famous as Boro' fans get; him a best-selling author and her, the displaced Labour MP who got a little caught up in the expenses furore.

Quirky fact time?

Back in the days of 'They Think It's All Over,' we featured on the round where the teams had to explain what was going on behind a celebration. If I remember rightly, we'd had a ballet teacher in and that prompted a mass display after a goal back around 1996 or 1997.

Best/worst Stevenage managers?

Graham Westley and Paul Fairclough are by far the most successful, while Mark Stimson got us playing some decent stuff and Mark Roberts remains unbeaten across two caretaker spells. For the worst, I can't think of a time since I started watching Boro' that was worse than Peter Taylor's. I don't want to say Gary Smith, but - like Wayne Turner back in the early 2000s, it just didn't work out for him at the Lamex.

Thoughts on ticket prices in general?

Not positive, shall we say. I get that clubs want success and it comes at a price, but leave the supporters behind and you don't have a club. It sometimes seems almost impressive that Premier League clubs still get people through the door when tickets can go for around £100. I don't know - maybe £20 week-in, week-out is what a club needs to charge to be competitive in the Football League. But that level seems to now be seeping into the top end of non-league and then the question is where will it end?

Name your Stevenage Dream Team?

One of my favourite questions, it's a shame I can only have 11. Okey-dokey, here goes (4-3-3)

Chris Day
Lee Harvey
Efetobore Sodje
Mark Roberts
Scott Laird
Dave Venables
Michael Bostwick
George Boyd
Barry Hayles
Steve Morison
Carl Alford

A BAD HEAD DAY IN HERTFORDSHIRE

Game #54: League Two - Tuesday 10th February 2015
STEVENAGE FC vs Bury - The Lamex Stadium (Broadhall Way)

You can't keep a good man down. That goes double for a keen groundhopper. Barely 12 hours after returning from the Bradford mis-adventure, and, by the power of paracetamol (to be taken every four hours) I passed a late fitness and sanity test to make the voyage to Hertfordshire. Just to make sure there wouldn't be a repeat of the previous night's painstaking voyage home, I arranged an overnight stay in Harrow with an old friend – Charlie Dehaan. Like myself, he was a fellow United fan, but couldn't be convinced to join me for some midweek League Two action. In truth, he was finishing up an evening course while the game was going on, although he kindly agreed to pick me up from the tube station after the game. It wouldn't take me long to travel back through London, plus I wouldn't be exposed to the wintry elements. It was a win-win situation. I neglected to mention to Charlie that I was under the weather. No need to complicate things with such minor details.

My knowledge of Stevenage was limited at best, so a crash course was needed. Upon their arrival into the 92 club in 2010, the club hastily dropped the Borough part from their name, although they're still affectionately known as the Boro by fans and stadium markings alike. Also, Giuliano Grazioli wrote himself into Borough...sorry, Stevenage folklore when he netted a famous equaliser in an FA Cup game with Newcastle United in 1998. While it's safe to say he wasn't still knocking around the Lamex looking for a game any longer, the club were still going relatively strong and did knock the Magpies out of the same competition in 2011. The Lamex Food Group took over naming rights to the stadium thanks to swelling the Stevenage coffers with a seven-figure sum.

Following a less than stellar tenure at Preston North End, Graham Westley was enjoying a second spell in charge at Stevenage and had them on the brink of the play-offs. Much like Eddie Howe at Bournemouth, it had been a homecoming of sorts for Westley and the pairing seemed a natural one from the outside looking in. Bury were making only their fourth trip to the Lamex, having not won on any of their previous three visits. With the Shakers also jostling for position in a crowded play-off picture, the game looked like having everything to play for.

I always pack plenty of reading material for any train excursions. This journey was no exception. A kind family member had bought me a subscription to football magazine 'When Saturday Comes,' for Christmas. I was busy leafing through a reporter's experience of Goodison Park when an Evertonian sitting opposite came to join me. Two random blokes can instantly diffuse any awkward situation by striking up a conversation about football. He was killing two birds with one stone - visiting his son and catching the Chelsea-Everton game the day after. While the football chat made the first leg of the journey go quickly, it also made me forget about my paracetamol window, which came back to bite me later on.

Thanks to signalling problems, what should have been a simple 20 minute journey from Finsbury Park to Stevenage turned into an hour's plod at snail's pace. It had gone 7:15pm when the train pulled in, so I needed to get my skates on. The station has a bridge over a dual carriageway. Once over that, the Lamex is only a mile from the station, so the bonus of having a midweek game means you can see the floodlights in the distance. The green surroundings from behind the stadium would be appreciated more for a Saturday afternoon game in warmer conditions. Following several fans through a subway got me to the ground just minutes before kick-off.

The stadium is half and half in terms of seating and standing. I figured there would be more of an atmosphere in the terraces. The bonus being I could move about freely with the idea of spending a half close to each set of fans behind the goals. The stadium is quite compact with low roofs, so I wouldn't like to hazard a guess how many balls go whistling out of the stadium during each game. The Bury fans were housed in the all seated South Stand and were relatively muted. For the home fans standing behind the other goal, only three quarters of the stand is covered. Thankfully, rain wasn't forecast, although it got a bit chilly as the night progressed.

The game was a massive disappointment. Both teams seemed content in the route one method of hoofing the ball in the air, which wasn't pretty. The state of the pitch did neither side any favours and was cutting up quite badly. In order to combat some of the boredom, I counted four balls which flew over the roof in the first half. I didn't win a prize. The Stevenage fans seemed fixated on pointing out that Bury forward Danny Rose looked like a 12-year-old. Rose was unfortunate not to win a penalty when he was manhandled by the lethargic boulders, which made up the Stevenage defence in first half stoppage time. When the fourth official signalled for two minutes added on time, a kid behind me laughed maniacally like Dr Evil.

I swapped ends as planned, but ended up trading Austin Powers' nemesis for fart noises and squeaky cockneys talking utter tripe. Most of the kids within my earshot made no secret of the fact they were Arsenal and Tottenham Hotspur fans who had decided to come to Stevenage for a cheap night out. Bury fans continued to sit on their hands, even when Andrew Tutte forced Chris Day into a flying save to pluck a free-kick from out of the top corner. Day ensured his side ended a run of three straight defeats when he got down well to save another set piece from Chris Hussey. While the club didn't lose any more balls in the second half, I felt like I had lost a lot more than the feeling in my gloveless hands.

The signalling problems still hadn't been sorted when I got back to the train station. An African lady tried to hand me a leaflet. "Jesus loves you," she said. "Ok, then why did he send me to Stevenage tonight?" I retorted just as quickly. She couldn't give me an answer. Washing down two (overdue) paracetamol with a bottle of water on the train, I was hoping to clear the bad taste of the game out of my system.

Charlie kindly picked me up from Northwick Park as promised. I appreciated the gesture and it felt good to travel to his neck of the woods for a change. All of our previous meetings had been up north for birthdays and Race meetings. A comfy bed and generous supply of fruit and bottled water helped keep the lurgy under control, and I can't thank him and his parents Mike and Rachel enough for the generous hospitality. I must apologise about the constant coughing through the night. Sorry if I kept any of you up. Passing through Wealdstone on the journey back, I didn't catch a glimpse of the Wealdstone Raider, but there's always next time. I'm not too sure when I'll next cross paths with Stevenage. All things considered, neither one of us were at our best. In hindsight, this would have been better suited as a weekend visit, but as first impressions go, unfortunately it had been a lame first experience at the Lamex.

Best chant: "You've got bigger tits than my Mum." A less than charming comparison made by one of the cheeky chappies standing behind me towards poor Stevenage centre-half Jon Ashton.
Match ticket: £16 student ticket for a Category B game. The dearest adult seat was £24.
Match programme: £3. The club included a report from the treatment room. Given the number of players Stevenage had on the injury list, it was certainly warranted. Graham Westley didn't bother with the generic welcome to the opposition blurb that every other manager seems to write in their programme notes. In fact, he didn't give Bury a mention at all. Mascot Boro Bear had his own cartoon strip, no doubt a result of him being something of a cult hero in these parts.
Cost of food: £2.50 for a pie (chicken or steak.) There was also a Boro burger with bacon and cheese for £5, or for those with a sweet tooth, vanilla cupcakes were sold for £1.50, with muffins slightly cheaper at £1.
Food rating: 1/5. I passed on a pie due to a queasy stomach, instead opting for a small sausage roll. It was the worst thing on what was otherwise a varied menu. Bereft of any flavour and tasted like a cardboard box. Just thinking of it makes my mouth dry and reach for some water.

Final Score
Stevenage FC 0
Bury 0
Attendance: 2,165

Getting to know Peterborough United
Mark Lea - Vital Posh
www.peterborough.vitalfootball.co.uk
Twitter @VitalPosh

Thoughts on Darren Ferguson?

He is without doubt one of the most successful managers in the history of Posh. Being a typical Scot and the son of the great Sir Alex, he was also very stubborn. If he fell out with a player or coach, that often meant the end of his career at Posh!

Best/worst players to pull on a Peterborough shirt?

Terry Bly, Bob Doyle, George Boyd, Lee Tomlin, Tommy Robson, Dennis Emery. There are too many for the "worst" category!

Best game you've witnessed at London Road?

Apart from the play-off semi-final win over MK Dons a couple of seasons ago, two 'recent' matches spring to mind and they both finished 4-4! The first was in 2009/10 when Championship leaders Cardiff City rocked up at London Road. They set their stall out early on and took the lead in the 6th minute. By half-time, the Bluebirds had a commanding 4-0 lead. No-one envisaged what would happen in the second half. Josh Simpson started the comeback in the 51st minute, before Charlie Lee pulled another goal back with 22 minutes remaining. There was no further scoring until a late double strike earned Posh a draw. George Boyd scored Posh's third after 89 minutes, before Simpson scored his second of the match in the 90th minute!

The second was in 2010/11 when Posh battled out the draw against Southampton in front of the Sky TV cameras. Striker Rickie Lambert scored two penalties in the match, one of which was won by Alex Oxlade-Chamberlain, but Posh battled back with two penalties of their own with the last one coming in the final minute of the match and was coolly scored by Lee Tomlin.

Ray Cole
The Posh Supporters Trust
www.theposhtrust.co.uk

Favourite memory as a Peterborough fan?

Walking up the tunnel into Moys End on the 3rd September 1966 (my first game). It was déjà-vu. Other than that, Wembley 24th May 1992 when we beat Stockport County 2-1 to get into the second tier of the Football League for the first time.

Best thing about London Road?

We still have terracing and so I can stand.

Thoughts on ticket prices in England?

Outrageous. £20 is more than enough.

Favourite away days?

Saltergate, Chesterfield and the Shay, Halifax (back in the 70/80's). They were real football grounds! Best ground lately has to be Old Trafford, beats Wembley hands down.

Famous Peterborough fans?

John Major when Prime Minister came and watched us one Boxing Day! I'm sure I've seen Warwick Davis at London Road too.

Quirky fact time?

Posh were demoted for offering bonuses to players to beat Sunderland in the 1966/67 FA Cup. They lost the game 7-1!

Name your Peterborough Dream Team?

GK: Mark Tyler
RB: Mark Little
LB: Adam Drury
CB: Chris Turner
CB: Simon Rea
RM: Chris Whelpdale
LM: George Boyd
CM: Billy Kellock
CF: Jim Hall
CF: Craig Mackail-Smith
CF: Robbie Cooke

They are my favourite eleven but not the best 11! They always gave 100%.

A POSH DAY OUT

Game #55: League One - Saturday 14th February 2015
PETERBOROUGH UNITED vs Rochdale - The ABAX Stadium (London Road)

Saint Valentine's Day! Stereotypically known as a day for hearts, flowers, expensive gifts and all that jazz, it certainly doesn't favour jumpers for goalposts and a kickabout. While I didn't have a fancy restaurant booked, I did have something of a 'posh' date to look forward to. Bucking the trend and sidestepping cupid's arrow, I set off to watch the club who shares their nickname with Victoria Beckham.

There were a couple of paths to get from Chester to Peterborough. Faced with a sensible and not so sensible option, you can probably guess which one I plumped for. Wanting a break from the London commute and keen to avoid a repeat of the Stevenage delays, I swerved the route through Hertfordshire in favour of a more unorthodox route via Yorkshire. Not for the first time, the journey brought plenty of drama.

Mingling with the rest of the weekend football folk at Crewe, I discovered that Arriva Trains Wales in their naivety had decided to only put two carriages on for its Manchester service. As a result, lots of angry Welsh commuters were left stranded between Shrewsbury and Piccadilly. It was standing room only, so I pushed my way into the aisle and hemmed myself in for a half hour trip to Stockport. One guy was comically banging on the driver's door asking when the sandwich cart was coming out. I didn't like his chances. From Stockport, I went through to Doncaster where I just about managed to catch a Kings Cross bound express train through to Peterborough. It's not a route I'm likely to repeat any time soon.

The good thing about Peterborough is that everything is signposted, with the town centre located pretty close to the train station. Bets were placed for the afternoon's action after I presented the necessary ID. To quote the bookie, "we have 12-year-olds with beards who come in here." There must be something in the water. Crossing a bridge over the River Nene, the stadium is tucked away behind a housing development. A bunny (Peter Burrow) and builder make up the club's mascots, thanks in part to shirt sponsors Mick George. Yes, the company that provide earthworks, concrete and demolition supplies are also responsible for Mick the Skip. Move over Bob the Builder!

Inside, London Road looks and feels like it has one foot in the past and the other in the future. Two stands have been modernised to replace former terracing, while the Main Stand still sports the old school wooden seats on rusted metal support and not much leg room. The solitary remaining terrace behind one of the goals looked like a massive shed. For those who are a bit claustrophobic, the canteen barely has enough room to swing a cat. An unenthusiastic adolescent let out a sigh when I asked what pies they sold. Hopefully he put more effort into his exams. I was bracing myself for him to throw the pie at me, although that would have required energy.

One man who certainly gives a damn is Peterborough chairman Darragh MacAnthony. The Irish chief had taken to social media to publicly lambast his misfiring players after a series of not so stellar results. For once, the manager - so often the scapegoat was spared, as MacAnthony threw his support behind under fire Darren Ferguson, whose second stint in charge had hit a rough patch.

The Posh have always subscribed to an attacking style of play, which explains why I almost always put them down as 'both teams to score' on my accumulator. The club's recruitment policy is also a shrewd one, plucking talent from non league and giving them a chance to flourish at a higher level. Marcus Maddison and Aaron McLean were recent success stories, with central midfielder Harry Beautyman also beginning to make some noise.

The League One table was so tight coming in, meaning one or two good results could put you back into the play-off picture, while a couple of bad results would have you looking over your shoulders at the relegation places. Peterborough couldn't have asked for a better start, going 2-0 up in less than ten minutes. Rochdale's inability to deal with crosses into the box was duly punished. Moments after Beautyman headed the Posh in front, Christian Burgess tapped in on the line after goalkeeper Josh Lillis made a hash out of catching a corner.

Beautyman almost netted a carbon copy of his first effort, but Lillis redeemed himself and Rochdale then gave themselves a lifeline. Full-back Joe Rafferty wandered forward, and decided to crack an effort into the top corner from 25 yards. Not a bad way to net the first league goal of your career.

Mick the Skip brought out a proverbial skip for the half time entertainment. Alas, there were no budding Andrea Pirlo's amongst the crowd, as fans failed to chip the balls into the skip from short distance. I was left disappointed that nobody stole the bunny's inflatable carrot and whacked him over the head with it. Relax, I'm just joking. Besides, that rabbit probably had a mean right hook on him.

With Peterborough's advantage halved, the home side became nervy. Meanwhile, the group of kids sitting behind me got restless. Their interest in the game completely disappeared. When they weren't planking between the seats, they were either clucking like chickens or playing on their iPads. My attention remained on the game, which I may note was anything but boring. Both teams seemed happy to attack, which translated into an entertaining spectacle.

Rochdale resorted to pumping balls into the box in an effort to find an equaliser, even throwing on lanky forward Calvin Andrew to cause the Posh some problems. Andrew - Dale's final substitute unwittingly caused his own side a problem when he limped off injured, forcing his side to play the final ten minutes a man down. Jack O'Connell was beginning a third loan spell at the heart of the visiting defence. Rotten luck saw the ball ricochet off his thigh and go over from a promising position at the back post.

Peterborough had scraped a victory to move back into play-off contention. However, a week is a long time in football. Fast forward seven days and Ferguson had gone. Two straight defeats without a goal scored saw the Scotsman fall on his sword and an announcement was made that Ferguson had departed by mutual consent. The Valentine's love had clearly faded, as academy and youth team boss Dave Robertson swiftly stepped in and won his first four games in charge. Just like in life, some partnerships aren't made to last. Sometimes, a change is for the best. As for me, I wouldn't change a thing about Peterborough and look forward to returning sometime down the line.

Best chant: "Darren, Darren give us a wave.'" One of the final times Ferguson found favour with the Peterborough fans.
Match ticket: £23 for an advance adult ticket. Terrace tickets ranged from £18-£21.
Match programme: £3. Vice captain Michael Smith apologised for colliding with the Fleetwood Town ballboy in a prior game. Lots of adverts made up the bulk of the 72 pages, although Jon Taylor scored a paltry 6/10 in a quiz based off a curriculum for a ten year-old. Not knowing who wrote Charlotte's Web or where the River Trent is sourced? Tut tut.
Cost of food: £3.10 for a balti pie. Steak and ale was the only other pie option.
Food rating: 3/5. Spicy puff pastry was slightly let down by the mild and mushy sauce inside. A very messy and crumbly pie, I managed to stop some of the chicken from landing on the lady sitting in front of me. That would have been a hard situation to talk myself out of.

Final Score
Peterborough United 2 (Beautyman 4, Burgess 7)
Rochdale 1 (Rafferty 24)
Attendance: 5,163

Getting to know Accrington Stanley
Robert Houseman
Supporter Liaison Officer - Accrington Stanley FC
www.accringtonstanley.co.uk

Favourite memory as an Accrington fan?
Gaining promotion at Woking on Easter Saturday 2006.

Best thing about the Crown Ground?
Friendly, close to the action and you can stand on the terraces.

Thoughts on ticket prices in general?
Different clubs have different reasons for their pricing. We rely on gate money on the day especially from away fans. We are often outnumbered by then.

Enjoyable away days?
Love AFC Wimbledon and Dagenham. Just like our club, friendly, community feel and spectators are close to the action.

Which club serves the nicest pies?
Morecambe and Lincoln City.

Famous Accrington fans?
David Lloyd, Jon Anderson (the band Yes), Julie Hesmondhalgh (Hayley from Coronation Street)

Quirky fact time?
We are the longest serving League Two club in the Division at the moment. This is our tenth season.

Name your Accrington Dream Team?
Marcus Bettinelli
Peter Cavanagh
Phil Edwards
Tom Aldred
Jimmy Ryan
Andrew Procter
Ian Craney
Gary Roberts
Paul Mullin
Romuald Boco
Bobby Grant

Game #56: League Two - Tuesday 24th February 2015
ACCRINGTON STANLEY vs Burton Albion - The Store First Stadium (Crown Ground)

"What are you doing tomorrow night Dad?"
"No, forget it!"
"But you haven't even heard me out yet."
"I'm staying in to watch the Champions League."

I needed to use some powers of persuasion to convince Dad to choose League Two over the European Cup. Thankfully, a work colleague helped sweeten the deal by selling me a Europa League ticket for Liverpool, which went a long way to getting my Dad to swap a warm sofa for a cold stand in Lancashire. I didn't charge him for the ticket either. One good turn deserves another after all, especially since the train timetable for midweek games isn't kind and I'd have no way of getting back.

"Shaun, there's no roof over the stand."
"It's okay Dad, that's where the Burton fans will be based."
"I hope for their sake it doesn't rain."

Despite being one of the twelve founding members of the Football League in 1888, Accrington had since collapsed, re-formed and made a dogged climb through the non-league pyramid, finally finding their way back to the Football League in 2006. Living by the moniker of "the club that wouldn't die," Accrington were saved from the brink of ruin in 2009 by former chairman Ilyas Khan, who supplied the club with the necessary funds.

Clearly one of the have nots of football, the club came agonisingly close to landing a plum money spinning FA Cup tie against Manchester United earlier in the season, only to lose a replay to Yeovil Town and miss out on a tidy payday. The club still printed commemorative tickets for a game that never took place and tried to sell them as souvenirs, which didn't go down too well.

Having Blackburn Rovers and Burnley in such close proximity means that an already small fanbase is struggling to grow. Back in October, the club recorded their lowest attendance in almost ten years when just 947 people turned up to watch them defeat Hartlepool United. It was the lowest attendance posted in the Football League since 849 watched a (pre MK Dons) Wimbledon game in 2002.

For the first time in four trips together, me and Dad didn't get lost, fall out or take a wrong turning. Passing through Blackburn, I decided to test Dad's knowledge of the lower leagues.

"John Coleman," he stated almost as soon as I'd asked who Accrington's manager was. He knows more than he lets on. Parking in a field next to the ground had its bonuses, not least for the low cost. A modest £2 is a far cry from the extortionate £5 - £10 most other clubs charge.

Dad wanted to get something to eat before the game, so we both headed to the Crown - a neighbouring pub rented to the club by the brewery which was very accommodating to both sets of supporters. There was a certain charm and immediate warmth from the staff as soon as we got to the ground. With the game being cash on the turnstiles, I enquired about getting a ticket as a souvenir. The guy running the club shop said to come back after the game and he'd sort me out. The chief steward then handed us both a teamsheet and pointed out to Dad some key players to look out for. If that wasn't enough, a Liverpool scout then approached us. He had been stood up by his plus one, so he handed us a free ticket. Talk about being in the right place at the right time.

Once inside, I realised why the ground is notorious for being one of the worst in the league. Less than half of the stadium is seated. Looking half completed, it's in desperate need of development or at least a makeover. The Whinney Hill side has had a few seats hastily installed to comply with Football League stadium criteria, but looks like a row of garden sheds. The roof on the stand is so low that is looks like you can easily bang your head when standing up. A new housing development overlooking this side basically gets a free view of the pitch, so they're not complaining. Behind one goal, the Sophia Khan Stand has terracing at the rear and a few rows of seats at the front. The small group of home fans gathered here were quiet and hardly living up to the banners of 'Pride not £££' and 'Stanley Ultras,' which hung above them. My heart went out to Winstanley, the club's K9 mascot, who was parading around a sparsely filled stadium. The away fans standing on the Coppice Terrace are chancing their luck, due to being exposed to the elements. On a Saturday game, you can turn around to get a nice view of the surrounding Lancashire hills. On a cold midweek Tuesday, not so much.

Distracting me from the aesthetics of the ground, Dad nominated yours truly to do a coffee run. Due to an open gap which splits the Main and Thwaites Stands, you almost have to go outside the stadium to come back on yourself in order to get to the concession stand. With my hands full, I wasn't aware of who was around me as I brought the drinks back.

"That's Dean Windass over there," pointed Dad. I looked over and there he was, with who I would imagine was a son or young relative. I hadn't looked at the teamsheet or the programme at this point, so thought it was a bit random as to why he was here. Maybe he was here on a scouting mission or in a working capacity for Sky Sports, although I couldn't see a camera, well apart from the one now in my hand.

"Hi Dean, would it be alright to get a picture with you?"
"Yeah sure," he said stoically with his hands lodged deep inside the pockets of a Hull City jacket.
"I'll take it," said the little sidekick. Perfect!

I proceeded to quickly tell Dean about my quest to the 72, but his expression didn't change and he continued to stare out onto the pitch at the players completing their warm ups. Dean did shake my hand and acknowledge my appreciation before I went back to my seat. Although he retired in 2012, he still looked in shape and like he could do a job. A striker never loses his instinct and sight for goal.

Seeing Josh Windass on the teamsheet may have exposed my lack of knowledge on current Accrington affairs, but it did allow me to join the dots. A father was simply coming out to support his son. Dean's presence rubbed off when Josh netted his first league goal midway through the first half. It was a goal that Windass Snr certainly would've been proud of. Windass Jnr cushioned a long ball before striking a fierce daisycutter which caught Jon McLaughlin by surprise, with the ball whistling into the bottom corner.

The goal knocked the stuffing out of Burton, who had come into this game on the back of a 13 game unbeaten run. All of a sudden, the small travelling contingent who were stood on the uncovered concrete slab behind the goal fell silent. The drum stopped beating and the swagger disappeared from Burton's play. Windass nearly notched a second, but McLaughlin did well to tip a free kick over the bar. Meanwhile, Piero Mingoia was turning the screw on the flank, putting teasing balls into the Burton box. It definitely looked like Brewers boss Jimmy Floyd Hasselbaink had underestimated the little club from Lancashire.

There was late drama when Rob Atkinson cut through Burton's Adam McGurk with a scathing post watershed tackle. The defender was very fortunate to escape with a yellow card. I'd seen people get sent off for much less. Gangly substitute Matt Crooks lacked the killer instinct to add to the lead towards the end. The defensive midfielder was put clear, but looked like he wasn't used to being so high up the pitch and ended up hesitating and turning back into Burton traffic.

As a game, it was far from vintage, but the win was a lot more comfortable than the scoresheet suggested. Burton certainly didn't look like a team topping the table. It's these kinds of games on a cold Tuesday night which are the makings of champions and I didn't see anything of the sort. To his credit, the guy from the club shop kept to his word and gave me a ticket at the end of the game. Sadly, it wasn't one of the Manchester United souvenirs. Accrington broke their own record for low attendance. It wasn't too surprising, given that it was a midweek game, plus the fact that Blackburn were playing down the road.

"You take me to some glamorous places," remarked Dad on the drive home.
"You're welcome. Port Vale are playing next Tuesday if you fancy it?"

Cue the silence and tumbleweeds.

Best chant: "Shall we sing a song for you?" The Burton fans before they lost their voices. The travelling band didn't bother tuning up again.

Match ticket: £15 student ticket, with adult tickets costing £20.

Match programme: £3. Small in size, but a very revealing edition. From Kai Naismith opening up about a personal tragedy, to Shay McCartan discussing how he acclimatised to living in digs after leaving his native Ireland, it gave this reader a real insight into the club. The Under 11, 12 and 13s became the first group from the club to travel into Europe, when they spent three days training at Paris St-Germain's training ground.

Cost of food: £3.50 for peppered steak pie and chips at the pub. £2.50 for a meat and potato pie inside the ground.

Food rating: 2/5. The steak pie was discoloured with no real bite and full of mushrooms, which I'm not too keen on. However, the chips and gravy were lovely and piping hot. The pie inside the ground had a crunchy crust, but the inside was too dry.

Final Score
Accrington Stanley 1 (Windass 23)
Burton Albion 0
Attendance: 919

Getting to know Hartlepool United
Ross Hamilton-Milburn
Twitter @RossHamMil & @HartlepoolStats

Best thing about Victoria Park?
I suppose the history of the place. It's been Hartlepool's home since the club was founded in 1908 and various local sports clubs had used it before then. Not many clubs in our league can say they play in a hundred plus year old stadium. It's a special place.

Thoughts on ticket prices in general?
Naturally I think they're too high, especially at the higher levels of the game. But you can understand the economics behind why Arsenal and Man United charge extortionate prices when you consider the fact that their games are guaranteed to sell out with 60,000-70,000 fans. But when you see a club like Middlesbrough charge £30 for an adult ticket and there's 10,000 empty seats left, there's something wrong there.

Enjoyable away days?
I like York's Bootham Crescent, partially due to the short distance and also because it has a lot of charm and character that you don't get with modern new-build arenas. I also liked Deepdale when I went last season. Like Victoria Park there is a lot of history there.

Which club serves the nicest pies?
I was a big fan of the famous Preston 'Butter Pie' when I visited Deepdale. Rochdale also do a very good, cheap pie for £2 which is excellent value.

Famous Hartlepool fans?
Aside from the obvious Jeff Stelling, Hartlepool can also boast American singer Meatloaf and Iron Maiden guitarist Janick Gers amongst its celebrity supporters. Film Director Ridley Scott is also a fan I believe.

Quirky fact time?
Hartlepool are one of three football league clubs who have never visited Wembley, along with Accrington Stanley and Crawley Town.

Name your Hartlepool Dream Team?
I'm not the oldest fan so this squad will all be fairly recent players.
GK: Scott Flinders,
RB: Michael Duckworth
CB: Sam Collins
CB: Scott Harrison
LB: Evan Horwood
RM: Nolberto Solano
CM: Ritchie Humphreys
CM: Antony Sweeney
LM: Andy Monkhouse
CF: Scott Fenwick
CF: James Poole

MONKEY BUSINESS IN THE NORTH EAST

Game #57: League Two - Saturday 28th February 2015
HARTLEPOOL UNITED vs AFC Wimbledon - Victoria Park

I couldn't recall ever going to the North East. Not even as a nipper. I have a distant Aunt who lives up there, but our paths had never really crossed. I'm not sure if that makes me a terrible nephew or not. She runs a guest house - *Altonlea Lodge* which isn't that far from Victoria Park, and by the looks of things has several cracking reviews. I emailed a few months before starting *Journey to the 72* to say that I'd pop in and say hello when I was in the area. Trust me to go and pick a weekend that she was away to come and watch Hartlepool. Some free advertising and a Christmas card would have to suffice.

To say it hadn't been the best season for Hartlepool was putting it mildly to say the least. Knocked out of the FA Cup on live TV by non league local rivals Blyth Spartans, while spending most of the season propping up the Football League made for grim reading. With the club eight points adrift from League Two safety coming in, the proverbial writing looked to be on the wall. Given my track record with some clubs, a visit from me looked like the last thing they needed, but surely when you're rock bottom then the only way is up.

I enjoyed mixed company on the various trains up north. Bumping into a work colleague helped pass the time to Manchester, although my patience was tested when I changed at York. An angry ginger guy plonked himself down opposite and began staring a hole through me for no apparent reason. His feeble attempts at twisting an empty Fanta bottle were more annoying than impressive, so I popped in my earphones and blanked him out.

A journalist from BBC London 94.9 was waiting on the platform to snap a photo of the first lot of AFC Wimbledon fans arriving. A photobomb didn't seem polite, so I set off to see some of the sights. Giant seagulls and a drunken hen party were the first things to catch my attention. Watching an inebriated Geordie still clutching a half open bottle of fizz while trying to walk on one shoe (don't ask me where the other one had gone) was comedy gold. You can't avoid seeing the HMS Trincomalee along the Hartlepool Marina or the Mecca Bingo unit on the way to the ground. If you look closely, you may even spot a Tesco trolley or two in the River Tees.

Blue silhouettes of footballers adorn the wall outside the ground, along with stickers to 'Gilly's Stag Do,' still proudly on display two months after the event. For all I knew, perhaps Gilly was still inside Victoria Park partying?

A programme seller was walking outside the ground trying to make a couple of sales before the gates opened. Picking up my copy, I attempted an icebreaker.
"Reckon Hartlepool will win today then mate?"
"Will we fuck!"
Such optimism! I hoped that the team didn't throw in the towel as easily, especially as they had won two out of their last three home games.

Victoria Park can house just under 8,000 fans with just over half of the capacity being seated. The Niramax Stand opposite to the dugouts is the only stand not to run the length of the pitch. With an open terrace at the front, its seating is made up of an odd mix of orange and green at the rear. The 'Tyneside Wombles' were just one of a many small pack of travelling fans situated behind the goal. Brentford may boast a pub on each corner of the ground, but Hartlepool just have the one. I'll let you guess where the 'Corner Flag,' bar is located.

I almost choked on my pie when 'Bird is the Word,' blared out over the speakers and club mascot H'Angus the Monkey was brought out in a wheelbarrow and pushed around the stadium. Nothing like some good old immature fun. H'Angus has quite the interesting backstory and is derived from the term 'Monkey Hanger,' which, believe it or not is a term of endearment to most Hartlepool folk. Back in the 19th century, a French ship was stranded on the Hartlepool coast. Legend has it that the only survivor was a monkey, allegedly in a Navy uniform. Rather than see the funny side, a bunch of locals held a mock trial on the beach. With the monkey unable or unwilling to co-operate, he was dubbed a French spy and sentenced to hanging on the beach. Odes, statues and monuments to this questionable fable are dotted around all across the city. Hartlepool United capitalised on the popularity of the 'Monkey Hangers' nickname and introduced H'Angus in 1999.

It didn't take long for the game to provide some entertainment, nor for all 16 stone of Adebayo Akinfenwa to get involved with the referee. However, when the man in charge went to confront the man nicknamed 'The Beast' about a foul, the dynamics changed. Akinfenwa put forth his argument while towering over the referee, who stayed silent and eventually cowered backwards. It was a smart move on his part. Oh and the yellow card didn't even come out.

In a game of few chances, both sides were denied by the woodwork, while Hartlepool's Connor Smith saw an effort headed off the line. The midfielder had already done the hard part by rounding the goalkeeper, but Dave Winfield came to the rescue for the Dons. Hartlepool were dealt a bad hand early in the second half when they lost playmaker Michael Woods to a serious leg injury. The midfielder suffered a broken leg and dislocated ankle after going down awkwardly from an innocuous challenge from Winfield.

Hartlepool recovered from the setback to net the only goal of the game. Jack Compton was afforded plenty of space down the left flank, with his cross tucked away from close range by Cambridge United loanee Ryan Bird. The frontman certainly made it a debut to remember to hand Ronnie Moore three priceless points. Pool survived a nervy finish to the game which included 12 minutes of added on time to compensate for the Woods injury. My mind drifted to the Sky Sports studio picturing Jeff Stelling jumping up and down begging for the whistle to blow. Much like the pre-match song, Bird was indeed the word in this part of the North East. To his credit, Wimbledon boss Neal Ardley proved to be gracious in defeat, coming onto the pitch instantly at the final whistle to applaud the travelling support.

I ended up running into the Wimbledon team back at the station, who were scheduled for the same train as me out of Hartlepool. Tracking down Akinfenwa by the vending machine, the gentle giant obliged a photo request and offered some words of wisdom for the remainder of the *Journey to the 72*.

"You'll enjoy it when you come to Wimbledon. We always win there, he boldly stated." I told Ade that I'd hold him to that statement. Ardley himself shuffled past on the train en route to collecting a sandwich from the on board shop, while several other members of the squad chatted along with fans to pass the time. At time of writing, Hartlepool staged a remarkable turnaround to pull themselves out of the relegation zone.

"Unbelievable Jeff!"

Best chant: "La, la, la Yellow and Blue. Yellow and Blue, Wombles!" AFC Wimbledon fans singing to the tune of "Hey Jude," by The Beatles.
Match ticket: £13 student ticket. Adult tickets ranged from £20-£25 depending on seat location/time of purchase.
Match programme: £3. Poor H'Angus was still waiting for a kind soul to sponsor him, as was club captain and goalkeeper Scott Flinders. Several players were grilled in Q & A features. Middlesbrough loanee Jordan Jones talked drinking Ribena as a pre-match superstition and the possibility of cars being able to swim in the future. Meanwhile, kit man Martyn Brown registered a perfect score to outwit defender Neil Austin in a head-to-head tournament on questions about Pools' season to move into the semi-finals of "Footballing Brain."
Cost of food: £3.00 for a steak pie.
Food rating: 3.5/5. The top fell off, but was salvaged before hitting the floor. Plenty of meat and commendable lashings of thick gravy to tuck into. The bottom of the pie was a tad crunchy and stuck to the foil tray.

Final Score
Hartlepool United 1 (Bird 73)
AFC Wimbledon 0
Attendance: 3,345

Getting to know Port Vale
Mike Williams - Friend and season ticket holder

Best Vale players in recent years?

Tom Pope will always get the headlines for the Vale, as our old fashioned centre forward, but the two players I would want you to see are Louis Dodds and Michael O'Connor. Dodds is a player who seems to polarise fan opinion, yet he is easily our most gifted technical player, capable of bringing the best out of all around him and allowing us to play quicker football. Unfortunately he is often say on the right and recently has spent too much of his time covering our right back. O'Connor is a centre midfielder who is capable of everything. His effort and drive mean an unstoppable work rate and he is also technically strong; picking passes and shooting from distance are two of his strengths. Keep an eye out for him after the ball has gone too just in case he fancies a bit of afters.

Best thing about Vale Park?

Well, that's a tough question. I would go with the playing surface or the friendly atmosphere. It's not a noisy or intimidating ground, but it has a real family feel.

Worst grounds you've visited?

Oldham Athletic is bad for League One standard, like nothing has been painted or worked on since they were in the Premier League. Accrington Stanley was an experience that has to be seen to be believed.

Best place to sit/stand at Vale Park?

In the Railway Paddock near the away end is probably where the noisiest fans are, but I am lucky enough to sit about 15 rows back right on half way and it is perfect.

Best game you've witnessed at Vale Park?

It's a choice between two. Either beating Burton Albion 7-1 to basically ensure our promotion two years ago, or beating Rotherham United heavily at home when Pope scored four. The look on Steve Evans' face was something that I will never forget.

Famous Vale fans?

Robbie Williams and Phil 'The Power' Taylor.

Quirky fact time?

Only Football League club which is not named after an actual place, good pub quiz fact right there.

Game #58: League One - Tuesday 3rd March 2015
PORT VALE vs Oldham Athletic - Vale Park

If at first you don't succeed, try again. Or something along those lines. Hurricane Gonzalo had prevented me from getting to Port Vale back in October, although I did get to meet John Hartson who had also been left in limbo at Crewe, so it wasn't all bad. Bracing myself for a second attempt at getting to Staffordshire, Dad spared me a scenic train route through Alsager and Kidsgrove by agreeing to come with me and drive. A week of negotiations had finally come up trumps. He drove a hard bargain, but I conceded the cost of a tea and a pie was worth it, although an 11th hour addition of a Big Mac and fries for the journey did blindside me. He may have still been coughing from the cold he picked up at Accrington the week before, but deep down Dad didn't want to see me get stranded again. I was more than happy to have company, well at least until we set off.

"Shaun, do you really have to put a bet on?" Dad isn't a big fan of the bookies.
Those familiar with me know that I like to have a tiny accumulator. If there's games on, then I'll be ready with my £1. I'm all about the hefty stakes. Go big or go home is my motto. To me, watching football without having a bet is like going to a steak house and just ordering salad. It adds to the fun plus I only bet what I can afford to lose. Checking the form guide, Port Vale were on a defensive roll with three consecutive clean sheets. Compare this with managerless Oldham, who were trounced 4-0 at home by Preston North End three days earlier. You didn't need William Hill to tell you that the smart money was pointing to a home banker.

Port Vale were one of the few clubs whose presence I had graced once before. On a random Tuesday evening back in 2012, I tagged along with Mike – yes the same Mike who accused me of putting a curse on his beloved club. I witnessed an entertaining 2-2 draw with Rochdale. From memory, I can remember ex-Chester bruiser Kevin McIntyre going overboard with the post watershed tackles. Oh, and it rained non stop too. The rubbery cheeseburger was memorable for reasons I won't go into.

It wouldn't be right unless there was a slight hitch in getting to the ground. Forget coming off at the wrong junction (sorry Dad) but an unhealthy noise from the engine was impossible to ignore. Pulling over at a garage in nearby Tunstall, it turned out that the car just needed an oil change. Breathing a sigh of relief, we followed the floodlights in the distance and parked up next to Vale Park.

Radio Stoke were out in force handing out 'I Love Port Vale' car stickers and urging passers by to get involved on the post match phone-in. Whenever I've tried to call, the lines have been jammed. No doubt that's because of Mike getting stuff off his chest. The elusive gent was in the vicinity, but doing his best to avoid me. Clearly, he still saw me as a bad luck charm. I was surprised to see the programme seller push the radio issue. So much so that he neglected to give me my change. An uncomfortable stand-off ensued.

"Can I have my change please?"
"I gave it to you just then didn't I?"
"Er no, that's what I'm waiting for."
"Oh sorry, my mistake. Here you go and don't forget about Radio Sto...."
"Yeah, I heard the first time."
"Thanks mate."
I wasn't his mate, but Dad was cracking up. I doubt he'd find it funny when I plastered the five or so Vale stickers tucked into my coat pocket over his car.

The ground was just over half full and the pitch was in pristine condition for the middle of winter. Legend has it that the Signal 1 Stand behind the goal was provided by Chester City when their old ground was knocked down. This was later confirmed to be true by a season ticket holder sitting in front. A small two-tiered stand which joins the Bycars Lane and Railway end looks like it's been wedged into the ground, but is actually part of the original ground structure. Most of Vale Park has had an uplift over the years, although part of the Lorne Street Stand is yet to be completed. A small area of concrete close to the away end remains unoccupied and is awaiting completion. Although he was still considered a novice, Vale boss Rob Page proved to be a throwback to the old tracksuit style manager. The Welshman was out with his squad completing the pre-match warmups rather than staying inside to preside over matters in a suit and tie. He looked like he still had the buzz and proverbial itch to play.

Right on kick off, a pack of half cut latecomers took up residence directly behind me and started talking about what they had for tea, how their wife's day at work had been etc. Basically, chatting about everything but football. It came as no surprise when resident midfield hardman Michael Brown gave away the first free kick of the game. If you haven't heard of the former Leeds United maestro, do a Google search. A delightful waist high tackle used to do the rounds and sums up the veteran's take no prisoners attitude. He makes Roy Keane look like a saint. Most players will welcome you to a game with a hearty handshake, while others opt for a crunching tackle. Brown certainly falls into the latter category. Vale goalkeeper Chris Neal almost gifted Oldham an early lead. After calling at his defenders to collect a ball, he backed off and Oldham's Jonathan Forte stabbed over from deep inside the box.

"He wouldn't hit the floor if he fell out of bed," shouted a voice from two rows behind. I wasn't sure if such wisdom from Mr Porky was aimed at Neal or Forte. Either way it was still funny. Oldham did find the net, albeit thanks to a bit of good fortune. Brown's reputation preceded him when he was pulled up for a foul, which to be honest was minimal contact at best. Mike Jones sized the ball up and put the free kick beyond Neal from close to 30 yards. Dad had a feeling it would go in and I turned to see him grinning back at me like a Cheshire Cat. It was a goal worthy of applauding. Talking about being happy, a young Oldham fan had rushed to the end of the away stand and was swinging his top over his head and bouncing up and down. It was probably the same guy I spotted at Boundary Park back in September. This time, the top stayed off for the rest of the game. Either this guy was immune from the cold, or high on adrenaline. My guess would be both of those said suggestions.

Vale's answer to going a goal down was to play the high ball....for the rest of the game! It didn't make for entertaining viewing to watch ball after ball being pumped forward to the hapless Tom Pope, who wasn't getting any change out of a tight Oldham defence. Aside from two efforts cleared off the line, Oldham saw the game out to hand caretaker boss and former player Dean Holden a priceless victory.

"They should be sued under the Trade Description Act for advertising football." Dad was far from happy on the way back to the car park. The guy arcing his piss up the wall next to our car didn't help matters either. Those Vale stickers still haven't seen the light of day, although I hadn't forgotten about the four times the Valiants had already entertained me on the road. Knowing what the side is capable of made the trip all the more frustrating, but there's always next time.

Best chant: "You're getting hired in the morning." Oldham fans chanting towards Holden, who was named new boss not long after.
Match ticket: £23 was the dearest adult ticket for the Lorne Street Stand. All other areas were £1 less.
Match programme: £3. Good old Michael Brown graced the front cover, yet was still to find sponsorship for the season. Club mascot Boomer the Dog had a page of jokes for the kids. Not a lot of Vale related features in the 68 page edition. Oldham received generous coverage including looks at past players and defining moments courtesy of two historians.
Cost of food: £2.50 for a steak pie.
Food rating: 4/5. Small in size, but it contained enough chunky portions of meat and a nice crunchy crust to get your teeth into. I enjoyed a second helping at half time.

Final Score
Port Vale 0
Oldham Athletic 1 (Jones 42)
Attendance: 4,423

Getting to know Plymouth Argyle
David Banks - Friend and longstanding fan

Favourite memory as a Plymouth fan?
Wembley play-off final 1996, beating Darlington 1-0, with a 35,000 Argyle allocation sold out of a total crowd of 43,000!

Best game you've witnessed at Home Park?
Unable to say just one. Promotion as champions from the now equivalent of League One to the Championship (2-0) victory over Colchester was a fantastic day in general. Best atmosphere was an FA Cup quarter final against Premiership Watford - lost 1-0 with a certain young Ben Foster man of the match in goal for Watford. We were so close to a semi-final against Manchester United.

Best/worst players to pull on a Plymouth shirt?
Best in my time: Mick Heathcote, Adrian Littlejohn, Graham Coughlan, David Friio, Peter Halmosi, Luke McCormick, Romain Larrieu. Worst: Peter Swan, James Dungey, Taribo West, Marvin Morgan.

Best thing about Home Park?
The ground being cited on a park overlooking Plymouth from beyond the Main Stand. I like that it is not in an industrial estate or run down housing estate like most grounds. I'm a fan of the charismatic grandstand - would love to see the old style design somehow incorporated when the new stand is eventually built.

Which club serves the nicest pies?
Don't tend to buy pies because they're overpriced and the generic Pukka pies are poor quality. The pie at Coventry was quite good though!

Famous Plymouth fans?
Michael Foot (Labour Leader in 80's), Bastille drummer Chris Wood.

Quirky fact time?
Pele (still in his prime) played with Santos against Plymouth in 1973 at Home Park. Third Division Argyle beat Santos 3-2 in front of 37,639 fans. Also, we hold the record as the first match to involve five players being sent off in a Football League game against Chesterfield at Saltergate. Players sent off included a young Kevin Davies for Chesterfield. In total it was three for Argyle and two for Chesterfield. Finally, Plymouth Argyle toured South America in 1924 with victories over Uruguay 4-0 (who went on to win the first World Cup six years later) and Argentina 1-0.

Thoughts on ticket prices in general?
Ticket prices should be set the same for each league with increments as you go up.

Name your Plymouth Dream Team?
Romain Larrieu
Mark Patterson
Paul Williams
Graham Coughlan
Mick Heathcote
David Friio
David Norris
Lillian Nalis
Adrian Littlejohn
Mickey Evans
Peter Halmosi

PILGRIMAGE TO PLYMOUTH

Game #59: League Two - Saturday 7th March 2015
PLYMOUTH ARGYLE vs Northampton Town - Home Park

The Proclaimers may have walked 500 miles, but I could trump that. Plymouth clocked in at 271 miles (each way) officially making it the longest journey thus far. Thankfully, help was at hand. Dave aka Banksy made good on a promise from his 30th Birthday bash back in November, putting himself forward to make the drive down to Devon and back. I appreciated the kind gesture and handed over an agreed £40 in petrol contribution - a fraction of what a return train ticket would have cost.

Banksy has family based in Plymouth and ties in a couple of visits each season with trips to Home Park. For this particular trip, his Dad Vic was joining us, while older brother Nick was meeting us at Plymouth. I was thankful at being able to gatecrash a family reunion and bag a lift for the five hour drive. Making good progress from a 7:30am pick up, we stopped off at Taunton Deane to stretch our legs and throw sandwich crusts at a couple of kids in Northampton shirts (just kidding.) Not long after being back on the road, a smooth nap and excursion was suddenly interrupted by Banksy turning the air blue. By Dave's own admission, he has some anger issues. For once, he had good reason. An idiot in a White Audi TT decided to channel his inner Lewis Hamilton and cut us up on the outside lane, weaving in and out of traffic as it were an F1 race track. Sheer good luck and quick reactions stopped the car from becoming a mangled mess.

As planned, Dave's brother Nick joined up with us at Plymouth. He had got the bus down from London and was booked on a midnight return ticket. Banksy had already booked a Travelodge close to his Nan's, so I checked in to a Guest House overlooking the West Hoe.

Parking up in a residential area close to the stadium, I quickly discovered that folk in these parts preferred pasties to their pies. Ivor Dewdney pasties to be precise. Voted 'Best Pasty' in 2002, the recipe and business has stayed in the family since the 1930s. Now offering a roadside service, this was one occasion when it was perfectly acceptable to handle hot goods from the back of a white van. Generously sized, I plumped for a medium Cornish pasty while the Banks family all went large.

Thanks to a Reuben Reid hat-trick, Plymouth had recently celebrated a 3-1 victory over fierce rivals Exeter City in the 100th Devon derby. Special #1-3 merchandise took pride of place in the club shop with various fans proudly displaying the slogan already on their replica shirts. The lack of Grecian love continued when Nick quipped "watch that piece of Exeter," as I turned to stop my foot stepping in a dog turd outside the turnstiles.

Steel framework hangs over the club's logo and name outside the ground. From a distance, it could be mistaken for scaffolding or the outside of a prison. Three sides of Home Park have been re-developed in recent times, with corners filled in and seating installed. The Grandstand has seen better days, looking quite neglected since the temporary seating used during the club's Championship tenure has been ripped out in favour of unused terracing. Sponsors Bond Timber have gone the extra mile in providing the wood which make up the two dugouts, while the club honours its past players with sticker like images emblazoned at the entrance to each section of the ground. From managers, to ex-internationals, all the way to famous FA Cup sides from back in the day, it seems like no player has been forgotten, although Banksy was struggling to spot the "legendary" Barry Hayles.

Argyle boss John Sheridan was known to commute to matches from his home in Yorkshire. It's "a fair old poke" after all according to the old Plymouth inspired car insurance advert. The ex-Republic of Ireland midfielder looked every bit pissed off as his tone suggested in his programme notes, deriding decisions that had gone against his team in recent games. Speaking of the programme, the back of 'The Pilgrim' proudly listed the 'Green Army' (aka the fans) as the 12th man.

Both teams were targeting the play-offs, although Northampton were light on attacking options. The mullet master John-Joe O'Toole had to be content with a place on the bench. Quite clearly, the hysteria surrounding the long haired wonder had died down somewhat since our last meeting.

Northampton's bald and physically imposing centre half Ryan Cresswell wasted no time stamping his authority on the game and on poor Argyle attacker Lewis Alessandra. Defensive tactics more accustomed to the UFC went largely unpunished, as did a handling offence outside the box by goalkeeper Matt Duke. When he did manage to wriggle free of his shadow, Alessandra fluffed a golden opportunity to score by sending a weak lob straight into Duke's gloves.

The hosts did take the lead when Bobby Reid (no relation to Reuben) unselfishly laid the ball off for Anthony O'Connor to drill a shot into the bottom corner. The referee failed to see the funny side of O'Connor's reveal of a Superman t-shirt in celebration and promptly booked the goalscorer. Northampton dominated possession, but their lack of a cutting edge up front was telling. Debutant James Gray along with substitute Ivan Toney (still sporting the Fresh Prince quiff) struggled to make an impression. Alessandra sealed the points for the Pilgrims late on. Drew Talbot cut the ball across the box, allowing the frontman to round Duke and tap into the net. From a distance, I detected a smile flash briefly across Sheridan's face. Even he would have admired the gutsy performance his team put in to grind out a difficult victory.

It had been a happy homecoming for the Banks family, plus a good decision by myself to stay over. Arranging a time and pick-up point for the following morning, we parted ways for the rest of the evening. Taking advantage of a fresh sea breeze and a leisurely stroll, the town folk were out in all their finest evening attire. Couples partied the night away along the pier, both on showboats and in one of the many offshore restaurants. There was a good vibe around the place, plus in the car on the drive back home. It may have been a fair old poke, but it's one I'd happily make again.

Best chant: "A.r.g.y.l.e, we are the pride of the West Country. With a knick knack paddy whack give a dog a bone, City fans can fuck off home." Plymouth fans reminding neutrals like me that they're not too fond of neighbours Exeter City.

Match ticket: £20 for an advance adult ticket.

Match programme: £3. The League Two mileage chart made for fascinating viewing. After Exeter, the closest away day for Argyle fans was Newport County, clocking in at a 278 mile round trip. Some clubs definitely have it easier than others. The programme writers liked to remember past masters, while youngster Tyler Harvey revealed the chefs make an "unbelievable" Lasagne. On the subject of food....

Cost of food: £3.00 for a balti pie. The pasty was a bit cheaper.

Food rating: 2/5 for the pie. Very greasy pastry and not very appetising. The pasty was more favourable. Lots of seasoning and potato.

Final Score
Plymouth Argyle 2 (O'Connor 28, Alessandra 86)
Northampton Town 0
Attendance: 6,501

Getting to know Middlesbrough
Jack Sargeant
Twitter @sargeant_j

How long have you been a Middlesbrough fan?
Since I was about nine years old, albeit with loyalties split between the Teessiders and Manchester United. I was born and grew up in Manchester to a Boro supporter, but the latter took precedence after the 2004 Carling Cup final win. Not many other Boro fans can claim to be glory hunters!

Favourite memory as a Middlesbrough fan?
The Carling Cup final would be the most obvious choice, but it's actually probably either the UEFA Cup quarter final or semi final from 2006. On both occasions Massimo Maccarone scored last-gasp winners as Boro came from four goals down; unbelievable scenes that earned a pretty underwhelming signing Riverside legend status.

Best game you've witnessed at the Riverside Stadium?
I've seen more horrors than I have classics! Barry Robson beating Hull with a last-minute rocket a few years ago was fun, I'll go for that.

Best/worst players to pull on a Middlesbrough shirt?
Best: George Camsell, John Hickton, Tony Mowbray, Bryan Robson, Juninho.
Worst: Branco, Phil Whelan, Mido, Afonso Alves.

Best thing about the Riverside Stadium?
The Ayresome Gates outside provide a very nice nod to Boro's heritage, but probably the magnificent view of the Transporter Bridge. Boro's industrial heritage is always in full view.

Worst grounds you've visited?
I'm pleased to say there really aren't any particularly bad ones that stand out.

Enjoyable away days?
I'm sure it's a popular choice, but one of my favourites is Craven Cottage. Lovely old ground, considerably more atmospheric than a lot of the identikit modern stadia.

Famous Middlesbrough fans?
The most notable is probably comedian Bob Mortimer, who goes to a lot of the away games and also apparently once trialled for the club. Otherwise, Chris Rea, Jeff Winter (unfortunately) and, according to the internet, England cricketer Liam Plunkett.

Quirky fact time?
You'll sometimes see a North Korean flag flying at the Riverside. That's because they trained and played their group games in the 1966 World Cup at Ayresome Park, and famously eliminated Italy there in one of the biggest shocks in football history. Ever since then, the Boro fans have occasionally been spotted waving the North Korean national flag.

Best/worst Boro managers?
The two standout managers are Steve McClaren and Bruce Rioch. The former led Boro to their first ever major silverware in the 2004 Carling Cup, to a record high finish in the Premier League, and to a European final in the 2006 UEFA Cup. It wasn't always pretty football, but his teams probably produced more unforgettable moments than anyone before or since. Rioch, meanwhile, led Boro through the most uncertain time in their history, coaching the team in parks and on school fields when they were locked out of Ayresome Park by the receivers in 1986. He brought through a team of local lads and let them to two successive promotions, and he could hardly be held in higher esteem.

Strong candidates for the worst have come over recent times. Gareth Southgate got Boro relegated from the Premier League after many years in the top tier, though his circumstances are slightly mitigated by the fact that it was his first managerial job - he shouldn't have been given it in the first place. His successor Gordon Strachan was even worse: despite his experience he saddled Boro with numerous terrible players (many brought in from the SPL), and was sacked with the club on the brink of relegation to the third tier. It's only over the last season or two that we've managed to recover from his legacy.

Thoughts on ticket prices in general?

Of course ticket prices are pretty ridiculously high, but I struggle to see how anything could transform the situation. Football is a business for those involved, and the clubs are no different. Many teams invariably run at a loss, and high ticket prices are clearly the best way for them to recoup some of the high expenditure on wages and other operating costs. It would probably take a dramatic restructuring of English football or the clubs for prices to drop, and there's no reason to believe that's in the offing.

Name your Middlesbrough Dream Team?

I've only drawn players from the last 30-odd years to make my task a bit easier! (3-4-1-2)
Mark Schwarzer
Gary Pallister
Gareth Southgate
Tony Mowbray
Christian Ziege
Gaizka Mendieta
Graeme Souness
Franck Queudrue
Juninho
Mark Viduka
Jimmy Floyd Hasselbaink

Game #60: The Championship - Saturday 14th March 2015
MIDDLESBROUGH vs Ipswich Town - The Riverside Stadium

Sellout games had been rare so far, although some matches still jumped out enough to warrant pre-booking. This was one of those occasions. Promotion chasers against play-off hopefuls with the business end of the season fast looming. I was sold and quietly confident that I'd picked the game of the weekend to come and see.

I opened negotiations with the ticket office. The club didn't do student tickets, plus the lack of a screaming child meant I was ineligible to go in the family enclosure. Placing my faith in the ticket clerk's hands, I asked to go wherever the best atmosphere was. "I'll put you in the South Stand," said Alma – a lovely lady, who was eager to hear about some of my trips. "There's a drummer nearby if you don't mind a bit of noise," she added.

This was music to my ears. I started to wonder if I'd be allowed to have a bit of a drum myself. The game was being televised, so was moved to a lunchtime kick-off. Setting off early had its advantages, specifically a lack of train changes and calling points. Adding on a small wait at Manchester for Greggs to open and provide breakfast, the total travel time was a little over three hours.

The ground is signposted as soon as you exit the station and is around a 10-15 minute walk. For those who are thirsty, the 'Lord Byron' is en route to break up the journey. Scores of home fans had already congregated outside the small pub, having brought their own beer to the party. The Riverside scrubs up well, as does the weird looking fishing net on display just outside. Despite being built 20 years ago, the stadium is still in pristine condition and has that relative new feel to it. Statues of former players George Hardwick and Wilf Mannion line the outside of the ground, along with the gates to Boro's old Ayresome Park ground. Former player and manager Tony Mowbray is celebrated as a 'Boro Legend,' on one of the flags that hangs on a post outside the ground, although his playing stint is more likely to be fondly remembered than his recent stab at the manager's job.

A good vibe was only made better when I saw the Queen's face staring up at me from the ground. Whereas a guy in front of me had just trampled over Her Majesty, I had no problem picking up a £5 note from the floor. I put the money (and a little bit more) straight back into the club with a purchase of the three P's - programme, pie and pizza. Yes, for the first time since Reading, I found a club that sold my favourite snack. I passed on trying a fourth P in a Parmo. What's that I hear you say? The Parmesan - a breaded chicken dish with cheese and white sauce is quite high in saturated fat and similar to a schnitzel. Created by American chef Nicos Harris in World War II, Nicos moved to Middlesbrough after being wounded in battle, opened a restaurant and started selling his creation. The original recipe has been in the family since 1958 and has become a favourite among North Eastern folk and its supermarket chains. There endeth today's history lesson.

The Boro ultras aka 'Red Faction' were putting the final touches to their pre-match preparations. Bags of white confetti were handed out, flags were ready to be waved and t-shirts were proudly on display. Not just any shirts, but special 'Fck Sky' (correct spelling) designs. Sky were not flavour of the month in the South Stand at all. From what I could gather, a small number of fans were unhappy at having their games moved at the broadcaster's whim. Their match at Brentford was brought forward after fans had already made travel arrangements, while Boro's next game at Bournemouth was also scheduled for a lunchtime kick-off. Proceeds from shirt sales apparently go directly into funding new colourful banners to display during games.

Playing the classic version of 'Three Lions,' plus AC/DC's 'Thunderstruck' poured gasoline onto an already rabid fire. The fans were on their feet and bouncing up and down to greet the two teams onto the pitch. Despite being an all-seater stadium, the South Stand opted to remain on their feet for the game, so I followed suit. The match took all of four minutes to burst into life. Ipswich goalkeeper Dean Gerken came for a cross and inadvertently knocked himself out after clashing with defender Christophe Berra. During the commotion, Daniel Ayala headed the Teessiders in front. There was an eight minute delay while medics tended to Gerken and stretchered him off. The whole stadium came together to applaud the Ipswich shotstopper, whose wife had only given birth the night before.

The delay didn't unnerve Ipswich. Quite the opposite actually. The Tractor Boys equalised direct from the restart. Dimitrios Konstantopoulos couldn't hold onto Jonathan Parr's shot and the rebound fell kindly to Daryl Murphy, who was never going to miss. Murphy was denied a second by the post before the home side lost Ayala to injury. Jonathan Woodgate entered the field to chants of "Johnny Woodgate is a red, he hates Geordies," a sentence I never thought I'd see myself type, let alone sing. Ipswich boasted a lot of height on the field and were relying too much on the high ball. The hosts were able to nullify that tactic and re-took the lead just before half time. A well rehearsed set piece exposed Ipswich, who weren't anticipating a short corner. A quick ball across the box was smashed hard and low into the net by pacy winger Albert Adomah.

From there Middlesbrough didn't look back. On loan Chelsea forward Patrick Bamford took the plaudits and the headlines with a sublime second half double. For his first, the forward beat the offside trap to run clear and effortlessly commit Bartosz Bialkowski to the floor, before slotting in. The second was pure genius. Bamford spun two markers with an exquisite dummy to run onto a high ball and fire an angled shot into the bottom corner. The South Stand were the conductors for the rest of the stadium to get up and start singing. I had the best view in the house, watching and listening to everyone from kids to pensioners getting behind their team.

The final whistle brought about a tinge of sadness. It was a game I didn't want to end. Buoyant Boro fans high fived and embraced, while excitedly making plans to fly down to Bournemouth the week after. One Boro fan was clearly feeling giddy on the first part of the train home, openly mocking a group of Ipswich fans still smarting from their defeat and readying themselves for a long journey back to East Anglia. Putting on his best/worst Suffolk accent, the portly fan started off with some light banter.

"There's no cars in Ipswich. Do you cycle home from the pub?" Canned laughter followed, so porky upped the ante. "Ooh, ahh, you've burnt down my barn. All my chickens have died." The six Ipswich fans shook their heads and I could tell they were quietly seething through clenched teeth. Fortunately for the fat man, his stop came up just as he was getting started on talking up Ipswich's fierce rivals Norwich City. Fight night was prevented and I could go back to my book.

While it wasn't a sellout, there was plenty of noise, a half time marriage propsal (she said yes) and a great game to boot. Lots of reasons why a return to the Riverside makes sense. Up the Boro!

Best chant: "Follow, follow, follow. We're the Red Army from Middlesbrough. And we'll stand and we'll sing, Stevie Gibson is King, we're the Red Army from Middlesbrough." The home fans showing their love and appreciation for club chairman/owner Steve Gibson.
Match ticket: £26.00 + £2.50 booking fee.
Match programme: £3. From fan tales with the super-friendly Juninho to ex-defender Curtis Fleming putting his name forward for a coaching job, the Boro edition was very generous to its former alumni.
Cost of food: £2.90 for a pie, £2.90 for a mini pizza. Very fast and efficient service too I might add.
Food rating: 5/5. At first glance, the pizza looked like a Chicago Town. Happily, it was a lot nicer with a soft crust. The tomato was bursting with flavour and oozed melt in the mouth cheese. Meanwhile the balti lent itself to being more of a chicken curry styled pie. Lovely marinated meat with enough spice, plus the pastry didn't stick to the tray.

Final Score
Middlesbrough 4 (Ayala 4, Adomah 30, Bamford 64, 79)
Ipswich Town 1 (Murphy 11)
Attendance: 18,909

Getting to know Millwall
Nick Hart - Achtung Millwall podcast
Twitter @CBL_Magazine

Explain the myth behind Millwall and their fans?

There's a certain aura around Millwall and its fanbase, which carries a negative stigma amongst other fans. Is that justified or a big misconception? The slogan of the fans is 'no one likes us and we don't care'. And it is indeed an aura that is at once our greatest strength...and our greatest weakness. Myself, I would lose all interest in the game if Millwall were ever to travel the 'half and half'/neutral fan stand route. Much as we will never challenge the bigger clubs in the financial stakes, I love The Den's partisanship, its no holds barred atmosphere and its unwillingness to partake in the corporate sanitised modern game. Is Millwall intimidating? Probably. Many away fans enjoy it though. For that reason I would describe it more as old fashioned - and I mean that in a positive way...

Thoughts on Ian Holloway's reign?

A total unmitigated disaster. Never has a man spoken so much and said so little worth listening to. An imposter passing himself off as a manager. Shall I continue?

Who have been Millwall's key players this season?

Genuinely, there haven't been any. Our leading scorer is Ricardo Fuller's zimmer frame...

Best/worst players to pull on a Millwall shirt?

Best - Teddy Sheringham, Terry Hurlock, Alex Rae, Barry Kitchener, Neil Harris. Worst - where do we start? The alcoholic Russians Kulkov and Yuran from the 90s, Dany N'Guessan more recently, the list really is endless.

Best game you've witnessed at the New Den?

The Huddersfield Town play-off game in 2010 was blistering in terms of atmosphere, the Mother's Day massacre of West Ham in 2004 will forever live in our hearts, the 4-0 defeat of Ronnie Moore's Rotherham in 2001 pretty much sealed the league for us that season. There was a good old Cold Blow Lane atmosphere (other fans would call it intimidating).

Best thing about the New Den?

Unlike any other modern ground and despite being totally different to Cold Blow Lane, it has somehow retained something of the old ground's capacity to overwhelm the opposition. All of this sounds laughable after this season's shambles when The Den has been the easiest away fixture for the championship to visit, but it is always there.

Best/worst grounds you've visited?

Best ground I suppose was Old Trafford in 2004 for the cup semi-final. I actually quite liked the Millennium Stadium in Cardiff as a venue. Otherwise, more modern stadia are bland versions of Sports Direct outlets and many look the same. The MK Dons bar code entry system always used to impress me, not so much now though as it's everywhere.

Which club serves the nicest pies?

Avoid the pies at The Den. Eat round London Bridge way.

Famous Millwall fans?

Danny Baker, Frank Harper of the Football Factory. Emilio Esteves has been pictured in a Millwall shirt. Denzel Washington claims to support the Lions. Oh yes, no mucking about us.

Quirky fact time?

I think our history and 'aura' mean that we're quite well known already and are the biggest small club in the world. Known in all sorts of odd places that you wouldn't expect. A quirky fact? Hmm ...we don't sell that many replica shirts and you will not be able to buy a half and half scarf at The Den. There just isn't any market for them.

ENTERING THE LION'S DEN

Game #61: The Championship - Tuesday 17th March 2015
MILLWALL vs Brighton & Hove Albion - The New Den

Boxing gloves? Check. Protective vest? Check. Sanity in question? Check. I was about to head into the Lion's Den. Quite literally. The most colourful away day had arrived. Millwall are a rather unique bunch with quite a history. Fans ripping up seats, meatheads putting bricks through windows, rioting on the pitch. You get the picture.

'No-one likes us, we don't care.' A rather blunt club moniker that summed everything up. Loved by a select few and revered by many, Millwall's reputation certainly preceded them. Armed with optimism, the signs were ominous when a big black hearse pulled out in front of me. I hadn't even left Chester yet. A midweek game would normally mean an overnight stay, but all of my friends were either away or otherwise engaged. A scan through Late Rooms brought about a less than favourable review of the South Bermondsey area. Reports of gang cultures and stories of accommodation which resembled a builders yard left me with little option but to book an overnight bus back to Chester. More on that later.

It had been a season to forget for Millwall, with relegation to League One all but confirmed. Without a home win since October, the club had just dismissed Ian Holloway - unpopular among the masses and promoted former striker Neil 'Chopper' Harris to the bench. Brighton had also shuffled their coaching pack since the last time we'd met, with Chris Hughton replacing Sami Hyypia. The Seagulls were struggling, but having poor performers such as Wigan and Blackpool below them had saved their bacon for another season.

The platform at London Bridge was overflowing with people. A quick scan of the area found two young Millwall fans. No sign of trouble yet. I could put the cricket bat away. South Bermondsey station was a simple five minute journey and overlooks the New Den. Directly outside the platform exit is a cordoned off area for away fans, who are given a special police escort around the back of the station and into the stadium. Much like herding sheep, a small Brighton contingent were already there and waiting patiently. I felt like I was running a gauntlet as I walked past them and continued along a straight path towards the station's exit.

I had unwittingly interrupted prayer time when calling into the local chippy. Peering over the counter to see why my order of fries was taking so long, the proprietor had taken his shoes off and was on his knees going through his daily ritual. Perhaps he was praying for a Millwall reprieve, although if he was then he was leaving it late. A disgruntled electrician was less tactful and complained loudly at having to wait ten minutes to complete his drilling. The fries were well worth the wait by the way.

The area surrounding the New Den was dimly lit. A couple of police vans were parked up, as was a special double decker bus, with the slogan 'let 'em all come down to the Den,' emblazoned across the bottom. Flyers were being handed out about a missing dog. I wondered if it had dared to venture onto the bus, never to be seen again. A Millwall player all suited and booted stepped out of a car to take photos and sign autographs with fans. Looking at the leg brace that the injured player was sporting, I couldn't help but think that one of the meatheads had gotten to him after a poor performance. Police on horseback were patrolling the eerily dark car park, so I quickly picked up my ticket and retreated into a lighter part of the stadium.

Tim Cahill, Dennis Wise and Kevin Muscat were all staring back at me in the corridor as I looked back at some of the finest thugs to grace a Millwall shirt. Arguably, if the current setup boasted a couple of midfield generals with half as much bark and bite as their past alumni, then maybe the club would be higher up the Championship ladder.

The pre-match mood inside the Den was surprisingly quiet, especially considering it was Harris' first home game in charge. The Brighton contingent filled half of their stand behind the goal and raised the decibels a few levels. Bizarrely, the red mist seemed to descend as soon as the match kicked off and Millwall suddenly found their voice. Cries of "Miiiiiiiiiilll" echoed around the stadium. I turned to see that flat caps were very much the headgear of choice in these parts. I didn't have to look far to see the stereotypical bunch of Millwall fans. A trio of charming gentlemen took great delight in yelling "queer," "puff," or "c**t," whenever a Brighton player got anywhere near the ball. Two older women were sat next to me, yet seemed immune to all the cussing going on around them.

Millwall goalkeeper David Forde did nothing to alleviate the bad blood from the stands. The shotstopper inexplicably came running out of goal to come for a ball he was never going to get. Stuck in no-mans land, Forde was lucky that Brighton's Craig Mackail-Smith's bearings were just as bad. The forward's weak attempt at a chip ended up going behind him and was cleared by a grateful Millwall defence. A bloke sporting half a tub of hair gel (maybe more) was quick to get up and offer words of encouragement.

"Wake up Forde, you fucking mug." I think poor David got the message loud and clear, as that was the last time he strayed from his line. Millwall were passing it round well enough. They just lacked the quality in the final third and someone who could apply a finish. Brighton were relying on set pieces and Millwall were grateful to have defender Shaun Cummings stationed on the line to clear a goalbound effort. Flashes of brilliance like Aiden O'Brien's mazy 40 yard run were few and far between for the home side. Joe Bennett struck the bar with a free kick for the visitors, but I got that sinking feeling that I wasn't going to see any goals.

The New Den used to be the backdrop for Sky One's fictional Football soap 'Dream Team.' Millwall's beanpole striker Stefan Maierhofer feebly stuck out a leg to send a pathetic late lob into the stand. Karl Fletcher he most certainly wasn't. Much like when half time was approaching, the smash brothers had upped and left to top up their alcohol intake. Many frustrated fans had followed suit minutes before the full time whistle went. Brighton seemed happiest with the point as it took them one step closer to safety. It was probably for the best that the video wall in the corner was out of use, as they would be scrambling to find many highlights to replay.

Like most away contingents at the New Den, Brighton fans were held back in the stadium until the home fans had filed out. The police weren't taking any chances either, keeping them fenced in at the station until platform staff radioed down to say the first few trains carrying home fans had departed. The night was still very much young for me. I had a five and a half hour coach journey to look forward to from London Victoria.

Settling down in a plush leather seat, most of the travelling contingent seemed happy to try and get some sleep - myself included. The silence didn't last too long. All the way from Birmingham to Stoke, ear screeching screams could be heard from the back of the coach. A lady in distress was complaining about stabbing kidney pains and had ignored doctor's advice not to travel long distance after just coming out of hospital. Vomiting was quickly added to her list of problems and it was decided to call an ambulance. The coach company were legally bound to stay with the distressed patient until said ambulance arrived, so it added an extra 45 minute layover at Stoke. I finally got back to Chester at 6am, half asleep and desperate for some shut eye. While I didn't need the boxing gloves, I still felt like I had gone ten rounds with Mike Tyson. I had survived the Millwall experience, but I'm unlikely to seek a rematch any time soon.

Best chant: "Super, super Neil. Super Neil Harris." Millwall finally have a boss they're happy with. Harris will need all of his superpowers to bring his current side back to prominence.
Match ticket: £27.00 for a Category B game in the upper part of the Barry Kitchener Stand. Category A games increased by £3, but members generally saved £3 per category.
Match programme: £3. Unsurprisingly, Neil Harris was all over the 84 page edition, which included a pull-out poster. A scouting report on Brighton proved to be pretty accurate, noting their strength being set pieces and their main weakness unable to finish scoring chances.
Cost of food: £3.30 for a steak and ale pie.
Food rating: 5/5. The food was the best part of the night and one of the nicest steak pies I've sampled. Firm pastry, good cuts of steak and a flavour which was constant in every bite. Piping hot and sat on the stomach well.

Final Score
Millwall 0
Brighton & Hove Albion 0
Attendance: 9,105

Getting to know Blackpool
Chris Walker
www.measuredprogress.co.uk
Twitter @onedavebamber

How long have you been a Blackpool fan?

Ever since I can remember. A lot of people can identify their first game, but when I was three-years-old my Grandad would sneak me and my brother in for the last 10 minutes when they used to open the gates to let people out. I've been going to Bloomfield Road since around 1990.

Favourite memory as a Blackpool fan?

Without doubt the play-off semi-final win at Nottingham Forest in 2010. There was only around 1,500 away fans there and to be among them that night was a privilege. We witnessed one of the best attacking performances I've ever seen from any team, not just Blackpool. Having led 2-1 from the home leg, we won 4-3 on the night and I knew we would win in the final.

How would you assess the season?

Entirely predictable. You know what they say, "fail to prepare, prepare to fail" and Blackpool's 2014/15 season is the ultimate example of that. We probably deserved to go down the previous season so we definitely got our just desserts. Jose Riga was dealt an awful hand by the owners, but was a model of dignity and stood firm on his values, not being afraid to speak his mind about the problems at the club and the help he needed from the chairman. Results were horrendous under Riga, as you might expect given we went into the opening day with just a handful of players registered, but you could at least see an ethos and with more resources I'm sure he would have made a good fist of it. In contrast, Lee Clark often attempts to cover up for the Oyston family and at the same time plays a truly awful brand of football.

Best game you've witnessed at Bloomfield Road?

A lot of my best memories of Blackpool are at away games or finals at Wembley or the Millennium Stadium, but obviously there have been exciting moments on home soil too. The final home game of our season in the Premier League was pretty special, when we beat Bolton Wanderers 4-3, on the anniversary of the 1953 cup win over the same opponents with the same scoreline. It meant we went into the final game of the season at Old Trafford with a decent chance of staying up, although good results for our rivals ultimately doomed us despite a strong points tally of 39 points, which is usually enough to keep you safe.

Best/worst players to pull on a Blackpool shirt?

Historically, there's obviously the likes of Stan Mortenson, Sir Stanley Matthews and Jimmy Armfield, although I'm too young to have witnessed any of those. In my early years supporting the club I got to see Trevor Sinclair close-up, and more recently Charlie Adam was a huge part of our success. The most skilful player I've seen in tangerine though is Wes Hoolahan. The ball just sticks to his feet and every week you'd see him do something extraordinary.

Best thing about Bloomfield Road?

There's not much about the ground in its current incarnation that is particularly great. Before all four sides were re-done, it had a lot of character and I have great memories of being on all four sides of the old Bloomfield Road. Compared to a lot of the new stadiums where all four sides are identical, our new build is at least a little different given it was constructed in different phases, and the compact nature of it can make for a good atmosphere when the team are doing well, although that seems like a long time ago now.

Worst grounds you've visited?

There is something to be quietly enjoyed in a lot of grounds that you might conventionally think of as bad, for instance Saltergate and Belle Vue were pretty disgusting, but filled with character, much like the old Bloomfield Road. The away end at Turf Moor is horrible though and Portman Road isn't much better either.

Enjoyable away days?
It's often about the day and not just the ground itself. Personal favourites include Griffin Park and Oakwell, but I've also visited quite a few in Europe and my favourites in Germany are Freiburg's Dreisamstadion and Union Berlin's Alte Försterei.

Which club serves the nicest pies?
I had an excellent steak pie at Everton. In fact, it was that good I went back for a second.

Famous Blackpool fans?
We don't have a great number of famous supporters. Jimmy Armfield is perhaps the main one but probably doesn't count given he's a former player. Bill Beaumont is meant to be a Blackpool fan, but his fame has been on the wane ever since he left Question of Sport.

Quirky fact time?
Blackpool have never won the top flight (we did finish 2nd to Manchester United in 1956) but we were top of the league in 1939 when World War II broke out and all fixtures were cancelled. Who knows, if it wasn't for Adolf Hitler we might have claimed our only title?

SCRAPPING AT THE SEASIDE

Game #62: The Championship - Saturday 21st March 2015
BLACKPOOL vs Leeds United - Bloomfield Road

Much like the town's famous rollercoaster, Blackpool Football Club had been through their fair share of highs and lows in recent times. Five years ago, they were the darlings of the Premier League. Now the laughing stock of the Football League, the Seasiders were on their way to League One and in danger of setting an all time lowest points total since Stockport County's meagre 26 back in the 2001/02 season.

The breakdown in relations between Blackpool's hierarchy and the club's supporters is the main catalyst for the club's recent decline. Much reported questions in the media over club funding along with alleged spats with supporters had made chairman Karl Oyston about as popular at Bloomfield Road as a Preston fan. The lack of care into the club's on field aspirations was made abundantly clear when Blackpool turned up for a pre-season friendly at Penrith with a team of trialists and had just eight registered players on their books the week before the season kicked off. Even shirt sponsors Wonga - whose own moral compass can be called into question at times, had decided to jump ship at the end of the season. The soap opera and nightmare for the poor fans certainly didn't look like coming to an end any time soon.

With tensions bubbling over and a reported mass protest planned before the game with Leeds, it was the ideal time for me to pack my bucket and spade and head to the seaside. Contrary to belief, I didn't see anyone shooting up by the seafront nor were donkeys being used as a mode of transport. I did however just miss a group of Preston fans celebrating their annual 'Gentry Day,' by dressing in suits, umbrellas and bowler hats for an away day. Ken Morley of Celebrity Big Brother and Coronation Street fame was also trying to go incognito along the platform at Preston station. Seeing through his disguise of an England baseball cap, I thought better of shouting "Reg" (Holdsworth) or asking for a quote for Safestyle windows and doors, instead leaving him to his own devices.

Blackpool has two main stations - North and South. The latter is the best option for those who are football inclined. Although some fans probably wouldn't blame you for turning back and going elsewhere. The club hotel situated next to the ground comes into view as soon as you leave the station car park and is barely a ten minute walk away. True to their word, an army of Tangerines had stationed themselves outside the club's reception. Armed with banners, megaphones and specially made 'Oyston Out' scarves, the Blackpool faithful weren't exactly backwards in coming forwards.

It all got a bit too much for one fan who, in his haste to catch up with his mate for an umpteenth pint ended up kissing the pavement. I bit my tongue. Honest. Luckily for him, there was an NHS unit on site. Wounded pride is easy to treat. There was a police presence, but they didn't need to interject themselves.....yet. That would come later on. As I went to collect my ticket, several Leeds fans started to file in with their bags of fish and chips and couldn't resist jamming a salty thumb into the eye of their scorned counterparts.

"You're going down with the Millwall."
"We're only here to send you down."

Like I've said before, the Leeds fans have a certain charm unlike any other. Most of the angry Blackpool mob carried out their threat of abandoning the Championship fixture in favour of going to watch non-league outfit AFC Blackpool take on Bootle in the North West Counties Premier Division. A half filled arena greeted me, which looked quite impressive until I clasped eyes on the pitch. The quaggy mud bath looked more suited to Glastonbury than anything else. Any hopes of watching some free flowing football went out the window. The majority of Bloomfield Road has been re-developed in recent years, although the makeshift East Stand looks a bit detached and is hampered by poorly placed supporting pillars, some of which obstruct seats in the front row.

Since replacing Jose Riga in the Blackpool hot seat, manager Lee Clark had strung together a starting eleven made out of loanees, youth players and free agents. Andrea Orlandi, Jamie O'Hara, Gary Madine, plus recent arrival Michael Jacobs were all proven individuals at this level, but the question remained whether any sort of a team could be forged to give the long suffering fans something to get behind.

Leeds came with a plan to contain and counter as they tried to get to grips with the difficult pitch. The hosts squandered a couple of chances to take the lead. Only Jacobs will know how he missed sliding in to connect with a tap in at the back post. Blackpool did find a goal right on half time. Orlandi's free kick was touched onto the bar by goalkeeper Marco Silvestri, leaving Madine with the simple task to head the rebound over the line. Leeds boss Neil Redfearn gambled on a double attacking change and it paid dividends. Substitute Mirco Antenucci made an instant impression on the game, ballooning over Gaetano Berardi's precise pass from 12 yards. I was still trying to work out how the Italian had missed when he popped up again and found the back of the net. The forward seized on a poor defensive header from Tangerines captain Peter Clarke to lob shot stopper Joe Lewis and bring his side level.

Play was halted when fighting broke out between rival fans behind the goal. Women and children looked on scared as stewards and police quickly intervened to drag a couple of the thugs over rows of seats to the floor. Wearing their cuts and bruises like badges of honour, the idiots were roundly jeered as they were dragged past en route to getting medical treatment, before being ejected and/or arrested. By this stage, the majority of fans had lost interest in what was happening on the pitch. A group of guys behind me were already on the whiskey and didn't bother looking up to see Silvestri fly across his goal to palm one final free kick from out of the top corner. Seagulls swooped down looking for crusts at the final whistle only to find nothing but dregs. This result didn't relegate Blackpool - the Easter Bunny delivered that inevitable blow during the Bank Holiday weekend.

A segment of fans went back to chanting their displeasure outside the stadium after the game. It didn't have the same effect. Most of the air had already been let out of the proverbial balloon. Kids fresh from an afternoon at neighbouring Pleasure Beach packed the train back to Preston. The attractions may have closed for the day, but the circus at the football club remains. The few fans left are sick of being treated like clowns by the ringleaders running the show.

Best chant: "How shit must you be? We're winning at home! Sea-sea-seasiders!" The Blackpool fans enjoying a brief moment to forget about their off-field problems.
Match ticket: £24. Adult prices were capped at £25. Supporters with an official membership could enjoy a £5 discount.
Match programme: £3. Lots of former players and managers joined the two clubs together. Blackpool staff had kind words for ex-assistant Steve Thompson, who was returning in the same role with Leeds (he would be suspended by Leeds for undisclosed reasons not long after this game.) Mascot Bloomfield the Bear revealed Lee Clark was joining junior members on an Easter egg hunt around the ground.
Cost of food: £2.50 for a steak pie.
Food rating: 2/5. Quite small in size and the meat was fatty. I returned for a cheese pasty and the abrupt staff gave me a meat and potato pie instead. Marginally better.

Final Score
Blackpool 1 (Madine 44)
Leeds United 1 (Antenucci 62)
Attendance: 11,688

Getting to know Luton Town
Kevin Harper - Luton Town programme contributor
Twitter @kevshat

Favourite memory as a Luton fan?
Dad decided I was too young to go to Wembley when we won the Littlewoods Cup in 1988, so my favourite memory is probably winning the Johnstone's Paint Trophy in 2009. That season was a tough one for Luton fans after we were given a 30 point deduction in the league before the season began. Realistically, we knew it was going to be a tough ask to preserve our league status, but against all the odds we battled through to make it to Wembley in the JPT and saw off Scunthorpe after extra time in front of over 40,000 Luton fans in a wonderful final full of great goals. We left the league a week later, but that was a wonderful memory to take with us.

Best game you've witnessed at Kenilworth Road?
Ironically the game that always stands out in my memory is one which Luton lost! Back in 2006, Liverpool arrived at Kenilworth Road for an FA Cup third round tie as the champions of Europe. We were a side on the up having won League One the season before and were determined to give them a game, and that is exactly what we did. At one stage, a Kevin Nicholls penalty saw us lead 3-1 early in the second half and the dream win seemed on, but like all good sides, Liverpool had a bench full of talent and turned the match around to win 5-3. Xabi Alonso wrapped up the match with a goal from inside his own half. The quality of football on show that night coupled with the amazing atmosphere made that a night I'll always remember albeit with an 'if only' at the end of it!

Best/worst players to pull on a Luton shirt?
Going way back in time, the best players to put on a Luton shirt would be the likes of Mick Harford, Ricky Hill – who should have had way more England caps than he managed – and Mal Donaghy. All three were key components to our Littlewoods Cup success in 1988 and are always fondly remembered by Town fans. Since then, key players have included the likes of Kevin Nicholls and the goal machine Steve Howard, while Andre Gray's goals will always be remembered as they were the catalyst for our promotion last season, although his exploits were obviously at a lower level to the rest. As for the worst players, sadly there have been a few that haven't cut the mustard with the Town down the years. Probably too many to name, but a couple that stand out were Taiwo Atieno and Pavel Besta. Both were signed by then manager Richard Money, but neither ever looked like they would be good enough even for Conference level. I couldn't tell you what happened to them since, although I would be surprised if either are still in pro football.

Best thing about Kenilworth Road?
The atmosphere! Kenilworth Road isn't the biggest ground in the world and it isn't the best looking one either, but on a big night there is nowhere I'd rather watch football. With the crowd right on top of the pitch, it can be an intimidating place for players from the opposition to play, especially when a packed stadium gets behind the Town. There is something quite magical about matches under the floodlights at Kenilworth Road and I always look forward to night games in particular.

Worst grounds you've visited?
Our non-league adventure took us to some pretty weird and wacky places. I think the worst ground I've been to would be Braintree's ground, but the likes of Alfreton, Grays Athletic and Hayes & Yeading's old ground would run it pretty close. Since we've been back in the Football League, I can't say I'm a huge fan of these new build grounds so Burton and Morecambe didn't excite me much.

Enjoyable away days?
I enjoy the older grounds. Anfield and probably Upton Park are two of my favourite grounds. Further back in the day, the likes of Maine Road was always a good place to go to. I went to Fratton Park for the first time this season when Luton played Portsmouth and that was another ground I enjoyed. I much prefer the older style grounds than the current new builds where the atmosphere seems to be missing.

Which club serves the nicest pies?
I've always thought the northern grounds do the nicest pies, so somewhere like Oldham or Rochdale would get that award. In League Two, I'd have to say Morecambe were top of that category this season.

Famous Luton fans?
Eric Morecambe is probably the most famous of them all, having been a director of the club back in the heydays of the late 70s and 80s. More recently, Nick Owen is now the chairman of the club. He is famous from his TV life and is a prominent person in the public profile of the club in the present day. David James is a big Luton fan despite his Watford background and I've regularly seen Catatonia lead singer Cerys Matthews at matches. Colin Salmon is another big Town fan and I've also seen England cricket captain Alastair Cook at the odd game too.

Quirky fact time?
LTFC celebrated its 130th anniversary on 11th April 2015.

Thoughts on ticket prices in general?
I think across the board, ticket prices are too high for the product people are served up. I'm a fan of a couple of other sports such as cricket and rugby league and you get much better value for money and a better product for what you pay in both those sports. It is something that football needs to address before ticket prices become totally unrealistic to the average man. Thankfully, some sides are starting to do deals on season tickets and hopefully that drops through the system to the everyday match tickets too.

Name your Luton Dream Team?
My all time Luton team (I've supported the Town since 1988) would be:
GK: Les Sealey
RB: Tim Breacker
LB: Matthew Taylor
CB: Curtis Davies
CB: Steve Foster
LM: Kingsley Black
CM: Kevin Nicholls
CM: David Preece
RM: Ricky Hill
CF: Mick Harford
CF: Brian Stein

Game #63: League Two - Tuesday 24th March 2015
LUTON TOWN vs Wycombe Wanderers - The Prostate Cancer UK Stadium (Kenilworth Road)

Two goalless draws and a coach trip that still sends a shiver down the spine. The last couple of midweek jaunts down south hadn't been too kind. Surely the third time had to be a charm. With another international break looming, options for midweek games were scarce. Wycombe were marking their 1,000th Football League game and the Sky cameras were knocking around, so I decided that was enough reason to go and have a gander at the stadium usually known as Kenilworth Road.

For one night only, Luton had renamed their ground after the Football League's official charity. A very classy gesture. The more people who sign up for Men United, the better the chance of fighting prostate cancer. Luton had been stuck in non league purgatory for a number of years, as a result of being deducted 30 points in 2008 for financial irregularities. Now back in the Football League, the Hatters had an eye on the play-offs, while Wycombe were going for automatic promotion. Orange shirts aplenty were on display coming out of Luton station, so it made sense to trail behind them to get to the ground.

Kenilworth Road is slap bang in the middle of a terraced housing estate and unlike any other stadium in the Football League. Old fashioned is a good way to put it. For starters, it's considered five sided. A family area was tagged onto the Main Stand at the beginning of the 1990s and named after late former player David Preece. One side is predominantly made up of executive boxes, with raised netting in place to try and prevent the number of footballs being kicked over into people's gardens. I didn't have to walk through someone's garden to gain entry. That privilege was reserved for the away fans en route to the Oak Stand behind the goal.

The club have reportedly been looking to move for several years, but plans have never really gone beyond the talking stage. A move to Milton Keynes was mooted in the early 80s. However, strong opposition from fans and the league meant that the MK Hatters never saw the light of day. Meanwhile the council's reluctance to allow any possible reconstruction to be built higher than the surrounding houses has led to a lack of current investment being made to Kenilworth Road. The TV trucks and trailers made an already compressed entrance area seem that much smaller. A Caribbean bar that is quite popular amongst the home fans was hidden away behind all the cables.

I was located in the Kenilworth Stand - a former uncovered terrace. Seating was quite compact. I mistakenly took my place in the lower tier, or what I thought was the lower tier when I was given a friendly tap on the shoulder. I'd unwittingly infiltrated some of the older generation's space in the upper tier, but was told it was a common occurrence. The gentleman in question wasn't going to be in attendance so me and my trusty rucksack were given a free pass for the night. Everyone within my earshot seemed to be on first name terms. How's the wife doing and all that jazz.

The match was barely a few minutes old when a wise man behind me complained about the tempo being slow. He had obviously seen into the future (or my midweek past) and glumly predicted a bore draw. Good job the players weren't listening. Within seconds, the deadlock was broken. Luton failed to clear a corner and a Sam Saunders half volley hit some traffic on its way into the net. The lead lasted barely four minutes. Wycombe goalkeeper Matt Ingram parried a long shot and Elliot Lee - son of former Newcastle and Wycombe midfielder Rob, tucked in the rebound. Lee was a ball of energy and dazzled with a mazy run into the box. The Wycombe defence were reluctant to put a foot in and give away an inevitable penalty. Luton did the exact opposite. Luke Wilkinson fouled Matt Bloomfield and Paul Hayes tucked his spot kick under the dive of Luton's Elliot Justham.

The visitors increased their lead when Alfie Mawson went on a darting run, before collecting a chipped pass and hitting a beautiful first time finish into the bottom corner. Once again, Lee proved to be a thorn in Wycombe's side. The West Ham loanee pulled a goal back with a close range volley. Five goals and it wasn't even half time yet. The interval did give everyone a chance to get their breath back. I began to wonder what delights the second half would bring. Naturally, there were no more goals, although Wycombe's Sam Wood should have filled his boots. The midfielder sliced wide then skimmed the bar with two efforts that frankly were easier to score than miss. Luton's failure to direct headers on target also let Wycombe off the hook. The Hatters slumped to a fifth consecutive defeat, putting their play-off push in serious jeopardy.

I could have swore that the flyover en route back to the station was rocking, as several hundred fans began to disperse. Good job I didn't look down. Damn vertigo once again. While the surrounding area of Kenilworth Road might not exactly be Bedfordshire's finest, I found the fans friendly and accommodating. Stewards couldn't have been nicer, helping to navigate around the outside of the ground. Five goals meant I was more than happy with my lot. Another curse safely put to bed. Thanks to a friend coming up trumps, I didn't have to brace myself for another through the night adventure with National Express. I ended up back in Harrow for another stay at Charlie's - this time without the sore throat.

Best chant: "Next time Sky want to put us on TV, tell them to fuck off!" One disgruntled and camera shy Luton fan on his way out of the stadium.
Match ticket: £20 for an adult ticket. Good value, although the club have now brought in A, B and C match categorisation.
Match programme: £3.50. A generous 100 page edition. Two Prostate cancer case studies were heavy hitting, but got the message across. Luton fan Kevin Harper clocked up the mileage, reporting on away trips to Portsmouth and Newport. Despite two defeats, his enthusiasm wasn't dampened. Talking of travel, Norwegian 'football fanatic' Einar Kvande completed a visit to all 92 league clubs. It took him 26 years, although he does live in Scandinavia. Well done Einar!
Cost of food: £3.00 for a balti pie.
Food rating: 4/5. Advertised as containing no hydrogenated fat, it didn't stick to the tray and went down quite nicely.

Final Score
Luton Town 2 (Lee 7, 38)
Wycombe Wanderers 3 (Saunders 3, Hayes pen 22, Mawson 31)
Attendance: 8,379

Getting to know Portsmouth
Steve Bone - Sports Editor for Chichester Observer
Twitter @stevebone1

Favourite memory as a Portsmouth fan?

It has to be winning the FA Cup. We lost in the 1992 semis to Liverpool and I think many then doubted if we'd ever actually get to the final in our lifetimes. When we did, it was an amazing experience. Even now, looking back, I find it hard to put it into context with the rest of our recent history. I have a DVD of the whole afternoon's coverage and I've never watched it and am not sure if I ever will. I just want to remember the day how I remember it now.

Best game you've witnessed at Fratton Park?

Tricky one. Possibly the 7-4 win over Reading in 2007 (which holds the record for the number of goals in a Premier League game). Or there was a 6-2 win over Derby in our 2002-03 promotion season. Or the night we nearly beat AC Milan in the UEFA Cup. Wouldn't want to not choose any of those three.

Best/worst players to pull on a Portsmouth shirt?

Best - for me - would include Alan Biley, Mark Hateley and Kevin Dillon from the 1980s; Paul Walsh from the 90s; and Robert Prosinecki and Paul Merson from the 2000s. Those are six - I could easily list 60! I wouldn't want to single out names under the 'worst' heading - there have been plenty of poor players who should never have played a game, but I like to think none of them ever set out to be rubbish. It's the ones who don't put the effort in that we don't like here.

Best thing about Fratton Park?

The fact that it has barely changed over the years is what I like about it. Fratton Park is Pompey. It's ageing but beautiful. If we were ever to move to a new ground, that would probably be the day I'd stop watching the team regularly.

Worst grounds you've visited?

The McCain Stadium (Scarborough) in 1988. Boundary Park (Oldham). And soulless St Mary's (Southampton). All awful in their own way and for different and personal reasons.

Enjoyable away days?

I love Anfield and used to love Highbury and Roker Park. I miss a lot of the old grounds no longer with us - of the newer breed, the Stadium of Light is my favourite. Oh and Wembley's not bad when you're winning the FA Cup.

Which club serves the nicest pies?

I sampled Morecambe's recently - £3.50 but worth every penny. Chicken and leek, with gravy. Worth making the 600-mile round trip for.

Famous Portsmouth fans?

Depends what you mean by famous - but how about Mick Robertson (once of Magpie), the TV commentator Ian Darke or ITV legend Fred Dinenage? Thank goodness we don't have to suffer 'celebrity' fans like Russell Brand.

Quirky fact time?

Pompey played in the first game thought to have had no corners awarded, and the first competitive fixture under floodlights, and of course held the FA Cup for longer than anyone else (1939 - 45)

Name your Portsmouth Dream Team?
GK: Alan Knight
RB: Warren Neill
LB: Ray Daniel
CB: Arjan De Zeeuw
CB: Linvoy Primus
M: Mick Kennedy
M: Kevin Dillon
M: Paul Merson
M: Robert Prosinecki
CF: Alan Biley
CF: Mark Hateley

I would be first in the queue for a season ticket if that lot were together!

FROM SHROPSHIRE TO THE SOUTH COAST

Game #64: League Two - Saturday 28th March 2015
PORTSMOUTH vs Shrewsbury Town - Fratton Park

It's just gone 9am and I'm standing under a shop canope in Shropshire. Fans a few feet apart were standing in groups happily chatting away. The rain wasn't letting up and I resembled something of a drowned rat as I waited for the bus to come. Portsmouth is a close second to Plymouth in terms of mileage, although adding on a commute to Shrewsbury and back probably puts it as number one in terms of away day voyages. Either way, it made sense from a cost perspective to join the Shrewsbury away travel contingent for the long poke to the South Coast.

Appliances were fully charged and plenty of books had been packed for the trip. I bagged a seat in the middle of the coach and we were away.....for all of 15 minutes. Just one more stop to pick up a couple of stragglers. A bloke with glasses got on and began to scan around the bus. Eyes fixed ahead, he walked straight down the aisle. Somehow I just knew that he was looking to speak to me.

"We've got a kid who wants to sit with his Dad. There aren't any double seats left. Would you mind going to sit at the front?"

Oh dear. I was caught between a rock and a hard place. The coach fell silent. I felt like the naughty pupil who was being made to sit next to the teacher. Once in primary school was bad enough. I wasn't feeling the vibe here either, but I couldn't exactly say no. Just when it looked like I'd have to suck it up and take my medicine, I was given a possible reprieve.

"There's also a seat right at the back if you would prefer?"

I was out of my seat quicker than Roadrunner. Door #2 was the much better option. I acquainted myself with the group of six lads at the back of the bus and breathed a sigh of relief at dodging a proverbial bullet.
Within no time, drinks were being passed out and we were shooting the breeze over several football themed quizzes. The serious competitions soon started. I quickly signed me and my team up for bus bingo and a general knowledge quiz for the grand prizes of free tickets and luxury coach travel to either Mansfield Town or Bury. The bingo took the form of large playing cards being pulled out. We didn't win and our claims for a re-shuffle were unfairly turned down. Despite pulling an admirable 34/40 in the music intros round, we fared little better in the quiz, having performed poorly in the earlier rounds. These were sufficient ways to pass the time. The books and iPod weren't needed at all.

Pulling over for a quick refreshment stop at Oxford, we heard a bang on the window from a neighbouring bus. A kid started mugging us off by lifting up his jumper to reveal a Leeds United shirt. Before you ask, yes he kissed the badge too. Kids at that age don't know any better, so I let him off. I doubt he even knew it was international break and that Leeds didn't have a game. It seemed that many footballing folk were at a loose end with the top two divisions not playing. Resident QPR badboy Joey Barton announced his intention via Twitter to take in the Portsmouth game, although he wouldn't RSVP to a kind invite to come and sit in the away end.

I've documented Pompey's issues in previous entries, but it still doesn't sound right when you mention Portsmouth and League Two in the same sentence. Throwing out an assortment of names amongst the bus- Kanu, Benjani, Robert Prosinecki, Sulley Muntari etc, it's amazing to remember the calibre of players to have graced Fratton Park in recent years. Not so long ago AC Milan were playing there in the UEFA Cup. The depth of Pompey's plight still boggles the mind. Stuck in mid-table mediocrity, the club were simply playing for pride, while Shrewsbury were bidding to bounce back up to League One at the first time of asking.

Almost five hours after setting off, we finally made it to Portsmouth and immediately got stuck in a big traffic jam. Kids cycling past were quick to flip the bird and give us all a warm South Coast welcome, as we passed through a residential area before parking up in a neighbouring industrial side street.

A retail park containing the usual eateries is across the road from the ground, but there was less than an hour to kick-off and I wanted to see some of the famous stadium.

Oozing character and charisma, Fratton Park is huge. The noise from inside was already deafening. The bell ringer was out in force, meaning the most famous Pompey fan of the lot - John Portsmouth Football Club Westwood was milling around. Antiquarian bookseller by day, mad Portsmouth fan the rest of the time, Westwood changed his name in order to include his beloved club in the title. His team's likenesses are engraved on teeth and various body parts while he's also synonymous by his top hat and curly blue wig.

Portsmouth may be floundering, but credit goes to the fans for sticking by them. They're certainly a loyal and long suffering bunch. I'd pre-booked a ticket to sit with the home supporters, but I now wanted to sit with my new acquaintances. More importantly, I didn't want to get detached and somehow miss the bus back. Walking past the Tudor style decor which forms part of the front entrance, the kind souls at the ticket office took sympathy and obliged my request. Fratton Park has been slightly modernised. Now an all-seated affair, the Milton End (where the away fans are based) has had a roof installed. As you walk along the back of the stand to get food or go to the toilet, you can see into the backs of all the neighbouring houses and their unkept gardens. Directly opposite, the Fratton End sports an outline of former player Jimmy Dickinson along with the club's logo in its seats.

The Pompey stewards were frisking everyone in sight and didn't look too happy. The club heavily underestimated the demand for food and only opened one kiosk for the travelling contingent. A quarter of an hour before kick-off, a queue of dismayed away fans (including myself) were told there was no more hot food left. This wasn't good. I had been looking forward to sampling the delights of a Pompey pie so went to put my case to the stewards by the turnstiles. I may as well have been speaking in Chinese. They point blank refused to open a gate and allow me to walk 30 yards to a neighbouring concession stand. Idiot #1 was as useful as a chocolate fireguard, while idiot #2 started laughing. The power of having a yellow jacket had clearly gone straight to his head. Some common sense finally prevailed when supplies were delivered, albeit begrudgingly from a man in a suit. On the plus side, I was fed and watered in time for kick-off and ready to take in the match.

Former midfielder and club captain Liam Lawrence was making a return to his former stomping ground. A popular figure in the Pompey dressing room, the midfielder left during the height of the club's financial problems. According to a feature in the programme, Lawrence accepted a settlement to terminate his deal, nobly waiving a large sum of money he was owed in the process out of respect for the club. He was given a mixed reception as Micky Mellon's side dominated the first half, looking every bit the title challengers that their league position suggested. Town's Jean-Louis Akpa Akpro's low drive across the box trickled inches past the wrong side of the post. Shrewsbury refused to let their hosts settle and were unfazed by the constant "Play up Pompey" chants echoing around Fratton Park.

Shrewsbury's dominance paid off midway through the first half when Bobby Grant opened the scoring with a fine solo effort. The Pompey defence backed off, allowing the on loan Blackpool midfielder to collect a return pass and curl an effort past Paul Jones into the bottom corner. It almost got worse for the home side. Portsmouth's Cole Kpekawa put in an important block to stop Cameron Gayle laying the ball off for an easy tap-in.

Normal service looked to have resumed after the break when Akpa Akpro saw an effort come back off the post. Aside from a bright ten minute spell, which saw Town's Mickey Demetriou throw himself in the way to block a shot, Portsmouth were outmatched and outclassed by their superior opponents. Grant was playing the game with supreme confidence. Chipping the ball over a defender, a speculative half volley went inches wide. Pompey failed to heed the warning signs and Grant soon bagged his brace. Afforded far too much time and space on the edge of the D, Grant coolly picked his spot and once again put the ball beyond Jones.

In Matt Tubbs, Portsmouth boasted one of League Two's leading strikers. He spent most of this match in Jermaine Grandison's back pocket. Poor old Westwood was still ringing his bell, but the rest of the ground had lost their spark. Shrewsbury's first victory at Fratton Park was now in the bag, prompting the travelling supporters to turn the screw. "Where's your famous atmosphere?" could be heard echoing around an emptying Fratton Park. Portsmouth had lost every game and failed to score a single goal on each of the three occasions I'd seen them play. It came as no surprise when under-fire boss Andy Awford stepped down a few weeks later. Where's good old Harry Redknapp when you need him?

Having missed out on sandcastles and ice cream on the South Coast, most of the Shrewsbury fraternity headed on to the 'Beach Bar and Club' back in Shropshire. The only shapes I wanted to throw were starfishes in bed. I rolled back in after an 18 hour day, with the faint sound of Westwood's handbell still in my ears. Ding ding. Good night!

Best chant: "You're just a bus stop in Bournemouth." A low blow from the 500+ Shrewsbury supporters.
Match ticket: £20. A fair price for home and away supporters.
Match programme: £3. "There are few things more demotivating for football fans than a season meandering away." Ominous words on the first page by Chairman Iain McInnes whose warning seemed to fall on deaf ears. Elsewhere, a Pompey addict takes BT Sport to task for invading the sanctuary of changing rooms and dugouts during games, arguing that football needs to preserve some of its backstage aura. It was a very well written argument.
Cost of food: £3 for a steak and potato pie.
Food rating: 1/5. I needn't have kicked up such a fuss about the pie. Burnt, dry as a bone and quite heavy on the stomach. I didn't bother finishing it. A cheese pasty at half time restored some flavour to the tastebuds (3/5)

Final Score
Portsmouth 0
Shrewsbury Town 2 (Grant 25, 66)
Attendance: 14,749

Getting to know Cambridge United
Louis Hrebeniak, Ben Dent, Dave B, Matt Faiers, Jordan Payne
Amber Army - Cambridge United Fans Club (Facebook)

Favourite memory as a Cambridge fan?
Louis: There are personal moments from recent memory such as training with the first team goalkeepers, playing in the development squad, Drawing Manchester United in the FA Cup and winning the FA Trophy 4-0 come close, but promotion to League Two has to top the lot.

Dave: I wasn't around for the 1991 play-off final, so it has to be the recent FA Trophy final and play-off final win for me. To get back into the Football League has been a long hard fight. but we've finally done it.

Thoughts on ticket prices in general?
Ben: Ticket prices for me aren't too bad, its either £7 or £9 for where I sit. I would rather pay these prices than pay to watch the Premier League any day.

Dave: It costs me £16 a game, which I don't mind as it goes straight into the club. Premier League is just a rip off and you're not as close to the players or club at that level either. I wouldn't spend thousands a season just to watch Arsenal or Manchester United play.

Matt: I work irregular work patterns, so don't get a season ticket anymore, but still get to a decent amount of games. Compared to away prices I pay, I'm more than happy. Don't think it has changed much if at all since Conference football, which is good for me.

Best game you've witnessed at the Abbey Stadium?
Louis: The 2013-14 play-off semi-final against Halifax Town. Trailing 1-0 on aggregate, I witnessed two great goals to take us to Wembley. Words cannot describe the utter pandemonium on the terraces when the second goal went in - the Newmarket Road End, where my Dad and I were standing, went absolutely crazy, and rightly so! It was what every fan dreams about and also I got to hug the scorer of both goals on the pitch at the end - Delano Sam-Yorke.

Ben: The Manchester United game. Excellent atmosphere, even through the poor weather conditions that Friday night, we still braved it.

Matt: We put a shift in against Manchester United and the reality was that we should have been destroyed. That aside, coming back from 3-1 down to defeat Stevenage in a play-off semi-final. Close enough to be a rival. Stevenage had booked their coaches for the final and team hotel. Nobody gave us a chance. Even some of the fans on the terrace weren't expecting much. They had a couple cleared off the line, we pulled it back to 2-0, went to extra time and got a 119th minute winner. That felt good!

Best/worst players to pull on a Cambridge shirt?
Louis: Kwesi Appiah was far too good for the Conference and, latterly, League Two. This fact showed; he's come on two seperate loan spells from Crystal Palace and, arguably, his goal contribution in those short times was what both got us promoted and will keep us up. My other favourite player has to be Chris Maxwell, a goalkeeper on loan from Fleetwood whose clean sheets drove us into League Two. Like Kwesi, his quality was plain for all to see by how terrible our defence was when he left. He hardly ever had a shot to save - his communication and domination of his area made sure of that. In terms of worst players, this "honour" has to jointly go to Issa Diallo (CM) and Matteo Lanzoni (RB.) Lanzoni was always played out of position, which was undeniably left back; in the dressing room, that is. After initially showing promise for all of 45 minutes, Diallo went on a run of terrible games and eventually was released due to injury. As for Lanzoni, we'll never really know what the situation was with him - just that he's gone now, and it's for the best.

Ben: Worst player? Has to be Matthew Barnes-Homer. Absolute shocking player, glad we released him.

Dave: Best would have to be people like Dion Dublin, Liam Daish, Trevor Benjamin, Jody Craddock, Danny Granville to name a few.

Matt: John Taylor is the king of the Abbey Stadium, Dion Dublin obviously for what he did and went on to achieve. Dave Kitson was a decent player, Ian Ashbee was with us for a while. We have had some names go on to higher things like Robbie Simpson, Michael Morrison, John Ruddy and Trevor Benjamin who all started youth team football with us.

Best thing about the Abbey Stadium?
Ben: The way the ground feels when there is a game. Oh and I do love the bacon rolls!
Matt: It feels like home. It's not that modern or fancy, but it's warm, it's familiar, it's all I've ever known. It's success when you win, it's despair when you don't. It's just what I want really.

Worst grounds you've visited?
Ben: Kenilworth Road, Luton. Turnstiles are where a front room should be, and the stairs into the ground are where someones back yard should be!
Jordan: I didn't enjoy going through people's back gardens at Luton, nor Northampton, as the stadium was still being built.
Dave: I hated Barnet's old ground, Underhill.
Matt: Histon when we were in the Conference. A few years ago, the Histon chairman didn't let away fans in so we had to watch on top of the hill for free.

Enjoyable away days?
Ben: I quite enjoyed visiting Northampton. Even though they only have three stands! However, a burger there is £4!
Matt: Anywhere that will have a laugh with us, primarily like the home fans enjoying a pint before the game. Bury were good for that when we visited Gigg Lane.

Which club serves the nicest pies?
Matt: Can I say ours?
Dave: Kidderminster Harriers by a mile.
Ben: Portsmouth have the best burgers!
Jordan: I normally just buy drinks as I take a packed lunch to games. Food is so overpriced at football grounds.

Famous Cambridge fans?
Matt: Max Rushden (of Soccer: AM fame) Is he famous enough?
Dave: Rory McGrath. Hoping the Prince George will follow them in future

Quirky fact time?
Ben: Near the Newmarket Road End there is an advertising board above the disabled area. It covers an old scoreboard from Ibrox, Rangers.
Matt: If we win a match, at the end of the game we play 'Coconuts' by Billy Cotton (I've got a lovely bunch of coconuts. There they are all standing in a row)

Name your Cambridge Dream Team?
Dave: This would be my team based on players I've seen play.
GK: Danny Potter
CB: Liam Daish
CB: Jody Craddock
RB: Andy Duncan
LB: Danny Granville
M: Ian Ashbee
M: Paul Wanless
M: Martin Butler
CF: Dion Dublin
CF: John Taylor
CF: Trevor Benjamin

I could have had a team of 30, but went with this and in that team every single one gave 110% in a Cambridge United shirt. I thank them all for their committment and hard work along with many memories.

A BURY GOOD FRIDAY IN CAMBRIDGE

Game #65: League Two - Friday 3rd April 2015
CAMBRIDGE UNITED vs Bury - The R Costings Abbey Stadium

Cambridge is famous for many things, although its university and the annual boat race are two facets which immediately spring to mind. The city also nurtured the talents of footballer turned "Homes under the Hammer" presenter Dion Dublin. From a football point of view, I was worried I had missed the proverbial boat in watching the U's play. Two opportunities to visit Cambridge earlier in the season weren't followed up on, resulting in me missing two emphatic victories (5-0 against Carlisle United and a 5-1 mauling of boating rivals Oxford United.) D'oh!

Back in the Football League after a nine year absence, Cambridge didn't look like they had missed a beat. Then along came Manchester United. The town was rightly swept up in FA Cup fever. Since the U's lost in a replay at Old Trafford, they'd been in a bit of a tailspin and suffered a downturn in form, picking up a solitary win in two months. Dreams of the play-offs had disappeared. Escaping the threat of relegation was now the club's main priority.

My timing for this game wasn't so great. However, games and the window of opportunity to visit were fast running out. Good Friday brought with it some bad news in the form of rail replacement works. With London being the main route affected and all roads to the Abbey Stadium seemingly running through the capital, I needed to find a different path. Step forward Bury and another adventure with the away travel bus. Coming hot on the heels of a fun trip with Shrewsbury, I was equally as optimistic. Purchasing travel and tickets through Bury saved me a bit of coin. I just needed to get to the JD Stadum for a 9am pick-up. You'd think that an early night would be the best way to prepare. Wrong! Playing squash and going for a quick drink turned into a few more drinks than originally bargained. It seemed like I was getting up almost as soon as I'd crawled into bed in order to make a 5:50am train and tram combination to Lancashire.

Just like the previous weekend, I found a small army of fans sheltering from the rain. This time, everyone was huddled under Bury's club shop. Two coaches turned up. Naturally, I followed the crew who were carrying the massive drum. Fatigue set in quite early and before I knew it, we had stopped at Peterborough services. The coach driver informed us we were less than an hour from the Abbey Stadium, so it looked like we would have plenty of time to wet our whistles with a pre-match pint. The ground stewards had other ideas. An ill informed staffer in a yellow jacket refused to let the coach in through the front entrance. Just like a Monopoly board, we couldn't pass go. After being sent back into the traffic and doing another lap of the area, we were shepherded off in the direction of a nearby industrial estate which backed onto the train tracks. Common sense would have been to let us off and then go and park the bus. The opportunity to have a pint with Hulk Hogan in neighbouring pub 'The Wrestler' wasn't possible.

Instead, we were made to wade through a boggy field and dodge the cows in order to gain entry to the South Habbin Stand at the back of the stadium. None of us had brought our wellies. Home fans packed the opposite terrace behind the goal, which only runs three quarters of the pitch and sits next to the supporters' club house. The Bury drum pretty much drowned them out for the majority of the game. There was a large area of grass between the pitch and the Stand (ala Newport County) so everything seemed that bit further away. Club mascot Marvin the Moose came over to wave cheerily. No-one seemed to give him any attention, so he tucked tail and walked off with his head down. If I hadn't been so high up and far away, I'd have taken a photo with you Marv!

U's winger Luke Chadwick stated he gets more excited lining up for Cambridge than he ever did when at Manchester United. His wife reportedly painted a Cambridge mural in one of the bedrooms while he was away during pre-season. Injury sadly prevented the veteran from taking to the field for his hometown club for this game. Cambridge came out wearing black t-shirts with 'United for Simon' written in gold lettering. This was after U's fan Simon Dobbin had been attacked following a match at Southend United a few weeks prior. At time of writing, Simon was still in a serious condition in hospital. All four sides of the ground united in a minute's applause during the game, while fans of both sides gave generously to a bucket collection to assist with medical costs.

Ex-Cambridge loanee Nick Pope was the first goalkeeper called into action when he tipped over Ryan Donaldson's 30 yard screamer in the opening minutes. Pope may have excelled at shot stopping, but his distribution was shocking. Cambridge's lack of a cutting threat up front meant that Pope wasn't punished for his sloppy kicking. Chris Hussey saw a free kick plucked out of the top corner, as Bury started to control the game. It didn't really surprise me when they took the lead. Captain Nathan Cameron was afforded too much space in the box and he punished Cambridge with a well placed effort past Chris Dunn. The Shakers sealed the points when they doubled their lead early in the second half. The Cambridge defence failed to close down Danny Mayor, allowing him to square the ball for an unmarked Tom Soares to place an angled drive into the far corner. Bury coasted to an impressive fifth consecutive away victory to continue their play-off push.

The cows stayed well away, as we made our way back through the field to the coach. A slew of home fans joined us in the mud and they were generally happy folk. Once we got away from the inevitable flux of matchday traffic, the trip back to Bury took just over four hours. This included a quick rest stop. Walking back from a toilet break, I turned to see an advert for Top Gear Live. Jeremy Clarkson's face had been covered up by a Bury sticker. It looked like a definite improvement. I got back on the coach to chants of "Jeremy is a Shaker." Who knew eh? Much like the year's boat race, Cambridge were sinking at an alarming rate, but they'd done enough in the earlier months and would be fine for another season.

A pitfall of travelling with the away contingent made me feel like I was kept at arm's length for the majority of my trip. In truth, I didn't get to find out much about Cambridge at all. Granted, the team didn't put in a memorable performance, but in the wake of the game, plenty of fans got in touch to alter that fact. Should the club land a plum FA Cup tie in the future, I'll make an attempt to return.

Best chant: "We hate Boro, we hate Boro. We are the Boro haters. Scum, scum, scum!" Cambridge fans weren't planning on giving neighbours Peterborough an Easter egg.
Match ticket: £19 for a pre-booked adult ticket. Adult tickets ranged from £16 - £22 depending on location/time bought.
Match programme: £3. A random article on the resurgence of Valencia was out of place and I skipped the club chaplain's piece talking about death. In depth travellers tales from Southend and Hartlepool detailed both grounds quite well.
Cost of food: £3.50 for a balti pie, although the kind lady only charged me £3.
Food rating: 3.5/5. Got better with each bite. What started out like a watery chicken curry turned into a nice pie. Spices baked into the crust, firm top, chewy meat.

Final Score
Cambridge United 0
Bury 2 (Cameron 23, Soares 53)
Attendance: 5,427

Getting to know Cardiff City
Phillip Nifield - Cardiff City FC Supporters Trust
www.ccfctrust.org

Favourite memory as a Cardiff fan?
I've supported the club through thick and thin for 50 years plus. Two memories come to mind. Beating Real Madrid 1-0 at home in the European Cup Winners' Cup and appearing at the FA Cup Final in 2008 – although we lost to Portsmouth.

Thoughts on Ole Gunnar Solskjaer's brief reign?
Ole was a bad appointment – given the job for his name rather than someone who could keep us in the Premier League. Far too inexperienced.

Best game you've witnessed at the Cardiff City Stadium?
For drama, beating Leicester City on penalties to reach the Championship play-off final (which we lost to Blackpool). Also, clinching promotion to the Premier League against Charlton Athletic.

Who have been some of the club's key players this season?
Bruno Mange has been the outstanding player. No others really stand out.

Best/worst players to pull on a Cardiff shirt?
Plenty of poor players whom I would rather not embarrass. But, the best include John Charles and Brian Harris, Ian Gibson and in more recent times, Craig Bellamy and Peter Whittingham.

Best thing about the Cardiff City Stadium?
Good view wherever you sit and, thankfully, none of the pillars that spoilt the view in some places at Ninian Park.

Worst grounds you've visited?
Darlington's old ground The Feethams and the Vetch Field in Swansea (both dumps)

Enjoyable away days?
Old Trafford and Wembley (despite three recent defeats)

Famous Cardiff fans?
Neil Kinnock, the former Labour Party leader and members of the Super Furry Animals.

Quirky fact time?
Cardiff City failed to win the First Division title in 1923-24, losing the title to Huddersfield on goal average.

Game #66: The Championship - Monday 6th April 2015
CARDIFF CITY vs Bolton Wanderers - The Cardiff City Stadium

Spring had arrived. The sun was shining and the birds were singing. Make that the Bluebirds. Yes, Cardiff were back playing in blue again. Gathering the remnants of my Easter Eggs and grabbing my passport, it was time to investigate if all was really well in South Wales.

Casting my mind back to the opening game of the season at Blackburn, I remembered the defiant Cardiff supporters singing "We're Cardiff City. We'll always be blue!" Three years of campaigning had paid dividends. Owner Vincent Tan finally realised that his re-branding of the club's colours hadn't gone down too well with the fanbase. Dwindling attendances and fruitful protests certainly forced Tan's hand. As an added extra, Tan had also promised to re-design a new club crest to restore the Bluebird in a more prominent position instead of the current tiny version underneath a big red dragon.

Following Ole Gunnar Solskjaer's decision early doors that life in the Championship wasn't for him, Russell Slade made the jump from Leyton Orient to take the Norwegian's place. Despite Tan's generosity with the purse strings, the results hadn't been forthcoming and Cardiff were marooned in mid-table, leaving hopes of a swift return to the Premier League in tatters.

Embracing the Bank Holiday, I couldn't have asked for better weather or a quicker train. The announcement of there being no stops after Shrewsbury ensured that I reached my destination in a respectable two and a half hours. I'd brought a coat out of habit, but that was quickly packed away as I stretched my legs around the sun kissed town. Welsh flags hung proudly outside establishments and the mood amongst the Cardiff folk was jovial. The Millennium Stadium is a stone's throw from Cardiff Central station. I wondered how many balls were floating around in the surrounding River Taff. On second thoughts, Gareth Bale doesn't miss the target very often.

Getting to the Cardiff City Stadium took just under half an hour on foot from the town centre. Ninian Park Halt station is a lot closer and a little under five minutes away, although that is only served by regional trains and services are infrequent on matchdays. Grangetown is another alternative and is a ten minute walk. It may have been walking weather, but the journey through a housing estate wasn't exactly flattering. This was evidenced by several boarded up council houses and a disused mattress attracting flies outside a block of flats. The masts of the Millennium Stadium could still be seen sticking out in the distance as I came towards Cardiff's new-ish stadium.

Cardiff moved to their new home in 2009. Following in Middlesbrough's footsteps, the club pay homage to their former ground. The gates from the now demolished Ninian Park are located outside the stadium. A plaque in remembrance of former Scotland and Celtic manager Jock Stein - who passed away during an international match at the old ground lies next to the gates. The Cardiff International Sports Stadium is also next door. Much smaller in size, that location is primarily used for Athletics and the lesser known Cardiff Bay Harlequins football team

As per usual with some of these new grounds, a retail park with all the usual suspects is nearby. With no sign of rain, I chose the perfect time to lose my footing on a curb and split one of my trainers. Luckily for me, no-one spotted the split second of misfortune and I was able to plod on.

Banners advertising luxurious getaways to the Philippines and Malaysia are used as decor for an outer part of the ground. These would certainly appeal in the middle of winter, although with the weather in Cardiff as hot as it was, they didn't have the same impact. The stadium and its fanbase are far from soulless. In fact, there were plenty of characters knocking around. What do you call a mullet haired, kilt wearing Welshman with a stuffed sheep hanging off his belt buckle? Why, none other than the programme seller, and what a friendly chap he was too. Before you ask, no, I didn't ask what was underneath his man skirt.

Pre-match entertainment came courtesy of a free concert being played on a makeshift stage just inside the turnstiles. Kids and parents snacked on their pies and pastries, while tribute act 'Hair of the Dog' belted out favourites from the Guns 'N' Roses, Alice Cooper and Feeder back catalogue. They weren't exactly PG, as evidenced by the lead singer proudly flaunting an 'Explicit Content' t-shirt and dropping in some colourful language here and there, but no-one seemed to object. The tattooed 50-year-old on the bass guitar looked like he was having a whale of a time. The band's 30 minute set was quite enjoyable and it sure beat listening to the usual pre-match riff-raff from Olly Murs and Beyonce etc.

It was great to see the sprinklers make a welcome re-appearance before kick-off. I congratulated myself on making it through a long and cold winter. Plenty of leg room between the rows of seats meant I didn't have to keep getting up to let people pass by. A comfy pew and a pitchside view were added bonuses. The multi-tiered stadium was a way off from being full, but the Cardiff faithful made their voices heard when the two teams emerged. Cardiff had tried out a multitude of front pairings in a bid to try and find a winning formula. An action shot of Kenwyne Jones still occupied a prominent position outside the stadium, even though the forward was out on loan. Another loanee, Adam Le Fondre was at Bolton and thus ineligible to face his parent club. January signings Eoin Doyle - still coming to terms with the step up to the Championship and Alex Revell - plagued by injury were the chosen two for this game. The latter's horrible luck continued when he limped out of the game early on.

Doyle was finding goals harder to come by since leaving Chesterfield. The Irishman hit a shot on the spin, only to see it cleared off the line by Bolton's Barry Bannan. There was a hint of handball, but it wasn't strong enough to convince the referee to award a penalty. Bolton relied on veterans Emile Heskey and Eidur Gudjohnsen for their predatory instincts. Both rolled back the years with vintage displays. Gudjohnsen cleverly played in Craig Davies, who fluffed a clear-cut chance wide, before Cardiff's Peter Whittingham - usually a threat from dead ball situations, disappointed by sending a free-kick wide from a promising position.

A segment of fans came down from the upper tier to get a closer look for the second half. Unfortunately for them, it was Bolton's old guard which brought the game to life. Heskey may have lost a bit of pace in his ageing legs, but he proved his footballing brain was still razor sharp by laying on two assists. The physically imposing forward expertly chested down a ball for strike partner Gudjohnsen to open the scoring by smashing an unstoppable shot into the top corner. It capped a fantastic week for the Icelandic hitman, who celebrated a goalscoring return at international level and welcomed a newborn baby. Congratulations!

Bolton's second came from a quick counter attack. Heskey's beautifully weighted pass unleashed Davies, who scampered down the flank. This time he got his angles right to place an effort beyond David Marshall in the far corner. Barely an hour had passed and the same fans who had switched seats now walked out in disgust. They clearly knew the drill, had become sick of an all too familiar script and weren't prepared to sit through any more. Davies heaped further misery when he netted again, collecting a long ball from Bannan and finding the same corner, albeit this time from a bit further out. Fans were now leaving in droves. Marshall got his feet in the way to prevent Davies completing a hat-trick, but it was scant consolation.

The travelling fans didn't let the fact they were sat under a Welsh flag deter them from singing "England, England" to the remaining contingent of home fans suffering in silence. Cardiff's players were booed off at the final whistle. However, not everyone was subscribing to the glass half empty theory. The tune of "always look on the bright side of life" could be heard in the distance as I exited the ground. Cardiff will look to go again and I'd certainly take in another game should the opportunity arise.

During the walk back to the station, I noticed that the mattress still hadn't been moved. It now had company in the form of a female model posing against a wall, while an eager male photographer snapped away. Unless they were planning on using green screen technology, I'd have shopped around for a more aesthetically pleasing backdrop. Stopping off at a Tesco to get some chocolate for the train, I walked out in the middle of a shouting match. I definitely had the knack for being in the wrong places at the right time. A young mother had abandoned her pram in order to exchange words with a group of kids in the street. Before you could say Jeremy Kyle, another hysterical woman entered the fray and started yelling. I didn't stick around to catch those all important lie detector results.

Nursing the sunburn on my head was painful enough. I wasn't too keen on copping a right hook from one of the undesirables.

Best chant: "Heskey for England." The Bolton fans weren't joking either.
Match ticket: £25. The club operated a zonal pricing system which differed according to whether the game fell in the Gold, Silver or Bronze category. Holy confusion Batman!
Match programme: £3. I was expecting parts to be in Welsh, but perhaps that was my ignorance. Eoin Doyle conducted his first Cardiff interview since his January arrival. There were a couple of player posters for the kids and the club recently ran a successful media programme for budding young journalists. Historians would appreciate the retro eight page programme enclosed from this fixture in 1957.
Cost of food: £3.50 for a steak pie.
Food rating: 2/5. A first chance to sample the Peter's Pies range. Presentation wise, it came in a box and had been foil wrapped. I had high hopes. There was plenty of content, as evidenced by the lashings of gravy that had pierced a small hole in the bottom of the pie. Sadly, it lacked any meaningful flavour and the taste was non descript. I wasn't prepared to pay £3 for a a small portion of chips either.

Final Score
Cardiff City 0
Bolton Wanderers 3 (Gudjohnsen 55, Davies 59, 73)
Attendance: 20,219

Getting to know Brighton & Hove Albion
Stefan Swift - The Seagull Love Review
www.theseagulllovereview.blogspot.com
Twitter @tslr

Favourite memory as a Brighton fan?

The new ground, after everything it was truly special - and has been on every visit since. Perhaps the day we finally got rid of the old board - the ones who sold the Goldstone Ground.

Best home game you've witnessed?

There are really so very many to choose from so this may take a while. The first game at Falmer when Will Buckley scored twice at the end of the game to win it was really quite special. That is up there, as is the last league game of 1991 when a late Dean Wilkins free-kick fired us into the (then) Second Division play-offs. But really the one that tops it all was surviving relegation to the Conference at Hereford in 1997.

There was, more recently, Nottingham Forest away the last game of last season when Leo Ulloa headed us into the play-offs for the (now) Championship play-offs - that was one of the single greatest moments. There was Walsall away when we clinched the League One title under Gus Poyet. Even that time when we drove to Hartlepool away, but didn't leave early enough and ended up watching us lose 3-1 on teletext in a pub on a Yorkshire industrial estate. Every memory is a favourite.

Best/worst players to pull on a Brighton shirt?

For the worst, Leon Best is doing his best at the moment. We seem to have had that with donkey strikers on loan such as Jon Obika last year. Looking backwards, there was Fran Sandaza - such a donkey but a bit of a cult legend - and he scored some important goals and looked like a horse. Colin Hawkins was an Irish central defender who scored one of the best own goals I have ever seen.

As for the best, the old people will tell you that is Peter Ward, but I never saw him play so can't be sure. In our era, it's generally the strikers, always the next one. So, that's Garry Nelson, Mike Small, Raphael Meade, John Byrne, Bobby Zamora, Glenn Murray and Leo Ulloa. Recently, Liam Bridcutt was wonderful. Personally my overall favourite was Colin Hawkins - we even made masks (I've never actually made a mask of any other Albionite).

Best thing about the AMEX Stadium?

Everything. The ground, the concourse, the toilets - I know, even the fucking toilets. The beer for sale, the pies, the way the bar stays open to all fans after the game, the green, green grass, the sleekily curved stand roofs, the tunnel, the smell, the feel, the legends wall, the museum, the club shop, the posh seats, the family stand, the big screens, the away end, the floodlights, even the police box, all of it. ALL OF IT!

Worst grounds you've visited?

Compared to ours, pretty much all of them. In fact we've become proper stadium snobs. Special mention should be given to that lot up the A23 - Selhurst Park is falling down and genuinely feels unsafe. In fact, many 'landmark' grounds feel like that now. Anfield was appalling, and the concourse is so tight it doesn't feel safe. The rest are much of a muchness - the space afforded to the new builds is good but most of them feel soulless, maybe Falmer would if it hadn't been such a frustrating battle to get there.

Enjoyable away days?

This is tough now I'm a stadium snob. I like the ones where you can stand, so the lower the better these days. I miss Peterborough's away terrace and now I'm looking forward to going down so we can play at Yeovil, Carlisle, Swindon, the few that still remain.

Which club serves the nicest pies?
Cambridge United's catering was always wonderful. The best pies are non-league really. Pukka are a mouth burning market for morons. I've heard Norwich and Bolton are good, though I haven't bought an away pie all season, for fear of sobering up and having to remember the football on offer.

Famous Brighton fans?
Norman Cook aka Fatboy Slim. He even gave us loads of money by selling so many records. There was an actor in that rugby film Up 'n' Under who was wearing an Albion shirt. Oh, and Des Lynam, but I think he's a bit senile these days and struggles to remember who he supports.

Quirky fact time?
Our heaviest defeat (18-2) away at Norwich on Christmas Day in 1942 is not quite as bad as it sounds. We only had eight players make the trip. The other players were taken from the crowd - including the Norwich end!

Game #67: The Championship - Friday 10th April 2015
BRIGHTON & HOVE ALBION vs AFC Bournemouth - The American Express (AMEX) Community Stadium

I'd made a lot of new friends on this trip, re-connected with old acquaintances and been reunited with old school pals. Now it was the turn of a former classmate, Graham Webb, to kindly offer me a bed for the night, which gave me the chance to come and watch Brighton under the Friday night lights. Since leaving school, Graham had led a somewhat nomadic existence, although we loosely kept in touch. A diehard Norwich fan, he had moved down to Brighton to study. Work commitments meant he was unable to join me for the game, but I was looking forward to a long overdue catch-up afterwards.

The American Express Stadium or AMEX as it's commonly known was one of the first grounds I had excitedly circled on the calendar back in August. Looking every bit of the £93million it cost to build, I couldn't spot a single supporting pillar from the pictures I'd pored over. The semi-circular roof design also draws comparisons with Huddersfield's humble abode. This is on a much larger scale, but also meant that due to my shaky relationship with heights, I wouldn't be going anywhere near the three-tier high West Stand.

With the Sky cameras in tow and Bournemouth coming to town, I left nothing to chance and bought a match ticket in advance. That also bought me a place into the Brighton secret society. The club email their fans a unique pre-match brief. As well as who's injured, current form and the rest of the norm, Brighton allow fans a sneak peek into the programme and reveal who's headlining in the bandstand outside the ground. If that's not enough, the chefs reveal what the guest pie will be. I'd missed out on the piglets breakfast and butternut squash options, so would have to make do with the chicken balti. I was also informed that it was a very special night at the AMEX....Curry night!

I had been promised a King's feast, yet felt a little bad leaving Chester on what was being reported as the hottest day of the year to date. Travel delays followed me all the way down to East Sussex. Train connections were running late and the London Underground briefly came to a standstill due to someone being taken ill and needing medical assistance. The good thing about London is that the next train is never far away. Just over an hour after leaving London Victoria, I made it into Brighton just as the after work rush was beginning to descend.

The AMEX is a couple of miles away from the train station, so the kind souls at the football club provide subsidised travel as part of the match ticket. Considering the price of a match ticket, it's a good thing they do. The ground is located in neighbouring Falmer, easily reached by bus or three stops away on a train. I opted for the latter. The stadium lies amongst the hills, peering out over the train station. It looks beautiful in the distance, especially on a warm sunny evening. A crazy activist yelling incoherently about the NHS was just an added sideshow. I'm not sure if he's there every week. There is a beer van outside the ground, but just like the Fish 'n' Chip stand, it proved both popular and expensive. I didn't fancy queuing for half an hour and being hit with a £7 chippy bill. I used my time a lot wiser, chasing club mascot Gully the Seagull, who was doing the rounds greeting fans. He seemed to enjoy giving me the runaround until I finally caught up to him to get a photo. Nice one Gully!

Murals of former players, including the likes of Charlie Oatway, Jimmy Case and even Mark Lawrenson are displayed on a blue canvas around the back of the stadium. Peering through an open door to the away end, Brighton had decorated the surrounding area with Bournemouth club badges and logos. Apparently, it's not uncommon for the club to display pictures of opposition players and even have food staff decked out in replica shirts of the side they're facing to give travelling supporters an extra special welcome.

I decided to take my seat early and was one of the first to do so. The entire capacity is made up of padded blue leather seats. I can concur they were very comfortable too. As the sun bounced off the transparent material used for the roofing, elevated video screens situated behind both goalmouths were replaying some of Brighton's best goals of the season. Since Chris Hughton took the reins, the Seagulls hadn't been known for their goalscoring exploits. Looking back at some of the strikes demonstrated that the players certainly had goals in their locker.

The Bournemouth fans didn't look too interested in the comfy seating and opted to stand for the duration of the game. The first half was a non-entity. So much so, that the two lads sat next to me started talking about Wigan. Like listening to two Sky Sports pundits, I was given a warts and all breakdown into the Latics' season. They were glued to their phones and preferred looking at score updates from Wigan's game at Fulham as opposed to watching the game taking place a few metres in front. I couldn't really blame them. Even Brighton's Joao Teixeira and Bournemouth's Matt Ritchie - two players bursting with creativity were having an off day.

Zorb football was demonstrated during the half time break. The Brighton players must have been watching, as they finally came out of their bubble and tried to impose themselves on the game. Poor finishing ultimately let the Seagulls down. Dale Stephens shot over from close range, before Leon Best collected a long ball and scuffed a weak effort straight at a grateful Artur Boruc. Brighton fans had their heads in their hands. Even the closet Wigan fans looked up momentarily. When Lewis Dunk committed a needless foul, Yann Kermorgant made Brighton pay by curling a 25-yard free-kick into the top corner.

To his credit, Hughton knew he needed a new gameplan. He boldly sacrificed Teixeira in favour of making a double attacking change and switching to a front three. It looked like it might pay dividends. Craig Mackail-Smith lashed a vicious snapshot wide of the post and Inigo Calderon was incensed not to get a penalty after Ritchie slipped and broke his fall by putting his hand to the ball. Ultimately, Bournemouth exposed the space left in midfield to grab a second and secure the three points. Callum Wilson turned poor Greg Halford no fewer than three times to carve open the necessary space and find the net with a low finish.

The players had barely left the pitch when two lawnmowers were already out providing aftercare to the pitch. It felt very much like the brand new trophy that had been on display and quickly needed to be put back into its protective case.

The AMEX had been chosen as one of the locations for the 2015 Rugby World Cup. If it was good enough for the egg, fingers crossed the FA give it good consideration for when England next hosts a football tournament.

Graham had kindly arranged a lift for me back into Brighton with a couple of season ticket holders he knew. With heavy traffic after a game, I was instructed to wait half an hour for the queues to disperse. Luckily, I spotted the Bournemouth coach pulling in towards the changing rooms and was able to get Boruc, Wilson and Harry Arter to scribble their signatures on my programme. The generous hospitality continued when I reached the pub that Graham worked at. The beer kept flowing and the conversation kept going until the early hours. AMEX - I raise my glass to you. Cheers Brighton!

Best chant: "Stand up if you hate Palace." The Brighton fans aren't too fond of the occupants over at Selhurst Park.
Match ticket: £38 + £1 booking fee. By far the most expensive ticket out of the 72. Around £5 made up the travel costs.
Match programme: £3.50. Contained a slew of player interviews in the 84 page edition. Gully's a busy mascot. In between matchday duties, Brighton's favourite seagull organises days out around Sussex for young people and adults with additional needs. Group packages to hire the stadium and full use of the club's facilities for a 90 minute game range between a cool £4,000-£8,000.
Cost of food: £4.10 for a pie. £5 for a pot of curry and a naan bread.
Food rating: 2/5. Disappointing. The pie wasn't too bad, although a little overpriced and the tomato didn't mix that well with the meat. The curry was foul. An oversized container of watery chicken with no flavour. Tikka Masala? My arse. The naan was rock hard and made for a great frisbee...into the bin!

Final Score
Brighton & Hove Albion 0
AFC Bournemouth 2 (Kermorgant 70, Wilson 81)
Attendance: 25,919

Getting to know Ipswich Town
Rob Freeman - Turnstile Blues (www.turnstileblues.co.uk)
Twitter @Turnstile_Blue

Favourite memory as an Ipswich fan?

Moscow, 2001 for the UEFA Cup. We hadn't qualified for Europe for almost two decades, and thought we'd never make it again. I don't remember much about the game, other than the fact we won. After getting back to the hotel, I got changed, got back in the lift to go back into the bar, and the lift doors opened to the sound of around 100 Ipswich fans signing "WOAH, the Tony Mowbray" [Tony Mowbray chant to the tune of the hokey cokey]

Best game you've witnessed at Portman Road?

A 3-2 victory against Newcastle United from April 1992. We were (unexpectedly) top of the league, Kevin Keegan had just returned to Newcastle, so the ground was full, and one of the last games at Portman Road before we went all-seater. The game itself had everything - goals, penalties, sendings off, both sides having the lead during the game. Fantastic!

Best/worst players to pull on an Ipswich shirt?

There have been regular polls over the years about best Ipswich player, and it was always a close run thing between John Wark (who had three spells at the club) and Kevin Beattie (classy defender, with a handful of England caps), but you could say that Arnold Muhren, Frans Thijssen, and Mick Mills weren't far behind. Matt Holland usually picks up most of the votes for those that missed the glory days of the Sir Bobby Robson era.

Late 80s centre half Chris O'Donnell was named Ipswich's worst player by a national magazine poll, but he played during the John Duncan days where we specialised in abysmal left backs like David Hill and Graham Harbey. Another left back - Amir Karic - is worth a mention too. I saw him play for Slovenia at Euro 2000, where he frightened Spanish winger Joseba Exteberria with an exceptionally clumsy challenge. Three months later we signed him for £700,000. He played three games in the League Cup, notably in the 2001 semi-final against Birmingham City, where it looked like his team mates didn't trust him with the ball, went on loan to Crystal Palace (who subbed him in the first half of an unimpressive debut and sent him back) and was never seen again.

Best thing about Portman Road?

Usually the view - there are very few restricted view seats at Portman Road. The atmosphere used to be great, but since the club rebuilt the Sir Bobby Robson Stand, the acoustics haven't helped the noise. The home fans can't hear the away fans, and the away fans direct their chants at the Sir Alf Ramsey Stand, which isn't a stand that makes much noise.

Worst grounds you've visited?

Any ground where the away end doesn't have a roof. Don't like St. James's Park (Newcastle), the away end is so far away from the pitch, it's like watching a subbuteo game. I managed to find a seat without a restricted view at Crystal Palace once. Just the once, though. The legroom in the away end at Kenilworth Road is so bad, it's uncomfortable to stand.

Enjoyable away days?

Anywhere we win! Seriously, I prefer old-style grounds – Highbury, the Dell, White Hart Lane, Upton Park, Villa Park. Most of the new grounds are identikit boxes on the edge of industrial estates, although the City of Manchester Stadium is really nice. You can tell it wasn't built for football fans, because it's like someone sat down and actually thought about it.

Which club serves the nicest pies?

I've not had a pie at a game for a long time! I do remember one at Stockport in the late 90s. The rain had been torrential from the moment we had left home until half an hour after the game finished, and there was no roof on the away end. All I know is that the pie was hot and full, and at that moment, that was all it needed to be.

Famous Ipswich fans?

We have a few - Brian Cant (Play School) is the one older fans remember. Bill Werbeniuk the Canadian snooker player, Keith Deller the former World Darts champion, Kevin Painter the current dart player, David Starie the boxer, and Georgie Bingham the TalkSport presenter come to mind.

Quirky fact time?

Ipswich have the longest unbeaten home record in European competitions. We've played 31 games in the European Cup, Cup Winners Cup and the UEFA Cup, and never lost. Not bad, when you bear in mind we've hosted Milan, Real Madrid, Lazio, Barcelona (twice), Inter, Feyenoord, Roma and a Saint Etienne side containing the likes of Michel Platini, Johnny Rep and Patrick Battiston.

Worst Ipswich managers?

Paul Jewell. Not only did we regularly concede lots of goals under him, he also had a habit of signing older players, and relied on loanees - Jewell signed more loanees in 21 months, than Sir Bobby signed permanently in thirteen years. Roy Keane had a poor record too, with the only high point in his tenure being the large number of youth team players making their debuts. However, Keane later wrote that he'd only done that because he had no other choice. Mick McGivern's football was unwatchable, unsuccessful and killed the confidence of the players. Ten men behind the ball, in the hope of drawing 0-0, then staying with the same tactic after going a goal down turned the club into a laughing stock.

Thoughts on ticket prices in general?

They're outrageous and don't reflect the quality on offer. The categorisation of games is shameful, given that (unlike other forms of entertainment) there is no guarantee that the game will be any good. My season ticket works out at just under £20 a game, which is a more reasonable price, but not everyone can make that sort of financial commitment.

Name your Ipswich Dream Team?

I just missed the glory days, so I'll give a lineup on who I've seen:
GK: Richard Wright
RB: Mick Stockwell
CB: Tony Mowbray
CB: Hermann Hreidarsson
LB: Mauricio Taricco
RM: Kieron Dyer
CM: Matt Holland
CM: John Wark
LM: Paul Mason
CF: Darren Bent
CF: Marcus Stewart

But an all-time lineup would be dominated by players from Robson's era and look more like:
GK: Paul Cooper
RB: George Burley
CB: Kevin Beattie
CB: Terry Butcher
LB: Mick Mills
M: Frans Thijssen
M: John Wark
M: Arnold Muhren
CF: Eric Gates
CF: Paul Mariner
CF: Ray Crawford

A TRIP TO SEE THE TRACTOR BOYS

Game #68: The Championship - Saturday 11th April 2015
IPSWICH TOWN vs Blackpool - Portman Road

From the pier of Brighton to the sights of Suffolk. I'd certainly chosen an interesting route for the second part of a weekend double header. Starting the day the right way thanks to Graham's full English breakfast, I made it out of rain soaked Brighton on a delayed train into London. Squeezing past an inflated number of weekend commuters, I was soon swapping views of Stratford and the Olympic Stadium for the Essex countryside.

Portman Road is visible as soon as you step outside Ipswich train station. Several Blackpool fans were tucking into a hearty pre-match meal at the 'Riverside Hotel' directly opposite. No doubt they were making the most of one of their final away days as a Championship club. A little further down the road, the 'Drum and Monkey' wasn't so accommodating. Away fans were clearly barred, as evidenced by a sign outside while an annoying and equally inebriated Ipswich fan was shouting incoherently at passers-by.

Former Ipswich and England managers Sir Alf Ramsey and Sir Bobby Robson are honoured with statues outside the ground. Both legends also have stands named after them behind the goals. State of the art floodlight pylons sit atop both said stands which were revamped at the turn of the century. They hang over the other two smaller stands at either side, despite the West Stand being a compressed three tier affair with a row of executive boxes sandwiching the middle and top tier. Coming out of the club shop, the likeness of Sir Bobby lies directly above, smiling down at you.

Ipswich had their own Megaphone man, parading up and down the streets before the game. Proudly wearing his personalised 'ITFC Big Fan' shirt, he's a part of the furniture in these parts and a definite contender to give the Wealdstone Raider a run for his money. Fans with clipboards were asking people to vote for their Player of the Season. Predictably, goal-getter Daryl Murphy was streets ahead of everyone else. I opted for Tyrone Mings. The young full-back had shown maturity beyond his years both on and off the pitch. Putting in eye catching performances which had Premier League clubs on high alert, the kind soul had also been giving tickets to hard-up fans, replacing replica shirts when his squad number was changed and settling his mother's debts. Top bloke!

On the subject of money, it was Grand National day. Which meant it was the day of the year when everyone instantly knew everything about horse racing, but just as quickly learnt everything about gambling. Ignoring the gee-gee's and musing over the football, the smart money - make that the only money was on an Ipswich win. The Tractor Boys were fending off rivals for a play-off spot, while Blackpool just wanted the season to end. Given Ipswich's defensive vulnerabilities, I thought goals for both sides looked the best bet.

Like many a horse, Ipswich were slow out of the gate and quickly punished. Jamie O'Hara's defence splitting pass allowed Henry Cameron to cross for an unmarked Andrea Orlandi to sweep the ball in and give the Seasiders a shock lead inside the first five minutes. The handful of Blackpool fans briefly stopped their chants of "Oyston Out" to celebrate some good fortune. Predictably, the lead didn't last long. It was Blackpool after all. As susceptible as Ipswich were at the back, they were lethal going forward.

Despite suffering the blow of losing Luke Varney to an early injury, Freddie Sears brought the two teams level with his 20th goal of the season. The tiny striker had enjoyed an upturn in form since his January move to East Anglia. Mings cushioned a header for Mears to confidently smash his effort into the roof of the net. The ex-Colchester United man was soon celebrating a double. A bout of one touch football bamboozled the Blackpool defence, before a lucky deflection fell kindly into the striker's path. Sears coolly slipped the ball under Elliot Parish from three yards. I had the perfect vantage point from my seat up high in Sir Alf's Stand, with the old school slate roofing either side of me shielding my eyes from part of the sun.

The game was providing sufficient entertainment for me to ignore the spotty teen throwing bits of rolled up paper at the back of my head. Junior was probably just letting off steam, thankful for a day off from asking people if they wanted to supersize their meals. On the pitch, Christophe Berra's abysmal defensive header almost led to a comical own goal. Mings then picked out Sears with a terrific long ball. The forward cut inside and looked odds on to bag a hat-trick, only to shoot straight at Parish. Blackpool punished Ipswich for their wastefulness by pulling the scores level. The Seasiders seized an opportunity when Orlandi was needlessly fouled by taking a quick free-kick. Gary Madine supplied the cross for Cameron to edge in front of his marker and poke the ball in.

Ipswich stuck to their bread and butter of using route one football to see them over the line.Their winner came from an unlikely source. Murphy turned goal provider, putting in a perfect cross for club captain Berra to head the ball over the line. Junior and his pals had already left - perhaps to start their shift, as a wave of relief spread around Portman Road. Berra was one of the last to leave the pitch. With fists clenched, he'd helped spare his side's blushes and kept Ipswich's play-off hopes on track.

The megaphone man provided a fitting farewell. Chatting away at the rate of a mile a minute, his echo could be heard all the way back to the station. I upgraded myself to First Class for part of the journey home. Complimentary cold snacks went down a treat, but a blissful sleep was interrupted by gatecrashers who invaded the peace, cramming three to a seat and flaunting the fact that they had no intention of paying for a ticket. The power of social media came to the rescue and I was given a generous reimbursement to compensate for the inconvenience.

Best chant: "If you all hate Norwich clap your hands." I didn't clap. I don't mind them to be honest.
Match ticket: £21.50 student ticket. The club operated a grading system and four separate price brackets depending on seat location. Buying in advance could save £2.50 in most parts, while premium seating could cost up to £62.50 for an adult ticket. Jeez Louise, that's steep!
Match programme: £3. Goalkeeper Dean Gerken recalled getting knocked out at Middlesbrough, while kit man Paul Beesley reminisced about washing his own match shirts, training on the beach and playing for Blackpool with an undetected broken ankle. Approximately 58 members of the Swedish Blue Army jetted in for the game. Hallå!
Cost of food: £3.20 for a pie.
Food rating: 2/5. I felt like a surgeon, pulling out unwanted ingredients. The chicken and ham offering had a glazed finish on top of the pastry, only to be spoilt with an overflow of chunky onions. The balti was a convoluted affair, needlessly stuffed with mushrooms, turnip and swede. Yuck!

Final Score
Ipswich Town 3 (Sears 24, 28, Berra 83)
Blackpool 2 (Orlandi 4, Cameron 63)
Attendance: 19,290

Getting to know York City
Joel Stern - www.yorkcitysouth.co.uk
Twitter @YCFCSouth

How long have you been a York fan?

Since 1995. I was sent to boarding school in York and used to go and watch City on a Saturday afternoon once school had finished. Having come from Newcastle and followed them for many years before, I followed both teams for a while until 2004 when, having become increasingly disillusioned with the money-focused Premier League, I switched my allegiance to York in full.

Favourite memory as a York fan?

Unfortunately I missed our Wembley play-off victory as my wife thought she was going into labour early and I had a tough decision to make - Wembley or hospital? In the end I went to the hospital. But my favourite memory was Northampton away at the end of the 2012/13 season when, faced with relegation back to the Conference in our first season back in the League, we went to Northampton who were unbeaten at home in 10 games and won 2-0 with an incredible support from the stands.

Best game you've witnessed at Bootham Crescent?

The 3-2 win over Everton in the League Cup in 1996 was really special. We'd drawn 1-1 at Goodison Park and Graeme Murty, who was coaching our school team at the time popped up to score the winner and send the Longhurst into pandemonium. Similarly, our play-off semi-final win over Luton in 2010 was pretty special. We've got a great group of fans who stand behind the goal, giving a really great atmosphere in the ground.

Best/worst players to pull on a York shirt?

There have been some pretty horrific signings in recent years, too many to name. A much acclaimed international Futsal player form Ireland, an Estonian international and the son of a Premier League winning manager have all failed to deceive and left almost as quickly as they arrived. Our all-time greats include Arthur Bottom and Keith Walwyn, and of course Richard Cresswell and European Cup winner Jonathan Greening both started out at Bootham Crescent.

Best thing about Bootham Crescent?

For me it's the ground itself. It's full of character and old (knackered) charm. It's one of those proper old football grounds that's located close to the city centre and has largely remained unchanged for many years. I'll certainly miss it when we move to the new ground.

Worst grounds you've visited?

We spent eight long years in the Conference, so there are some high contenders here. The Dripping Pan in Lewes was pretty bad, although we had a great day out there. For me though, I think Ebbsfleet's Stonebridge Road takes the award for worst ground. The open terrace facing the Thames estuary always seemed to save its worst weather for us. I can recall plenty of mangled umbrellas on the terrace following our visit and a lot of very wet York fans.

Which club serves the nicest pies?

Kidderminster, no competition!

Famous York fans?

Commentators Jon Champion and Guy Mowbray are both City fans. As is comedian Richard Herring. Shed Seven frontman Rik Witter performed a benefit concert when we almost went out of business. The Archbishop of York, John Sentamu is also a huge fan.

Thoughts on ticket prices in general?

Too high and too inconsistent. In League Two, you can pay anything from about £16 to £24 - usually the more expensive ones are the bigger clubs who probably need the money less and who will stick you on a freezing open terrace. I think about £18 is a fair price for League Two football.

Game #69: League Two - Tuesday 14th April 2015
YORK CITY vs Morecambe - Bootham Crescent

"Don't York play at KitKat Crescent?"
"No Dad, they fell out with Nestle and it's back to being Bootham Crescent."
"Sarcasm doesn't suit you Shaun."
"Tell you what Dad, I'll buy you a KitKat if you fancy tagging along with me to York?"
"No thanks. Enjoy the game."

With hopes of another father/son trip dashed, I was flying solo for the final midweek round of the season. Just the one ticket please. Around 20 years ago, the Minstermen famously thrashed Manchester United 3-0 at Old Trafford in the first leg of a League Cup tie. Although the Red Devils won the second leg, York snuck through 4-3 on aggregate to record one of the club's most impressive victories. Cue the taunts in the playground at school the next day. Not forgetting the unbearable Maths teacher who also coached York schoolboys. I hope his training methods were better than his teaching. Sorry Neil, I mean sir.

York needed a win here to ensure survival. Some things never changed. Even back in 1995, York were battling relegation. Following an eight year tenure in the Conference, they returned to the Football League in 2012. A lone police officer was standing outside the train station. He didn't need any back-up to control the crowds. Truth be told, there weren't any other football fans in the vicinity at 5:30pm on a Tuesday evening. Talk about being an eager beaver.

The York Minster cathedral - one of the largest of its kind in Europe was sticking out in the distance and inviting me to take a closer look. Standing tall in the early evening sun, there were a few tourists still milling around, but overall there was a relaxed vibe around what is a beautiful city. Short cobbled roads in the middle of Tudor buildings allow you to walk freely without worrying about cars coming from behind. I chose to take the scenic route towards the stadium via the city walls. The ground is at the end of Bootham Crescent - largely a residential area with Edwardian terraces and a couple of guest houses.

Bootham Crescent was old school in more ways than one. Lots of the elder generation were chatting outside, while inside was a mixture of seats and terraces. Just under half of the current capacity is seated, with away fans situated in an uncovered terrace not too dissimilar to the one at Accrington. The club staff hooked me up with a great spec close to the press pit. Rows of journalist tables looked like something out of a grammar school. No doubt each reporter was praying that the small tubular light was in working order for when the sun went down. The wooden seat awaiting me looked like it had some stories to tell and the stand I was in only ran two thirds of the length of the pitch. The partnership with KitKat ended amicably several years ago and the club are soon to sever their ties with Bootham Crescent too. Plans for an 8,000 capacity stadium four miles from York have been green lit, with construction work beginning during the close season. The York Community Stadium will play host to both ball and egg shaped games and is rumoured to be costing in the region of £37million.

Morecambe's small, yet loyal fanbase excitedly affixed a 'Sardines on Tour' flag, while poor ground staff seemed to constantly be running around the back of the ground to retrieve wayward balls during the warm-up. I'd lost count the number of times Morecambe had cost me money on failed accumulators during the course of the season. Impossible to work out, they seemingly won games most wrote them off in, then lost to a struggling side.

York looked to have found some form at the right time of the season. Coming into this game, they were unbeaten in five. Just twelve months prior, Manager Russ Wilcox masterminded an impressive 28 game unbeaten streak which saw Scunthorpe United get promoted. A week after getting the boot and his P45 from the Iron, he joined the Minstermen. Talk about swift movement.

Wilcox's players looked lost when the match kicked off. Treating the ball like a hot potato, they couldn't string two passes together. Physically imposing defender Stephane Zubar looked uncomfortable at left-back and was chasing Shaun Beeley's shadow. It came as no surprise when Morecambe took an early lead. A quick passing move was finished from close range by Paul Mullin.

Shaq Coulthirst came to Zubar's rescue to cover the left hand side. His pace started to cause Morecambe problems, with York soon levelling from a corner. Who else but Zubar! The on loan Bournemouth defender climbed highest to send a header in at the far post. Morecambe cried foul to no avail. Zubar wheeled away motioning to the bench "look boss I scored with my head."

York looked the more likely of the two sides to conjure up a winner. Jake Hyde's screamer went just over, while the striker's next attempt was headed off the line by a well-placed Kevin Ellison. The third effort proved to be a charm. York finally hit the front with a spectacular effort from their captain. Morecambe failed to clear a corner and the ball fell invitingly for Russell Penn. The midfielder made amends for earlier giving the ball away which led to the Morecambe goal by smashing an unstoppable shot into the top corner from 35 yards.

Euphoria took over and it was man hugs all round. I'd briefly shared polite chatter with the season ticket holder sitting next to me. Now we were jumping around like girls at a One Direction concert. A young kid behind me was repeatedly asking his Dad how Penn managed to score. Nobody knew nor cared. I just wanted to bottle the feeling. Football has a way of bringing people from all walks of life together, be it a special occasion, derby game, or a flash of brilliance like Penn's strike. It was a definite Goal of the Season contender. Had Sky Sports bothered to send a camera crew then Chris Kamara would have gone crazy with hysteria. Every time Penn touched the ball after that he was encouraged to shoot. He obliged the crowd on a couple of occasions, yet unsurprisingly couldn't replicate his earlier effort. No-one was complaining. It may have only been York's fifth win of the season in front of their own fans, but what a way to retain your Football League status!

The party atmosphere continued on the train home. Fresh from thrashing Bradford City 6-0 on their own patch to seal promotion to the Championship, a group of jubilant Bristol City fans sung merrily all the way onto the platform at Manchester Piccadilly. I must have been the only one who didn't mind the noise, as several late night commuters groaned loudly at not being able to sleep. It ended up being another 2am arrival back home, with a wake-up call scheduled for just four hours later. It was all worth it to be a part of some midweek magic.

Best chant: "We all hate Leeds scum." Since Scarborough's demise, York haven't had anyone to banter with. Morecambe fans comically joined in with the singing, proudly jumping on the universal bandwagon against the West Yorkshire club in the process.
Match ticket: £14 student ticket. Adult tickets ranged from £18-£21. Very reasonably priced for League Two.
Match programme: £3. 'The Citizen' contained some forewarning as to how the night would go. In his captain's column, Penn was quoted as saying "if you don't shoot, you don't score," while Zubar was the poster boy in the centre pages.
Cost of food: £3.00 for a meat and potato pie.
Food rating: 3.5/5. Crumbling like the Berlin Wall, I regretted not asking for a fork. At times it felt like I was bobbing for apples just to consume my savoury snack. The extra effort was rewarded with what turned out to be a tasty pie.

Final Score
York City 2 (Zubar 34, Penn 51)
Morecambe 1 (Mullin 10)
Attendance: 2,854

Getting to know AFC Wimbledon
Haydon the Womble - AFC Wimbledon mascot
Twitter @HaydontheWomble

Favourite memory as a Wimbledon fan?

My first game was on Boxing Day 1983, a 1-1 draw against Mansfield. I dont know if it was fans wrapped in tinsel, the panda pop, or the football, but I was hooked The FA Cup final has to top everything. I didn't know until the morning of the game that my dad had got us tickets, and wow, walking down Wembley Way, it was mainly red, but then we got in the ground and our area was just a sea of yellow and blue. I dont remember much of the game, I think I was just looking all around Wembley just pinching myself.

Best game you've witnessed at the Cherry Red Records Stadium?

Been too many to single out, but beating Pompey 4-0 has to be up there.

Best/worst players to pull on a Wimbledon shirt?

I think it's harsh to say anyone has been terrible as a lot of them were young and are still in football, and I would not want to knock any players' confidence. Best at the time, Rob Ursell, in non league excited me every time he touched the ball. As a kid I loved John Leslie, Terry Gibson, Michael Hughes and Robbie Earle.

Best thing about the Cherry Red?

Maybe a little cheesy, but as they say in 'Cheers,' everybody knows your name. I love the family atmosphere, like we had at Plough Lane.

Worst grounds you've visited?

I loved Plough Lane, whilst everyone hated it. Your own ground has charm that only you can see, but Barrow and the open air bog has to be up there. A 14 hour round trip to pee in a gutter!

Enjoyable away days?

I love Wycombe's view (off the pitch) love Plymouth Argyle and their away team branded ice cream, but over the years nothing has been such an atmosphere for me as my first time to St James's Park (Newcastle)

Which club serves the nicest pies?

Sorry to break the mould, but I'm not much of a pie eater. Prefer a fry up!

Famous Wimbledon fans?

We have Alun Armstrong and his son Joe, both actors, plus Mumford and Sons.

How did it feel crowdsurfing during the Liverpool game?

Brilliant. I was a little hesitant, as I didn't want to distract the players, but I had to celebrate such an occasion. I had faith in the fans, well I did until they dropped me on the crush barrier!

Who's in your top five of English mascots?

Haha so many characters, but Peter Burrow, Pete the Eagle, Captain Blade, Hangus the Monkey and Howie the Hornet (Horsham) have to be my favourites.

Quirky fact time?

Apart from the fact we breed wombles. Well no one person owns more of the club than any other. We all have the one share. Erik our chief executive is paid one guinea a year (he thought it sounded posher than a pound.)

Thoughts on ticket prices in general?

For me, ticket prices in England are too expensive at the top level, considering the money they make from TV and sponsors etc. It would be nice to make it more affordable, especially for families. The lower leagues are more affordable despite a smaller pot from TV. I do feel League Two should not be more than £20, but quite a few clubs charge more. Being a loyal fan is getting harder and harder especially for families. At AFC Wimbledon we do keep under 16's prices quite low, something I'm very proud of.

Name your Wimbledon Dream Team?

GK: Dave Beasant - Never has a goalkeeper seemed so tall, but so friendly. He really was the big friendly giant to 11-year-old me, and when Dave went up to lift the FA Cup I was there.

LB: Terry Phelan - So fast, so skilfull, until he got near an opponent's box.

RB: Barry Fuller - I've seen many players play for Wimbledon, and it may have been Warren Barton had he not played for the franchise, and refused to answer my interview questions, but Barry Fuller is Mr Reliable, full of passion for the cause, something every fan loves in a player.

CB: Chris Perry -The rash as he was known. Won so many headers he had no right to win, and often gave a striker a yard advantage and still won the ball. Came through the ranks and is still a fan now.

CB: Matt Everard - Yes it was the CCL & Ryman Leagues, but I've never seen a centre back score so often with such pinnache.

LM: Michael Hughes - One of the most skilful players in a Dons shirt. The fact he was forced against his will to leave the club by the Norwegians says it all.

RM: Wally Downes - His blonde locks, the way he always looked to cause mischief on and off the pitch meant he was a teenage fan's favourite. He was a decent player too.

CM: Robbie Earle - A real box-to-box player, who ran like a leopard about to stalk its prey, but popped up with numerous important goals. Sadly, his career ended too soon by injury.

CM: Vinnie Jones - A real marmite player. If he played for you, you loved him. Much better than his disciplinary record suggests. Scored great goals against Luton, Millwall, Arsenal that if Eric Cantona had scored would still be shown now.

CF: Terry Gibson - As a teenager, us signing a striker from Manchester United filled me with excitement, and he lived up to it. Full of energy, Terry was the workhorse for John Fashanu and veteran Alan Cork.

CF: Alan Cork - Would have been Fashanu, but too many things off the pitch meant he stopped being a favourite. Instead I've gone for Cork. Only recently he seems to have said AFC Wimbledon are the real Wimbledon after sitting on a fence so long splinters must have taken root up his bum. But, a player coming through every division and scoring important goals in every one, I'm willing to ignore (hey us football fans are allowed to be fickle.)

Game #70: League Two - Saturday 18th April 2015
AFC WIMBLEDON vs Wycombe Wanderers - The Cherry Red Records Stadium

From FA Cup winners to fighting off the MK franchise, AFC Wimbledon have proved that it isn't the size of the womble in the fight, but the size of the fight in the womble. Five promotions in nine seasons saw the newest incarnation of the Dons become the first club to be formed in the 21st century to make it into the Football League. Now under the guide of former Crazy Gang defender Neal Ardley (one of their own), the time had come to do a bit of womble spotting in sunny Kingston upon Thames. The club may not currently play in Wimbledon, although plans are in place to eventually move back to spiritual former stomping ground Plough Lane.

Since their re-formation in 2002, Wimbledon had entered into a ground share arrangement with non-league Kingstonian. The Dons had since secured full ownership, with Kingstonian leasing it for a nominal fee. It may not be a massive arena like their namesakes in Bletchley, but it's home for now. Chief executive Erik Samuelson runs the phoenix club for the equivalent of a £1 a year, such is his love for the Dons. I'd bumped into the Wimbledon squad on their way back from Hartlepool back in February. Beastly striker Adebayo Akinfenwa confidently predicted a Dons victory whenever I decided to come and visit him and his mates. I kept those words firmly in the front of my mind as I travelled into London on a blazing hot Saturday afternoon.

"Oh no, it's that time on a Saturday again," said a middle-aged woman, whose nose was crinkled so high it was almost tickling the roof of the train. Clearly she wasn't a football fan. Her husband/male accomplice gave off a perfect poker face and remained neutral. Dons and Wycombe fans aplenty joined me at Vauxhall for the six stop journey to Norbiton. The Wycombe fans were considerate enough to wait until getting off before the singing commenced. Chants of "we are going up," filled the air, as the crowds marched through what looked to be a usually quiet housing estate.

The Chairboys were clearly in town for a promotion party. It was quite a remarkable turnaround for a club who only escaped relegation by the skin of their teeth on the final day of last season. Bristol Rovers were the unlucky ones who lost their league status on goal difference - a tidbit visiting fans hadn't forgotten, based on several less than flattering songs towards the Gas filling the air. Residents came to their windows to see what all the racket was. The singing came to a momentary halt while a group disappeared up a side alley to give a lucky man's fence a fresh coat. I'm not talking about Ronseal if you catch my drift.

The club shop proved to be a snug affair. Best to avoid for those who are claustrophobic, although there was a cracking deal on the latest installment of Football Manager for those inclined. The kind souls at Sports Interactive have sponsored the team since its inception and were offering mates rates for £10. An absolute steal!

Independent music label Cherry Red Records took over naming rights of the stadium from the plain sounding Kingsmeadow. The upside to that meant that my ears appreciated hearing the new Jimmy Somerville song over the umpteenth playing of Taylor Swift or Beyonce. Just under half of the stadium is seated. I opted to stand behind the goal in the Chemflow Terrace. After all it was the scene where mascot Haydon the Womble defied the laws of gravity and became the first crowd surfing womble in history during the sell-out televised FA Cup game against Liverpool. I say the first, as I doubt Great Uncle Bulgaria can match Haydon's feat given the state of his knees these days. They're completely knackered from what I hear.

Getting food felt like running the gauntlet on an episode of Takeshi's Castle. The non-Wimbledon forwards were lining up for shooting practice. One texter failed to cotton on to the warning signs of the walls thudding around him and almost had a close encounter. Security weren't safe either. Guarding a small uncovered space which made up the shortfall for the low hanging Golf Travel Terrace, they were ducking and diving just as much as the fans were.

Ardley and opposite counterpart Gareth Ainsworth were former Wimbledon teammates and shared a friendly embrace before kick-off. The Wycombe players didn't return the sporting gesture. Let's just say they didn't make the short trip to play football. Their tactics were as hideous as the ridiculous fruit salad style shirts they were decked out in. Play acting and conning the referee with flimsy fouls was a far cry from the Wycombe side which I'd seen dismantle Luton Town a few weeks prior.

Wycombe lost Matt Bloomfield to injury in the first ten minutes, but went back to their unscrupulous style of play. Wimbledon went to clear a ball and a defender got an elbow in the face. The referee gave a corner. Cue the chants of "where's your labrador ref?" Good question. Unsurprisingly, Akinfenwa posed Wimbledon's greatest attacking threat. He rose highest to head against the post. A bloke in front clearly had the big guy as the first goalscorer. The poor guy was kicking every ball, willing the big man to score. Truth be told, the Wycombe players used all Akinfenwa's girth against him, bouncing off him like a pinball and getting all the decisions. Another Wycombe injury - this time Nico Yennaris led to six minutes of first half stoppage time being added on. Wimbledon's Adebayo Azeez broke clear, only to be thwarted by an alert Matt Ingram and his legs.

Haydon was doing his best to keep the crowd's spirits up. Sadly, there was to be no crowd surfing today, but scores of fans still lined up to get souvenir selfies with the cheery mascot. Wimbledon's Craig Tanner should have earned a penalty from Aaron Pierre's foul. Maybe with a different referee. However, the Wycombe defender did push his luck one too many times and was sent off late on for a second bookable offence. Wimbledon's Jake Goodman headed over from the resulting free-kick. I wasn't destined to see a goal. Akinfenwa's prediction may not have come true, but at least Wimbledon tried. The Wycombe fans sung merrily after the game, seemingly having no shame after seeing their side turn in such a poor performance. To top things off, a bird crapped on my shoulder back at the station. It was somewhat ironic that the pesky pigeon's aim was about as accurate as Wycombe's attempts on goal. On the plus side, the poop missed my hair and was easily brushed off.

Best chant: "You're gonna lose in the play-offs." Yours sincerely, the Wimbledon fans.
Match ticket: £11 student ticket. An absolute bargain and great atmosphere to boot in the Chemflow.
Match programme: £3. A pleasing read to see so many volunteers and the Dons Trust Board rally round to do their bit for the club. Every little clearly helps.
Cost of food: £3.50 for a bacon roll. There wasn't a pie in sight inside the ground.
Food rating: 2/5. As much fat as there was bacon and not worth the costly price.

Final Score
AFC Wimbledon 0
Wycombe Wanderers 0
Attendance: 4,535

Getting to know Yeovil Town
Oliver Marsh - www.olliemarsh.webs.com
Twitter @ollie_marsh

Favourite memory as a Yeovil fan?

It has to be getting promoted to the Championship at Wembley. Nobody thought we would make the play-offs that year, and we did. Nobody thought we would get to the final that year, and we did. And nobody thought we would win the final, and we did! The play-offs is probably the best way to get promoted and for 'Little Old Yeovil' to reach the second highest level of football in the country was something quite special.

Thoughts on Gary Johnson/Terry Skiverton's reigns during the season?

I think most people think all Yeovil Town fans worship Gary Johnson; that isn't the case. While there's no doubting he's one of Yeovil's most successful managers in history, he also had the ego that came with that, leading to fall-outs with the fans and the players. After a dismal season this year, he can't complain about getting the boot. On the other hand, Terry Skiverton has almost exactly the opposite problem. While he lives and breathes Yeovil Town, and is seen as a club legend, who can do no wrong, he's not cut out to be a manager.

Best game you've witnessed at Huish Park?

There's a few to choose from but the one that sticks in my mind is a 3 - 3 draw with Norwich City in 2009. At the time, Norwich were at the top of League One and looking pretty much unbeatable, but Yeovil were proving more than a match for them, and in second half stoppage time Jonathan Obika put the Glovers 3 - 2 up. Astoundingly, Norwich then still found time to equalise, but although this was disappointing, it's by far one of the most entertaining matches I've ever witnessed.

Best/worst players to pull on a Yeovil shirt?

While it's difficult for a club like Yeovil to make big-name signings, they've had a lot of success in the loan market. Steven Caulker, Andros Townsend and Ryan Mason all made their league debuts at Huish Park, and all have gone on to be capped for England. Constrastingly, one of the worst players has to be a young lad called Alistair Slowe. Despite comparing himself to David Beckham, Slowe only ever played (badly!) for Yeovil in reserve and county cup games, and it later emerged that his father was paying his wages for the club. When Gary Johnson took over from Terry Skiverton, Slowe disappeared without a trace, never to be seen again.

Best thing about Huish Park?

I'm a fan of unique grounds. Yes, it would be nice to have a shiny new stadium, but I much prefer grounds with character as opposed to soulless bowls. In other words, it's not perfect but it's home.

Worst grounds you've visited?

I don't remember ever really disliking a ground, but one does find it rather hypocritical when Bristol Rovers fans complain about the facilities at Huish Park when you look at their rather dismal excuse of a stadium!

Enjoyable away days?

Every stadium is different and that's what makes them appealing. There were some obvious highlights during our Championship season, with us getting unprecedented chances to visit Reading's Madjeski Stadium, Derby's Pride Park and Leicester's King Power Stadium to name but a few. But then again, I enjoy being in the "cowshed" away stand at Southend's Roots Hall just as much!

Famous Yeovil fans?

Trevor Peacock from The Vicar of Dibley is often at games, and James Purefoy from the American TV shows 'Rome' and 'The Following.'

Quirky fact time?

In 1933, they beat the Czechslovakian national team 8 - 3 in what has to be one of the most bizarre friendlies ever!

Thoughts on ticket prices in general?

Pretty much the same as any other fan - they're too high! At Yeovil there's been enough proof through 'Kids for a Quid', 'Green and White Tuesday Nights' (a two-for-one offer), and other promotions that cheap ticket prices equal a rise in attendance. Sadly, it's going to take a very confident chairman to lower ticket prices substantially enough to see this rise. The "suits" upstairs forget that for away supporters, travel, food and possibly overnight accommodation also have to be bought. Add an expensive ticket price to that and you've almost reached the £100 mark. Who's going to pay £100 to watch a football match?

Name your Yeovil Dream Team?

GK: Wayne Hennessey - The hardest position to pick as I was choosing from the likes of Asmir Begovic, Alex McCarthy, Marek Stech and Stephen Henderson to name a few. I went for Hennessey because the others were generally youngsters during their Yeovil spells - some fantastic performances including a memorable double save from a Nottingham Forest penalty proves that Hennessey was still in his prime when wearing the Glovers shirt.

LB: Nathan Jones - Jonesey has been picked for being the most committed and passionate Yeovil player I've ever seen. You can have all the talent in the world but if you don't have the right attitude then you'll never achieve the same things that Jonesey did. Also assistant manager during his time at Yeovil, he has a promising career ahead in coaching.

CB: Terry Skiverton - How can you not pick Mr Yeovil Town? Skivo first joined the club when they were non-league and captained them during their meteoric rise up the divisions. Eventually retiring to focus on managing the club, he signed some of the best players to ever play for the Glovers, some of whom are on this list.

CB: Steven Caulker - One of Skiverton's signings, Caulker was a Tottenham Hotspur loanee who shined in his first season in professional football. Great tackler, great on the ball and great discipline meant he was destined for the Premier League. While his progression has stalled a little in the last couple of seasons, I'd still back him to become a regular in a top flight team when he decides on a club to settle down at.

RB: Luke Ayling - Another Skiverton signing and another fans favourite, Luke Ayling was more of a wing back than a full back, going forward at any opportunity with lightning pace and great crossing ability. In the summer of 2012, he turned down offers from numerous Championship clubs in order to win promotion at Wembley with Yeovil.

LW: Andy Welsh - A hard working winger with experience in the Premier League before his time at with the Glovers. His skill developed as he became more confident, eventually becoming able to get past defenders with ease.

CM: Ryan Mason - While Mason was a bit younger and a lot scrawnier than he is now, he still displayed the flair that is currently impressing Spurs fans in the top flight. The highlight was probably a spectacular volley away at Exeter City on a Tuesday night.

CM: Ed Upson - One of the most improved players Yeovil Town has ever seen. At first he came to the club as a benchwarmer, but a lot of work with coach Darren Way (who also could have taken this position on this list) made him a mainstay in the side that won promotion to the Championship.

RW: Andros Townsend - Still being cited as 'one for the future', he displayed the same skills and trickery that have excited football fans all over the country while on loan at Yeovil.

CF: Paddy Madden - An obvious choice, but you can't argue with a player who finished League One top scorer despite only joining Yeovil halfway through the season. A bust-up with manager Gary Johnson ended his time with the Glovers.

CF: Leon Best - Another obvious choice, whose goals inspired Yeovil to the League One play-offs in 2007. Maybe had he of been in the side for the final against Blackpool, the Glovers could have gone all the way.

WEEKEND IN THE WEST COUNTRY

Game #71: League One - Saturday 25th April 2015
YEOVIL TOWN vs Port Vale - Huish Park

The penultimate weekend of the season. So close to completing the 72, yet so far away at the same time. Yeovil was not one of the easiest places to get to for a non-driver. A daunting six hour commute via London didn't look too appealing. Away travel wasn't really an option this time either. Vale Park isn't remotely close to any train stations (30 minute walk from Longport or four miles from Stoke-on-Trent) plus by the time I'd get back into Stoke, it would be too late to make a connection back to Chester. Splitting the journey up over two days was a much better solution. Luckily, Ben was able to put me up in Bristol overnight meaning I'd have just under a two hour commute on matchday. He even got the beers in. I think he felt bad for bailing when I was in town to see Bristol City back in December.

Yeovil's fate and demotion to League Two may already have been sealed, but the Glovers were making sure they were going down swinging. Back-to-back relegations saw Gary Johnson - the mastermind behind the club's recent rise to the Championship, fall on his sword, while former player Terry Skiverton was unable to stop the rot during a caretaker spell in charge. Step forward Paul Sturrock. The Scot famously led Plymouth Argyle to two successive promotions at the start of the century and had already guided Yeovil to two morale boosting victories over play-off contenders Swindon Town and Sheffield United since being appointed. Port Vale weren't mathematically safe from the drop, so I was expecting to see a competitive game.

Well rested and refreshed, despite an evening sampling some of Bristol's finer craft beers, I squeezed into a small gap on a mid-morning train bound for Weymouth. First Great Western hadn't felt the need to put on more than two carriages. Like a lion scoping his prey, I pounced on an empty seat as soon as the crowds started to disperse after leaving the Avon area. Passing a seemingly endless row of greenery, the fear of being dropped off in a field and navigating to the ground on the back of a tractor looked like a possibility. Alas, it was just my overactive imagination running wild. Even though I was approaching Wurzel territory, I didn't spot a single scarecrow in the field.

Yeovil Junction and Pen Mill make up the town's two railway stations. I arrived at the latter. For what it's worth, both are quite a way from Huish Park. A shifty looking taxi driver offered to drop me off in town. Being kidnapped and locked in a car boot didn't appeal, so I sought solace in a neighbouring sandwich shop until the undesirable drove off. A country park links the station to the city centre. It was all quite civilised. Park benches were free from tramps, dogs were kept on leads and a nice looking golf course could be seen peeping out during a pleasant walk through rural Somerset. Next time I'm in town I'll bring my clubs and work on my handicap.

A well-placed Wetherspoons lies on the cusp of the town centre. I joined several travelling fans for a couple of jars and to enquire about getting to the ground. Huish Park is on the other side of town, so it's strongly advised to catch a bus from the neighbouring station. Fortunately, a frequent service runs on a loop, stopping directly outside the ground. There wasn't a cloud in sight, as I strolled into the car park and purchased a programme from one of the many wooden huts dotted around. A healthy crowd had gathered to watch Yeovil's kids play on a state of the art 3G pitch. In contrast, some of the older generation had converged on one of the various metal containers converted into a greasy spoon behind one of the terraces.

Images from the club's 2013 play-off triumph at Wembley were displayed around the outside of the stadium, while a half and half Manchester United scarf commemorating January's glamorous FA Cup tie was the marquee item on display inside the club shop. Both represented memories of happier times for the football club, although my lasting memory of the club shop will be the grass tiling they used to decorate the floor. 100% hayfever proof too.

In a rare show of solidarity, Vale's mascot Boomer the Dog joined up with home counterpart the Jolly Green Giant and Little Green Giant to greet fans before kick-off. It wasn't that long ago the poor old Giant was punched in the nose by an inebriated Nottingham Forest during half time in a Championship fixture. A repeat wasn't likely, although having a trusty K9 in close proximity no doubt deterred any drunken idiots thinking of doing anything stupid. I wasn't too far from the dugouts and could see Vale boss Rob Page chuckling away at some of the chants aimed his way. Come to think of it, they were all coming from a large Yeovil fan a few rows back. Sporting an array of badges on his hat and a replica shirt a few sizes too small, Mr Yeovil was desperate to get a reaction. "Sit down Rob before your toupee falls off," was yelled repeatedly, albeit in vain. The bald as a coot Page didn't bother turning round and the only rise the fan got was from the shirt riding up his chest.

Despite boasting a tall strapping centre half by the name of Stephen Arthurworrey, Yeovil were given plenty to worry about early on. After losing winger Sam Foley to injury, they seemed to go a goal down when Tom Pope headed in. Huish Park breathed a sigh of relief when the effort was disallowed for a foul. That relief didn't last. Pope made his next effort count, firing the Valiants in front with a low shot. The travelling fans were clearly enjoying their day out in Somerset. They didn't care about the imminent rain. Stood in the uncovered Copse Terrace, they stopped singing about goalkeeper Chris Neale's well coiffed hair and turned their attention to the toiling Yeovil team. Afro wearing frontman Gozie Ugwu was one who was picked out and labelled as a "shit Danny Welbeck," by the rabid away following. If anything, the physical resemblance was uncanny.

A big black cloud - both literally and metaphorically was now hanging over Huish Park. Rain started beating down and I remarked to the fan sat behind me that Yeovil were missing some fighting spirit. The words had barely left my mouth when the Glovers equalised with an acrobatic overhead kick from close range. The scorer – you guessed it, none other than Ugwu. It was en effort that Welbeck would have been proud of and the Vale fans were well and truly silenced.

Yeovil looked to have given their fans something to cheer about. I was still eating the portion of humble pie generously served from the fan behind me when the home side gave away an innocuous looking free kick right in front of me. Enter Port Vale's resident midfield hardman Michael Brown to cause a ruckus in the box. Michael O'Connor flighted the ball in and it was none other than Brown who turned the ball in amid a goalline scramble. Say what you will about Brown, but his bite was exactly what Yeovil had been missing all afternoon. The Glovers weren't coming back a second time.

Most fans opted to leave at the final whistle, missing out on the club's end of season awards being presented on the pitch. A few of the diehards stayed behind and faint clapping could be heard from the bus stop. Lining up next to glum rain soaked fans, I was shocked to hear the topic of conversation being League Two survival. Blimey! Three straight relegations would be some unwanted record. Morale was worse than originally thought. Once back in town, season ticket holders embraced and shook hands, wishing each other well. Long sighs and the words "see you next season," were uttered with as much gusto as waiting to go and see the dentist.

The arduous journey facing the Glovers mirrored the one I had getting back to Chester. Setting off at 6:15pm, a stream of delays meant that it would be a race against time to make my connections. The last train out of Bristol Temple Meads heading my way left at 8:30pm. Arriving five minutes before departure time at the other end of the station led to a frenzied but successful sprint. Further connections at Birmingham New Street, Stafford and Crewe were less eventful and I made it back to Chester at 11:45pm. It had been a very long poke indeed. Needless to say, it was probably my first and last trip to Yeovil. Well, unless someone offers to drive.

Best chant: "Sam Foley oooo-oooo, Sam Foley oooo-oooo, he came from non-League shite to play in Green and White." Foley earned cult hero status on the turnstiles and the club's Player of the Year award. Foley repaid the faith by rejecting a new contract and signing for Port Vale.

Match ticket: £28. With nothing but pride to play for, I was shocked at such a steep price. No student discount or flexibility, although I could have saved £2 had I bought a ticket in advance.

Match programme: £3. It read more like a eulogy, as players, fans and officials tried to rationalise a poor season. We all know that football is a drug. Two years out of the game can make a manager do some crazy things. In Sturrock's case it was taking up the Yeovil hotseat in order to get his latest "fix." Wayne Rooney battling for possession with a Yeovil player was used to try and entice fans into purchasing reduced priced season tickets for the following campaign.

Cost of food: £3.20 for a balti pie.

Food rating: 2.5/5. One from the bargain bin. A hastily arranged sign warned that food stocks were low given that it was nearing the end of the season. The contents were bursting out of the slightly burnt and uneven crust, resulting in me wrestling with rather than eating the pie. No spillage on my cream jumper, which was surprising.

Final Score
Yeovil Town 1 (Ugwu 80)
Port Vale 2 (Pope 13, Brown 82)
Attendance: 4,127

Favourite memory of being a Charlton fan?

I've been a fan for pushing on 65 years. Getting to the Premier League in that memorable game at Wembley in 1998 was a great memory. Following our double relegation from the Premier League, promotion from League One at Carlisle in 2012 was a wonderful memory too.

Thoughts on ticket prices in general?

Premier League prices are ridiculous, others are reasonable, but some lower division clubs charge crazy prices. I seem to remember Ipswich charging over £40 for Championship games a year or two back. West Ham's price reduction policy is an excellent initiative.

Best game you've witnessed at the Valley?

A 7-6 win over Huddersfield at The Valley in December 1957. Back then there were no substitutes. Charlton were reduced to ten men when Derek Ufton was injured and went 5-1 down. There will never be another game like it.

Best/worst players to pull on a Charlton shirt?

Andy Hunt, Clive Mendonca, Stuart Leary and Sam Bartram were greats. George Tucudean, Pawel Abbott, Alan McCormack less so.

Worst grounds you've visited?

Brighton's Withdean Stadium had the worst away end ever. Kenilworth Road and Roots Hall offer poor views too.

Enjoyable away days?

I like 'real' football grounds more than the massive Premier League stadiums. Spotland, Prenton Park and Exeter's St James Park are favourites of mine.

Which club serves the nicest pies?

Lancashire is the pie capital of the world. Oldham and Rochdale are supplied by Clayton Park. Wonderful pies. 'Leavers,' opposite Ewood Park, make the best pies in the environs of a stadium.

Famous Charlton fans?

Jim Davidson and Gemma Arterton are probably the most famous fans at the moment. Jim is a regular, both home and away.

Quirky fact time?

Just after the last World War, the club planned to buy out a builder whose yard was close to the North West corner of the ground. Had they been successful, there were rumours at the time that the club planned to turn the pitch round and make The Valley the country's first all-seater stadium.

Name your Charlton Dream Team?

GK: Vince Bartram
RB: John Hewie
CB: Richard Rufus
CB: Marvin Hinton
LB: Paul Konchesky
RM: Mike Kenning
CM: Scott Parker
CM: Claus Jensen
LM: Johnny Summers
CF: Andy Hunt
CF: Darren Bent

PEAKS AND VALLEYS

Game #72: The Championship - Saturday 2nd May 2015
CHARLTON ATHLETIC vs AFC Bournemouth - The Valley

All good things must come to an end...unfortunately! The last nine months had been an absolute blast. Casting a wistful eye back to that first Friday at Ewood Park in August, I was on the cusp of something special. Having travelled the length and breadth of the country, braved sub-zero conditions and survived the tale, just 90 minutes stood between me and the end of my quest. However, it wouldn't be me without a bit of last day drama. Not for the first time, it was proving a tad difficult to get my hand on a matchday ticket. Charlton had endured a mediocre season and had only come close to selling out their 27,000 stadium once all season. Just as I was about to laud former player/manager Chris Powell's talent to bring the fans flocking back when he brought his Huddersfield team to town, I realised much of the increase in numbers was due to an attractive 'Football for a Fiver' initiative.

Sadly, that offer was no longer valid and a restricted ticket sale ruled me out. Surely the fine folk at the Football League offices had heard of a little trooper going up and down the country and would be sympathetic to his plight? Apparently not.

Shaun,

Thank you for your email.

Whilst we appreciate your circumstances, unfortunately The Football League cannot assist with obtaining any match tickets and the sale of these is purely handled through the home/away clubs. While it is obvious that this game will be well attended, we can only advise you contact the home club on this occasion and explain the background to your attendance and see if they can assist.

We wish you the best of luck.

Thank you for contacting The Football League.

Where there's a will there's most definitely a way. Plan B proved to be more successful, with Charlton selling me a ticket over the phone and guaranteeing me a good seat. Yes just the one seat. Due to location and the fact that all Championship games were kicking off at the earlier time of 12:15pm, I couldn't rope any friends into joining me for a 5am wake-up call. Oh well, sleep was overrated anyway. Even though my ticket was for the home end, I threw on my Bournemouth shirt underneath a jumper. Barring a 19 goal swing in Charlton's favour then the Cherries would be promoted. Besides, I wanted to be ready to join in the celebrations at the end.

Maintenance work up and down the country meant that most trains were being diverted. I'd barely left Crewe and the train came to a screeching halt. I peeped out the window to see the sign for Alsager staring back at me. No offense to the quaint Cheshire town, but an eerie sense of déjà-vu immediately took my mind back to the very same spot on a cold and wet October evening when the winds of Hurricane Gonzalo literally derailed me from getting to a Port Vale game. Thankfully, the delay was a short one and was due to being stuck behind a slow moving local train.

A myriad of football shirts came from all directions walking through Euston station. That was a sight I was going to miss during the close season. On the flip side, the sound of someone having a white christmas in the toilet cubicle certainly wasn't. A Lone Charlton fan found himself amongst a cluster of travelling fans at London Bridge.

"Really happy for you lads. You deserve to go up," he said. Not a bad way to ingratiate yourself to the opposition and ensure a pleasant 20 minute journey. It was barely standing room only on the crammed train with almost everyone decked out in a Bournemouth shirt.

Fans were spilling out of the pubs and onto the street. Suddenly everyone stopped to cheer and clap. I wasn't aware the Queen was passing through. I turned to see a blacked out bus making its way down the road slowly. It was the Bournemouth team bus. It may not have been royalty, but judging by the stellar season the club had enjoyed, they were more than worthy of the applause. I had a gut feeling that I was on the cusp of seeing something special unfold.

The Valley is no more than a five minute walk from the station and partially hidden by terraced housing. Talking of hiding, the programme sellers were doing a good job of that. Queues of fans were instead diverted to the alternative matchday magazine by way of Charlton fanzine 'Voice of the Valley.' The seller, a guy named Rick had no problem finding his voice.

"Those programme sellers are useless and lazy. No different than the last lot who got sacked," he stated. Ironically enough, no sooner had the words left Rick's mouth, the programme boys put in an appearance.

I was apprehensive to discover my seat was high in the upper tier. As evidenced earlier on in the season at Bradford, me and heights don't really get on. Instead of passing through a door and scaling the steps, the stairwell was external, meaning I couldn't help but look down at the people becoming smaller as I slowly negotiated the winding path into the upper echelon. It was completely safe, clearly evidenced by non-vertigo suffering fans casually leaning over the edge texting or drinking.

Finally at the sun kissed summit, the pitch was in pristine condition. Three sides of the Valley have been re-developed in recent years and undergone a facelift to house more spectators. The corners have been filled in apart from the South Stand (named after famous player Jimmy Seed) which stands alone and is dwarfed by its modernised neighbours. The away fans are normally housed here, but Charlton kindly gave up their biggest North Stand to accommodate a large portion of the 4,000 travelling support.

A shortage of savouries meant that I missed out on a pie. The concession stand resembled something of a cattle market and I had to settle for a large sausage baguette instead. Based on recent attendances, it's not surprising that the supply barely met the demand. Charlton were heavily pushing their new kit and manager Guy Luzon's press conference on the video wall. The softly spoken Israeli coach was hard to hear and he seemed like he was focusing on next season. Home fans politely welcomed back old faces Yann Kermorgant and Simon Francis, while Harry Arter returned to the club that released him as a wet behind the ears 19-year-old after playing just the one game.

Bournemouth fans had brought their beach balls and other inflatable toys in anticipation of a promotion party. Both sides emerged from the dugout - oddly situated by one of the corner flags, with the away side wasting no time in stamping their authority on the game.

"Arter's going to come back and haunt us today, I just know he is," said a chorus of worried looking Charlton fans within earshot. The midfielder and brother-in-law of another ex-Athletic alumni Scott Parker must have heard, as he helped his side go 2-0 up inside the first 12 minutes. After Matt Ritchie cannoned an effort in off the post, Arter dispossessed a clumsy Yoni Buyens before tucking the ball in from close range. The midfielder was dictating the play with a Pirlo-esque performance and was clearly enjoying his football under Eddie Howe. Much of the Bournemouth team were doing the same and it was beginning to look like a training game.

Charlton barely threatened. Igor Vetokele missed an open goal and injured himself in the process. Bournemouth's Callum Wilson had trouble shaking off a streamer which had got stuck to his boot. In truth, it gave him more trouble than markers Roger Johnson and Tal Ben Haim did, who both looked like they were sucking wind. The lively Ritchie was chomping at the bit, chipping the ball over a hapless defender and seeing an effort come back off the woodwork. Charlton's players were dropping like flies. Frederic Bulot joined the treatment table, before Tony Watt took himself off and left his team down to ten men. Fans had gone from cheering "Tony Watt, Watt, Watt," to wondering *watt* was up with the striker's seemingly soft exit. Ritchie swept in a third goal for unforgiving Bournemouth late on after an initial effort was blocked.

The Charlton fans showed their class when they gave Kermorgant a standing ovation when he was substituted. Those cheers were soon trumped when the away fans went potty. Sheffield Wednesday had netted a last gasp equaliser at Watford. Bournemouth were officially crowned champions. The prestigious Championship trophy, which had looked bound for Watford was now making a sharp U-turn and heading towards South East London.

Following a brief address to say goodbye to their supporters, Charlton rolled out the red carpet, giving the new champions a guard of honour and free reign of the pitch to begin their celebrations.

"Cause a few upsets and we'll see you in two season's time," came a bold and cheeky final statement from the Charlton PA announcer, who graciously handed over MC duties to a Bournemouth counterpart. Stewards allowed anyone in the home end to stay behind, film and take pictures at will. A quick change in the toilets meant I could finally show my true colours and blend in with the crowd.

Police had cordoned off the main entrance to the train station after the game. A controlled fencing system was in place to gradually allow the jubilant away supporters a way back into the capital. The look of horror on a female commuter's face was priceless as an empty train pulled in, soon to be filled with boisterous football folk blasting out 'Champione' at the top of their lungs.

Walking back through London, people were stopping to acknowledge the travelling party. A guy having coffee with his wife pumped fists with passers-by, while strangers simply nodded and smiled as they walked past. My heart dropped a bit when 95% of the fans inevitably turned southwards to continue the party while I set off in a more northernly direction. There was still some fun to be had at Euston. Passing by two Sheffield Wednesday fans on the elevator, they noticed my shirt. "You've won the league because of us, congratulations," they said. Moments later, two Watford fans walked past, shaking their heads. Sorry lads, but at least your team got promoted too and that's nothing to be scoffed at.

All the goals, memories and magical moments came flooding back during a reflective journey home. I'd achieved what I set out to do. It felt weird to say the least when I arrived back in Chester. The hysteria and hype of the day was beginning to die down and a thought flashed through my mind.

If only there was one more game.

They say you should be careful what you wish for. It just might come true.

Best chant: "Let's all laugh at Millwall. La la la la." Charlton fans revelling in rivals Millwall's relegation misery.
Match ticket: £24.00. The club were kind to waive the booking fee.
Match programme: £3.00. From University (of Greenwich) Challenge, to historical pieces, to a message wall. Quite a varied edition, but no mention of a certain someone completing the 72.
Cost of food: £4.50 for a long sausage baguette. Not to be confused with a £3.60 hot dog.
Food rating: 2.5/5. Just missing that bit of HP Sauce to make it go down a bit better.

Final Score
Charlton Athletic 0
AFC Bournemouth 3 (Ritchie 10, 85, Arter 12)
Attendance: 21,280

A FITTING FINALE

Game #73: League One Play-Off Final - Sunday 24th May 2015
Preston North End vs Swindon Town - Wembley Stadium

Congratulations!

As part of the Sky Bet Play-Off ticket competition you entered last week, you have won a pair of tickets to the Sky Bet League One Play-Off Final taking place at 5.30pm at Wembley on Sunday 24th May.
Your tickets have been posted to the address you provided when you entered the competition and should definitely arrive by Thursday of this week.

Congratulations again on winning this competition, we hope you enjoy the game!

Best wishes,
Dave

Boom! The news I'd been waiting for. Bits of burger went flying as I shouted out loud and punched the air in delight. I'd quite clearly forgotten my surroundings for a brief couple of seconds. I haven't been able to show my face in McDonalds since. A hopeful entry via a Twitter competition had come up trumps. Either that or the Football League had finally recognised my groundhop achievement and wanted to reward me. I wasn't complaining. It was all aboard the Wembley train. No longer would I have to stare out of the train window for a fleeting look at England's home of football. The more I thought about it, the more it actually felt like the proper way to round off an exciting season.

The first order of business was that timing and logistics had to be taken into account. Planned rail strikes may have been called off, but a 5:30pm kick-off still meant it would be impossible to get back on the same day. Drivers were in short supply. Dad was 24 hours removed from a holiday and didn't fancy a near 400 mile round trip. Thankfully, Charlie ended up coming to the rescue once again. Wembley is near enough on his doorstep, much like Chester FC is for me, although there's no comparison. A free ticket was the least I could do to thank him for his generous hospitality throughout the season.

Leaving Chester with plenty of time ended up being smart. The express rail route limped along and added an extra hour onto the journey. A sea of white Preston shirts alighted next to me at Euston, with passers-by shaking hands and offering words of encouragement. They provided good company on the short commute to Wembley Central. All of us had beer on the mind. The pubs knew this and weren't taking any chances. Drinking dens within the vicinity were deemed for Preston or Swindon fans in the windows. Basically, if your voice didn't sound right then you weren't getting in. Luckily, my northern accent helped me gain entry to the 'Liquor Station.' Once inside, the bar staff were having difficulty understanding the thick Lancashire drawl from the other side of the bar. It was funny hearing them ask two or three times "can you repeat that?"

The Preston fans were getting re-acquainted with London prices. They'd lost all nine of their previous play-off campaigns, so naturally the fans were a bit pensive and keen to have a few shandies. A couple of champagne Charlies were stood at the bar talking about the previous evening's antics.

"Spent £200 on booze in the West End last night."
"Best not tell the wife."
"It's ok, I'll put it down to expenses."

Might want to hide that credit card statement too mate. Just a friendly suggestion. I digress. Supping all of my modestly priced pint in a plastic glass, Charlie had text to say he was at Wembley Park - which is basically in the concourse of the stadium. Following the crowd, my stomach turned at the sight of the half and half scarves hanging on display. No-one was buying, at least within my view. A lone Swindon fan was locking his car and sarcastically applauded when he spotted a group of red reinforcements approaching.

"Beginning to think I was the only one here," he muttered. The mood was positive and both sets of fans were mixing and comparing travel stories. Programme sellers dotted around each of the alphabetical checkpoints/entries were doing a roaring trade.

The famous Twin Towers may have been demolished, yet the arch which towers over the stadium can be seen for miles on end and adds to the ground's unique character. The badges of both clubs were illuminated high up along the top of the stadium. I took the opportunity to play tourist and get a picture next to the Bobby Moore statue outside. Despite extortionate ticket prices and less than ideal travel arrangements - especially for Swindon fans, Wembley Way was occupied by a steady stream of people. Over 40,000 filled two of the three tiered stadium. PA announcers from both clubs whipped up a frenzy and the seating arrangements have to be commended judging by the evenflow ring of red and white shirts around the stadium.

We took our seats and it was just my luck to be sitting next to a guy who looked like he needed an instruction manual to wave a flag. Wanting to retain both eyes and 20/20 vision, I got up and went on the search for my final pie of the journey, while Charlie mused over an in-play bet.

"Jermaine Beckford to score first and Preston to win. What do you think Shaun?"
"Go for Joe Garner. He scored all three the last time these two met."
"You sure mate?"
"Yeah certain pal."

Swindon and Charlie's bet couldn't have asked for a worse start. Beckford won a free-kick inside the first few minutes, then turned in Paul Gallagher's delivery from close-range to give the Lilywhites an ideal start. Sorry Charlie. To rub salt into the wounds, Swindon lost captain Nathan Thompson to a leg injury, as the defender failed to block Beckford's effort. Another Gallagher delivery led to a second goal in quick succession. This time, Paul Huntington was left unmarked and with the easiest of tap-ins. Swindon's shirt beared the slogan 'Imagine Cruising.' With less than 15 minutes on the clock, Preston actually were cruising.

The rogue sitting next door was still oblivious to the fact he was caressing my face with his flag. He soon had an angry mob to deal with when he refused to sit down.

"Excuse me mate, can you sit down please? I've got a six-year-old who can't see. We've paid a lot of money for these seats." This was a perfectly reasonable request from a father looking to appease his young son's request to be able to see the action. An expletive laden rant which was uttered in retaliation came as quite the shock. The idiot feebly pointed up to the screen in the corner and said "it's not my problem, I'll do what I want." A steward briefly came over, but decided he wasn't going to offer any assistance. Two lads from a few rows back finally intervened. It's amazing what a few raised fists can achieve. The simpleton finally sat down, but brooded terribly. He reminded me of Muttley the Dog from the Wacky Races, given the constant cursing under his breath. Despite me nailing a perfect impression of Muttley's trademark laugh, Charlie still wasn't keen on swapping seats. It was probably payback for my lame betting advice.

Michael Smith spurned a golden chance to bring Swindon back into the game, glancing a header wide from close range. The Swindon fans groaned, they knew they'd wasted their golden chance to get back into the game. Naturally, Preston and Beckford kicked them when they were down. The striker bagged his second of the afternoon when he curled the ball in from the edge of the box. A man with no top came running over like it was Christmas morning. It was hugs and high fives all round, complete with a waft of body odour. 3-0 and not even half time. One side of Wembley was riding the crest of a wave, the other knew there was no way back now.

One lucky Preston fan won a Fiat during the break. Shrugging off the minor detail that he couldn't drive, the generous soul passed the car onto his Mum. Preston let their foot off the gas slightly, but Swindon couldn't find a way past inspired goalkeeper Sam Johnstone. At the other end, Beckford ran clear and fluffed a one-on-one. He was just finding his range. Moments later, the striker made amends with an almost identical chance to collect the match ball. In the process, Beckford became only the fifth man in history to net three times in a play-off final. With all the imminent celebrations going on around me, I couldn't help but spare a thought for the Swindon fans, who had already started to leave. I held no animosity towards them. In fact, I'd enjoyed a great day out at the County Ground earlier in the tour. Having edged a 13 goal thriller with Sheffield United just to get to Wembley, it ultimately proved a step too far for the Robins.

Of course, I stayed behind to see Preston revel in their celebrations. At the tenth time of asking, their fans finally had some happy memories to take back from Wembley. There was a mad scramble when Beckford launched his boots into the crowd. The flag waving freak put in a slide tackle in a weak attempt to catch the boots. Much like a striker's challenge, he completely missed the target, as evidenced by me when a sharp jolt of pain shot up my leg. I couldn't have chased him even if I'd wanted to. My one and only injury right at the end of the season. Typical!

"Come on mate, time to go now," said Charlie. It was almost throwing out time.
"They think it's all over. Well it is now."

Best chant: "Are you Blackpool in disguise?" The Preston fans being far from complimentary to their Wiltshire opponents.
Match ticket: £0.00. Ticket would have cost a staggering £62 at face value. Ouch! That doesn't include the booking fee and several other add-ons. Still, a great experience and one I'm extremely thankful for.
Match programme: £6.00. Bigger in size and price. Included an A-Z guide to play-off finals, a plethora of stats, plus numerous League One personnel got together to pick their highlights of the season. Both managers came under the spotlight via in-depth interviews. We won't mention the typo in Swindon boss Mark 'Copper' sorry Cooper's name. Whoops!
Cost of food: £5.00 for a pie. The choice was beef and angus ale, buttered chicken balti or cauliflower cheese. I went with the first choice.
Food rating: 3/5. The pie crumbled as easily as the Swindon defence. Gravy went everywhere and the lack of forks meant I resorted to using my hands. Like baby's feeding time, but a nice pie nonetheless.

Final Score
Preston North End 4 (Beckford 3, 44, 57, Huntington 13)
Swindon Town 0
Attendance: 48,236

SLOCOMBE
1
DARBY
2
HUNTINGTON
4
ELOKOBI
5
MINGS
3
POWER
8
ARTER
7
WOODS
6
CLUCAS
11
POPE
9
MURPHY
10

Groundhop Team of the Season

Goalkeeper

1) Sam Slocombe (Scunthorpe United)
Denied Chesterfield a famous FA Cup comeback with enough saves to fill a DVD. Just days after his heroics, the shot stopper broke his arm and was then released at the end of the season. Sam, you're always welcome to have a game with me and my mates on a Sunday night. A cracking keeper!

Defenders

2) Stephen Darby (Bradford City)
A buccaneering full-back, who was as comfortable crossing the halfway line as much as putting in a crunching tackle. The ex-Liverpool academy player didn't put a foot wrong in front of my eyes and it's easy to see why he's worked his way up to captaining the side.

4) Paul Huntington (Preston North End)
Being voted Player of the Year by his own fans and scoring a goal in the play-off final at Wembley is all well and good. However, the lanky defender is best remembered by me for his dubious hand of god-esque goal at Notts County in the JPT. A towering centre half, Huntington remained composed and was an integral part in getting his side promoted to the Championship.

5) George Elokobi (Oldham Athletic)
Lancashire's version of Rambo (complete with headband) made it his mission on a baltic Tuesday night in the JPT that Bradford's attack shall not pass. Many a ball were hoofed into the heavens, but the hapless attackers were no match for Elokobi's strength and girth. Mission accomplished and Oldham progressed.

3) Tyrone Mings (Ipswich Town)
Plucked from non-league for a measly £10,000 the fresh faced youngster is proof that nice guys still exist in football. Settling his mother's debts, buying hard-up fans match tickets and replacing out of date shirt sales, plus becoming one of the Championship's best left backs was all in a day's work. Mings's greatest asset is his peach of a left foot and demonstrating an assured touch and maturity beyond his 22 years.

Midfielders

8) Max Power (Tranmere Rovers)
One of the few shining lights in a miserable season for Rovers. The homegrown midfielder often took games by the scruff of the neck, sometimes single-handedly making and scoring goals to try and keep his side afloat. He may not have kept Tranmere in the league, but he rarely put a foot wrong on the several occasions I went to watch Tranmere.

6) Ryan Woods (Shrewsbury Town)
Shropshire's equivalent to Paul Scholes, and not just because of the Ginger hair. Also, Dad's one and only pick. The Shrewsbury academy graduate covered every blade of grass at the Greenhous Meadow, playing with a fearlessness and hounding many a Norwich player off the ball. Woods put in a Man of the Match performance en route to dumping the Canaries out of the Capital One Cup.

7) Harry Arter (AFC Bournemouth)
Free-kicks, 30 yard screamers, netting against your former club. Whenever I went to see Bournemouth, Arter's performances caught the eye and made him a joy to watch. His workrate was second to none, which is crucial for a midfielder. Open a gate to a field and I have no doubt that Harry would run through it.

11) Sam Clucas (Chesterfield)

No player was more versatile than the former Mansfield Town man. From left back, to the flank, to leading the line up front, it didn't matter. Supplying the ammunition to keep his side in the FA Cup, Clucas also scored a wonderful solo goal at Swindon which almost got me in trouble for over celebrating. Bigger things are clearly in the pipeline. He barely finished his cup of coffee at Chesterfield before being poached by Hull City in the close season.

Forwards

9) Tom Pope (Port Vale)

The gangly forward did exactly what the fans chanted. When the target man was fed sufficiently enough, Pope responded in kind with goals by the bucketload. Vale tailored their play to suit their star man and will have to adjust accordingly now that Pope has taken his goals and services to Bury.

10) Daryl Murphy (Ipswich Town)

A typical centre forward who knew exactly where the goal was. One of the main reasons for Ipswich getting into the play-offs. Murphy notched a sublime double to almost single handedly defeat Nottingham Forest. Whenever I came to see Ipswich play, if Murphy took to the field, he was odds on to find the net.

Thanks to determination, a favourable winter, plus unwavering support from family and friends, I was able to complete my quest. Travelling thousands of miles, I was lucky enough to see 190 goals ripple the net, witness seven red cards and digest an unhealthy number of pies to boot. More importantly, I re-discovered my love of going to a game. Swapping the sofa for the turnstile and the buzz of watching a live match is something I've become addicted to. Weekends (and windy Tuesday nights) will never be the same again.

Before signing off, I just wanted to mention a select few people who really helped with *Journey to the 72*. From coming to games, offering a bed for the night or helping with tickets, your help has been very much appreciated.

Steve Cook, Dave Singh, Dan Broadley, James Sellers, Mark Parry, John West, Heidi Scammell, Roger and Angela Scammell, Mark Field, Rich Ward, David Banks, Charlie Dehaan, Rachel and Mike Dehaan, Vic Banks, Nick Banks, Graham Webb, Ben Fotheringham

Not forgetting my dear family. Thank you to my parents Cyril and Elaine, plus sister Sarah-Jayne. You guys were my biggest support network through all of this and I love you all very much.

Throughout the journey, people constantly asked how much the project cost. Truthfully, I hadn't kept a running tally, primarily because I didn't want to know. It's been so much fun and one of the best decisions I've ever made. Besides, you can't put a price on happiness.

That being said, out of sheer curiosity, I'll attempt to break down some of the numbers for you.

Cost of tickets: £1, 382.50
Cheapest ticket: £5 - Preston North End vs Port Vale, Coventry City vs Plymouth Argyle
Dearest ticket: £38 - Brighton & Hove Albion vs AFC Bournemouth
Cost of programmes: £207.50
Cheapest programme: £1 - Preston North End
Dearest programme: £6 - Wembley
Largest attendances: 48,236 - Preston North End vs Swindon Town (Wembley) 26,673 - Derby County vs Ipswich Town
Smallest attendance: 919 - Accrington Stanley vs Burton Albion
Best mascots: Harry the Hornet (Watford) Rammie the Ram (Derby County) H'Angus the Monkey (Hartlepool United) Haydon the Womble (AFC Wimbledon) Boomer the Dog (Port Vale)
Best steak pies: Bury, Millwall, Swindon Town, Sheffield Wednesday, Blackburn Rovers
Best balti pies: Sheffield United, Crawley Town, Reading, Middlesbrough, Birmingham City
Best meat and potato pies: Nottingham Forest, Fulham, Morecambe, Carlisle United, York City
Best cheese pies: Preston North End, Rochdale
Best pizzas: Middlesbrough, Reading
Worst pie: Leeds United
Best matchday programmes: Scunthorpe United, Bury, Shrewsbury Town, Middlesbrough, Northampton Town

Five of the best games
Dagenham & Redbridge 4-2 Carlisle United
Rotherham United 1-5 AFC Bournemouth
Scunthorpe United 2-2 Chesterfield
MK Dons 4-2 Gillingham
Middlesbrough 4-1 Ipswich Town

Five of the worst games
Leeds United 0-0 Reading
Stevenage 0-0 Bury
Newport County 1-0 Portsmouth
Accrington Stanley 1-0 Burton Albion
Leyton Orient 0-0 MK Dons

Top five grounds
Brighton & Hove Albion
Preston North End
Nottingham Forest
Rochdale
Rotherham United

With another season already underway, fresh adventures are there to be had, additional chapters are ready to write and new grounds are calling out to be visited. Time to crack on with completing the 92!

Excuse me, while I go check the fixture list and train timetable......

Epilogue

Setting out on a journey to do the 72 like this requires dedication, ambition and bags of commitment. Out of the fans who embark on such quests we will never know the number who are successful but all will have been on a journey that, although started about football, became so much more.

Anyone can watch a game on television, with so many viewing providers such as Sky and BT Sport there is pretty much a game on every day. From the high definition picture quality, to multiple camera angles, to the variety of slow motion replays, the armchair fan never misses a thing on the pitch.

However, these fans are missing out on the bigger picture - the whole experience of football. Shaun enjoyed 'the experience of football' 72 times as he completed his journey to all of the Football League grounds. A feat such as this in a lifetime is commendable, but to do it over the course of just one season, travelling the length and breadth of the country? That is a truly remarkable achievement.

Journalist and pundit Tim Vickery hit the nail on the head, revealing he liked to take public transport to travel with the crowd to and from games to soak up the atmosphere. And the key point was the reason he gave why. The game starts from the moment you leave your front door and doesn't finish until the moment you get back in and shut that door.

It's thanks to the dedication of football fans like Shaun that the92.net was born - created from the need of football lovers to embrace a challenge that not many will achieve; to visit all 92 league grounds. Of course there is debate over what counts and in all honestly that is up to the individual, but the website aims to standardise these rules and offer a platform for those that want to keep track. It also gives fans the chance to share their tips and give feedback on the good, the bad and the ugly from their travels as well as capturing key information regarding pints, pies, atmosphere, location stewarding and more.

Peter Briers www.the92.net

8519047R00160

Printed in Germany
by Amazon Distribution
GmbH, Leipzig